The Eastside Devotional

Pirate Parrot Press

Fullerton, California

THE EATSIDE DEVOTIONAL

Copyright © 2008 John C. Hendershot

Edited by Rebekah M. Hendershot

Published by Pirate Parrot Press
1201 N. Concord Ave.
Fullerton, CA 92831

www.BecomingCloser.org

ISBN-13: 978-0-615-26245-1

Third Edition: December 2008

"Blessed is the man who does not..."
Psalm 1

Your mother was right. Character counts, and it does matter who you hang around with.

Note the character of the man so blessed. He does not walk in the "counsel" of the wicked—in other words, he's careful about where he gets his advice. Think about it: the last time you got into a lot of trouble, were you taking good advice from an evil friend?

He does not "stand" in the way of sinners. You won't find him standing at the bar getting drunk, looking for tonight's bedroom companion. Think about it: the last time you got into a lot of trouble, were you in the wrong place at the wrong time—with the wrong friends?

Nor does he "sit" in the seat of the mockers. Much of our humor is nothing but a sneer at what is reviled as "Puritanism." Honesty is sneered at as being impossible, chastity unthinkable and humility beyond imagination. We proclaim virtue on Sunday morning after laughing at it Saturday night. Think about it: do your kids see you as a hypocrite—for a reason?

It is not sufficient, however, to "not do." How does this man so blessed keep himself? First, the Psalmist tells us, is that his "delight" is in the law of the Lord. Do you see reading the Scripture as a chore, or do you seek the blessing of the word of the Lord? It is not enough just to read the Bible; you must practice delight in it, too.

Indeed, we are shown, that such a man meditates on it day and night. Perhaps you do not delight in it because you do not meditate upon it. When you read, do you ask yourself, "What is the Lord saying to me here?" Apply it to yourself personally!

God desires the companionship of each of us. He speaks to us through the Scriptures, but (so the Psalm says) he also "watches over" the way of the righteous. In his great love for us he cares for us, taking our human efforts to walk in his way and magnifying them by his power. If we will walk in his way, he will care for us greatly. Even when times of trouble come, he will not allow us to wither away. The tree planted by the stream of life itself cannot wither, no matter how hot the trials of the day.

The Fear of the Lord
Proverbs 1:7

"The fear of the Lord is the beginning of knowledge," says the Proverb. We often misuse this passage. Surely, we say, God would not want us to be afraid of him, would he? Not the loving God?

But it is so. If you have raised a child, you understand this proverb in all its truth. One of the first things you must do is to teach your child to fear. Being a child, they do not see the reason for your teaching them to stay out of the street. They do not have the knowledge of traffic accidents yet—but you do. So to substitute for their lack of knowledge, you place your authority on them, and forbid them to play in the street.

It is most necessary to fear the Lord, for if you do not fear him, will you not be tempted to scoff at him when you sin? "He is the loving God; he will forgive me, so I can do anything I want." It is not so. He is the Lord God Almighty, Sovereign and Awesome, and he need not take such insolence from you.

Indeed, fear can be a most useful thing. How many of us have been prevented from sinning simply by the fear of discovery? "What if my wife were to find out?" If the fear of your wife (or husband) is motivation to remain faithful, how much more motivation should come from the fear of God the Omnipotent?

But note that fear is the "beginning" of knowledge. It is necessary, but it is not sufficient. The child grows up and learns about traffic. Your relationship with your spouse cannot be built upon fear; neither can your relationship with God. Once having begun upon the road to knowledge of God, you must go as far as you can. Soon you will pass from fear to delight, for the Father loves you deeply. An automobile is a dangerous thing, to be greatly feared as an instrument of destruction—but once you know how to drive it safely, it is a great convenience. You must not lose the fear of it, or disaster will strike, but you need not cower before it either. With God the relationship is so much better. Do not lose the fear of God, but rather grow in knowledge and in love. Then you will see that all those things which you rightly fear now stand guard over you. The dog is fearsome or lovable depending on whether you're the burglar or the owner. The Father is fearsome to the wicked and pure love to the righteous.

Three Temptations
Matthew 4:1-11

The ancient scholars divided sins (and thus temptations) into the three categories shown in this passage: the flesh, the world, and pride.

Sins of the flesh are Satan's first weapon. Why? Satan does not wait until old age to begin his evil work, and the hormones of youth are fertile ground. Such sins also produce the quickest spiral of damage—teenage pregnancy, the despair of alcoholism. The damage lasts a lifetime and is quickly inflicted. But perhaps most telling of all is this: if Satan can destroy you with the sins of the flesh, the destruction is most certain—for the sins of the flesh produce no virtue along the way. No one ever developed patience along Lover's Lane; good work habits do not come out of the bar.

Time, and some residue of virtue, may force Satan to escalate. The sins of the world come next: greed and envy. A receding hairline and expanding waist may end lust and gluttony, but the lure of the BMW continues for life. How good it feels to have influence and power! Indeed, these are respectable sins. Greed can masquerade as "entrepreneurial spirit." Envy may wear the label of "social justice."

But if these fail, then Satan resorts to the weapon that produced the Pharisees: pride. It is a telling point that our civilization considers pride a virtue, not a sin. We look up in admiration at athletes who regularly look down on others. But think: if you are looking down on others, how can you look up to God? If you think yourself so great, and others so small, what will you think when you compare yourself to God?

The Christian has a sure defense against all three, and Christ uses it here. All three temptations are hurled at Jesus; against all three he uses the defense of Scripture. No wonder we are told to hide the word of God in our hearts!

It is characteristic of God that the angels minister to Jesus *after* the temptations. God is raising us up to be sons and daughters, to be mature in the faith. After the storm of temptation comes the calm of God's comfort. In the meantime, resist the devil—and he will flee.

Answer Me
Psalm 4

The Psalmist expresses here a common problem. We cry out to the Lord that the wicked are everywhere. They turn the glory of the Lord into shame, taking what is holy and mocking it, making it a subject of humor. They love delusions, seeking after any form of spirituality that does not acknowledge God. Magic on one hand and materialism on the other; the world chases its illusions.

But know this: the Lord has set apart the godly for himself. Oh, yes, they will be mocked. They will be pitied as those whose beliefs are "obsolete" (when does truth become obsolete?) or "old-fashioned" (when does righteousness have a fashion?). But still, the godly belong to the Lord.

What does that mean? First, it means that the Lord will hear them. The world may not notice. The prayers of the righteous will be answered, even if the world calls it "coincidence." God still reigns, and his will indeed prevails.

Then, what shall the righteous do in such times of trial? First, we must abstain from anger. It is so easy to mount the pulpit and condemn the world and all who do not believe. But Christ came to seek and save the lost; shall we then go out and condemn them? No, we should not be angry, but rather use the weapons of godliness to triumph over the weapons of the world.

Even as we meditate on our beds, we should not give way to anger. Rather, in the quiet of our own souls, we should examine ourselves and see if there is any wickedness in us. We too are sinners, and such an examination should keep us from opening our mouths in condemnation.

The world asks, "Where is this God?" The Psalmist tells us that we are to reflect him in our faces. Do you celebrate the goodness of God, or are you the sour taste of curdled righteousness?

We are also to show the joy in our hearts, particularly in things which are not material. Some will rejoice in riches; we should rejoice in the things of God.

Finally, there is the matter of fear. A world which does not know God knows only power and corruption—and fears any greater power. By our confidence in God we should show how his perfect love casts fear out of our lives, and fills us with the peace that passes understanding.

Leave Your Gift
Matthew 5:23-26

One of the more astonishing misconceptions in Christian life is this: if a sin is old enough, no repentance is required. Indeed, the sin can become a grudge; the grudge then becomes a point of principle; the point of principle becomes a point of pride. For this reason our Lord says, "if you .. there *remember*"—even though the sin is an old one, if the Spirit brings it to your mind, then waste no time in making it right. You do not know if you will ever get the chance again, for which of us is sure of life or death tomorrow? Be reconciled immediately.

Indeed, we are commanded to leave the gift behind to do this. This too is no accident. We often think that repentance means that we must confess and be sorry before the Lord. It does mean that, but it also means that we must confess and be sorry before the one whom we have offended. Do not for a moment suppose that your sorrow before the Lord excuses you from confession and repentance before your brother. He will accept no gift from a sinner who will not repent. The Lord God is Holy.

We are told to settle matters quickly, even on the way to court. This is not just good legal advice, but superb spiritual advice. Have you ever had a grievance that festered? A wrong done to you that has eaten into your soul? Then you know the terrible impact it can have upon your soul. Would you inflict such a spiritual wound upon your brother? If you settle quickly, the wound is slight and heals early. Let it fester, and the healing is slow, and the bitterness deep. This command is given that you may not inflict such injuries on your brothers.

It is also given that you may avoid the lesson. God is not mocked. He will use the courts of justice—formal or informal—to work his will. If you will not learn to settle quickly, being willing to concede the material to obtain the spiritual, then God will teach that lesson to you. One method is to let you take your adversary to court—and lose. Then you will see how harsh justice can be. It may be that you will then learn to love mercy, first for yourself and then for your brother. Blessed are the merciful, for they shall obtain mercy.

Abram and Righteousness
Genesis 15:1-21

We sometimes gather the impression that the great men of faith never had the slightest doubt or argument that the Lord would indeed keep his promises. Abram (later Abraham) shows us the opposite here. God speaks to him in a vision, and Abram's first thought is that God does not know what he's talking about.

It's a logical point. Abram is an old man, and childless. How then can his descendants be so numerous?

Abram debates the point with God, but in the end he believes what God tells him—and God credits him with righteousness. In this we have a picture of the faith Christ has shown us in the New Testament. It is not that Abram has earned this righteousness by his own actions; it is that he took God at his word. He trusted him.

Note, too, that Abram could not see the fulfillment of these prophecies in his own lifetime. Indeed, God specifically tells him that his descendants will be incredibly numerous, that they will be in slavery for four hundred years and then delivered, and that the land he sees is given to his descendants. Abram must have known that he could see none of these things in his lifetime. Yet he believed.

We have a similar situation. Two thousand years have come and gone, and we still have the promise (but not the delivery) of the resurrection and judgment. We have the evidence of the Resurrection of our Lord. We have the word of God, but this is still a promise, not yet a delivery. If we want to claim that promise, we must trust God. If we do, he will credit us with righteousness—the righteousness of Jesus Christ. What he did for his Son, Jesus, he will do for all his children— raise them from the grave to eternal life with him.

The issue is still the same. God does not force us to believe, either by power or physical evidence. He offers us evidence, adds to that his unbreakable word, and invites us to trust him. The deepest personal relationships have the deepest trust, and that is the type of relationship he desires with us. The question is, do we intend to have that relationship with him—and will we trust him for it?

Is Anything Too Hard for the Lord?
Genesis 16:1-18:19

There is one constant sin shown here. We will not trust God; we will arrange things for him, and when things don't work out the way we plan, we get mad.

Sarah (Sarai) has an ingenious idea. God has said that through Abram (Abraham) all nations will be blest. But she is old, and well beyond childbearing years. Instead of trusting God to do his will, she arranges matters for him. In accord with the custom of the time, she arranges for Abram to sleep with Hagar, her servant. Hagar gives birth to Ishmael. A childless woman in those days was a sorry thing, and soon Hagar despises her mistress.

What does Sarai do? She blames Abram! (How quick we are to say that we are not at fault!) Abram replies, quite logically, that she may do as she pleases with her servant. So then Sarai takes it out on Hagar, who flees.

But note what the Lord does. He does not punish; he redeems. Because Abram is the friend of God, he will make of Ishmael a great nation—and he will also bring that child to Sarai. God starts this process by giving Abram and Sarai new names—Abraham and Sarah. He is the God who renews all things. In his redemption all things will be made new.

Our reaction would probably have been much like Abraham and Sarah. They laughed. Abraham laughs, but does what God says. He circumcises himself and all in his household, thus showing his faith that God can do not only the impossible but the ridiculous. The foolishness of God is greater than the wisdom of man.

When Sarah hears about it, she too laughs. This provokes the Lord to ask the question: "Is anything too hard for the Lord?" It is a reminder. Whenever we become "amateur providences" and arrange things in such fashion as we think God would want, he tells us by his actions that we are not wiser or stronger than he. He arranges for his will to come—in his way, not ours. But in the steps of doing this, he redeems our failures and turns them into his triumphs.

Is anything too hard for the Lord?

Righteous Judgment
Matthew 7:1-5

A story is told of Robert E. Lee. He was riding past some soldiers who were scheduled to be tried for various crimes, including desertion, which carried the death penalty. As he passed one soldier, Lee noticed that the man was crying. He leaned down from his horse and said, "Don't fear, my son, I will see that you get justice." "General," replied the soldier, "that's exactly what I'm afraid of!"

Most of us learn at an early age that there is such a thing as justice, and we quickly develop a two-edged attitude toward it. When we are the one in the right, we want justice, swift, sure and unmerciful. When we wrong someone else, it's all too clear that there are circumstances to be considered.

Our Lord here gives us a special case of the golden rule. God is quite fair about these things. If you use a rule for judging others, God will use it on you. You like to measure other people; fine. God simply will use your own yardstick to measure you!

This prompts Jesus to give us some wise advice. Most of us have a sufficient sense of right and wrong to condemn others quite often. Jesus tells us not to do so, for that same standard will be applied. The choice is simple: either give up your standards of right and wrong (interesting where *that* might lead) or stop applying them to everyone else. Otherwise, out of your own mouth you will stand condemned.

Worse yet, most of us are very good at being extra strict with others while quite lenient with ourselves. It is exceedingly useful to remember at all times that you, too, are a sinner. It seems to be the only qualification for becoming a Christian; thus, to say you are a child of Christ is to say you are a sinner too—a forgiven one.

But let us take that standard a bit further. Take your yardstick for forgiveness—the one you use on yourself—and apply it to your brother. Do you ask your Lord for mercy on your own behalf? Then do so on your brother's behalf as well. May your yardstick for mercy be generous—and your yardstick for judgment be hidden away, unused. Then when God comes to measure you, he will have only the generous, merciful yardstick to use. Blessed are the merciful, for they shall obtain mercy.

The Lord Will Provide
Genesis 22:1-18

Character is revealed in action. The character of Abraham had many faults, but his great virtue is revealed here. He loved God so much that he would sacrifice his own son at his God's command.

The story is fascinating for us. It is a picture of God's own love for us, shown at the Cross. Like Abraham, God there sacrificed his own son. In Abraham we can see the anguish more clearly, for Abraham was a man like us. We can understand the thoughts that must have raced through his mind.

How could he have held his courage together in such a circumstance? One clue we have. As Abraham and Isaac leave the servants behind, Isaac asks where the sacrifice is. "God himself will provide the lamb," is Abraham's reply—even though he knows that Isaac is to be that lamb. A long life with God—Abraham is well over a hundred years old at this time—has taught him one lesson: the Lord will provide.

How much we need to learn that lesson! Is there any spiritual disease so common in our time as that of worry? We go to church on Sunday and proclaim the greatness of God, and the rest of the week we act as if we had to carry him. So often we look at our circumstances and say, "I just don't see how God can provide for me in this. I just don't see it." He never says that you will see it. He only says that He will provide. He will give you example after example (consider the lilies of the field!) of his provision, but you must trust him.

Such trust must be wholehearted. We cannot trust him on Sunday and think him unreliable on Monday. On the wall next to my bed is a needlepoint work—the first thing I read each morning. It says, "Trust in the Lord with all your heart." We need to be reminded.

Abraham understood that too. As a reminder, he named that place Jehovah-jireh, literally "the Lord will see (to it)" or "The Lord Will Provide."

The hill so named is Mt. Moriah, the mount on which the Temple was built. On that same mountain, just outside the city walls two millennia later, God did indeed provide the sacrifice. He provided his only Son, the lamb of God. Now we know that He really loves us, for He did not withhold his Son, His only Son. The Lord provided then. The Lord Will Provide.

A Man Under Authority
Matthew 8:5-13

There is a certain directness to this centurion—a leader of a hundred men in the Roman army.

First, despite his position as a leader in the army, which is occupying Israel as conqueror, he does not even attempt to command this Jesus. Rather, he addresses him as "Lord." This alone makes him unusual among the conquerors. It is the title of one who must be obeyed.

He also seems to know enough about Jesus. He tells him he is not worthy to have him under his roof. What an attitude of humility this is! As his own words show, he is a man accustomed to wielding authority. He tells people what to do every day. By right of conquest he should be able to tell this carpenter what to do—but instead he approaches him in complete humility.

We work with what we know, and this man works with authority. He recognizes that authority in Jesus. He knows how authority is supposed to work, and therefore he knows what Jesus can do.

He is also a man of compassion. His request is not for himself, but for his servant. The servant is paralyzed, and is in terrible pain. So, knowing that the Jews have no dealings with the Gentiles, having no standing with this rabbi, but loving his servant, he comes to this Jesus with his request.

Jesus replies—it is only one of two such occasions in the Gospels—that the man has great faith. Do you see the ingredients of such a faith?

He recognizes Jesus as Lord.

He approaches him in complete humility.

He knows that Jesus can do as he desires.

He approaches him in intercession for a friend, not for his own selfish wants.

Jesus calls this attitude "faith." Perhaps the reason our faith is so weak is that we do not do as the centurion did. Do you recognize Jesus as Lord, or just friend? Do you come to him in humility, or in pride? Do you genuinely believe that he can do far more than you could possibly ask? Do you approach him in an unselfish, loving way?

Perhaps our lack of prayer power stems from us, not him!

Wise in Your Own Eyes
Proverbs 3:7-8

There is a temptation that is very strong for the experienced Christian. Someone comes to you with a problem, and instantly you think you see a clever way to rid them of their difficulties. You don't stop to consult the Lord; nor do you stop to pray for them. You just give them good advice. It almost always backfires.

The reason is rather simple. God is teaching you not to be "wise in your own eyes." The issue is not whether or not your advice is good. Of course it is—or so you think. But any advice may go astray if the Lord opposes it.

The Lord takes great delight in this. He will go to marvelous lengths to make sure you see that his way of dealing with the difficulty is so much better than yours. This is not because he wants to convince you that he is wiser than you are. You know that. He has a much deeper purpose.

He wants you to rely on Him. In this situation there is a great temptation for those who are learned, for those who are experienced, and for those who are intelligent. Those who are none of these things naturally lean on God—what else could they do? But those who have ability say, "Thanks, God, but just watch me handle this one."

It should not be so. Not because you are stupid, or naive, or uneducated, but because you should lean upon the Lord.

Always remember that he is so much wiser than you. Always remember too that he wants you to lean on him, to become more like him. Remember that you are the imitator of Jesus Christ, your Lord— who could do nothing except that which the Father showed him to do. Constantly consult his Word. Be ever in prayer before him, not to give him advice but to give him your self in obedience.

If you do, what will happen? Solomon, the wisest of mortals, says it will bring health to your body and nourishment to your bones. Indeed, more than that, it will bring you the sweet fellowship of Jesus himself, the wisdom of a caring heavenly Father and the deep indwelling of the Holy Spirit. Do not grow in your own wisdom; rather, grow in wisdom and the grace of God.

Authority
Matthew 9:1-8

Guilt is a fact in everyone's life. We go to psychiatrists to have them convince us that it's just an abnormal way of thinking. We puff up our chests and declare our own righteousness, in the hope that hearing it will make it so. We flock to religions that demand from us mighty works to atone for it. In all these things we forget to ask, "Just who gave you the authority to wipe away guilt?"

It is the key point. The psychiatrist can try and convince you there is nothing to feel guilty about—but on what basis? Does he create right and wrong? Our own self-righteousness is its own condemnation. Religions that demand human atonement are never satisfied. Guilt will not go away.

Consider: when we sin, we offend not only another human being (who, after all, is a sinner like us) but also the God of creation. How do we offend God? His eternal character is shown in his creation. Part of that creation is the certainty of right and wrong, of good and evil. There is no victimless sin, for God is always the victim.

Now, it is easy to see that if I offend you, you have the privilege of forgiving me—you, and no one else. The principle is simple: only the one offended may forgive. God is offended at each and every sin, and therefore has the privilege of forgiving.

More important, he is the innocent one offended, for he is righteousness itself. Unlike my fellow sinner, he comes to the question with clean hands. I can say to the one I offend, "You are guilty too." But I cannot say that to God. So when God forgives, I am forgiven indeed. He indeed has the authority. Jesus merely demonstrates the power of that authority here; it is yet another statement that he is God in the flesh.

Ah, but will God forgive me? He is righteousness; I am a sinner. How can pure righteousness have anything to do with a sinner such as I am? The answer to that was given on the Cross. The atonement no human could attain was made for us at Calvary. By the blood of Jesus, in his sacrifice, God has made a way for me to be forgiven. Guilt cannot be reasoned away, nor blown away with pride, nor worked away by any means. It can be dissolved—utterly and completely—through the forgiveness made freely available through Jesus, the Christ. Here is the only authority available. Here is the only one I need.

The Lord Disciplines Those He Loves
Proverbs 3:11-12

Discipline is like a diet. You're the last person to know you need it.

For the Christian, discipline is a sign.

It's a sign of God's love for you. Think of it this way. Have you ever seen a child whose parents did not take the time to discipline him? The child "acts up" to get attention—for what is often a lack of love. Children who are well behaved are usually those whose parents love them enough to take the time to discipline them.

It is a sign of son-ship. When you see a child misbehaving in public, the temptation is to "set him straight." But you don't do it—unless it's your own child. So when God disciplines you, it's a sign that you are his child.

It is a sign that you will avoid the condemnation due to the powers of this world. Those who reject God he may allow to continue in wickedness, but he corrects his children now to keep them from judgment on the Day.

How, then, should we respond to such discipline? We are often given to complaining about such things.

First, we must not make light of them. Some of us have the idea that we can shrug off anything—"I can take it." This is not the way to treat a gift from God.

Next, look back. You know that good times seldom make a good story. But when you tell stories at parties, they are usually about your troubles and trials. They seemed great at the time, but now you see what God was doing, and you are glad. He has not changed his methods.

Then, look forward. Hope in the Lord. You know from the Scriptures that the trial does not go on forever. It will end soon, in God's good time. So keep your chin up and thank him for what he's doing in your life.

In all such trials remember that you are a member of the family of God. Discipline is in love; accept it as such. Trust your Father, for he cares for you.

Flawless
Psalm 12

One of the great uses of the Psalms is to express the groaning of the human heart. This Psalm should get a lot of use in our day.

The Psalmist describes a time in which things which are vile are honored. Does that sound like our day? If it doesn't, consider the test he gives us: when such days happen, the wicked strut. Not that they show up in broad daylight; they strut. In this day that which has been vile for thousands of years is now "an alternate lifestyle;" adultery is now "liberating your marriage." The wicked strut indeed.

The character of the wicked is worth some study, for it is by their tongues you will know them here:

They are double minded, and therefore practice flattery and lies. When the wicked strut, the lie with the wink in it is everywhere.

They proudly proclaim themselves master of their own fates. Listen to the commercials for expensive cars, and see if you don't hear that "I can handle anything" rugged individualism proclaimed.

In action comes the test: they oppress the weak and the needy. Neither government nor charity need care for the oppressed; after all, they don't deserve it. Would Christ have said that?

But the words of the Lord are flawless; like pure silver, they reflect light upon our path.

The words of the Lord reflect the perfection of God. Unlike that of the wicked, his mind does not change.

The words of the Lord reflect the faithfulness of God. When He promises, it is to be done. You can count on it. More than that, you can count on Him.

The words of the Lord reflect the righteousness of God. He shows no favoritism toward weak or mighty, rich or poor. His favor rests on the pure and contrite heart.

Listen to your words today. Do they reflect flattery and lies, and the spirit that says, "I am my own master?" Or do they reflect the child of God? If you are his child, how refined are your words? Do they show his perfection, faithfulness and righteousness?

Remember—you are the image of Christ someone will see and hear.

A Prophet's Reward
Matthew 10:40-42

Old friends can be a blessing. My wife and I once spent six weeks living in a camper on the driveway of an old friend of the family. How they put up with us I shall never know. When we arrived, they were friends of my parents. When we left, they were friends of ours.

Now that I am a father, I see the principle. If you do a favor for one of my children, you do me a favor. This is true for our heavenly father as well; if you accept his son, you accept him. If you honor his son, you honor him. Jesus extends that principle to his disciples: to reject the disciple, the ambassador of Christ, is to reject Christ, and to reject Christ is to reject God.

The principle may be extended further. The church is the body of Christ. Our Lord was sent by His Father; we are sent by our Lord. We are sons and daughters of God, and our acceptance flows back to Him. In that light, how should we behave?

We need to remember the principle of the Sower. If we are generous in God's work, God will be generous with us.

Note Christ's example here: even to children. In that society, children were the least of all people. He extends his care even to the least, and we should too.

Some will object that the world does not seem to work this way. Many of the faithful labor away, caring for the least, and see no sign of the reward. But God is not finished with us yet. He has not yet closed his books, desiring that none should perish.

There is judgment to come. When the Lord returns, he will punish those who have rejected this Gospel.

But at the same time he will reward those who have heard the Gospel and taken it to heart. Those whose lives show the love of God in their hearts will be richly rewarded. Indeed, a prophet's reward for receiving a prophet.

God is just. We may think that we have not had the opportunity, or the call, to become a missionary, or a prophet, or a preacher. These we know God will reward richly. But God will judge on the basis of our opportunities as well. You were not a missionary? Fine; how did you receive the missionary I sent to you?

God is just. The time for his return is approaching, and his reward is in his hand. Let the reader prepare.

The Burden is Light
Matthew 11:28-30

Nothing is so characteristic of Christ as the invitation. Have you ever wondered why God does not "make" the world behave as He wishes? Someday, at the renewal of all things, He will. But it is His good pleasure until then to invite, rather than to command. He wants not your outward obedience but your entire self, and that can be gained only if you give it.

Who does He call? He calls the burdened ones.

Those who are burdened with guilt. Guilt that to them cannot be forgiven or forgotten, guilt that presses them down. These he calls.

Those who are burdened with the chase of this world. Whether for fame, or justification, or just to keep up with our own desires, these are burdens indeed. These he calls too.

Those who labor in their own righteousness, those who want to work their way into heaven. Their burden is extremely heavy. These he calls too.

Indeed, he calls all of mankind. There is only one qualification for becoming a Christian: you have to be a sinner first. So far, this has not posed any practical difficulties.

To what does he call you? To rest. Rest from the things of this world. Rest from the burdens of this world, whether the burdens of the flesh, or of worldly things, or most deadly of all, the burden of pride. You cannot give them up while you are your own master, but in his yoke it is easy to part with them.

You see, he truly is gentle and humble. He knows (who better?) that power is best clothed in gentleness. All know that the truly strong do not have to brag about it. The small dog barks the most often. God has no reason nor desire to make you miserable; rather, he loves you and wants to share with you.

That is why his yoke is easy and burden light. The yoke is easy because he is pulling it with you. He is our comfort in time of trouble and strength in time of need. Our troubles here are but momentary and our reward eternal.

If your burden today is heavy, perhaps it is because you have not shared it with your yokefellow—Jesus Christ. Take your burdens to the Lord in prayer, and he will indeed give you rest.

Never Be Shaken
Psalm 15

Some of the shortest of Psalms can have the most punch. This is one. Hebrew poetry rhymes in thought, and in the echoing stanzas of this Psalm we see a test of righteousness which still applies to us today.

A blameless walk: where have your feet taken you today? Have you been where you should not have been? Many times our sins start with being in the wrong place at the wrong time. But it is not sufficient just to stay away from trouble. We must also actively do what is righteous. What have you done today that would show that to the world?

Speaking the truth from the heart: it is difficult to see from the outside whether a man is really speaking from the heart. From the inside the view is a little clearer. Are you a truthful person? More than that, check that tongue one more time to see if the temptation to slander someone is there (even if you're sure it's true).

Do your neighbor no wrong: this is a milder form of the Golden Rule—but note also that we are to cast no slur on our fellow man. Sometimes the wrong is in words as well as deeds.

Despise the vile: we like to think we are "open-minded." But as Calvin Coolidge once remarked, sometimes being open-minded is just being too lazy to make up your mind. When you encounter someone who is openly wicked, are you properly outraged? Even more difficult, do you honor and praise those who fear the Lord? Or do you snicker at the righteous and admire the wicked for what they have?

Keep your oath—even when it hurts. As my father taught me, if a man's principles don't cost him anything, they aren't worth very much.

Lend—without usury: how do you handle your money? Do you freely give when called on, and freely lend in need? That's one side. The other side is this: can you be bought for favor or money?

Hear the word of the Lord: if you pass these tests, and that means by doing, not just by saying, then you will never be shaken. Why? Because you have the Lord as your foundation, and that foundation is eternal.

The Great Divide
Matthew 12:22-32

There is a common thread among those who oppose the Gospel. It is this: any explanation, no matter how implausible, is preferable to acknowledging that Jesus Christ is the Son of God. The Pharisees show this here. Christ drives out the demons, and they say it must be by demons that he drives out demons.

Their argument is simple: the reason he can drive out demons is that he is possessed by a stronger demon. Jesus points out the fallacy of that thinking. Satan's kingdom stands only by the ways of this world. No one in his kingdom entertains thoughts of being unselfish; everyone is in it for himself. So therefore, if one demon drives out another, Satan's kingdom is (obviously) fractured.

God, however, is one. Integrity is God's characteristic: "Hear, O Israel, the Lord your God is One." His kingdom is not divided, and his power is set against Satan. Therefore you must choose: either Satan's kingdom is fracturing and falling apart (hallelujah, but not much chance) or the kingdom of God is upon you.

That forces a choice. As long as things are in doubt, you are permitted to sit on the fence and wait and see. But now the demons are driven out, now the lame are healed, and now a decision must be made. If you fail to decide, you will be left out. So you must decide, even by not deciding. But how are you to do this?

Christ gives you the key: a tree is recognized by its fruit. You see in front of you what claims to be the kingdom of God. Do the actions of these people look like those of God?

Do they care for the poor and lost? Do they spread the word of God and the love of God in comforting others?

Do they show the righteousness of God? Is their word something you can trust, or do you need to get it in writing?

Are their words gentle and kind, sorrowing over the wicked and rejoicing over the good?

Jesus clearly tells us that the heart of man is the essence of the matter. If your heart is in God's keeping, its bounty, its overflow will be from God. Your words and your actions will show all that you belong to him.

It is a good test—for a church congregation, and for a Christian. How do you fare at it?

Agriculture and Evangelism
Matthew 13:1-23

The parable of the soils and the Sower is a frequent subject of sermons. From a teacher's point of view, however, the four souls shown in the four soils are also seen in the classroom:

The seed on the path, Christ tells us, represents the one who does not understand. Note, please, that he does not say this is the one with the hardness of heart, as it is so often interpreted. This is one who just doesn't "get it." We see him often, brought in by the advertising and confused by the service. Is his lack of understanding really just a reflection of the fact that he has no one to guide him? Is his lack of a guide a reflection of our lack of concern for the lost?

The seed on the rocky soil has no root. This is a cruel trick to play on the teacher, for such people often come in appearing on fire for Christ. They are really on fire with the idea that all their troubles are over. Their troubles are not over. When the next one surfaces, it's obvious enough to them that Jesus Christ is not the painkiller of choice.

The seed among the thorns fills our churches. The teacher sees them every week. They sit in the class, listening to the lesson, approving or nodding quizzically—and then they go home and do nothing about it. They are hearers of the Word, not doers. But they don't think themselves hypocrites. They know that there are many real-world problems they have to face, and they don't have time for Christ. They are lost—among the weeds. Until they pick up the sickle of the Scripture and apply it to the weeds, they will not be found.

But—the teacher's blessing—there are those in good soil. Not always visible from the world's perspective, their lives show the power of God. How? Everyone they touch knows that these people have blessed them; they leave a little bit of themselves, as Christians, with everyone they befriend. If you look around them, you will see those who imitate them, as they imitate Christ. Of such is the kingdom of God.

Is it that you don't understand? ASK! Do you think God will keep you from all pain? Think again. Is there no time for Christ in your life? Cut the weeds of materialism, and see. Are you fruitful for Christ? God bless you (and the teacher thanks you)!

Word from the Enemy
Matthew 13:24-30

The current notion is that all opinions concerning religion are equally valid. Nowhere is this notion so cherished as in America. It is the perversion of a hallowed precept. Our nation was founded with the idea that the government had neither the right nor the duty to prescribe a religion. Indeed, the power of God was held to be such that His blessing was to be sought, and the government was not to dictate how He was to be worshiped. But no more.

There is a difference between saying, "You and I have a right to our opinions " and "Our opinions are equally true and valid." If I believe the earth is flat and you think it is round, we are both entitled to our opinions. But one of us is ignorant, or worse.

The truth is there to be found, but the enemy of mankind, Satan, sows the seeds of deception.

Satan cannot create; only God can. But Satan can distort. So many of his lies are distortions of the truth.

- One such distortion is the idea that I can work my way into heaven. Surely God honors and desires the acts of charity and righteousness of his saints. But these are not to be confused with the sacrifice of Christ on the Cross.
- Another such is the idea that God wishes to bless us—and therefore is nothing more than a cosmic blessing generator. The "name it and claim it" method comes from this, and ignores the righteousness of God and the sinfulness of man.
- Satan is also a liar; indeed, the father of lies. So he tells us that (as reasonable people, of course) we cannot possibly believe in that comic fellow with the pitchfork and tail. Since Satan does not exist, obviously God doesn't either. But nowhere in the Bible does Satan appear as a comedian.
- People everywhere seek comfort in understanding "psychic forces"—the power of magic. A benevolent force that can be harnessed for my profit is always welcome. A God who is righteous and demands honor is not. The Force is with us, and it is not a blessing.

The lies of Satan are long known, and long since refuted. But each new generation hears them again, and the tempter grows his weeds among the good grain of the church. But those who love the Lord will listen to his word, and his word alone.

Preparation Justified
Genesis 42-43

Many of us have the idea that while we have a goodly amount of trouble with the small things of life, we would certainly do well if God were to provide us a major challenge. We would rise to the occasion, we think.

It is not so. God trains his servants in the small things of life so that, if and when the time comes, they will be faithful in the grand things of life. Joseph is an example.

Think of the temptation to take vengeance on his brothers. These are the men who had him sold into slavery. Now they are starving, and he is in charge of the food. But what lesson did Joseph learn with Potiphar's wife? Resistance to temptations.

There is also the fact of criticism. The Scripture plainly tells us that the Egyptians thought it despicable to eat with Hebrews. Joseph commands that a banquet be made for them. How much easier just to treat them like scum! Joseph risks scorn to accomplish God's purpose.

The greatest temptation is pride. How grand it would be to lord it over them, reminding them of his visions, and sneering at them now!

How did God train Joseph to resist these temptations? By suffering. See what suffering has brought to Joseph in the way of virtues:

First, there is humility. He has been sold as a slave. No longer can he look at others with unsympathetic eyes. He knows what it is to serve, and to rule—and who made the trip between possible.

There is also patience. When he interpreted dreams in prison, don't you think he anticipated that his "friend" the cupbearer would remember him? When he didn't, God was teaching him patience.

Most of all is this: Joseph was faithful in little things—in Potiphar's house, in the prison. So God had tested him and knew that he would be faithful in much.

We like to dream that God will call us to do great things. Indeed He may. The real question is, will we be faithful servants in the things to which He has called us? Only then can we know that great things could be ours.

The Cost of Forgiveness
Genesis 44-45

In the 1850s, Dan Sickles was a prominent Congressman, elected via the Tammany Hall machine. He moved in the graft-ridden circles of Washington, wheeling and dealing. One of the men he dealt with was Philip Barton Key, an attorney and the son of Francis Scott Key. Key did legal business for Sickles, and soon the two men became fast friends.

This would be unrecorded except that Key also became friendly with Mrs. Sickles. Too friendly, to the point of adultery. One day Sickles walked into the shabby downtown apartment the lovers kept for such trysts and shot Key through the head. He then went to the Attorney General's office, handed in the gun and surrendered himself.

The trial was a national sensation. His defense attorney was Edwin Stanton, later Secretary of War under Lincoln, who used—for the first time, evidently—the defense of "temporary insanity." He used it successfully. Sickles was acquitted.

When he returned to the halls of Congress, every other member publicly ostracized him. No one would sit near him; when he spoke, all the other members would leave. Perhaps you think this is the just treatment of a murderer who got off on a technicality like that. Perhaps it is just. But murder was not the reason that Sickles was treated like a leper. The real reason: he forgave his wife, and took her back. Forgiving murder in love's name is one thing. Forgiving adultery is another, or so they thought. Perhaps he loved her.

Forgiveness costs. You will certainly pay the price of foregoing revenge; you may pay the price of having your friends think you crazy; you may even pay the price of having to forgive again. And who pays the price of forgiveness? The innocent one.

Joseph could have taken vengeance. No doubt his servants thought him completely mad to forgive this way. And as his "don't quarrel" remark shows, he knew that this would not be the last time. But he did it.

We are the imitators of Christ, the ultimate Innocent One. He paid the price of our forgiveness at Calvary. He forgives again and again those who repent. Without his innocent sacrifice, we could not be forgiven. How then can we not forgive? He loved us to the Cross; surely we can love and forgive in His name.

The Canaanite Woman
Matthew 15:21-28

It is no accident that this section is sandwiched between two episodes with the Pharisees. She is the contrast; she is the right answer. Consider her not so much as the example of faith as the contrast to the Pharisees:

The rules are all against her. The Messiah, the Christ, was sent to Israel alone—and you got that right from the source. "What part of 'no' don't you understand?"

She has none of the merit of the righteous—and claims none. There is not a word of how deserving she is, how innocent her daughter.

But note this well: she begs. She begs in the face of rejection. The grace seeker turns even rejection into grace!

Here is the cure. How often have we had Jesus reject our prayers, only to see us go away and sulk. Our pride will not allow us to take his rejection as a way of humbling us—for if we will not humble ourselves in his sight, he will do it for us—so we sulk away. Look at the example of faith! Rejection brings humility; humility bases itself on grace—and God is gracious.

How, then, do we become humble? It is not something to be found in the various self-help books so constant today. Indeed, we need to seek it as it has been sought in the past.

Practice! Humility is not a theory; it is the deliberate work of a Christian. Place yourself in situations where humility is a requirement.

Prayer. In meeting the Almighty, you cannot help but understand that you are the creation, He the creator.

Reading. Both in the Scripture and in those Christian authors who speak to you, hear what God is saying to you.

Application. Do not let the lessons of prayer and reading be merely toys of the intellect. Deliberately apply them to your daily life.

If your pride will not permit you this, consider that you may indeed borrow his humility. Jesus became humble, submitting himself to man—to the point of death on a cross—so that you might become humble enough to submit yourself to God.

Seeking a Sign
Matthew 16:1-12

One of the constants of Christian discussion in our time is this: we seek the miraculous. "If only I could see one miracle," we say, "my faith would be so strong." It is not so. There were those who saw Christ in the flesh who did not believe - to the point of crucifying Him.

Why do we seek a miracle? It is not a question of evidence for the faith; there is plenty of that. I submit that there are two reasons:

> We have abandoned the idea that God is the ultimate authority in things spiritual. Man now presumes to be the ultimate authority on all things. If someone comes along and says that we are wrong, he'd best have a great deal of evidence! Would even a miracle suffice to burst this presumption?

> Our lives are based upon our works, not upon faith. We believe, especially in America, in self-reliance. A life based upon works must stand by itself. There can be no gaps in our works, any more than we could overdraw our checking accounts. Every detail must fit together in our self-mandated perfection. There is no room for the miraculous, for that would not fit our perfection.

We did not reason this out. It has come upon us slowly, like yeast working in bread. We do not see the yeast doing its work, only the result of that work. The bread is puffed up, but there is no more nutrition in the fluff than there was in the dough. Our egos are now so puffed that we believe ourselves the ultimate authority in the universe. Such an authority cannot stand the challenge of God's miracles.

What shall we do? Go to God and demand miracles? No, the sign given to a generation such as ours is clear. The "sign of Jonah," the risen Christ, is all the sign we need. We need to go before our maker in humility and prayer, asking his forgiveness for our presumption. We need to beg his mercy and grace for ourselves, for our nation, for our generation. We ought to show our faith and repentance by honoring his name, both in word and in action.

Then indeed you will see the miracle—the miracle of grace. God is merciful indeed; he will swiftly forgive those who turn to him. Then indeed you will see healing—healing of the spirit of the land in which you live.

The Transfiguration
Matthew 17:1-9

There is a wonderful sense in which God is an artist. Note the beginning of this passage: "after six days..." Why six days?

One reason might be that the Artist who created the universe in six days is now using the exact same timing to show his disciples the prime element of the creation—as it will be when it is renewed. Six days for creation; six days to see the new creation.

The motif is repeated at Jericho. Six days the Israelites marched around the walls. On the seventh day, the walls of this universe fell down, and the disciples saw the Truth unveiled indeed.

In the mystic vision of Ezekiel, the measuring rod of the Temple was six cubits. Six days for the measure of all things?

Whatever the reason, here is the original "mountaintop experience." It brings us to the question: why can't we stay in that kind of experience? Certainly the disciples wanted to; why would Jesus not allow it?

Peter provides the answer by asking to build three shelters, or tabernacles in older translations. This comes from the Feast of the Tabernacles—which reminds the Jew that he is a traveler through this world. We cannot stay; this world is not our home.

Indeed, the experience is on the mountaintop—but the work is in the valley below. Where should the servant of God remain, but in the work God calls him to?

The purpose of the mountaintop is vision. Near my home is a year-round creek, rare in Southern California. It flows year round because of a dam upstream. The mountaintop is the dam that provides the vision—which flows in the valley year round. Carry the vision to the work.

The reaction of the disciples is quite typical. It is likely that they have seen the pre-Incarnate Lord, the Angel of the Lord of the Old Testament. Angels usually begin their announcements with "fear not." So their fear is a normal thing. Consider, however, that all mankind will someday have the same experience. The Risen Lord is coming again. When he returns in this glory, will you be one to "lift up your head, for redemption draweth nigh"?

Sons Are Exempt
Matthew 17:24-27

There is a running question among Christians in any age: how much respect is due to the authorities of the day? In this episode—which, by the way, shows the divine sense of humor quite nicely—Jesus shows us two things:

> The authorities are, in general, to be obeyed—even when oppressive. This tax is being collected "out of season" (it's fall; this tax was supposed to be collected in the spring).

> This respect for authority is, however, a exercise in trivia.

Simply put, the tax is not in conflict with God's command, and thus should be paid.

However, to make the point clear, Jesus does ask Peter from whom taxes are collected. Remember that the Romans rule Palestine as conquered territory, and view it as one more territory to enrich Rome. The implied point is this: should the temple of God tax the Son of God? To show his estimate of how important this issue is, Jesus tells Peter to go fish.

Why is this? The phrase "so that we may not offend them" is the same Greek phrasing translated elsewhere as not causing them to "stumble." The Greek word is *skandalon*, from which we get our word "scandal." Even the tax collectors, looking for an occasion to accuse Jesus, are not to be given a reason to stumble.

You see the point, of course: it is better to pay the tax, no matter how insulting, than to give someone else a point on which to stumble.

The striking thing in the passage, however, is the insouciance of Christ. In our terms, He would be thumbing his nose at the IRS—all the while staying within the tax laws. There is a key point in this: just who's running this world? The bureaucrats and politicians think that they are. And they are—just as far as God permits. This often gives rise to the arrogance of politicians and bureaucrats. The child of God must see "greatness" in a very different light. Nations and kingdoms, statesmen and politicians, bureaucracies and agencies—all these are temporary things. Only the things of God will endure forever.

The Greatest
Matthew 18:1-22

The best leadership is always by example. Ask your kids!

Christ, the master teacher, is always willing to use the example at hand. This is not the only time he will use a child in this context. From this picture we must see what he means:

A child signifies "family" to us. This is an early indication of the family of God. Indeed, Christ might be signifying that whoever receives his child, receives him.

In the family, the Father is the head. If we are to follow his leadership, we must see with his eyes. If He sees the unimportant as important, so should we. We must therefore "do the best for the least."

Even the unimportant may be an ambassador of the great. We are the body of Christ; He is the image of God; therefore, whoever receives a child of God receives Christ, and therefore God. (Think of it this way: how do you feel about the way other people treat your children?)

The example suffers in our time. Children are no longer "seen and not heard." Society values youth and despises age; but it was not always so. Then, to be a child was to be at the bottom of society.

This is a warning against pride. Of all the difficulties faced by a Christian, pride is the worst. We should work hard at righteousness, for our Lord commands it. But a part of that righteousness is that pride has no place in the Christian's life. Examine the face of a little child basking in a father's praise. The glow of accomplishment is wonderful. There is no sense of "I am better than you are"; rather, there is the sense of accomplishment and of pleasing the person you most want to please. That same sense should be the Christian's goal: pleasing our heavenly father.

My father often told me that he was "easy to please, but hard to satisfy." Our Heavenly Father is like that. He is well pleased with our efforts to be like him, but nothing less than the righteousness of pure perfection, of our Lord Jesus Christ, will satisfy him. By his grace, we have that perfection, given to us at the Cross. Therefore, we have nothing to brag about, but every opportunity to please. We are his children; let us make every effort to please him.

Personal Church Discipline
Matthew 18:23-35

There is a price to church discipline that is not often seen. Most of us know the steps of church discipline. In particular, the first step is to go to the one who has offended, in the name and power of Jesus Christ, and point out the sin. As this is usually taught, we think that the person going is a minister, a teacher, or some other person of authority in the church. This is not true.

That person comes only as the second step in discipline. The first step is usually taken by one particular person: the one who has been offended. This carries implications:

As the "offended one" our usual reaction ("I need to talk to someone about this") is wrong. We need to do like my mother did: bring up the offense immediately, and in terms of the offender's relationship to Jesus Christ. (I can still hear my mother's voice: "If you consider yourself a Christian, ...")

The cost may be very high: forgiveness. Worse yet, that forgiveness may involve my relationship with the church; I may have to call on them to help me forgive. Am I enjoying my anger so much that I will not forgive, but instead "turn him over to the church?" Or worse, "turn him over to the Lord?"

No wonder Peter wants to put a limit on this! Christ's reply is in the form of a parable: that means he wants us to remember it well (it's a teacher's favorite technique). The ten thousand talents represents our debt to God; the 100 denarii the debt others owe us. The proportion is about right; every sin I have ever committed is first against the one who is Righteousness. The message is clear: there is no forgiveness for me unless I forgive others.

We often forget that forgiveness costs the forgiver. It certainly cost our Lord at Calvary. More than that, we forget that the price may seem insignificant to others, but be very painful to us. We very often cherish the offenses others commit against us. Is there any anger so delicious as the anger of remembering past sins?

We are the imitators of Christ. At the Cross he purchased our pardon, our forgiveness, from the one who is Righteousness. We must not imagine this to be a trivial or easy purchase. Indeed, forgiveness is costly, for Him or for us. I do not say forgiveness is cheap. I only say that it is required.

Why Did He Ask?
Matthew 19:15-24

The fascinating thing about this man is that he asked the question. The tragedy is in his response. One must ask: why did he ask? The answer is quite simple: something was missing in his life. But what was it?

Like Linus in *Peanuts*, he was sincere. This is no hypocrite. But sincerity alone is no guarantee of eternal life. The Thuggees, the sect in India that gave us the English word "thug," sincerely believed that murdering travelers sent them on their way to a better life.

Nor was it a lack of obedience. Christ does not challenge his statement that he has kept the commandments. He has known the joy of the obedient life.

Ultimately what was missing was his willingness to pay the price. He would not risk all on God; only a part of him was available. Something else came first in his life. He has missed the opportunity of a lifetime, and the lifetime of divine opportunity. "He is no fool if he would choose to give the things he cannot keep to buy what he can never lose."

Note how Jesus handles the commandments: He does not quote all of them—only those that deal with the relationships between people. He also does not quote the commandment about envy—which is typically the sin of the have-nots.

He places before him the ultimate in choice. "Why do you call me good?" No one is good but God. The man before him is God in the flesh, or so He claims. That claim may be denied, but can it be ignored? So now Christ tells the answer:

Get rid of the thing that stands ahead of God in your life: the money. But this is not sufficient.

Then, follow me. No great feat of service, no grand sacrifice. The sacrifice is not even in the money; that's just disposing of the obstacle. The service is simple: follow me.

There it is. Rich or poor, the claim is simple: follow me. The answer is equally simple, and here, equally tragic.

Ambition
Matthew 20:17-28

It's important to note that James and John are following the custom of the time. Influence is gained by the back door, or by family connections. However that may (or may not) have changed, we need to note that they did this *after* Jesus announced again his upcoming death. They did not understand what was going to happen—but they understood who he is. By Christ's teaching, John will now learn the lesson he will apply later.

Our Lord, in his response, makes three points:

First, you don't know what you're asking for. How often we tell God what we want, rather than trusting to his wisdom to provide for our needs!

Next, it is not his to give! Indeed, our Lord is a servant, and in this he sets us the example of the servant in the kingdom of God.

Finally, though you will not (necessarily) get the place, you will get the service—which is much more important than they thought.

The other disciples are indignant with this, of course. But it is interesting to see how Jesus handles that reaction. The disciples have started with the idea that to be first is to lord it over others. Jesus corrects this misimpression.

He reveals to them the great secret of the kingdom: service. In the kingdom, you don't take charge—you take care. Yours is to serve, not caring who gets the credit—for Christ should receive the glory. "It is amazing what you can accomplish when you don't care who gets the credit," the sign goes. It's even more amazing when Christ gets the credit.

Think of it this way: can you be indignant with a servant leader? One who cares for you, works hard to see that you are able to perform your tasks and sees to it that you are credited for it? It is impossible. Now, if you so much appreciate that kind of leader, what kind of leader should you be?

Each of us, in some way, is a leader in the kingdom of heaven, for each of us is a servant. So then, be the kind of leader, the servant leader, called for. Indeed, follow the example of your Lord. His leadership was that of the Servant King, who went to the Cross—for you.

Blind by the Road
Matthew 20:29-34

There are three sets of actors in this little drama. The crowd is the first, following Jesus. Note how they resent the beggar's interruption. We can learn from this attitude:

They were not expecting Jesus to do anything for the beggars. They were expecting him to teach. Does our world today look to the church for action, or words?

Indeed, his teaching was not expected to be given to beggars. They would not be socially acceptable to most people. The crowd expects Jesus to teach only the "right" people.

But when Jesus stops and takes charge, the attitude changes. We hear no more from the crowd.

Could it be that the world looks the same way at the church as the crowd did at her Lord? Are we expected to stay in our place and teach politely to those who are socially acceptable? But what if we don't?

The beggars had a much simpler role in the drama. They begged for the mercy of healing. Please note that they did not come to him with a full understanding of their sinful nature, with a complete teaching of correct doctrine, ready to be baptized. They didn't say anything about forgiveness or grace. They had one mission in life. They were blind; they wanted to see.

Jesus ignored all their deficiencies and lacks. He did not care about their lack of theology or unrepentant attitude. He did not stop to instruct them on baptism. Indeed, you might just notice here how unscrupulous our Lord truly is! It seems he will talk to anyone, from any layer of society. It seems he does not demand a correct understanding of doctrine. Indeed, it seems that the only factor of importance here is that Jesus had compassion.

Something in Jesus drew the blind men. Their motives may not have been the purest—indeed, they may have been purely interested in themselves—but they came to the right man. In simplicity and honesty they asked for their sight. They received it. But note what comes next.

They followed him. All the gaps of doctrine and learning, the need for prayer and teaching, all could be remedied in time. The essential thing was that they follow him.

Follow Jesus. Everything else is just a detail.

Authority in Things Religious
Matthew 21:23-27

Jesus begins his discourse here by responding to the Pharisees, asking them about the authority of John the Baptist. It brings up a question for us. We go through our lives relying on authorities. I don't have a medical degree; I see a doctor. My doctor relies on a dentist, and so on. In matters religious, then, we often rely on authority too. Why is John the Baptist an authority?

First, he seems free of the material reason for getting into the "religion business"—he's definitely not in it for the money! And we reason that anyone who is preaching, and not for the money, must have some other motive.

Next, there is a consistency of his life and message. He speaks like a prophet—and wanders the desert like one, too. We believe a man whose life matches his message.

But most of all there is the sense of conviction that he produces. When he speaks, people are convicted of sin—and repent. The common man knows who this John is, for the common man is a sinner, and a sinner knows when God calls.

The Pharisees have difficulty with this question. They're stuck. They know that John was indeed a prophet—but if they admit it, Jesus will simply ask, "Then why didn't you believe him?" If they deny it, they run up against the convictions of the crowd, and lose debating points. So they say they don't know.

Jesus cuts off the debate at that point. This is one of those situations where it's interesting to see what Jesus does *not* do. He does not take this and slam home his debating point. He cuts off the discussion right there. Why?

Perhaps it's because he is not debating. The Pharisees are playing at religious debate, trying to win theological points with this upstart rabbi. Jesus knows that it's much more serious than that. At stake here is eternal salvation, heaven and hell—for the Pharisees. To continue the debate would be to say that debate is all it is. It is not.

The Christian must know this and live this. We are not to be concerned with intellectual debating points but with the salvation of those around us. The command is not, "Look good with style points" but, "Make disciples." We need to remember who we are and how little time we have left.

Fox Trap
Matthew 22:15-22

The trap in these verses is cleverly constructed. If Jesus says to pay the tax, he loses favor with the people by siding with the Romans. If he says no, then he is a revolutionary—and the Pharisees may have him disposed of by the Romans.

Jesus' reply is indeed shrewd. Note that he first asks *them* for the coin. Perhaps he doesn't have one, but more likely he wants to make the point out of their own purse.

> The point is simple. If you use the king's money, you are acknowledging his authority in your daily actions. If you don't, you're saying it's worthless here.

> The same point applies today. Suppose you have a genuine Confederate dollar bill. Show it to someone, and they're bound to ask you, "How much is it worth?" No matter how much you love Dixie, you measure its value in Yankee greenbacks.

> Even in our day, the government owns the currency (you own the value of it). It's illegal to "deface" the currency of the United States, for example. It belongs to our government, and every day we use it we acknowledge their authority over us.

The debate over church and state has gone on for two millennia now, and it will continue until the Lord comes. When does the Christian owe allegiance to a state? The issue is complex, but one thing may be said: the weapons of the state and the weapons of the Christian are quite different. We are to overcome evil with good, not with more evil.

In a very real sense the world can perform Christ's test on us. We are Christians, the imitators of Christ, the sons and daughters of God. We, as Christians, are made in the image of God. We are the coinage of his kingdom. Just as Jesus told them to use Caesar's coins to pay our debt to Caesar, so we must use God's coin to pay our debt to God. We are debtors; "Let no debt remain outstanding, except the continuing debt to love one another," Paul said. And how is such debt to be paid? Only in the coinage of the kingdom, the lives of the saints. "Not with sword's loud crashing, nor roll of stirring drum; with deeds of love and mercy the heavenly kingdom comes."

The Standard You Carry With You
Matthew 22:34-40

Despite all the things I have done (my sins are both boring and dreadful, so I will not repeat them to you), I have never had the slightest difficulty in loving myself. In fact, I rather think I am the life of the party and an all-around wonderful fellow. I usually am quite willing to ignore my sins and go on with a smile.

Our Lord, in his infinite wisdom, has seen fit to apply a particular cure to this problem. First, he insists on repentance (for He is Holy). Next, he insists that I apply exactly the same standard to everyone else (for He is both just and love). Indeed, that is the literal meaning of "love your neighbor as yourself." I love myself; God simply insists that I apply the same standard to everyone else. This is not easy.

The standard is a convenient one. Unlike rule books and manuals, I carry it with me at all times; it is easy to consult and (since there is only one person who is the real expert) it is never ambiguous. So why, then, is this world such an unloving place, even among those who bear the name of Christ?

> Because of our lack of integrity, our oneness. This method requires that we look at ourselves and ask the question, "what grace would I like to receive?" Instead, we look at others and ask, "what do they deserve?" Integrity is required if love is to prevail!

> Because we will not love with all of our selves. We want to do part of the job, not all of it. We are lukewarm. God is not, and we should imitate him.

> Because we are feeble in our efforts; we quit too soon. We give it one or two attempts, but we don't really put our persistent, strong efforts into it. Any discouragement will serve as an excuse.

> Because we are not in close touch with Jesus. If we are in sweet fellowship with him, we imitate him. He went to the Cross for us; and what an example that is!

But take heart; there is forgiveness for this too. Remember that each new day brings us a chance to begin again to love as Jesus loved. Examine yourself; ask if you are loving those about you with the same standard to which you love yourself—and then commit yourself to do so, as Jesus has done for you.

The Tenth Commandment
Exodus 20:17

The Ten Commandments are set in a particular order. First come those commandments that relate a man to God—for without that, there can be no true relationship between men. Even these start with the most basic—no God before Him—and work down to the keeping of the Sabbath. It is likewise with the commandments regarding our relationships with each other. So in some sense the tenth commandment seems to be the last and least.

It is unique in one other regard. Of those that deal with men, there are six. Five relate to our actions; one relates to our desires. That one is the tenth. You shall not covet....

It is written in the style of the times. But even today the most expensive thing that most of us own is our house. So even after all these years we can see an example that applies to us.

To covet: to desire, to want, to lust after, to envy, to long for. Your neighbor has it; you see it; you want it.

Sometimes this is a matter of status. He has a new car; you need a new car to match him.

Sometimes this is a matter of jealousy. He has it; you want it not for yourself but just to prevent him from having it.

Sometimes it is a matter of lust. She is beautiful; her husband (or your wife) is a terrible inconvenience.

Sometimes it is a matter of pride. You are in competition with him; how unfair that he should have and you should not!

Sometimes it is just a matter of longing. The excitement is in the chase. Once you have the thing longed for, it bores you and you begin to chase something (or someone) else.

All of these are matters of the heart. Clausewitz said that the heart is the starting point of all things military. We are in a war with Satan, and the heart is his starting point too. We often watch our actions, if only for propriety. Do we watch our desires?

Chrysostom said that wealth is the state where our possessions are more than our desires. When we envy, we think ourselves poor and needy. As Christians we are indeed rich if we will but recognize and accept our riches. That will often mean that we must bring our desires into subjection to Jesus Christ. Do the desires of your heart show the love of Christ, or the lust of the world?

Misplaced Sympathy
Exodus 23:1-3

Exodus, and even more Leviticus, seems at places to be just a list of rules and regulations. But this is God's work, and even in the list of rules can be found the inspiration of God. In these few verses comes a warning.

It is an often repeated warning—indeed, the next few verses are such—that we should not side with the wicked rich in order to win their favor and money. Such conduct is understood to be wrong, though often practiced. The opposite conduct is also wrong. We are not to side with the poor just because they are poor, but rather to render honest justice. We see that here.

First, we are not to spread false reports. How often are we tempted to repeat (and nicely embellish) the rumor of the day? Is it not a temptation to feel that you are the one "in the know?" And of course the one in the know cannot help but add a few "facts." This is falsehood. The end does not justify the means, and in most cases the end is unknown; the motivation is just the sense of self-importance that spreading the rumor gives.

Next, we are not to be malicious witnesses. So often the temptation arises to be a "witness" to what we did not see! We know the accused must be guilty of something, so we soothe the conscience with that thought. Honesty is still the best policy.

More commonly, though, we follow the crowd. Most of us are sheep. The thought here is that of a civil lawsuit. Most of our neighbors will side with the poor against the rich, but that is not always justice. What the crowd thinks is of no matter to God, and it should be of no matter to the child of God.

Indeed, we are not to show favoritism to the poor simply because they are poor. We may show charity to them, as our Lord commands, but we must not bend our testimony or administration of justice in their favor. In our time we see lawsuits with enormous awards from "sympathetic" juries. Sympathy and mercy are commendable—at one's own expense. They are not the same thing as justice.

My father taught me that "if a man's principles cost him nothing, they aren't worth very much." Sometimes our principles must be displayed even in an unpopular cause. Righteousness still means something, even in this world.

Praise for Anger
Psalm 30

It is a curious thought: the Psalmist here encourages us to praise God for "his anger lasts only a moment." Often the Old Testament pictures to us the wrath of God. This is a problem to Christians who see God as love; in this passage there is a remedy.

Have you ever had to remove an adhesive bandage along with some hair? The swift pull is often the best way, just as swift surgery is often the best cure. Our Lord's swift anger is often the correct cure for our sinfulness.

Such anger serves as a corrective. If we see it properly, it produces what Paul called "godly sorrow." That produces repentance, and our Lord seeks that in us.

The Psalmist pictures us as weeping for the night. Surely this is the cry for mercy. We must not attempt to bargain with God, but rather appeal to him for mercy. The process is painful, but short.

Indeed, our Lord assures us that those who mourn are indeed blessed—for they shall be comforted. If we mourn for our own sinfulness, shall we not be comforted with his forgiveness?

Contrast this swift action with the favor of God, which lasts a lifetime (and beyond). This is a reflection of God's character.

God is love. Love may rise up in anger to correct the sin of the beloved, but it swiftly dies down and resumes its blessings.

God is eternal. Therefore, his desire is to bless us eternally. If we will hear his voice, this will be his pleasure.

We are the children of God. From this brief Psalm we can learn much. If we do, we should come away from the lesson ready to do His will. For example,

We should praise him because his anger is so brief. He does not punish his children forever, but only long enough to produce repentance.

We can imitate this characteristic of God. "Let not the sun go down on your wrath," as the King James Version had it. If anger is called for, let it be brief—and followed by forgiveness and love that last a lifetime.

Parable of the Talents
Matthew 25:14-30

This is a rich parable (pardon the pun). It can be taken in so many ways: as dealing with money; or (taking the fortunate English translation) as dealing with talent; or for that matter dealing with anything we have. This story is about using what we have, and we all have something.

Now, there is a curious point to this parable, often missed. What was the motive of the third servant? Fear. He has misunderstood his master's thought. Out of fear he hides the money in the ground.

In the kingdom, responsibility and authority come together. When God gives you something to work with, he has handed you the responsibility, whether that be a checkbook or a singing voice. He also hands you the authority to use it, for (as the world would say) it is "your own." All the complaints of the workers of the world (I'm responsible for failure but don't have the authority to do the job, or I have the wherewithal to do the job, but somebody else has the task) are nonexistent here. If you have the responsibility (i.e., you have the money or the talent) you have the authority to use it as you see fit.

Indeed, God is the ideal manager. Not only does he match authority and responsibility, he rewards those who perform. Very richly too; the bonus program in the kingdom of heaven is exceedingly generous. But God works on the same principle you do when you pick out a mutual stock fund: he rewards the ones that perform.

One interesting side note: this is an example of why we are to "judge not." We have no idea what God may have given the other servant.

But if God rewards, it is only fair that he withdraw that reward from the servant who does not perform. Indeed, it is a hard part of a manager's job to tell the poor performer of his reward; it is never pleasant. The third servant presents his excuses, and expects to be rewarded for them. God doesn't work that way.

Sadly, there are many in the kingdom who see their main purpose as sitting in the pew and watching. Examine yourself. Has He given you "talents"—monetary or otherwise—that you are not using? He is coming again, with your reward. Beware.

The Most Terrifying Passage
Matthew 25:31-46

We come now to what C. S. Lewis once called "the most terrifying passage in the New Testament." It is the separation of the sheep and the goats.

The story would have been familiar to anyone of the time. Sheep and goats are normally separated when grazing. The application is to all of us (it is not specific to ministers, deacons, teachers, etc.)—when Christ comes again, there will be the final divide. Some of us who call ourselves Christians will be sent to hell. The dividing point will be our treatment of others.

A curious point arises here. Note, please, that neither the sheep nor the goats know what is going on. Both groups object to the division on the grounds that they never did, or failed to do, anything for Christ. Neither group saw the face of Christ in the face of the poor. Why then did one group give, and the other not?

I suspect that those who do not give make one of two mistakes:

They do not distinguish an objection from an excuse. It is entirely possible that the man with the cardboard sign by the roadside is a fraud. Because frauds exist, they believe they are relieved of their duty to love their brothers. Counterfeit money exists too—but we continue to spend the real thing.

There is also the desire to judge. "They don't deserve it," goes the cry. Possibly they don't. But even the example of the Old Testament cries out here. The edges of the grain field were to be left to the widows, orphans and aliens. Fault did not matter; poverty and want did. Judge not.

Will you please note what is not used as criteria here? Jesus passes no sentence on the sign on the church door (did you belong to the right denomination?); no mention is made of church doctrine (though this should be as sound as we can make it); and worship style seems unnoticed. These things may be good, but we must not neglect the "weightier matters." If you are truly a child of God, then His Spirit will be in you. You will imitate him, as seen in the person of Christ. He fed the hungry; he healed the sick; he cared even for the undeserving, the sinners. He asks no miracle of you. The hungry, the thirsty, the naked, the stranger, the sick, the prisoner—all these are within our reach. But will we reach out to them?

The Lord's Passover
Matthew 26:26-29

It is clear from any number of pictures that Passover is a forerunner of the sacrifice of Christ. Jesus, at this supper, transforms the Passover meal into what we now call the Lord's Supper. In so doing, we can see many things that were in the Passover that are shown in His sacrifice at the cross:

The Passover lamb was to be "without defect." Jesus was our sinless sacrifice—as John has it, the Lamb of God.

The house was to be purged of yeast, a symbol of sin. This is also symbolic of our Lord's sinlessness.

Blood was to be applied to the doorposts and lintel so that the angel of death would "pass over" that house. We know that it is by the blood of Christ that we are saved, that judgment "passes over" us. Interestingly, it was applied using hyssop, which was also used during the Crucifixion.

Only the circumcised (whether Jew or alien) could partake of the Passover. Similarly, only the baptized believer should partake of the Lord's Supper—but it is open to all such.

The Jew was instructed not to break any bones of the lamb—just as none of Christ's bones were broken.

Interestingly, the Jew was instructed to leave none of the meat until morning—he was to burn it up if necessary. Just as Christ stayed on the cross only for one day, Good Friday.

All the people were to participate. It was not sufficient for the religious rulers to condemn Christ; they had to get the crowd with them. "His blood be on us and on our children!"

They were to eat the meal in haste, clothed for a journey. We are to eat it until he comes again—a coming about which we are warned to be ready.

And like the ancient Jew, God "passes over" us in judgment, not for our merit or good works, but because of his grace.

In Passover, God painted a picture of what was to come: the sacrifice of Christ. It is a measure of the importance of the Cross that God called out a people to himself by means of this picture. When we consider the sacrifice of Christ, we should remember that God drew us a picture fifteen hundred years earlier—so that we might know the genuine Lamb of God.

Blessed Forgiveness
Psalm 32

There is a sweet relief in confession of sins, so much so that the Psalmist calls it blessed.

Do you know the sensation of having a splinter removed from your foot? There is that terrible anxiety; then the relief that the pain is gone. Confession is like that.

There is a grand sense of "it's over." The event, the sin, is now history. We can go on.

There is also the sense of a relationship restored. It's like getting a hug from God.

But note, please, that this is not a mechanical action. You cannot go through the motions and please God with this. There must be no deceit.

Most of us, like the Psalmist, begin our reaction to our sins by keeping quiet. If I'm quiet enough, and no one notices, then maybe God will just let it slide. This is like cancer. It is an internal ache; "my bones wasted away," says the Psalmist. The feeling is one of something dying on the inside while putting on a brave face. It manifests itself as a weariness; in particular, a weariness of living. Life does not seem worth the living when there is secret sin in it.

But there is hope! Confession is readily available; indeed, it is useless to try to hide anything from God. Confession does not tell him what he does not know; confession tells him that you have acknowledged the evil of it. God's reaction to pure confession is that of a loving father: forgiveness. But beware—there is a sense that God must be sought swiftly ("while he may be found") so that the infection of sin, the splinter of evil, may not fester and breed more evil.

And after confession comes goodwill. The restored saint goes forth to proclaim God's goodness and mercy. Learning from his own experience, he teaches others the same truth. It is so much simpler to learn from the mistakes of others; it is also so rare.

Finally, after confession, repentance, forgiveness and goodwill comes rejoicing. The fully restored saint knows the joy of his salvation. The unity of Father and child is restored.

Seek Him now, while He may be found. He is merciful and swift to forgive, showing love quickly and restoring his children.

The Word of the Lord
Psalm 33

It is a distinct fact that many of the Psalms consist of exhortations to praise the Lord. It is not sufficient for the Psalmist to praise him; he must have you praise him too. In this Psalm he gives some of the reasons relating to the word of the Lord.

The word used for "word" here is the spoken word; until the time of the New Testament it would have been difficult to see the Christ in this. But the characteristics are there, for they are the characteristics of God:

The word of the Lord is "right"—this word can be translated "straight" as well. We still speak of someone as being a "straight arrow" to imply that he is a truthful man, and this is the sense of this word.

The word of the Lord is "true"—the original meaning has to do with firmness in the literal use, or security and faithfulness in the figurative sense. It is unchanging, and can be counted upon.

These are certainly characteristics of Jesus, the Christ. We also see what the Lord loves:

"Righteousness"—the word might be translated "rectitude" or "virtue." It is a sad comment on our times that this word now seems reserved for the church.

"Justice"—the word in the original carries with it the idea of a judicial sentence, much as we might say that "justice was done" when we hear of a fair sentence upon a criminal.

The Psalmist says that the earth is full of his unfailing love. Then comes what for the Old Testament is a curious point: The word makes the heavens and the earth. God spoke, and the worlds began.

Not until the time of the New Testament would this make complete sense. The original meaning was that God created the universe out of nothing, by his word. We know now that he created it by his Word—Jesus, through whom all things were made and in whom all things have their being. We borrow the very concept of existence from Jesus Christ. We are, because he is "I AM."

It is easy to see Jesus as friend; wonderful to see him as savior. To see him as Lord is sometimes difficult; but consider—he is Lord of all things. Even you, if you will accept him.

Pontius Pilate
Matthew 27:15-31

Pontius Pilate is, by all accounts, an able administrator. A bureaucrat by trade, he has been given one of the more difficult of Roman provinces. Pilate has been warned about this man, and this trial:

He has been warned by his sense of justice. The Romans were not particularly great philosophers, but they had a stern sense of justice. Indeed, it was their pride that they brought justice to a barbarian world. Surely here was the test case: the emotions of the Jews opposed to the calm justice of the mighty Roman Empire.

He has been warned by his conscience. Even at the end he tells the world that he finds no fault with the man. Why, then, the condemnation by the man with the troops?

He has been warned by his wife's dream. In those days these things were taken seriously. His wife has taken particular care to send him a message to keep his hands off.

Pilate, alas for his reputation before history, is a man of half measures. He is looking for a compromise to please all. He will not find it, but he will make two attempts:

He offers to flog the man and let him go. Surely this would satisfy the bloodlust of the crowd?

He gives them the poison pill option: which would you prefer? I'll release this man—or the local murderer, Barabbas. Surely you law-and-order types would not want that?

But nothing works. He falls back upon the politician's tool: the ceremony. In full public display, he literally washes his hands of the matter. The priests and the crowd, tragically, accept the offer. The blood of Christ has been upon their children from that day to now (which is no excuse for persecution of the Jews).

But even out of such a great evil God can make a great good. Jesus is condemned to the cross, and to the cross he will go. But from the grave he will rise, and in the cross and resurrection he will bring salvation to all who believe.

No matter how desperate the circumstances of your life, remember this: God took the evil of Pilate and the Jews, and turned it into the glory of the Resurrection. Trust him: he will do the same for you.

He Knows How You Feel
Matthew 27:32-66

Have you ever been down to the point where the government had to get someone else to carry your load? A welfare case? Simon of Cyrene carried the cross for Him. He knows how you feel.

Have you ever been down to the point where those around you can think of nothing more to say than, "Buddy, I'll buy you a drink"? They offered Jesus drugged wine. He knows how you feel.

Have you ever been to the point where the world takes away even your clothes? Have you had to watch total strangers pick through what used to be your clothes? Bankruptcy and the last garage sale, perhaps? They gambled for His clothes. He knows how you feel.

Have you ever been in trouble with the law? To the point where the criminals around you gave you a hard time about it? They crucified Him between two thieves, and even they insulted Him. He knows how you feel.

Have you ever been the victim of the insults of the mob? Just those looking on, laughing at you and calling you names? "Come down from the cross," they called to Him. He knows how you feel.

Have you ever had the "righteous" people insult you, calling you names and letting the world know just how rotten they think you are? Even the religious leaders insulted Him on the cross. He knows how you feel.

He knows how you feel, for it all happened to Him. Even though He had lived a sinless life, deserving none of this, that's how they treated Him. So when you feel the world coming down on top of you, whether you deserve it or not, remember: He knows how you feel.

Take your troubles to Him. Go to Him in prayer and tell Him how it is within the depths of your soul. There is nothing you can say that He does not understand, for He is human just like us. There is nothing He cannot comprehend, for He is God. There is nothing He cannot forgive, for He went to the cross for you, that you might be forgiven. There is no hurt too deep for the Christ, by whose wounds you are healed. Love, in its purest form, awaits you. He knows how you feel.

The Resurrection
Matthew 28

C. S. Lewis once remarked that Christianity could almost be reduced to one doctrine and one fact. The doctrine would be redemption by grace; the fact, the Resurrection.

Indeed, it is at once obvious that the physical, literal fact of the Resurrection of Jesus Christ is absolutely essential to any real form of Christianity. Every attempt to separate the Resurrection from the faith has produced a dead church, as many liberal denominations are finding in our own time. The early church was quite explicit on the point. Indeed, without the Resurrection, why would you bother with anything Jesus of Nazareth had to say two thousand years ago?

The most telling evidence for the Resurrection is, interestingly, the church itself. That Jesus was crucified was undoubted. All theories that hold that he was not, or that he did not die, ignore one tremendous fact. The disciples went from men who were depressed, in fear, and completely lost to men who boldly went out and turned the world upside down. Men do not do this for a lie. Indeed, all but one of the apostles, to the best of our knowledge, died painful deaths for the faith—as did millions of others. Men do not die for what they know to be a lie.

The manner of death, however, is a telling point. The early church was quite confident of the Resurrection. Indeed, they were so confident in it, and in the resurrection of all who believe when Christ returns, that martyrdom used to be considered the most honorable of fates for a Christian. To die for the faith was considered a mark of honor, a sign of God's favor. Indeed, Athanasius (about the fourth century) used this fact, which he declares was known to one and all, as proof of the Resurrection of Christ. After all, he argues, if Christ is not risen, then who would dare to die for his church?

How times have changed. The church no longer turns the world upside down, but tries to fit into it. Christians consider death not simply "absent from the body, present with the Lord" but a terrible thing. We think ourselves wise in this. Perhaps not; perhaps the preceding generations will rise up and condemn us as fools, not knowing the power of the Resurrection yet claiming the name of Christ. What is death to you? The end, or the gateway to the presence of the Lord? And does your life show it?

The Holy One
Mark 1:21-26

One of the unusual titles of Jesus occurs in this passage. It is "The Holy One." The title itself comes from the Old Testament, in particular the prophetic book of Isaiah. The meaning is clear: this man is the Messiah; this man is also God. What is unusual is the one doing the proclaiming: the demon.

It is a common reaction in cases of demon possession as recorded in the New Testament. It is quite clear that the demons wish to announce this title for one and all to hear—and equally clear that Jesus does not wish it made known by them. Many reasons have been suggested; perhaps one of the best is that our Lord does not want our faith to rest on the word of a liar.

But it is clear that the demons believe—at least in the sense that they know exactly who Jesus is. Believe, and shudder, as James says.

Why do the demons announce him by this title?

It is the name by which they fear him. Everything they are not, He Is. He is holy, separate, pure, beyond the touch of sin. They are steeped in it. Cockroaches fear the light; demons fear the Light.

It is the name by which they hate him. They have chosen to rebel against the Lord God Jehovah, the ruler of heaven and earth. Jesus is the ultimate example of obedience to that God of heaven and earth. He is all that they are not—and envy gnaws at their vitals.

"What do you want with us?" they ask. They know their doom; they fear it has come.

Hypocrisy is unmasked here. The demons see, glaringly, the Truth. But they will not serve; their lord, Satan, has infused them with pride. As Milton had Satan put it, better a ruler in Hell (which he is not) than a servant in heaven.

How about us? Are we among those who acknowledge Jesus as Lord—but refuse to obey his commands? Does our pride prevent us from humbling ourselves to serve him? If so, then we are no better than the demons, and have chosen their side in the ultimate war. God help us! Send us repentance, and then forgiveness—so that we may serve the Living God. The war is on; the choice must be made. Even the demons believe—and shudder.

Faith in Intercession
Mark 2:1-12

One of the most interesting facts in Scripture is this: we often see faith as the enabler of God's power, or the lack of faith as its limitation. We have seen how Jesus could work no major miracles in his hometown because of their lack of faith. This limit sometimes puzzles the new Christian, for it seems that it contradicts the omnipotence of God. I make these observations:

God *voluntarily* limits himself—to achieve his own purposes. If you want your kid's room picked up, rent a bulldozer. If you want the kid to pick it up—ah, that's a bit more difficult.

Likewise, God *voluntarily* enables us—the intrinsically powerless—to do great things. He usually (but not always) requires us to have faith, however, to do this.

One of the reasons God so enables us and limits himself is that he wants us to practice intercession for others. All through the Scripture the mighty works of the saints and prophets are not designed to inflate their egos but rather to build up his kingdom.

Such faith, and such intercession, are seen in this example. We are not told that the paralytic had faith; rather, that his friends did. They had to clear away a thatch roof (no small task) and lower him down on ropes to get him to the Healer. This was at no small risk to themselves, both in terms of physical danger and in terms of what the house owner might say about his roof! Here we have a true example of intercession—faith in action on behalf of others.

So often we pray for others and despair at our lack of effectiveness. We know that we must have faith when we pray on our own behalf. Do we have that same faith when we pray for others?

There might be a reason why we don't. When things look desperate for us there is the thought that says, "I might just as well commit my entire hope to God—because nothing else is working." Our "faith" comes out of our desperation as much as our belief. We have, personally, no options.

But when we pray for others, the temptation is always to ask for a wiser doctor or more powerful medicine. But if we truly love our brothers as ourselves, would we not be as desperate for them as for ourselves? And intercede with equal faith?

Sin Offerings
Leviticus 4

When reading through the entire Bible it is tempting to quit when one encounters Leviticus. The array of ritual laws seems endless, and pointless. But (buried in all the details) there are some things that we may learn:

Even the unaware can be guilty. The question of guilt or innocence is not a matter of feeling or emotion. One can feel guilty and be innocent; it is more common to feel innocent and be guilty. You may not even be aware of the fact ("But Officer, I never saw that stop sign."). Guilt, or innocence, is a fact.

Confession is required of the guilty. Once you find out that you are guilty, you need to admit it. Why does God command us to confess? First, so that we will not have our mental fingers crossed ("I have to say I'm sorry, but I'm not"). God knows we are guilty; it is important that we truly know it also. Second, so that we may be held accountable by our fellow Christians—and obtain their aid in keeping sin away from the door.

The penalty varies by the offender. The priest's sin costs the same penalty as that of the whole community. The leader's sin is more expensive than the follower's sin. Privates pay for generals' mistakes in war. God is just. He has the generals pay.

God provides a way for all. You can't afford a goat or a lamb? Then you may bring two pigeons or doves. You can't afford pigeons or doves? Then you may bring plain flour. Even the poorest have a way provided for them.

Atonement is required for all. Without atonement there is no remission of sin. Whether intended or accidental, known or unknown, all sin must be atoned for.

The Christian today sees these same principles. We are to examine ourselves for sin. We are to confess that sin, and make what restitution we can. For all our sin, for each of us, no matter how poor or vile, God has provided a way: the Atonement of Christ. At the Cross all the law was completed, for the perfect sacrifice was made. Atonement is required for all—and Jesus has atoned for all.

Do Not Fret
Psalm 37

Some commentators hold that this Psalm was written by Jews in captivity in Babylon. Imagine that you have been taken from your home to be the slave of those you know as wicked! How easy is the temptation to envy!

The Psalmist tells us not to fret or envy, for they will soon be gone. But the temptation is with us today. We can feel the same force today when we look at those who are the rich and wicked. Envy is the sin of the "have-nots" against the "haves." It's a common enough thing; what's interesting here is that it is not directed against those who are merely rich, but those who are wicked and rich.

The reasoning is simple enough. We're the good guys, the righteous ones, and we're supposed to win. That's how we see it. Whether it's "work hard and you will see your reward" or any other motivation, we view the wicked rich as those who do not deserve what they have—and of course we do. But consider: is it the Lord's will that you have such riches? He cares for you. He also knows that you are meant to be eternal. Riches are temporary. Did Mother Teresa have a good life?

The Psalmist raises the problem, and provides us the cure:

Trust in the Lord. Echoed in the next stanza as "commit your way" to him, it calls for our full-hearted trust—not just words, but pure-hearted devotion.

Do good. The echo in the next stanza says that your righteousness will shine. It will be very dull indeed if you will not do good. It is by practice that we acquire our habits, and by practice we polish righteousness to brilliance.

Delight in the Lord. Echoed as "be still," this could be taken to mean that we must practice the prayerful presence of God, always being glad to hear his voice and speak with him.

Refrain from anger. How often has your anger done you any good? How often harm? Is that not lesson enough? It leads only to evil.

When you live in the sight, or even in the house, of the evil rich it is a temptation to snarl beneath your breath in envy. Instead, trust God and do his will. He knows your temptation. He will reward your work.

The Vantage Point of Years
Psalm 37:25-26

The Psalmist continues his recital of comparisons between the wicked and the righteous. In the middle of this he makes a personal observation. He is now old; he remembers being young—but he has never seen the righteous forsaken.

It is not to say that he has never seen the righteous troubled—particularly by the wicked:

The word picture here is of the evil plotting against the righteous. Our law knows of a crime called "conspiracy." It means to plot together to commit a crime. Have you ever noticed that most of the evil people in this world just have to have someone else to plot with?

The next word picture is of the victim of such: the poor and the needy. It is a tragedy but true: the con man plots against the poor, probably because the rich can afford a lawyer.

The righteous are not encouraged to rise up and destroy the wicked. We are not to use Satan's weapons to defeat Satan, for then we are with him, not against him. The patient endurance in "times of disaster" is the mark of the righteous.

There is a telling phrase here: "in times of famine they will enjoy plenty." I remember my mother telling me of the Great Depression; how poverty was everywhere and many lost all their savings. Yet she always was pleased to point out that no one ever left our house hungry. It is the wicked who, assuming that all are like them, must borrow without intending to repay. The righteous know better; they give generously.

The truth of the matter is simple, and it can be found in this Psalm. The wicked rely on their own strength; when it fails, they do not hesitate to cheat and steal. The righteous rely on the strength of the Lord. The Lord loves such people and will not forsake them.

There is a lesson in here for us. So many of us are seeking security that we forget its source. God alone gives true security. If you trust in your own wealth you will find it fails you. If you trust in the Living God, He will never fail you. If you are old, and you remember being young, I ask you: have you ever seen the righteous forsaken, or their children begging for bread? Trust in the Lord with all your heart.

Divine Humor
Mark 4:35-41

It is just possible—despite generations of preachers to the contrary—that God has a sense of humor. Humor is best when you suddenly see the absurdity of the situation. The situation here is absurd; it's just that the disciples don't see it.

A few notes are in order. Jesus is a carpenter; the disciples are fishermen. He is their leader, and therefore has the seat of honor (the one in the back, upwind from the smell). He is asleep. We know that Mark wrote much of what Peter preached, so I suspect the disciple who awakened Jesus was Peter. Perhaps he felt that this was the time he showed the Man that he, too, knew a few things. Just perhaps.

Can you picture it? Peter, desperate because the boat was about to sink, yells, "Why don't you get up and help?" So Jesus takes him literally. He gets up, tells the wind to die down and tells the waves to be quiet. As if they were disturbing his slumber.

On a serious note, however, look at Jesus' reaction to the disciples: "Why were you so afraid? Do you still have no faith?" He is upset at their lack of faith! What did he expect them to think? He expected them to believe that He is indeed God in the flesh, the one through whom all things are made. "No water can swallow the ship where lies the master of ocean and sea and skies."

They are terrified at this. Like a man who discovers that his house was built over an unexploded bomb, they suddenly realize the immense power of the man in the boat. They have been screaming at the Lord of All, telling him what to do in a tone of voice that you and I would use toward a lazy son. If he calms the waves with the merest suggestion, what else might he do?

He, on the other hand, thinks the exercise a trivial one. You can imagine him going back to sleep afterwards.

Why did he permit this storm? Was it to increase their faith? Indeed, was it to increase ours? Perhaps it was to break them free from thinking of him as just a man; a prophet, no doubt, but a man like the rest of us. They had good reason to think that; He is indeed such. He is also God.

When you pray, do you remember who He really is? Do you converse with the gentle Jesus of the parables but forget the Lord who calmed the sea? Consider well. The fear of the Lord is the beginning of wisdom. Be wise in your prayers.

February 21*

The Pain of the Sinner
Psalm 38

One of the many uses of the Psalms is to put into words the pain the sinner feels. This Psalm is just such an expression. In the agony of the soul, the Psalmist pours out his heart, and in so doing gives us words we can use in our own time of trial.

He begins by stating just how he feels:

He is feeling God's wrath—he knows that God is punishing him, and it hurts.

Beyond that, he feels the pain of his own guilt. His conscience troubles him, and he pours this out to God.

Above all else, there are the longings of his soul. The light is gone from his eyes, his heart pounds—and all this is naked before God.

Is this all? No, he sees the reactions of others around him. They know his guilt too, and their reactions tell the tale:

Those who are innocent, his friends and neighbors, now avoid him. He is in agony, but they know he deserves it. They avoid him.

But those who are evil are closing in for the kill. This is a man who has tried to live a righteous life. Now he has failed, and failed publicly. Those who hated him for his righteousness now say, "We have him!"

What can he do about it? Of his own strength, in his own voice, there is nothing he can do. He cannot defend himself; he is guilty. But he can go to the Lord of Creation—and beg.

He acknowledges the state he is in. His pain, his wrong, his troubles and enemies, he pours them all out before God, pleading for help.

He confesses his sin, admitting that he is wrong. He does not ask for help by his own merit, but on God's mercy.

Indeed, he begs for help, and help quickly.

There is a model here for us. All of us sin. All of us at one time or another find ourselves begging for help. We can take the words of the Psalmist to heart. We are not the first; we will not be the last. Let us come before God, acknowledging our sin, admitting our pain, dismissing our pride, and ask God for his help. Indeed, Lord, come quickly.

54

The Number of My Days
Psalm 39

David, the Psalmist, is almost unique among the kings of the earth. He shared with us not only his triumphs but his agonies and doubts. Here is one such.

You can picture the situation. David is in the presence of evil men. We are not sure when this was written, but he had ample opportunity. Have you ever been in a situation where you are the only Christian, and you wonder what to say? That's about where David is. So he decides that the only safe thing to say is nothing. He'll shut up. This, too, has its drawbacks, for now he can say nothing good, either. Eventually the pressure builds within him in this tense situation, and he explodes to God with his cry.

"Show me, O Lord, my life's end and the number of my days."

Why that particular cry? Well, suppose God were to tell you, right now, just how many days left you have on this earth. Suppose he told you how you were going to die.

Wouldn't you tell him that you didn't think that this was enough time? How many more things you'd like to accomplish in your life? In fact, wouldn't you say, "That's too short"?

When you thought a little further, would you not realize that much of what you are doing—especially in piling up wealth—is a vanity? In fact, you would look at yourself and decide that you needed to use that time wisely.

Wisely? How? What would that mean? David tells us:

Hope in God – and no one else.

Ask him for mercy. Go to him and ask that you be relieved of the burden of his chastisement, for he is merciful.

Acknowledge to him that you are "just passing through" this world.

A wise old rabbi was once asked when a man should repent. He answered, "On the last day of his life." His student complained that no one knows which is the last day. "That's why you should repent every day," answered his teacher. God knows the number of your days; it's just that he hasn't told you. Use them well and wisely. Hope in him; ask his mercy; acknowledge his care.

Waiting Patiently
Psalm 40

So often we pray for the salvation of a loved one; so often we are disappointed that it does not come immediately. This Psalm can be seen (among other interpretations) as a lesson for that. It shows us the way in which God answers our cries—and the good and proper response we should have.

I waited patiently

Wait with whom you wish, but wait for the Lord. No one else is so faithful. See what he does here:

It begins with action, taking the sinner from the pit of sin and lifting him to the solid Rock of Christ.

This changes the sinner's attitude – a new song is born.

The change in the sinner cannot be hidden. Others see the change and know that God has moved in this life.

Blessed is the man

What is the life of this man now saved? First, he makes the Lord his trust. Note the phrasing: it is a choice, it is an action of the sinner. He chooses God to be the one source of reliance.

Thus, he must reject the proud. How often we admire the ones who strut the most! Not so the man of God.

He rejects the "false gods" - in our time these would be the desires of the flesh, and the things of the world.

But this is not the life of the legalist. It is not "sacrifice and offerings" but "my ears you have pierced."

What does that mean? In these days a Hebrew slave was to be set free after seven years. But if the slave was happy with his life, he could voluntarily remain a slave for life. The sign of this was piercing the ears. Paul often remarked that he was the bondservant of the Lord; this is just such a thought.

Such a life cannot be hidden. The actions of such a man reflect the law "within my heart." If the actions are there, then the words will be too—and they will be heard.

But it all begins with waiting patiently for the Lord. Your situation may be difficult. When times are tough it is hard to be patient, but patient you must be. Wait upon him, and he will turn and rescue you. The experience will strengthen you, and you will be blessed—as you make the Lord your trust.

The Scapegoat
Leviticus 16

The word "scapegoat" entered the English language, like so many others, from the pages of the Bible. The concept is quite simple: it is an innocent person who takes the blame for others. Here we see the origin of the term. We also see that it is a picture of what Christ has done for us.

  Note that there are two goats. One is killed and sacrificed; the other is let go in the desert. Which is which? It is chosen by lot. This signifies that they are really the same. One is a picture of Christ's death for our sins. The other is the picture of his carrying our sins for us, the remission of our sins. This goat is said to be "used to make atonement."

  Aaron is told to confess the sins and rebellions of the people over the head of the scapegoat. This, symbolically, transfers those sins to the goat. This is a picture not only of the transfer of our sins to Christ—he who had no sin, who was made sin for us— but also of our confession of our sins to him.

  The goat is then taken to a solitary place and released. This is like our sins being taken far away from us, never to return. They are remembered no more. The goat lives, just as Christ lives forever.

  The entire episode is done only once a year—on the Day of Atonement. This is a picture of Christ's atonement being sufficient for us once and for all.

The pages of the book of Leviticus often seem dull and dry, full of endless regulations for a people of three millennia before. But it is not so. God was teaching the Israelites just what kind of God He is, and what was to come. Many of these regulations point to the Messiah.

As they do, we need to remember that Jesus is our scapegoat. He bore the penalty in his body—as did the goat sacrificed. He bore our sins away from us, never to return, as did the scapegoat. It is unlikely that the Israelites ever worshiped the goat. They were to worship the God who provided the goat as a means to purge them from sin. We too should worship God, who provided us with a scapegoat—his own son, Jesus, the Christ. He has provided for us what the blood of goats could not: forgiveness. Worship the Lord who loves you.

While There is Time
Psalm 41

In the first verse of this lovely Psalm the writer gives us the secret of God's mercy: "Blessed is he who has regard for the weak." Does that seem strange? Consider this: God consistently uses your own standard by which to judge you. If you are one who cares for the poor, the weak, the sick; if you are one who seeks justice for all; if you are one who is merciful, then God will be merciful to you.

It is the only sentence in the Psalm that even hints at the actions the Psalmist has done, but it is a powerful one. In times of plenty the Lord will bless him:

He will bless him by deliverance from danger and pain.

He will bless him "in the land"—in his daily activities.

He will not surrender him "to the desires of his foes"—or, he will triumph in those contests between the good and the evil.

Even in sickness, God will restore him.

These are blessings indeed, but it is in time of sin that we need such things most. When we are walking in a righteous path there is almost a presumption of blessing. When we sin, and we acknowledge it, we want mercy. The time is a dangerous one, for those who hate us see our sins; they spread them and exaggerate them. Have you ever had those who hate you rubbing their hands together in glee, waiting for you to die? What a horrible feeling!

But God is merciful to those who are merciful. The darkness will last for the night, but then comes the morning when God rescues his people. Hold fast for the dawn.

Examine your life today. Each of us is polite and kind to those who are rich, those who are in positions of influence. How do you treat those who are poor? Particularly, how do you treat the invisible poor, those who go through life around you in positions of service— the waitress, the busboy, the clerk at the store? Are you demanding of them, or kind? The operator on the phone, the clerk behind the post office counter, all these are God's children as well as you. Do you "have regard for the weak?" If you do, then rejoice in God's blessing, for you love his children. If you do not, then reach out for God's mercy this very day.

I Am the Lord Your God
Leviticus 19:9-10

It is a curious but significant fact that many of the commands given to the ancient Israelites end with the statement: "I am the Lord your God." It is as if God is telling them, "The reason I gave you this command is because of myself; I am the Lord your God." Something in God's own character is revealed, therefore, in this command. This can be seen in this command concerning the harvests of the Israelites.

They are not to harvest the fields to the edges. It is as if God is saying to them that he is more than sufficient for them, they need not cut down all the grain. His provision for them overflows their needs—if they will trust him.

They are not to gather the gleanings. Gleaning means to go back over the fields, vineyards or orchards a second time so that you may get anything you missed the first time, or something that ripened too late. God is revealing a central part of his character here. He gives each of us one life, one opportunity to worship him. The opportunity he gives is more than sufficient, but you will never get a second one. Make the best of the one you have.

They are not to pick up any fallen grapes. Think of it this way: would you purchase bruised, dirty fruit at the market? Certainly not. Would you even think of serving this to family and guests? It is absurd. God's provision for you is quite the same. There is no need for you to pick up fruit from the ground. You are his children, and you will be fed as befits the children of the King of Kings.

Of course, whenever there is a spiritual lesson there is an application, which is rooted in practical, charitable work. If we are not to harvest to the edge, nor glean, nor pick up, who will? The poor we always have with us. Note how gently God deals with them. We are not to harvest these things and give them away; rather, they are to come and harvest them for themselves. In this way we do not humiliate them.

Do you trust God's abundant provision? Are you making the best of your life's opportunity? Are you a child of the King of Kings? Then do as his children do. Feed the poor and the alien, at your Father's command. His bounty is sufficient for you—and them.

If You Can
Mark 9:14-29

One of the frustrations of modern Christians is that they feel they should be able to work miracles as Jesus did, as if on command. The disciples felt the same way—only more so, for they indeed did work miracles. So this story must have shown their frustration.

The Disciples

Despite the power that Jesus has shown and shared with them, they still are unbelieving. They trust only what they have seen.

Therefore, they are powerless here.

They are also without a clue as to why. They are looking for the magic formula, and it seems lost.

The Father

It is easy to understand the father in this story; he is almost modern in his thought. First, he is a loving father, for he has cared enough for his child to take the chance that this strange new rabbi, Jesus, can do something for his child. Indeed, he gets to the point of begging, or the attitude of "whatever it takes." This is contrary to his nature, for he does not really think that this Jesus can do anything. But just in case there's even a slight chance he can, he'll give it a try.

Jesus

Jesus reacts to this as he often did: he condemns their lack of faith. The magic formula sought by the disciples, the wild chance of the father, both result from this lack of faith. It is not how to do it, but who will do it. "If you can?" answers Jesus. He makes it clear that the limitation is not on the power of Jesus but the faith of the father (and of the disciples).

The father gives us the first great lesson here. He believes—but not enough. So he turns to the ultimate source of faith and asks for help. Have you ever done that? When doubt assaults you, have you turned to God and asked for faith? He gives it liberally.

Jesus gives us the second lesson. Such things are not done by repeating a "faith formula." They are done by going to our knees in prayer.

Combine these two, now. Go to your Father in prayer, and with fervent heart ask him to increase your faith.

In My Name
Mark 9:33-41

One of the most disturbing aspects of Christ's teaching is found here. It seems that he does not have the finely tuned sensitivity we so cherish when it comes to who is important, or doctrinal correctness, or the practical aspects of charity.

He tells us to welcome small children in his name. Children in his day were the lowest members of society.

A child, after all, is a burden.

A child can do you no favors.

A child is a major responsibility.

But despite this, he tells us that welcoming such a little one is the same as welcoming Him! This tells us much about Jesus; he is indeed Son of Man, and understands even the neediest among us.

He also seems to be indifferent to which particular denomination is your own. This fellow driving out demons did not have the right credentials. But Jesus sees spiritual warfare as black and white: you side with God, or you side with Satan. There is no fence on which to sit. So all our disputes about baptism, liturgy, creeds—what are they? And all our reluctance to fellowship with those who hold the "wrong" views—where are they? Perhaps the only thing which truly matters is, "Who do you say that I am?" For he who is not against him is for him.

Finally, there is the immense importance that Jesus places upon the physical side of charity. Just when we have convinced ourselves that mere works are nothing and our spirituality is all that Jesus wants, he tells us that even so small a thing as a cup of water, given in his name, will not go unrewarded by God. It seems as if our means are not nearly as important as whether or not our hearts' desires lead to action. Faith without works, it seems, is quite dead.

There it is. This side of Jesus is not often remarked on in our day. But he spoke of it frequently. Do you welcome the poor, the helpless, indeed the small children? Is there time on your lap for the infant? Will you fellowship with the fellow from the other church? And do you practice the practical side of Christian charity on a regular basis? Have the poor eaten at your table? Does the water from your faucet flow like the water of life? Your Lord fed the five thousand; have you fed the five?

The Little Children
Mark 10:13-16

Background

It was the custom of the time for mothers to bring their children to any famous, visiting rabbi to have him lay hands on the children and bless them. We have something of the same idea when we say we've shaken the hand of someone famous.

Humility

Jesus uses this occasion to teach a lesson—symbolically. He knows that we learn well with an example. The child is the symbol of the poor and helpless of his time; they were the lowest members of that society.

Such lessons are memorable. I once had a boss who insisted that he was too important to make coffee—even after taking the last cup in the pot. One day a secretary spoke to him about it. He turned on her and let her know, vigorously, that this was her job. While he was yelling, *his* boss (a vice-president) quietly came up and made the next pot. Lesson without words, volume 1.

The disciples

The disciples thought they were doing a good thing. Indeed, they were doing a good thing; they were keeping distractions away from their Master. What they weren't doing was the *best* thing, which was to follow their Master's will.

So how were they to know? From Jesus' reaction we can see that he expected that they should have known. Perhaps it is this: they were so busy with the details of life that they did not remember the mind of their Master. To know his Mind is to do his will.

Jesus

Jesus was indeed "indignant" (the word is also translated "sorely grieved.") This is not surprising. God frequently proclaims himself (in the Old Testament) to be the defender of widows and orphans. Jesus is God in the flesh; the disciples had missed that point. So it was that they were keeping the children away in favor of those who were more powerful in society. And thus they missed the mind of the Maker.

How often we are impressed with "Oz the great and powerful!" How seldom we regard "Dorothy the small and meek!" Yet to God this is not right. We must be his imitators; we must take care for the powerless around us. We must make a way for even the little children to come to our care.

Allegory
Psalm 45

Allegory has a bad name among many Christians. For a variety of reasons they associate it with a style of interpretation which denies the truth of the Scripture. This is a recent attitude. Most Christian scholars of most times have considered allegory a form of the truth, and a very high one indeed.

This Psalm is an example of such. At first glance, it appears out of place; it seems to be a wedding song. But we must remember that the most common allegory for the church is the Bride of Christ. Seen in that light, almost all commentators agree that this Psalm is an allegory—something that can be understood on an earthly level (a wedding song) and a heavenly level (the Bride of Christ). God does this in several places; Song of Solomon and Hosea are two notable examples.

In this allegory there are two people pictured. The first is the King. This is likely to be Solomon in the literal sense, but in the allegorical sense it is, of course, Jesus Christ. We see three key attributes of the King:

He is a conquering king – over all nations and enemies, displaying awesome deeds. This can be seen as the spread of the church, or the conquest to come when he returns.

He is one who loves righteousness and justice.

He is described as being above all companions, superior to all.

The bride, too, is shown to us in such pictures.

She is a royal princess. We are a royal priesthood.

She is arrayed in the finest gold; we are rich in Christ beyond price or picture.

She takes the King not only as husband but as Lord. The church always acknowledges Jesus as Lord.

In the picture of the Bride of Christ, God calls us to devotion to our Lord and Savior. This is the measure of devotion that we are to have, that of a bride on her wedding day. The Lord and King the church takes as husband loves her, even to the point of death, death on a cross. That is his love for you, o church; what is your love for him? Is it indeed the passion of the bride for her husband on their wedding day? Love him with all your heart.

The Unusual Miracle
Mark 11

When we first read of the withering of the fig tree it seems unusual to us. Indeed, had it been a recently discovered fragment we would think it a later addition. It seems that such destruction is unlike the loving God. Certainly, God would not do such a thing in what appears to be a fit of temper. One other curious fact: the withering happens overnight, not instantly like other miracles.

We need to understand the agriculture and the symbolism. This particular fig does produce fruit in the spring—but only if it is planted in sheltered areas. Otherwise, only leaves are produced. This fig is in the wrong place.

The fig tree, however, is a well-known symbol in the Old Testament for the nation of Israel. Jesus is painting a lesson for his disciples, a lesson concerning the house of Israel. Certainly the history of the Jews since the time of Christ has indeed been tragic.

There are lessons in this tree for us too, however:

If you will not produce fruit, you will wither—from the roots (that is, Christ) up.

It will not be because you cut the root; rather, the root will reject you.

It will not be an instant withering, but it will not take long either.

So how then do we avoid such a fate? Christ's answer to the disciples' comments here seems almost out of place. "Have faith" does not sound like the answer to Peter's remark. But it is the answer to the symbolic side – it is the way to avoid being withered from the roots up.

"Have faith"—not perform great works, though these will come to those who have such faith. They will move mountains, our Lord tells us—but the point is, "Have faith." Have faith in the one Who Is. Have faith that He hears the one who calls out to him, and rewards those who seek him. Have faith in the one who is faithful and just to forgive you when you repent.

The warning is clear to the one who considers himself a Christian. If you will not have faith, if you are only going through the motions, the curse will strike. Therefore, "Have faith."

The Artistry of God
Numbers 2

It often seems that Numbers was placed in the Bible to prevent you from reading through the Bible in a year. Who cares how many of what tribe camped where?

But there is a curious "coincidence" in this chapter. The camp is not arranged in a circle, nor a large square – it is in the form of a cross! Note that (for example) on the Eastern arm the tribe of Judah is next to the Tent of Meeting. Just to the East of them is Issachar, then Zebulun. The total number of men is 186,400. This is the long arm of the cross. The short arm (to the West) is 108,100. The Northern and Southern arms are, respectively, 157,600 and 151,450 – in other words, about the same length. Seen from the air, this camp would be a cross whose base would be to the East (which in itself has symbolic significance).

Why? There is no reference to this point in the New Testament. Is it possible that God was laying out for us a picture of what was to come? We cannot say, for without confirmation it must remain a speculation. But it does raise some thoughts:

God is eternal; He never changes. His purposes never change. He planned from the beginning that Jesus would go to the Cross for the sins of the world.

God is the creator. Like the artists we know in our own world, he uses the same themes more than once, and so creates order in variety. He uses various pictures in the Old Testament—whether the Temple, the Tabernacle or various people (for example, Hosea)—to portray what is to come in the New Testament.

While we may groan at genealogies and lists of tribes, they have a purpose too. They are proof that we are not dealing with some misty legend, but the true history of a real people, the Jews. In this instance, it may be something more.

At the very least there is this: by reading through the Bible in an orderly manner you train your mind to value even the most boring parts of Scripture. Often you will find that what is meaningless today suddenly takes on a new meaning years later, when the Spirit has prepared you to receive it. All Scripture is inspired by God—and all of it is profitable. Some of it now, some of it later, but like God, it is all good. You know the workman by the work!

The Resurrection of the Dead
Mark 12:18-27

The Sadducees are a remarkably modern lot of people. They are very similar to many we see in the church today:

They consider themselves "advanced thinkers." The merely orthodox will no doubt soon fade away, to be replaced by their new thought. (Have you heard of Sadducees lately?)

They are not so much "for" a doctrine as against others. They are the professional doubters.

To show how advanced is their thinking, they are very fond of the "test case." That's what we see here.

Christ's reply gives us the answer to these "advanced thinkers." There are two key points:

They do not understand the Scriptures. If you give me liberty to pick and choose among verses, and to construct what I will with them, I can concoct almost any theory you like. But if I must consider the Scriptures as a whole as well as in detail, things are greatly different. Does it not depend upon motive?

They do not understand the power of God. Because they are the great thinkers, it is obvious that God would agree with them, wouldn't he? And wouldn't he be bound by their limitations? I think not!

So then, for the Christian the question comes down to these two: how do I gain understanding of the Scriptures, and how do I know the power of God?

To understand the Scriptures you must first read them! It is not sufficient to read about them, or to follow the latest Christian bestseller. You must read the Bible. Then you must accept the discipline and love you find there. When you have, then this must flow through your life into your witness to others.

Power can best be understood in one of two ways. You can see power in resisting it—as we see when we sin, and God chastises us. Or you can understand it in observing it. Consider the great things God has done, both in the physical universe and in the province of your life. Meditate on these things, and give him thanks.

"Advanced thinkers" fade; the word of the Lord endures forever.

Watch Out
Mark 13:1-13

For the Christian the world can be a frightening place. The disciples come to Christ and ask him about his statement that the Temple would be destroyed completely. Jesus, as is his custom, does not answer any question they should not have asked. Thus he will not tell them when this will come about. Indeed, he answers the question they should have asked.

What question is that? Even Christ himself was not to know the time of his return. That knowledge is reserved for the Father alone. Therefore it is presumptuous for us to inquire about it. But we might ask this: what will happen around us, and what should we do about it? This question bears upon our Christian conduct, and Christ answers it.

He tells of four things that will happen—indeed, have happened many times in many generations:

There will be those who claim to be Christ. The number of leaders who have claimed to be divine, or claimed to be a particular prophet with divine guidance, is legion. They are all frauds— so watch out!

There will be wars, famines, earthquakes—natural disasters of all sorts. Christ's injunction: don't be alarmed. Expect it.

The Christian will be persecuted by the government of the day. Our faith is to be so strong that Christ passes over the pains of imprisonment and torture and tells the disciples not to worry. Why? Because the Spirit will give them the words they will need in their own defense. It is this attitude—that before you put me to death you will hear about Christ from me—that makes the blood of martyrs the seed of the church.

The Christian will be betrayed by his own family. All earthly bonds will be ruptured for the cause of Christ. The Christian will be hated. Christ's command? Stand firm until the end.

Is your faith weak? Do you feel that your prayers are of no great concern to Almighty God? Perhaps it is because your vision of things to come is too dim. The day is coming when all Christians will be tested by such things. We must be prepared. We have been warned of what is to come. Perhaps your faith is too weak because your peril is too small.

If I Were Hungry
Psalm 50

In one of the earliest and most graphic descriptions of the Lord's coming we have the picture by the Psalmist. This Psalm can refer to nothing but the return of our Lord. Note how he begins:

God comes, and summons to himself both heaven and earth.

He calls together the consecrated—those who are set apart from the rest of the world to him. This can be none other than the church in our day.

They are set apart by a covenant of sacrifice. You can see that the sacrifices of the old Jewish worship did not establish this covenant—"If I were hungry, I would not tell you." The sacrifice of this covenant is Jesus Christ.

God calls all to the judgment, the righteous and the wicked. But note the difference in his warnings. To the righteous he says:

I don't need your works. In this time, this would be the animal sacrifices at the Temple. Even then the Jews knew that God had no real need of these sacrifices; rather, they were the acts of worship and devotion that symbolized the real devotion in their hearts.

Rather, he calls on them to be honest, to fulfill their promises. In addition, he tells them: "call on me." Rely on me; trust me; have faith in me. This is pleasing to God.

To the wicked, however, he denies the right to call on God. The point is simple: have you ever seen a news report of a lawyer using a point of law designed to protect the innocent to shield the obviously guilty? How we despise such men! God says the same: what right do you have to cite my laws when you ignore them?

Just in case you were in doubt as to who God might have in mind, he lists them: those who hate his instruction, those who steal, who slander, the adulterers. Note that first one--those who cannot stand to be taught in righteousness.

There is a serious, solemn point to this. The Lord God Almighty will someday return in power, and before him you will stand, to receive reward or punishment. To those who call on his name, he will be both merciful and rewarding. To those who despise him, he will be a complete terror. The choice will not be available on the day of his return. It is available now. Choose you this day whom you will serve.

Have Mercy on Me
Psalm 51

David was said to be a man after God's own heart, but even such a man sins. So it was with Bathsheba. But David repents as God would have him do; being a poet, he writes this Psalm about it. In that, we can see the steps by which the sinner comes home.

Repentance

> David begins by admitting his guilt. Not just a vague feeling of guilt, but the specific transgression. He knows he has done wrong, and that the wrong is against God Himself.

> David then expands that theme to show that he is indeed a sinner, and has been all his life. No one is righteous but God, and David is no exception.

> More than that, he confesses that God is the source of righteousness, and that he needs that source.

Restoration

> Restoration begins with cleansing. It is the purging by God of the sin. The illustration of being washed clean is most common, and very powerful; sin, like dirt, needs to be washed away.

> But this is not sufficient. Forgiveness he needs, but also a return to the fellowship he had before--the clean heart.

> Beyond that, he longs for the joy he once had, the joy of salvation. The sinner should not sorrow forever, but be restored to gladness.

Renewal of Service

So often when a sinner repents we are willing to forgive, but not to restore—and certainly not to allow them to return to a place of service to God. This should not be. Look at David's plea:

> He will teach others God's way. Is there anything so powerful to an addict as the testimony of a former addict?

> He will give praise to God, not for David's righteousness displayed in sacrifice, but God's righteousness.

> He will offer the true sacrifice: humility and contriteness.

The return to God runs down the road of repentance, stops at the station of restoration and delivers service renewed. But it begins with the sinner saying, I must return to God. He is always willing to run to you—if you will turn to him.

Prayer in Trial
Mark 14:32-42

In no other moment than this does Jesus so show us how truly human He is. His favorite title is "Son of Man." Here, like any other man, he faces the moment of his death—and deeply desires that it would not happen. With this deepest and most natural of human desires in his heart, he goes to his Father in prayer.

First, note that he goes in prayer three times, not just once. It is scarcely possible that He thinks the Father will not hear him. It is very likely that the agony of his heart is such that he must repeat himself. There is one other possibility, however. It is just possible that Jesus, with the loving care he always had for his disciples, is teaching them one last lesson in prayer. They are falling asleep; he awakens them so that they will see persistence in prayer one last time.

Jesus somehow gathers strength from this. Luke's parallel account says that an angel came and strengthened him. But there is no doubt that he was strengthened. He entered the garden overwhelmed with sorrow; he left his time of prayer with an attitude of grim determination. The strength he gathers reminds us that prayer is designed to bring us closer to God. Sometimes we don't want the power that prayer can bring. Sometimes we would prefer to remain weak—and by our weakness excuse ourselves from our duty.

Note too the trust that Jesus has in his Father. He appeals to him as a little child would, with the word *Abba*. It is an intimate, personal relationship. He begins with a confession of God's power—that all things are possible to him. But such is his trust that he does not argue with his Father. He asks to be relieved of the burden, and ends his request with, "Yet not what I will, but what you will." Was his mind going back to Abraham, bringing his son Isaac to what is now the Temple mount, to sacrifice him? Did he see Isaac's trust in his father too? We cannot know, but we can see the complete trust Jesus had in his Father.

Here are the secrets to deep prayer. We must persist in the depths of our hearts. We must draw strength from prayer to do God's will. We must trust our heavenly Father. Our Lord did so—and the strength took him through Calvary to the Resurrection.

A Wrong Repentance
Numbers 14

Most Christians are firmly of the opinion that if they ever saw a miracle, an undisputed miracle, their faith would be absolutely rock solid. The evidence to the contrary is found here.

The Israelites have sent out spies into the Promised Land, and ten of the twelve came back discouraged. They saw the men in the land. The other two saw the land, and knew the power of God. So which prevailed? The fear of men, or the proven power of God? You can read the answer. Despite all the miracles, they still did not believe.

There is an interesting epilogue to their unbelief. Moses goes before the Lord and begs forgiveness (again) for the people. God grants this, but declares that no one of that generation will enter the land, except the two spies who gave a good report. Look at the reaction of the people then.

They say, "We have sinned." They mean, "We got caught at it." Their repentance is not motivated by godly sorrow but at the penalty that has been imposed.

They treat God as if he were an impersonal force—like the law of gravity. Since this God objects to our lack of belief, we will change our minds and do what he wanted in the first place— despite what he just told us. Note the presumption in this! They are telling God the conditions of their repentance, as if he had offended them by punishing them.

Despite yet another warning from Moses, they go up to war with the inhabitants—who promptly rout them. God is not mocked; he is a person, not a force. You cannot treat him with presumption; you must approach him with fear and reverence.

Three thousand years have passed, but these lessons are not yet in our minds. When God tells us to accomplish something, or to stand for something, we count the forces opposing in human terms and forget that he is God—the battle belongs to the Lord. Then, when God deals with us as we deserve, we feel "found out." We make a show of repentance, trying to bargain with God. Now that we understand, how willing we are to do what we should have done! Come to him in true repentance, and he will swiftly forgive. Come to bargain, and you will see that he is still God.

Charity Without Hope of Reward
Mark 15:42-47

We know very little about Joseph of Arimathea. He is a minor character in the account of the Gospels. Interestingly, though, he is mentioned in all four Gospels—quite a rare thing. He goes to Pilate—after Jesus is dead—and begs the body. By Mark's account we learn that he is a member of the council. By Matthew's, we learn that he placed Jesus' body in his own tomb. By Luke's account we learn that he had not consented to the crucifixion. By John's account we learn that he was a secret disciple of Jesus. John's account may have been written after Joseph was dead, and thus have posed no threat to Joseph.

Other than these facts we know very little about the man. But Mark tells us that he was waiting for the kingdom of God to come. (John tells us that Nicodemus, who visited Jesus by night, also was with him). What may seem curious to us is that Joseph waited until Jesus was dead, and then took courage to speak up.

Joseph is acting in the finest traditions of Jewish charity. He knows quite well that the favor of placing the body in the tomb is one that Jesus cannot repay. It is an act of charity without hope of reward. By all earthly standards, there is no possible method by which Jesus could bless Joseph in return. By the standards of the Jewish leaders, Jesus had no intrinsic merit. For that reason the charity stands out as being completely selfless.

There is a point in it, however. Proverbs 19:17 tells us that he who is kind to the poor lends to the Lord, and the Lord will repay him. It is in this sense that Joseph has acted. So we note first that any reward for this act must come from God.

But that is not all. The act is one of great courage. If Jesus had been a man popular with the authorities no doubt this act would have been honored (and not at all risky). But this act risked his reputation. It therefore took great courage—we read that he went boldly to Pilate—and is all the more a sign of devotion to God.

There are the two tests of great devotion to God. Are you willing to do something that the world holds to be completely without hope of reward? Are you willing to do so at great risk to yourself? The sons of this world will tell you that you are foolish. But you are not a son or daughter of this world. Or are you?

Wings of a Dove
Psalm 55

The Psalms often puzzle the new Christian. It seems they jump about; there are certainly thoughts in them that seem unfitting for a Christian. But this has a purpose: it shows us that our fears and anxieties do not have to be pious and pure to be brought to the Lord. Consider the Psalmist here:

Is there a better picture of anxiety than verses 2-3? All the pain is within; it is his thoughts that trouble him. You can picture how his mind is tortured with the slightest glance of his enemy.

Have you ever had the temptation to run away from it all? Have you ever thought, "I could run away to Mexico or Tahiti, change my name and leave all this behind." Look at verses 6-8. Running isn't sufficient; he needs wings.

Do you feel that you're living in hostile territory? Does it seem that the streets are not safe for honest men? Do you have the feeling that just walking out of your home to get the newspaper is a threatening experience? See verse 11—the threat of the gang is not a new one.

Most hostile of all is betrayal. It is one thing to be threatened by your enemies. It is entirely another to feel that you can't trust your friends, that they are just waiting to betray you at the worst possible moment. Verses 12-14 and verses 20-21 show us exactly such a hostility.

The fears and terrors given by the Psalmist are not new. They were not new in his time either. They are recorded so that you may know that God will listen to such fears. How often our prayers concern only the sick, and do not touch on our inmost fears! When stress racks our lives we often feel that it's not appropriate for us to pray about it—after all, real Christians don't fret, do they? Aren't we supposed to live serene, worry-free lives?

Troubles within, panic, threats and lies, betrayal—all these things will come. The Psalmist asks the Lord to strike at his enemies, but he ends with this thought: ultimately, you must cast your cares upon the Lord, for he will sustain you. Cares you will have. Deny them you may, but they will still come. Give them to God. As an old friend once put it, "You might as well give your worries to God. He's going to be up all night anyway."

Zechariah
Luke 1

It is a common point about angels: their first words are often "Fear not." They must indeed be a terrifying sight. Evidently they are not the fluttery creatures of our paintings, but rather stern visitors from God.

Yet they often bring good news. We must understand that in those days a woman who could not have children was considered at the least unfortunate. More often she was thought of as being punished for her (or her husband's) sins. So being childless was not only unfortunate but disgraceful. For a righteous couple like Zechariah and Elizabeth this must have been difficult to bear. Even the future would be bleak. Women most commonly outlive their husbands, and in those days would need to depend on their children for food and shelter.

But good news! Your wife, Mr. Zechariah, is going to get pregnant. Not only that, but the child will be someone special. He will be a joy to you; he will be a joy to many:

He will be filled with the Holy Spirit. In Old Testament times this was a rare thing, and a sign of great favor from God, or some special purpose.

Many will turn back to the Lord because of him. Can you imagine a greater gift to a righteous couple living in such an unrighteous time? Often they would have prayed for God to redeem their land; now their son would lead many to the path of righteousness.

When a Jew of this time heard the names "Moses and Elijah" he thought of Law (Moses) and Prophets (Elijah). Elijah is the quintessential prophet; Elijah comes before the Christ; now your son will be that Elijah.

In the face of this terrifying visitor, filled with all this good news, Zechariah fails. He doubts. He is quite familiar enough with how children are conceived. Medicare does not cover pregnancy. It cannot be done. It is impossible.

Do you wonder why your prayer life is so small and unfruitful? Here is a clue. When God says it will be, do not tell him your difficulties. Rejoice that he will make it so. So often we doubt what God tells us must be. If we are his children, we must trust him. Fear not, but rejoice.

Magnificat
Luke 1:46-56

"Magnificat" is the first word, in Latin, of the psalm that Mary delivers in this passage of Scripture. Translated "glorifies" here, it is sometimes translated "magnifies." There is a good sense in that.

We often forget that our worship of God must begin with the acknowledgement of who He is. He is the "Mighty One" Mary so praises here. The most honored woman in history (and with cause) is not proud of her selection to be the mother of Jesus. Rather, her mind goes immediately to her Lord. Her worship of God is a model for us.

She acknowledges Him as God, but more than that she rejoices in Him. He is the Mighty One; but that is a source of joy for the people of God.

Mary, of all people, has reason to praise Him. She is a young girl in Judea, one of many and of no particular repute, when God selects her to be Blessed. You see no claim to virtue in Mary's praise; rather, she admits her humble state and thanks God for what He has done for her.

She has praised Him for what He has done for her; now she praises Him for what He has done for Israel:

Time and again he has brought Israel—when faithful—to military victory. In particular, it is victory over the arrogant.

For a time the arrogant ruler was invincible—but God brings him down by means of the humble.

He is the one who feeds the hungry; he is the one who is merciful to his children forever.

How often when we begin our prayers we begin with "God, I want." We forget that the Lord's Prayer starts with God's praise and holiness. Have we really acknowledged what God has done for us? Both for us personally and for the children of God?

Do we, like Mary, admit our humble state—or do we go to God with the attitude that we are so righteous that He owes us something (and we've come to prayer to collect)?

We often hear the joyous command to "Praise the Lord!" It is indeed a joy to do so. It is also a requirement of true worship. So when we pray, let us begin with who He is, and who we are—and thus "Praise the Lord!"

Zechariah, Reprise
Luke 1:57-80

Imagine, for the moment, that you are mute. You cannot speak. Think of the inconvenience. Now imagine that your first child has just been born—and your wife wants to name the baby after someone you've never heard of.

That's what Zechariah's neighbors perceived as his problem. They hand him the tablet; he writes, "His name is John," and thus confirms his wife's strange choice. He has been silent these nine months; the choice of the name seems strange—and we have Zechariah's words, a psalm of praise.

It is interesting what Zechariah did *not* say. He did not praise God for the fact that he was now a father (at such an old age). He did not even praise or thank God that he had his speech back! I suspect he had thought about what he would say.

He praises God:

First, that God has remembered his covenant with Israel and has sent the Messiah at last. This is the most important thing he has to say; it takes up half the Psalm, and it comes first. For a devout Jew of the time, no greater news could be found than this.

He praises God that his son, John, will be a part of this new thing. He is delighted that his son will "go before the Lord." His son will have the privilege of serving the Messiah himself. Indeed, the service he will perform is of great importance. He will give his people the knowledge of salvation through forgiveness of sins. Sometimes we forget that the word "gospel" means "good news."

He praises God for his tender mercy.

Zechariah had eight months to think about this speech. It is the result of the Spirit filling him, but he knew what to say. Do we?

Do you rejoice that God keeps his promises? Do you even claim those promises for yourself?

Do you know the joy of service? Every great saint considered serving Christ a joy; can you feel that same joy?

Do you hear the cry of this world for salvation, and do you hear God's tender mercy in reply?

Hear the words of this devout Jew, blessed by God. Shape your words to praise God for his promises, service and mercy.

Simeon
Luke 2:25-35

Have you ever considered that the principal actors in the birth of Jesus, other than mom and dad, are very elderly? Elizabeth and Zechariah, Simeon and Anna are all elderly folks. There might just be a reason for this:

Who among the Jews is most likely to be devout? Perhaps those with the most practice?

In a greater sense, they represent the last of the Old Testament—those bound by the Law.

But there is no conflict between old and new—for the old blesses the new, and then departs.

We see in this story a man, Simeon, who is great in the Holy Spirit. In the old covenant, the Spirit comes and goes as He pleases. In that covenant, the Spirit rests upon someone for God's purposes. In his old age he does not know why, but he has been told: you will not see death until you see the Lord's Anointed One, the Messiah. So, day after day, he goes to the one most likely spot: the Temple. Then one day a young girl brings in a baby, and the Spirit moves Simeon to prophesy.

There is a dark side to the prophecy. We see the Christmas season as a time of joy, but Simeon sees, through the eyes of the Spirit, the darker points.

He sees that the time has come for the rising and falling of many. No longer may those who waver sit on the fence. The man of decision is born, and decision must be made. The Messiah is here; you are for or against him.

He sees also the years of persecution. To carry the name of Christian is to be persecuted. Sometimes mildly, sometimes to death, but always there is persecution. The wicked abhor the light of righteousness, and the Christian is the light of the world.

Touchingly, he sees the pain that Mary will bear. She will see her firstborn son crucified like a common criminal. Neither she, nor anyone else, will see the Resurrection beforehand. The pain of this will be hers, a sword in her side.

The prophecy remains. Decision is here; the righteous will be persecuted. Pain will come. But then the Resurrection! The time to decide is now; choose wisely.

Child in the Temple
Luke 2:41-52

There is a measure of the devoutness of Mary and Joseph in this passage. It tells us that every year they went up for Passover. This was a long journey from Nazareth. Only the males were required to make it, but the devout women were permitted as well. Mary and Joseph made it annually.

> Do we take our children to worship, even worship that they might not yet be old enough to understand? Do we show them by our example that the worship of God is something extremely important? Or is it just something that we do when we can fit it in? And then only if the sermon topic looks interesting?

> When we do go, do we look like the Psalmist who said, "I was glad when they said to me, let us go up to the House of the Lord"? Do we appear to be glad, or are we rushed, harried and worried? Is it a joy, or a chore?

Each of us naturally desires that our children will be well behaved and polite. But zeal for the Lord is another matter!

> Do our children have the zeal for the Lord that is shown here? Does the name of Jesus enter into their conversation often? Do you hear them at prayer?

> How do we react when we encounter zeal in our children? If your child comes home and announces that his junior high class will be fasting for 24 hours, do you smirk? Or do you praise your child for caring?

Christ, in this only story of his childhood, shows us the example of one who must be obedient to God above all else. The ties of family, however precious, cannot precede the love of God. Thus our Lord must be in his Father's house. But note that after his parents came for him, he went down to Nazareth with them and was obedient to them. The example of their devoutness could not have been missed. As the Suffering Servant, our Lord submitted to the rule of his earthly parents. Could this have been done if they had been disobedient to God?

Parents must remember that our example will be seen, and often followed, by our children. What is your example to your children? Do they see one who loves the Lord and worships Him, or one who views worship as painful duty?

Prepare the Way
Luke 3:4-6

Prepare the Way

It is a clear fact that our Lord will not force himself upon anyone. Neither at the time when you first come to know him, nor as you walk in the Christian walk, will he use force to bring you to his way. The persuasion of your circumstance, the pleading of family and friends, the Scripture itself, conscience—all these will press on you. But Jesus is the lover of your soul, and he will not force himself upon you. Therefore, he must be welcomed, or he will not come. You must prepare the way for him to come to you.

How?

Every Valley

When we think of the "valleys" in our life, we think of those times when we are at our lowest.

> There is the valley of doubt. This we must fill in with the mountain moved by faith.

> There is the valley of despair. Can Jesus love one like me? Over and over he whispers, "I can—and I do."

Every Mountain

The mountain is a high point, a point of exaltation in our lives. In one sense, this may be understood as pride. If we spend our lives looking down on others, how can we look up to God? If you will sacrifice your pride and humble yourself, he will come to you. There is another sense: the mountaintop experience. The spiritual exaltation of one moment sometimes blinds us to the call of our Lord in day-to-day living. Come down from that mountain.

The Crooked Straight

Jesus only once told someone to be born again; but "repent, and sin no more" came to sinners often. If you will not try to cast the sin out of your life, how can the Holy One come in?

The Rough Places Made Smooth

Pride, envy, greed—and so much more, all of our sins—are the rough places of our lives. We must try to smooth them out. Why? Because we walk by faith, not by sight. If you will not walk by sight, you must walk as if blindfolded. If you are to walk blindfolded for any distance, the path must be smooth indeed.

The voice is calling in the desert, prepare the way for the Lord. Will you prepare that way for him?

Deceptive Wages
Proverbs 11:18

The Book of Proverbs contains some meaty advice. Here is a good example.

Deceptive. The word means tending to deceive, to be fraudulent, a sham. How can wages be a sham? We view wages, quite rightly, as proper compensation for our work. Indeed, the very concept of wages is that someone has earned them. There is nothing unjust in this proverb. The wicked work their wickedness, and receive a reward in kind.

Interestingly, God stressed throughout the Old Testament (and even James has something to say about it) that the wages of the laborer were to be paid promptly. It was sinful to hold them even so long as overnight, for the day laborer lived from day to day on them. The wages of sin is death, as Paul told the church in Rome. It seems that God is merciful in withholding such wages for a short while.

This is the nature of wickedness: they earned it. A thief considers it no wrong to steal from another thief. When a man turns his way to the wicked, he is only assaulting himself.

One way is this: when a man falls in amongst thieves, he runs the risk—and eventual certainty—of being their victim as well as their comrade. Just being around such people makes you vulnerable to them.

Another way is this: how do you quit? The rewards of sin are a lure; soon you become accustomed to the life of stolen wealth. Then how do you turn around and become an honest man? Will your "friends" not turn you in? What will you do to earn a living? Sin is bondage, stronger than any chain.

Does wickedness affect you alone? I have often visited people in prison for their crimes. The saddest sight is to see a young mother, with two or three small children in tow, going to see their father in prison. How does a four-year-old explain that Daddy is in jail? How does a mother explain it to the four-year-old? The pain of sin is not yours to bear alone.

The temptation is always there. Cheat here, steal there—who will know? You will know. Satan knows, and now has a lever to push you further into sin. God knows; God cares. For this Christ went to the Cross. Will you cause Him further pain?

The Shadow of Your Wings
Psalm 63

David evidently wrote this psalm while he was hiding in the desert, probably from Saul. It is a common fact that our faith is deepened most when our troubles are deepest. David looks at the desert around him and finds the word-picture he needs. He seeks the Lord with all his being; his soul thirsts for God, his body longs for him.

To what does David turn? To the memory of better days. His mind turns back to a "mountaintop" experience where he saw God in the sanctuary. God allows us such experiences for just such a purpose, that we might remember the days when his glory was revealed to us, and so be strengthened when going through desert days. Indeed, David shows us here that the knowledge of God far exceeds all physical things. This is the power of worship remembered, and for that alone the Psalm is exceedingly comforting.

The nights are long and clear in the desert. Was David looking up at the clear stars of heaven, so hidden in our modern world, as he remembered God in the watches of the night? Have you ever lain awake at night, asking God for his favor, asking for his protection? So often when we do we complain to God, but David remembers and clings to God.

Then, in the midst of the cold desert night and the evil all around him, David produces a masterful phrase. "Because you are my help, I sing in the shadow of your wings." In other Psalms he has taken refuge in the shadow of those wings, but this night he sings. David rises above his troubles, remembers the Lord he saw in the sanctuary, and like Paul and Silas in jail, begins to sing. Out of the terror of the night comes the joy of the Lord.

This is triumph indeed. How puny is our faith! When the slightest trouble comes we complain to God. If our troubles should happen to be related to our witness to him, we double our complaint (as if he hadn't warned us!) But David shows us the true path. He has been persecuted, but it is of no consequence. God will deal soon enough with those evil men, of that David is sure. What is important? That God be praised. That David clings to him. That we rejoice in him.

Rejoice in the Lord always, said Paul. Sing—in the shadow of his wings, for he cares for you.

March 21

I am a Sinful Man
Luke 5:1-11

Three times—a symbol of completeness—Jesus will call Peter to be his disciple. This is the third time, and in this little story there is much to see in Peter, and in our Lord.

The boat

The boats used for fishing on a lake of this size are necessarily of shallow draft. They would therefore be quite useful for a speaker who wished to speak from a few yards offshore, and so Christ used them.

> There are some who think that God must reject human means. It is not so. Christ uses the boat for a pulpit. The nets are the tool of the miracle. The right use of human means is to place them at the service of the Lord.

> But human means alone, without the Lord Jesus, are of no use in the kingdom. His presence, his command, these turn our small means into his great works.

The Awesome God

Do you remember Isaiah's vision of the Lord? His first reaction is to be stricken in his conscience. He is a man of unclean lips, and he fears death at the hands of the Awesome God. It is not the only instance in the Old Testament, by any means. The Jews had a clear sense that the presence of God, the Holy One, was fatal to sinners.

Peter shows that same sense—and begs for his life. That is why he asks Jesus, his Lord, to go away. Have you ever done the same thing? Perhaps there is something in your prayers that you will not mention, because you don't want the Awesome God.

Christ raises the sinner

Peter falls to his knees, but Christ brings him back up. Peter is a sinner, but Christ will use him. Why?

> Peter was a fisherman; Jesus, a carpenter. Yet at his command Peter let down the nets. Obedience is the habit of the true disciple.

> Obedience is carried through as Peter and the others leave everything and follow Jesus.

There it is. The Awesome God has come in the flesh. He has called you and all you have . If you will be obedient, he will raise you up too—even at the Last Day.

82

Cities of Refuge
Numbers 35

The early books of the Bible are a window on a time very distant from our own. Sometimes the conception of justice shown in those books seems primitive and harsh by comparison to our own. We must remember that God was establishing this system not only to ensure justice but to teach Israel what was to come. The cities of refuge are just such an example.

Shedding of blood

Central to our understanding of the cities of refuge is this. Any time blood was shed, even accidentally, the land was considered to be defiled. This was a great sacrilege, for the land was considered to be the land where God lived with his people. Unsolved murders were to be atoned for by the elders. Murders in which the murderer was known were to be avenged by the kinsman redeemer. We are most familiar with this person as Boaz, in the story of Ruth. The same relative was also charged with the duty of being the avenger of blood. But what if the killer was innocent of murder? What if it was an accident?

The cities of refuge

To deal with this, God instructed Moses to designate certain cities as cities of refuge.

- Each of these cities was a city belonging to the Levites, the priestly tribe. Not all Levite cities were cities of refuge.
- Only the innocent slayer could obtain refuge there; the elders were to hand over any murderer.
- Even the innocent one could not leave until the death of the High Priest. His death was considered atonement for the blood that had been shed.

The lesson for us

Sin is still sin. Each and every one of us is a sinner, and as such we have defiled the land of God. We must have a place of refuge, and we must have atonement for sin. Jesus Christ has provided both. In His kingdom of priests, the church, we find refuge from our sins and help for their consequences. In His death on the Cross, as our High Priest, we find the atonement needed for sin.

Note, however, that the refugee still had to run to the city of refuge. We too must come to the church, the refuge of God, and claim the atonement of the Cross.

The Character of Our Witness
Luke 5:29-39

There once was a congregation most determined to "preserve the character of our witness." To this end, all who wanted to be members of this congregation were carefully examined by the elders, to ensure that no deviation—in character or doctrine—was to be admitted. None but the finest of souls were allowed in. I flunked.

Levi, also known as Matthew, was a tax collector. He would probably have flunked also. Tax collectors in those days were the scum of the Roman Empire. They were Jews who cheated other Jews (in excess taxes) on behalf of Rome. Strangely enough, Jesus called him, and he followed. His first act on behalf of his new Master was to throw a party. It is referred to as a "great banquet"—evidently Levi knew all the other sinners and tax collectors of the area. The Pharisees complained of this. Though their complaint was addressed to the disciples, it was answered by Jesus.

His reply defines the church in a way. It is composed of sinners. As such, it is a disreputable organization. Think of it this way: the only qualification known for becoming a Christian is that you must be a sinner first. Each and every Christian proclaims this. Then some of us complain about the quality of the people who seem to be joining.

May I suggest something to you, by Jesus' example? If the church congregation you love has nothing but lovely, happy people, possessed of good character and strong morals, there is something tragically wrong. You are in a health club for saints. The church is a hospital for sinners.

Is the unwed mother welcome in your Women's Fellowship? Is the drunkard or drug addict, struggling desperately to be free, welcome in your Bible study? If not, consider the example of Levi. Perhaps your standards for entrance are too low; you should consider setting a stricter standard of sin for entrance.

We must not, in any sense, condone sin. Nor can we condemn the sinner who has appealed to Jesus for salvation. We too have made the same appeal. Rather, we must be the open arms of the body of Christ, open to the sinner. Really, are we all so lovable and they so ugly that we cannot see in them one for whom Christ died?

Vengeance is Mine
Luke 6:27-31

The temptation to vengeance is a common one. Christ here commands us to do the opposite—rather than seek vengeance, we must love our enemies, bless those who curse us and pray for those who mistreat us. In anger the Christian may ask, why?

The children of God

We must not take vengeance because we are the children of God. Like him who causes rain on the just and unjust, we must be loving. You can also look at it this way:

> Your persecutor is, at least in potential, a child of God also. Do you think it wise to pursue vengeance on someone whose Father is so powerful?

> You—and your persecutor—will have body and soul reunited at the last day. What will you say to the judge? To one who is now your brother?

> Your righteousness must exceed that of the greatest legalists. How can you then take vengeance?

Vengeance belongs to God –

And if you take it, you're stealing from him. Indeed you are stealing what is his:

> How can you be as just a judge as he—or as merciful?

> The passage here relates mostly to material things. But consider: is anything *really* ours? If it is material, we will lose it at death anyway. Even before then, as Christians we have surrendered all things to Christ. Shall we now pull them back?

Using Satan's Weapons

To take vengeance is to pick up the weapons of Satan—which is to join Satan. Why would you do this?

Is the cause of your vengeance really significant—in eternity?

As the imitator of God, is this how he treats you, when you sin?

God has reserved vengeance for himself, for only he can judge justly. Christ took no vengeance, though he was innocence itself, wronged by man. We are the followers of Christ. His example is before us. Should we not follow it?

Not Above His Teacher
Luke 6:39-49

Christ makes it clear in this passage that we are not to pass judgment upon our brothers. If his command were not enough, there is his example: the Son of Man came to redeem the world, not to judge it. So why then do those who claim to imitate him seem so judgmental?

Why do we judge?

First, as a cover for our own sin. Little children have been known to complain, "He hit me back first!" But do recall King David—and Bathsheba. How angry David was at the man in Nathan's story! Was this not his own guilt coming out as judgment?

Christ here gives us another reason: spiritual blindness. If we will not examine ourselves (as we are taught to do at Communion) then we can blindly say, "Let me help you" to one who should be helping us. It sounds so "Christian" but it is so false.

There is also the matter of a blasphemous lack of faith. "Poor Joe, he's a hopeless drunkard." What that really means is, "Even God couldn't help Joe." We condemn the man and give up on him at the same moment.

The Principle of Lordship

How do we avoid falling into this deadly trap? One way has already been shown: self-examination, regularly. But most important of all is the principle of lordship. We are his students; he is our teacher. We are not above him. If he did not judge, then how do we dare to claim that privilege?

Indeed, we are taught that in regard to our weaker brother we are not to judge—but to uphold that weaker brother, even if we disagree with his rules and regulations.

If our brother sins, we are to gently restore him—watching all the while that we don't fall into the same pit.

In all our works, we should have mercy triumph over judgment. It is this standard that the Lord expects of us—and that we want him to use when he returns.

By what measure you measure, you will be measured when he comes again. Measure mercifully, tenderly and generously.

The Awesome Nature of God
(various)

If there is a major failing of the Christian of our time it is that he does not know the awesome nature of God. A friend of mine once expressed this as "me and Jesus in the telephone booth." We forget that God is indeed awesome, holy and sovereign.

Old Testament: Deuteronomy 5:23-27

It is with a sense of awe that the elders of the Jews realize the fact that one can actually see the glory of God—and not die. Recall that throughout this period—Isaiah is a good example—the most common thought about the awesome nature of God is that we cannot see it and survive. Even Moses is hidden in the crack of the rock, and cannot see the face of God. Isaiah must have his lips purged. It can be survived; but, as the elders point out here, it's not very likely. Certainly it is not something to be sought out, but rather avoided. The central idea of these people is that they want someone else, a representative, to talk to God for them. The High Priest is such a person—and he could approach the Holy of Holies only once a year. This accurately reflects the awesome nature of the Almighty One.

New Testament: Luke 17:18-28

The ultimate representative of man is also the ultimate representative of God: Jesus Christ. The dilemma is resolved; one man is the bridge between the awesome nature of God and the human nature of man. John the Baptist is the greatest among men, but inadequate in the kingdom—because the Cross has not yet come. So the awesome nature of God has been brought down to our level—and we can see him face to face, and adore him.

Psalms 68:32-35

We forget the awesome nature of God in our time. We have lost the sense of awe that possessed the ancient ones. Like them, we need to remember that the first reaction to God is one of awestruck worship. As the Psalmist says, we should sing to God, and proclaim his power.

If you truly wish to have a personal relationship with someone, it must begin by knowing who that someone truly is. If you will not see who God is, that he is awesome and powerful, righteous and holy, you cannot see how generous is his mercy at the Cross. Open your eyes; see the Lord of Heaven and Earth.

The Prostitute
Luke 7:36-50

It is part of our popular culture to be very sympathetic to prostitutes and prostitution. This is more the symptom of our time than righteousness, for the prostitute is an agent by whom Satan fractures homes and lives. The Pharisees understood this, and so should we. Prostitution is sin. This story is not about sin; it is about forgiveness.

The Prostitute

There are two things that stand out concerning her:

She has genuine faith—she believes that Jesus can and will forgive her.

She is repentant—in great humility.

Simon, the Pharisee

Simon suffers in this telling of the story. He is not so much a hypocrite as he is class-conscious. This woman is well beneath him. The fact that Jesus does not reject her means to him that Jesus does not know who she is. But there are two mistakes in Simon:

He condemns the sin—but along with it, the sinner.

He does not see the value of repentance.

But he is willing to learn. He did not invite this rough carpenter into his home to ridicule him.

Guilt

Simon and the woman share one view: that she is a sinner. That is undeniable; the question is, what to do about the guilt?

The modern trend is to insist that guilt really doesn't exist. No one is guilty; it's just a feeling. See your therapist.

The more traditional method is much more common. There is such a thing as guilt—but I have an excuse.

There is only one thing that genuinely works—the method used by the prostitute, repentance.

Jesus

Two things are clear concerning this Jesus: first, that he has the authority to forgive sin. Second, that he is willing to forgive the repentant sinner.

The only remaining question has been the same for two thousand years: are we willing to repent?

Now, O Israel
Deuteronomy 10:12-13

Moses has come to the end of his life, and is delivering his farewell speech. Have you ever wished that you could leave a message to your children from beyond the grave? Moses knew the place of his death; he had such a privilege here.

ASK

Note, please, that the Lord asks his people.

He does not force them, like robots, to obey. He does not want the unwilling servant; rather, he wants the one who is committed with a whole heart.

He does not even demand. There is no sense of hammering the people into submission.

Indeed, in kindness and mercy, He asks. It is not his will that any should perish, but that all should voluntarily come to his presence.

So then, what does the Lord in such meekness ask?

Fear the Lord

The first thing he asks is that your fear the Lord. Take account of him in your comings and goings; factor him into your calculations; make sure that you please him in all your doings. It is a little thing for so mighty a God.

Walk in His ways

By his mercy and grace he has given you his instructions. They are meant for your salvation. Is it so great a thing that he asks you to follow them?

Serve the Lord with all your heart

It is not sufficient for you to serve the Lord. Indeed, he needs no service of any kind; if he were hungry, would he ask you? No, he desires the service of the complete heart. The partial service is worse than useless.. But how can you do this?

Obey his commands and decrees

Surely you have read his commands; surely you know his word. Is this so hard? Especially since these commands are given for your own good?

Three thousand and some years have passed, but God has not changed. Serve the Lord, obey his commands—these are still the same. What's new? You. The question is, will <u>you</u> obey?

Be Careful
Deuteronomy 11:16-21

Moses is giving his last warning to the people of Israel. Like a father sending his son off to college, the warnings are repeated. One of them may seem strange to some.

Be careful

Note the phrasing: "or you will be enticed." Many of us today think that because we were tempted to go astray, the blame and the guilt lie upon the tempter, not ourselves. We quickly seek to rationalize our own sin by saying, "Oh, I was tempted by ..." as if this excuses us from all responsibility. It is not so. Moses tells the children of Israel to "be careful", or they will be enticed. The failing is not with the one doing the enticing, but with the one who failed to be careful. So then, how are we to "be careful?"

On your heart

Moses goes directly to the point. If you are to be careful for these things, you must fix the word of God on your heart. Over and over you are encouraged to read the Scripture—and not just read, but cherish it and plant it in your heart. Here is the reason why! If you don't, temptation will come and sweep you away.

Tie them on your hands

Moses is no fool. He knows that you can study the word and still be tempted. You need a reminder to carry with you. To this day, in obedience to this command, the devout Orthodox Jew carries the Scripture on his body. We need to be reminded minute by minute of who we are and what we believe.

Teach them

Nothing so strengthens the faith as being a teacher. But not all of us have the gift of teaching. Many of us, however, have the gift of children. They are a precious responsibility. Both for their sake and for our own, we need to teach them the Word.

Write them on the door

Christian bookstores do a brisk business in cute plaques to hang on the wall. It would be so much better if the plaques were not so cute and much more Scriptural. The method, however, is sound: put the word where you can see it.

We are amphibians: part animal, part spirit. The animal requires reminding so that the spirit may remain in God. Do not neglect the Word—in body, in child, on the wall.

Be Openhanded
Deuteronomy 15:1-18

Bible reading in a yearly plan tends to bog down in two places. One is the seemingly endless list of who begat whom; the other is the lengthy list of regulations. But among those regulations are some true gems.

Note here how the poor of the land are to be cared for. This is not the only such section, but it is representative of God's commands. It is clear from this section that:

Debts were to be cancelled every seven years.

The Jews were to be openhanded and generous to the poor.

If they were, God would richly bless them.

Why did God so command the Jews in this?

Test of faith

First, there is no visible connection between being openhanded and generous to the poor (despite the warnings) and the increase of your wealth. This promise can only be taken by one who genuinely believes. Our usual response is that we don't think the poor deserve it, or perhaps they are frauds, or any other excuse. His point is that he will bless you as you bless them. The question is, do you believe his word?

The Yardstick Principle

God makes it clear that he is very fond of measuring you by your own yardstick. If you forgive others, he forgives you. If you bless others materially, he will bless you. You have your own yardstick; you use it every day; he just borrows it to measure out your blessings.

The Practical Side

Consider it this way: no government, no committee could possibly use the money as efficiently as someone who knows the poor man personally. By making it a loan there is a sense of obligation—and preservation of self-respect. What bureaucracy could do better?

God's children

Finally, there is this. Note that repayment may be demanded of a foreigner, but not a Jew. The Jews (at this time) are God's children. They are his family, as we are now. A favor to my children is a favor to me. So it is with God. Even the slightest kindness, done in his name, will not go unrewarded.

Who Do You Say That I Am?
Luke 9:18-27

A dear friend (who was, incidentally, a priest) once remarked, "There is only one question: who do you say that I am?" By this he meant that the one thing that unites all Christians is their conviction that Jesus is indeed the Messiah, the Christ of God. No other question really matters. If he is Christ and Lord to you, all is ultimately well. If not, you are doomed. But in the meanwhile there may be a little spot of trouble. If you will follow your Lord, you must go on the path he picked out.

Self-Denial

Could there be any greater example of self-denial than this? Jesus, in the form of God, made himself man—not a regal man, but a common man, born to suffer and die for sins he did not commit. This is the ultimate in denying the right to be what you are. If you wish to follow your Lord, you must do likewise. You must give up all "rights" and think only of the love he had for you, that you must share with others.

Take up your cross daily

Most of us are convinced that if the moment of glory came, we could be entirely self-sacrificing. Would you jump in front of the speeding car to save the helpless baby? Of course. But that is not the test Christ gives you. You are to take up your cross *daily*. Each day, are you patient and kind with the impatient and unkind? Do you love those who cannot love you in return? Do you endure with kindness the unkindness of others? Daily—the cross must be carried.

The power of paradox

If you wish to save your life, you must lose it. If you lose it, you will save it. At face value it is nonsense—but these words have inspired the greatest of saints. If you play it safe, keeping the things of this world in your hands, you will lose all. If you gamble all on Jesus Christ, taking him at his word, you will gain all. That is his claim. He will have all of you, or nothing. The choice is yours, but no half measures will suffice.

Reward

He understands you; you will work for reward. He promises you great things upon his return—and sacrifice and suffering here. Sacrifice and suffering you will have anyway. Do you trust him completely? Who do you say that He is?

Envy
Psalm 73

Humility used to be considered a virtue. It is now considered (by the world) to be a fault. Arrogance (called pride) is now thought by the world to be a virtue. This has the advantage, at least, of avoiding hypocrisy. No longer is hypocrisy the tribute vice pays to virtue. Now the rich and powerful consider it righteous to flaunt themselves.

Asaph, the author of this Psalm, lived in such a time. He was a priest in a time when such a calling was not well paid. Truly, envy is the sin of the "have nots" against the "haves." One of the uses of the Psalms is to express our feelings, and Asaph has captured the feeling of envy very well in this one.

Why does God allow the wicked to prosper so? Leaving aside the presumption of asking God any such question, it is one that rings true in our time. Asaph has been a righteous man, and where has it led? He is poor; they are rich. He's been good; they have not. The gnawing begins. As one writer (Buechner) defined it, envy is "the consuming desire to have everyone else as unsuccessful as you." This envy is gnawing away; it is all Asaph can do to keep from complaining aloud.

He asks the question, and the question is oppressive—until he enters the sanctuary. It is when he comes close to God that he realizes his point of view is incorrect.

First, there is a point of perspective. The wicked are prospering—today. But man is designed to be eternal. God sees the eternal end of man.

Next, it is not God's desire that anyone should perish. Have you never fallen into temptation? If he were to immediately destroy anyone who sinned, where would we be then? Rather, he is gracious and desires everyone to have all opportunity to repent.

Finally, there is the question of judgment. It is not ours to judge; it is forbidden to us. God will judge them; we need not even think of it.

There is one other way to look at this. Consider things this way: if this is the way that God treats the unrighteous in this life—with such blessings that we envy them—how much more will he give to those who love him when he comes again?

Three Men Called
Luke 9:57-62

We meet three men here. Each desires to follow Jesus; each has a problem.

The Scribe

(Matthew's account labels the first man a scribe). Have you ever considered that your abilities and talents might be a *barrier* to your wholehearted devotion to Christ? This man is an expert in the Jewish law; he is also respected in the community. He could have said to Jesus, "Lord, think what I could bring to your movement." Note, however, that he volunteers; Jesus did not call him. He thinks he is doing Jesus a favor, but the servant is not above the Master. This man's undoing is his love of status; Jesus tells him the life he must live—that of a hobo. Did the man follow anyway?

Bury My Father

The second man asks a reasonable thing, and one commanded by the Law. He wants to do a good thing. But the good is often the enemy of the best. Indeed, have you ever used a poor excuse to get out of your duty—when a good excuse was at hand?

Jesus' reply seems harsh, but he is talking about the spiritually dead. They prefer the easy path of following rules and regulations to the absolute commitment to Jesus Christ. Was this man able to break his lukewarm bonds?

Let me say good-bye

The story has an echo of Elisha joining Elijah. The life of a prophet was no easy one, but this man seems to have accepted that. But the man makes a mistake: he wants to carry the past with him. He wants to go, but not make a clean break from his past, in this instance his family. Don't look back; the past is history, and history belongs to God. Did this man break free into true freedom?

Who followed Jesus? All? None? We don't know. But we do know who can follow Jesus:

Those who will give up all to follow him.

Those who are spiritually alive

Those who don't look back.

Are you one of those?

Love Undeserved
Luke 10:25-37

This just might be the greatest short story ever written—the Good Samaritan. It concerns itself with the most unpopular concept in the Bible—love undeserved.

You think the concept is not unpopular? I ask you to consider this: she is young, pretty, pregnant and single—or even has had the child. How much help does she deserve?

None, if you're the typical taxpayer.

Everything, if you're the grandparents.

So consider, then, the traveler. This is not a man of sense. The road to Jericho was a notorious haunt for robbers—even into the twentieth century. A man who went that way alone was a fool, and deserved what he got. This traveler, then, was a man looking for trouble—and found it.

It is the Samaritan, however, who commands our interest. We must first remember what the Samaritan and the traveler would agree upon: the Jew hated the Samaritan. It was bad enough to be a Gentile, but to be a half-breed Jew with no true respect for the Law was outrageous. The prejudice was deep.

But consider our Samaritan!

He came prepared to help others. Have you ever passed the man with the cardboard sign, feeling guilty, but knowing you had nothing to give?

He followed through. He did not promise to call the police; he took action himself.

Note one thing about his life: his credit was good! The innkeeper evidently trusted him.

Indeed, he was willing to make what appears to be an unlimited commitment to the innkeeper. What an exquisite parallel to our Lord's unlimited sacrifice!

He was not concerned that his own efforts might not be sufficient. He was willing to trust the innkeeper—as we should trust the church.

Above all this there is one great parallel to Christ. Despite the rejection that was sure to come, despite the hatred of this man, he cared and loved. The traveler did not deserve this. We do not deserve Jesus Christ. He loves us in spite of that.

Mary and Martha
Luke 10:38-42

The story is a familiar one to most women. Somebody has to do the dishes.

For the men, therefore, we must present Martha's point of view.

First, there are no good hotels in these days. Inns are likely enough houses of ill repute. Travel depended upon staying with friends. Hospitality was considered a great virtue, not just a sideline.

Think of it this way: if the preacher asked you if you could put up a visitor—named, say, Billy Graham—would you refuse? And how quickly you'd go home to clean house!

There is also the natural irritation of someone working hard—while watching someone else sit still.

Women very often see "Christian charity" as something they do; men often see it as something they put up with. To Martha, Mary is neglecting her duties. Likely enough, Mary is her little sister, and that may have had some influence too.

So she does what so many of us do when confronted with a situation in which we feel abused or let down by someone else. We go to God and tell him how to fix the situation. It never occurs to us that he does not know about the situation, or might even know better what to do—we're sure he needs our advice. So Martha gives it to him.

Jesus' reply has the sweet tenderness of our Heavenly Father. We need to be careful about his answer:

We are not to conclude that the Christian life is one of laziness and pure contemplation. Action is required.

Indeed, for some of us, this will be the calling of God. "The sons of Mary lay their troubles on the Lord—and the Lord, he lays them on the sons of Martha." (Kipling).

What Jesus is telling us is this: the life of devotion is the pure life in Christ. What I accomplish is nothing to him—he created the universe, after all. My relationship to him is everything. From that relationship will spring action, but that relationship must come first, above all else. The "good" is often the enemy of the "best." Sadly, too often we fail in this. We try to substitute action for devotion, and miss the sweet fellowship of our Lord and Savior.

The House Divided
Luke 11:14-36

Jesus in this passage gives us three important spiritual principles.

There is the principle of *spiritual vacuum*. Just because you rid yourself of one spiritual problem doesn't mean you have triumphed. Consider the "donut diet": I will just stop eating donuts, and surely I will lose weight. Maybe I will—if I also change my other eating habits.

There is the principle of *power and authority*. One of the key methods of distinguishing good from evil is shown here. In the kingdom of God, power and authority always go together. If I claim to be a prophet, but have no vision, I am a fraud—no power, no authority. If I use deceit and force to proclaim my version of the Gospel, I am a fake—no authority, no power for the kingdom.

There is the principle of *spiritual discernment*. Each of us is responsible for discerning the truth in matters spiritual. It does not matter that we sincerely believed something false—if the evidence was before us, we should have seen it. So how, then, does one have spiritual discernment?

Jesus gives an example that would have been familiar to his listeners but not so much so to us. Permit me to vary the metaphor. In every campsite there should be a tree. On that tree, at a height just about as high as a man can reach, there is always a nail. Why is that nail there? It's to hang your camp lantern on. Someone selected that exact spot because it is the one place to put a lantern to shed light over the entire campground.

Now, that lantern is like our spiritual discernment. It does us no good if the lantern is broken, or out of fuel. It would be completely foolish to light the lantern—and then put it back into its box! But Christians often do these things:

Is your relationship with God broken by sin? Your lantern will not work.

Do you study the Scriptures and apply them to your life? If not, your lantern is out of gas.

Do you come to church on Sunday, and forget everything about it the rest of the week? Your lantern is in the box.

Take the lantern out of the box; fix it; fill it with gas—and see!

Pharisees and Lawyers
Luke 11:37-54

The Pharisees do not get much good press in the Scripture. With good reason; they have missed the point of the Law itself. Here are some symptoms we should watch for:

They concentrated on external things. The closest modern example is the baby-kissing politician. This has two issues:

First, they had no real charity. They gave money, but charity, help for the poor and unfortunate, was far from their minds.

This does not mean that we can neglect the external observances. There is a temptation to say, "What you do doesn't matter, as long as you have true faith." What you do does matter—it is a reflection of your faith.

They loved the admiration of others. It is not wrong to be a role model. It is wrong to pattern your life in such a way that others feel obliged to praise you. It is not the praise, but the love of the praise of which Christ is speaking. This makes this particular symptom very hard to see in others.

They were full of hidden unrighteousness. What they did in secret was not what they did in public.

The Lawyers

The lawyers also give us some tests of darkness.

They laid burdens on others. They made the religious law so complicated that others found it difficult to keep. But they knew the loopholes. So they put these burdens on others, did nothing to help them carry these burdens—and refused to carry them themselves. In our terms today, this would be the person who insists that every man must wear a tie to church—she's quite sure of it.

They make yesterday's wrongs today's right. This is what is meant by "the tombs of the prophets." These are those who insist that hymns must be sung from the hymnbook, rather than praise songs from the screen (or vice versa).

They take away knowledge from others. By adding rules to what God said, they make faith something that cannot be understood by the ordinary man.

The sad test is this: these men thought they were the most righteous and religious of all. Those who claim the name of Christ must examine themselves—to see if there is any Pharisee or Lawyer in them.

Consider the Lilies
Luke 12:22-34

At first it seems absurd. How can I not worry about the things of this world? A great portion of my life is spent in earning them, and another portion in enjoying them. How then can Christ tell me not to worry about them?

Why not?

First—as he plainly tells you—such worry gets in the way of the kingdom of God. Worry chokes out the Gospel, slowly. It does not seem much at the time, but it is fatal. First things first—and the first thing is the kingdom.

By the act of worrying we deny our Lord. He said we need not worry; he commanded us not to. By our actions we say that he didn't know what he was talking about.

Such worry—as with all sin—hinders our prayers. Oh, I'd like to talk to God about all this worry, but not right now.....

God tells us not to worry, that He will provide. When we worry, we deny both the faithfulness and the power of the eternally faithful and omnipotent God.

How do I do that?

It's easy to read the Scripture and say, "I should not worry." It's hard to keep worry away. So how can we do this?

First, cast your cares upon God in prayer. Confess this sin to him, and give him your troubles.

Next, do not be afraid—take courage! What is it that drives out fear but perfect love?

This is primarily an issue of faith. If you lack faith, go to God and ask for it; he will give it to you liberally.

You—or God

It has been my experience that if you worry about a problem, God will not. If you give it to him, he will handle it. If you take it back, he will let you. Perhaps you should decide which of the two of you is better suited to the task! As an old friend of mine once put it to me, "You might as well give your troubles to God to worry about—after all, He's going to be up all night anyway."

April 8

The Art of Waiting
Luke 12:35-59

The art of waiting is something not practiced in our time. We want something; we want it now. Our Lord, however, commands us to wait—until his return. To understand the meaning of this we must examine this passage, for waiting is not a passive state to the Christian.

Be dressed

To the Jew of this time the instant picture would be that of Passover. The Jew is to eat the Passover dressed and ready for a journey. That journey—from Egypt, the picture of sin, to the Promised Land, the picture of heaven—would be the first thought. But the word used for "dressed" can also be translated "prepared" —as we say that someone dressed the turkey. So how do we prepare?

We prepare our minds for action, by the careful reading of the Scripture and study to defend the faith.

We prepare ourselves with self-control, as an athlete would.

We prepare ourselves with hope in the Lord's return.

Lamps burning

The lamp burning is a common metaphor in the teaching of Christ for our good works. Consider this: if the lamp you use for reading begins to flicker, do you not change the bulb? So then, you expect a lamp to provide consistent light. Our Lord expects no less of our works: that they be consistently performed. It is not sufficient that we occasionally attempt great things. He much prefers that we always attempt good works within our grasp.

Thief in the night

The most common word-picture for Christ's return is the "thief in the night." How do you prepare for a thief?

Since you don't know when he might strike, there is no great fuss— but you do lock the door. Then lock the door to sin in your life as well.

You would also put away your valuables, things easy to steal. So you should also put out things that Christ would condemn.

Do we know the hour of his coming? Certainly not. But he said we would know the season. Look around you, and consider the times— and keep watch!

Blood Mingled
Luke 13:1-5

There is an enduring myth among us. Whenever someone suffers, particularly when we can see no immediate cause for the suffering, the temptation is to say, "God is punishing them for what they did. I don't know what it is, but it must have been something awful."

There are a number of things wrong with this. The first is that it is judgmental. It presumes upon the prerogative of the Lord God Almighty—to pass judgment on another human being. It says, "I know that you are guilty, because God has stricken you." But we know from the Scripture that there are other reasons:

Job, we know, was stricken so that the Lord might triumph over Satan—and that we might have an example of innocent suffering.

The man born blind was stricken not for his own sin, or for his parents' sin, but that we might see the glory of God.

God no doubt has other purposes too—in particular, the use of suffering in preparing one of his children to be an instrument for his particular purposes. So there is no reason for us to pass judgment; it is false when we do.

But why do we persist in it? The answer is given here. These Galileans were killed by the Romans in what appears to be an overzealous suppression of revolt. The others were killed in what we would call an industrial accident. The people of that time, however, judged and said that they must have been guilty. Jesus tells us the truth:

Yes, they were guilty. They were sinners, and as those who sin against the law of God, they deserved to die.

But so do we! All of us are sinners; they just happened to get what they deserve.

And unless we repent, and soon, we will be like them.

Not one of us is perfect. Not one of us can say, "I don't deserve to be punished by God." But God is merciful; a repentant heart coming to him is treated like a long-lost son coming home. Do not think that his mercy is automatic. It is a gift, and a gift at his option. He chooses to give it to those who genuinely repent and turn to him. So then, do not despise his mercy. Turn from your ways, and turn to him.

April 10

The Narrow Way
Luke 13:22-35

One of the most difficult concepts in Christianity is here: the door is narrow. We spend so much time proclaiming that the door is open that we forget that it is narrow. Much grief is caused by this.

First, we forget how the door appears to the world. "If this is such a good thing, if this is truly the way, then why isn't it more obvious? Why isn't it clearly marked as such?" It is clearly marked; it's just narrow. Just because one way is a six-lane freeway and the other a country road does not mean the freeway will take you to the right destination. The real complaint is not the marking; the real complaint is that it is hard. Because it is hard, it is the "road less traveled," — not because it is unmarked.

People raised in a democracy abhor the idea that anything can be so exclusive—and then seek after the exclusive. A consistent theme throughout the Scripture is the concept of "the remnant." The history of the Old Testament nation of Israel is largely one of God taking a people out of bondage in Egypt and refining them. Over the years many are lost, but always there exists the remnant who are faithful to God.

This passage most certainly contains references to the return of the Lord. In Isaiah we are told that one of the characteristics of the end time is that Israel will return to her land. This is phrased in terms of "the remnant." The point is clear; God is seeking that remnant in faithful men and women. What, then, should we do as we "watch and pray" until the Lord returns?

We need to remain faithful, to be in fellowship with him, doing his works at all times. It will not matter to such a faithful servant when his Lord returns.

We need to remember that we are working for a heavenly reward, not an earthly one. Times will be tough.

Those who take the freeway to hell, the lost, will be greatly surprised. It will be a bitter taste, and it will be difficult for them to believe that God has made it final. But final it will be. We, therefore, must exercise "tough love" towards them. There is no sense, and even less love, in telling people that God will forgive no matter what you do. Repentance is required; salvation must be accepted and the new life begun. The faithful remnant must lead all who will—through the narrow way.

God is Just
Luke 14:12-14

A central aspect of God's character is that he is just, or righteous. As little children might understand it, God is "fair." This helps explain this passage, in which Jesus commands us to feed (indeed, to feast) those who cannot repay us. For it is the way of the world that if I scratch your back, I expect you to scratch mine. Good manners alone tell us to return dinner party invitations. But if I invite those who cannot return the favor, then what? Have I wasted the banquet? No indeed, says our Lord. The God who is just will repay us.

God also is love. The blind, the poor, the lame, the crippled—these are God's children too. If you are kind to my children, I consider it a favor just as if you had done it for me. This is because I love my children. God loves his children far more, and when you bless them, he will bless you.

Why, then, do we hesitate to provide such a meal? The man by the roadside with the cardboard sign saying, "Hungry—please help" experiences rejection from car after car. Why do we refuse to obey our Lord's commands in this?

"I'm afraid; he might be violent." Perfect love, the Scripture tells us, casts out fear. Indeed, have you considered what an honor it is should you experience harm *just because* you were doing what God commands you?

"They're all frauds." Really? All of them? How could you know that—without becoming involved in their lives? But suppose it is so. Our Lord commands us to overcome evil not with evil but with good. And where is the good in letting the hungry starve?

"Surely there are churches with soup kitchens!" Ah yes! Our God is infinitely rich, and surely he can find someone else to feed the hungry. Surely he can, but did he? Or did he find you, and charge you to feed this one particular hungry person?

"There are so many!" Did God ask you to feed the world? Or did he place you in contact with this one, so that his church might feed the hungry around the world—one Christian at a time?

"Although they cannot repay you, you will be repaid at the resurrection of the righteous." God is fair; God is just. Fear not, but rather keep his commandments.

The Greatest Short Story Ever Written
Luke 15:11-32

A writer once called The Prodigal Son "the greatest short story ever written." Shall we look at it as an author might? See how the character of the prodigal son is given to us in actions—the sign of a great storyteller.

"Father, give me..." He demands, so that he might do as he pleases. Me first.

By his actions he rejects his father, and all that he stands for.

He comes to his senses, not through theology but hunger. His system doesn't work, and he knows it.

As he prepares his repentance he teaches us two lessons:

He has sinned not only "against heaven" but against a person—and to that person he will confess and repent.

In his repentance he retains the necessary sense of being unworthy. So should we.

God, portrayed by this father, shows his character in action too.

He sees "a long way off." Long before you see God's mercy, God is looking for you.

God reigns in majesty, rides the wings of the storm, but only to seek the lost does he ever run.

He does not *allow* his son home; he welcomes him with joy.

We would miss much if we did not look at the older brother:

He is proud—proud of hard work, and his comparison to the younger brother shows it. He is the better son, but that is not even remotely important now.

He is ignorant—of his father's heart. Instead of joy, there is pain.

But even at this God's heart does not give way to anger. Does the father rage at the older brother? No. He rebukes him gently.

It is not that God prefers the wicked; it is that he seeks their repentance.

All that is his, is yours. Indeed, if we suffer with him, we will reign with him.

"But we had to celebrate and be glad..." Your brother comes home. Do you welcome the sinner with open arms, or do you complain of how the church will let *anybody* in? Indeed, Christ's body is open to all; the angels rejoice at one sinner coming home. Do we rejoice with them?

God and Money
Luke 16:10-12

If you really want to understand men, become a Little League coach.

Little Leaguers are men—in training. You can see their attitudes, and in them you can see the attitudes of adult men. It is for that reason that the coach stresses over and over, "You practice like you play; you play like you practice." It is so easy for the team to fall into the habit of saying, "I'll do it right on game day." But you won't.

God does the same. This world and its riches are practice for the next world and true riches. God knows that your trustworthiness in this world is a sure sign of your trustworthiness in general. In this passage our Lord teaches us the true use of worldly wealth.

First, in the use of worldly wealth we are to show ourselves trustworthy. Do you believe that God controls this world? If you do, then you know that He determines who is wealthy and who is not. One factor in this (by no means the only one) is the trustworthiness of the one who holds the wealth. It is indeed possible to cheat on your expense account; it is even possible to deceive the tax man. It is not possible to do this and expect God to trust you with more.

More than this, there is true wealth. Money belongs only to this world. There are no pockets in a shroud. God will bless you as you are able to receive it. In nothing is this more true than in the world to come, where all things will be revealed. Your blessings in the world to come depend on your stewardship of whatever you have in this.

Indeed, in that world to come you will receive the wealth which is truly yours. What you "own" today is but a stewardship. You think not? Will you own it in a hundred years? Two hundred? Of course not. Your time is fleeting on this earth, and it is a time of trial. Pass the test. Handle that which God has chosen to give you in a worthy manner, and the greatness of his riches in the world to come will be yours for all eternity. The amount you have in this world is not the test. What you do with that amount—ah, that he will measure with care.

Lazarus

Luke 16:19-31

Is there anything that makes your suffering worse than the sight of someone else who seems to have no problems?

Some of us can rise above that. The Scripture does not say that Lazarus envied the rich man. It does say he was hungry, and wanted to eat what fell to the floor from the rich man's table. In this, Lazarus shows us an admirable self-control. Being hungry is biological; envy is spiritual. So many of us spend our lives looking at those with a little bit more than ourselves, wondering how they got so lucky.

Many will point out that this is America, the richest land on earth (at least materially). The proper comparison is not with the neighbor next door but the poor of the world. Perhaps the comparison is useful, but may I suggest a better way?

How is it that Lazarus, despite his condition, shows no sign of envy or anger? Indeed, the reader of the story would see his high position in that he is at Abraham's side—the sign of a truly righteous man. And in his time it would have been hard for him to find someone worse off than himself. Perhaps the virtue of Lazarus is not that he compared himself to someone else in a lower condition. Perhaps he made no comparison at all! Is it just possible that he practiced contentment with what God had given him? Is it at all likely that he trusted the God of justice to give to him all that he deserved—in God's own time, place and way? Could it be that faith in God's character—his righteousness, his loving kindness, his care—triumphed over the temporary problems of life?

It is well said that wealth is the state in which your possessions exceed your desires, and poverty that in which your desires exceed your possessions. Neither state has anything to do with the amount of money you have, nor your health—just their relationship to your desires. Perhaps the reason we feel so stricken is not that God has not blessed us—but that our desires exceed the blessings he has given us. Do you see the utter presumption in that? We are saying to God that we want more than he chooses to give; that our passions should triumph over his wisdom. Should we not rather listen to our Father, and tame our desires instead?

Ten Lepers
Luke 17:11-19

Faith does not necessarily imply gratitude. You will please note that the Scripture says, "as they went" they were cleansed. So it appears that all ten of the lepers had faith, for they all went to the priests to present themselves as cleansed.

It cannot be concluded that the other nine were ungrateful. After all, Jesus had commanded them to go that way. He never issued a command for them to return and give thanks; he did not proclaim his lordship over them. He merely commanded them to go.

Obedience is necessary. It is the foundation stone of faith. You say you have faith, and the first question is, "Do you obey?" But it is only the first question.

My children were trained, in their youth, to obey their parents. The slightest disobedience was treated as rebellion. But as they grew older we kept telling them, "I am raising eagles to fly, not chickens for Colonel Sanders." By this we meant that they were to grow in the faith and become mature, thinking for themselves and no longer obeying blindly. Their obedience was still required, but it is now obedience to our God. The next step in maturity is to go from obedience to adoration.

Adoration cannot be commanded. But it is the natural result of meeting the living God. The tenth leper evidently knew that. There were many things on his mind, no doubt—how do I get back to family and friends, how do I begin my life again, what shall I do for a living now that I can no longer beg—but the first priority was to give thanks.

It is more amazing yet—the man was a Samaritan, and the Jews and Samaritans hated each other. There is a grand virtue here. This man was so humble that he would cast aside all the passions of racial prejudice to perform the simple act of courtesy: "thank you." Perhaps he was amazed that he was included.

I often have the same feeling. Why did God choose me for such a salvation? I am not one of those whose lives have been a model of righteousness. Indeed, my astonishment overcomes my pride and I say to him, "thank you." Wonderful grace of Jesus, greater than all my sin! You do not need to understand "why" or "how" to understand that grace has been extended to you—and to say "thank you" to the King of Kings.

April 16

God be Merciful
Luke 18:9-14

We spend much of our lives in comparative adjectives: fatter, thinner, taller, younger, older... It seems that we are never content with what we are. One way we avoid the guilt in our own eyes is to look upon others.

The Pharisee is doing that. He is comparing himself to the tax collector. Now, the fact is that the Pharisee is much more righteous, in the eyes of most of us, than the tax collector. He is more educated in the Law of Moses; he follows the strictest of rules. But as he stands before God, in the one spot on earth where God has put his name, his entire statement is one of comparison of his virtues to the tax collector's vices.

His virtues are undoubted. Jesus does not challenge them. The vices of the tax collector are obvious and admitted. All that is said is true—and misses the point. The Pharisee is making the wrong comparison. He is looking down on the tax collector when he should be looking up to God.

The tax collector, however, has sense enough to realize what a sinner he is. Perhaps it is his good fortune that there is no one around who is worse than he is! His comparison is to God, and to the Law, and at such he recognizes himself as an abject failure. He may be a crook to the citizenry, but he admits it to God.

Nor does he plead for mercy on the grounds of what good things he may have done to make up for it. He does not tell God about the money he might have given to charity, or the beggar he may have fed, or the mercy he showed to some other person. He is neither proud nor bargaining.

Instead, he begs. He begs from the creator of the universe one thing: mercy. No arguments as to why, no virtues advanced—just the plea for mercy. It is utterly humiliating to him, for there is not a shred of justification for such mercy. He cannot ask, he must beg.

Christ then tells us the secret. This man goes home justified. Why? Certainly not for his virtue, nor for his charity. He goes home justified because he has acknowledged what he is, and has humbled himself.

Humble yourself in the sight of the Lord, and He will lift you up.

An Undivided Heart
Psalm 86:11-13

It is the mark of the pure in heart, says our Lord, that they shall see God. Indeed, one might say that the pure heart is the instrument needed to see God clearly. The Psalmist in these three verses makes two requests. The first of these is that the Lord would teach him his ways. One of the characteristics of the pure, undivided heart is that there is no self-deception in it. The pure heart knows its needs. So the true lover of Jesus asks instruction. But not just for the sake of knowledge alone, or for the glory of being known as wise. No, the teaching of the Lord is meant for action. The disciple must walk in God's truth.

There is a test in that. We often read of the Pharisees being so strictly obedient to what they thought was the Law. From this we conclude (erroneously) that obedience is not necessary. Far from it! If you are pure in heart, you will walk in God's truth. If you are not walking in God's way, then this purity is far from you.

So it is that the Psalmist asks for an undivided heart. There are those who are pious on Sunday while Monday reveals a new man. Many believe that they have fooled others; this may be true. But who can fool God? Indeed, the Psalmist understands this, so he asks for this undivided heart so that he may fear God. God is love, but he is also the God of power and righteousness. He is not mocked. If you fear him, you will not try to deceive him by first deceiving yourself.

But the fear of God is the beginning of wisdom. What begins with fear goes on to praise, pure-hearted praise. Not the praise of a sly man hoping for a favor, but the praise of a man with genuine adoration for what God has done for him.

This praise comes to its highest point when it rests on God's love. God is love, and God's love towards us is great. Here, hundreds of years before Christ, the Psalmist has touched the highest point of love: that God has delivered us from the grave.

Have you learned from the Lord today? Have you taken his instruction, learning in the fear of the Lord? Have you praised his name to others today? Have you acknowledged your salvation?

Are you one with an undivided heart?

The Hope of a Sinner
Luke 19:1-10

"Zacchaeus was a wee little man," the children sing. Being children, they know what it is to be short in a tall world. Perhaps they understand Zacchaeus better than we do; how many of us would climb a tree to catch a glimpse of someone passing by?

Being short caused Zacchaeus to climb the tree. Being curious, and perhaps even hopeful, caused him to go to the parade. In this Zacchaeus tells us something about Jesus: he is always the hope of a sinner. Zacchaeus, unlike some of us, knew quite well that he was a sinner. His society reminded him of it every day.

Now, every other mortal in Jericho with him was a sinner too. But society considered Zacchaeus to be the real thing, for he was a tax collector on behalf of the conquering Romans. Their society, like ours, divided sins into the acceptable and the unacceptable.

ur society too? Yes, certainly. Divorce no longer causes a stigma in our culture; greed can masquerade nicely as "being an entrepreneur;" and idolatry as fashion or sports. All these are acceptable sins. They are just as much sin as murder or child abuse, but they are acceptable.

So Zacchaeus knew he was a sinner and did something about it. Jesus came to seek and save the lost, so he came to Zacchaeus. The crowd, the keeper of acceptable sins, muttered against this. In our day we would find the unacceptable sinner politely ignored. Do you think not? What would your reaction be if you found that the lady in the next seat was a prostitute? How would you react to the news that a man who had abused his children had joined your Sunday School class?

Jesus is not willing that one should be lost. Throughout his ministry he went to the homes of those who were "religiously incorrect." He partied with the sinners and welcomed them gladly. He called them to repentance, and they heard him gladly. Is not the kingdom of God the richer for it?

For our part, we need to imitate our Lord. Should we not put aside our prejudices, our fears—and even our good manners, if need be—and welcome all into the Kingdom of God? The church is more than a health club for saints; she is a hospital for sinners. We are the nurses with the Great Physician, healing the rift of sin between God and mankind.

The Stones Will Cry Out
Luke 19:28-48

There is no getting around it. Jesus of Nazareth had a very high opinion of himself—and he revealed it in complete humility.

Here, at the Triumphal Entry, we see just one sentence that tells much. Jesus comes before the people of Israel, as prophesied, presenting himself as the coming King. The moment is a joyous one for all but the Pharisees. Evidently dignity and decorum must prevail! So they tell Jesus to rebuke his disciples.

The reply is astonishing. "I tell you, if they keep quiet, the stones will cry out." Can you imagine such a thing?

Yes, indeed. God tells us, in Job, that when he formed the worlds the stars sang together as the angels shouted for joy. Here, in this specific place and time, comes a man who claims the same control over the universe. Not just that he could command the stones to shout—that they would shout of their own accord.

We forget that the universe need not exist. All things were created by God, and in Him they have their being. It is quite literally true that you and I borrow the very concept of existence from the great I Am. But the Scripture tells us more: they tell us that Christ is the very agent of that creation, that he is before all things, and in him all things hold together.

Consider it: why are there laws of physics? Why does the universe work today the way it did yesterday? Is it not a reflection of the workman who put it together, who is eternal and unchanging? All things continue as they are because He wills it—until He comes again. Then He will make all things anew.

The Carpenter of Galilee, the Man of Sorrows, is also the creator of heaven and earth. His creation holds together by his will. So it is not at all a surprise to hear that his creation will recognize him as creator. Paul indeed tells us that the whole creation awaits the return of its Lord and Creator, held in bondage until his return.

So I ask you: do you see in Jesus the Lord of Creation, or just a nice teacher? Here again he tells you who he is. If your relationship to him does not acknowledge this primary fact, then you do not know him very well. Perhaps the reason he does not take your good advice—sometimes known as your prayers—is that you are the creature and he is the creator. It is well to recognize who you are—and who He is.

April 20

Render Unto Caesar
Luke 20:20-26

In this short answer Jesus lays down the principal method by which Christians must be governed. Caesar—that is, the state—has his place. Within his proper functions he is to be obeyed.

It is interesting that this passage tells us that Jesus saw through their duplicity. That word, *duplicity*, has its roots in the idea that they are double-minded. With one hand they raise rebellion against the Romans, and with the other they use Roman coins.

The matter is much the same today. The pieces of paper in your wallet actually belong to the government (hence it is illegal to deface the currency) but the value of them belongs to you. By using them you acknowledge the legitimate claims of the government of the day. So did they. Only the double-minded can preach rebellion on one hand and claim the use of the government's care on the other.

There is another, deeper principle shown here: the principle of performance. You may measure a man by what he performs. If he accepts the currency, he accepts the government. "By their fruits you will know them," says our Lord. It is a good test today. You don't like what the government does? What are you doing about it? If you accept what they do and do nothing about it, your actions belie your arguments.

The problem was simple, then. There was one government. The Romans were noted, in general, for their sense of justice. But persecution came eventually, and men had to decide: God, or Caesar?

The rule for the Christian has always been: God first. This is just the specific case of it. Many of us loudly repeat this doctrine. In our time this is a safe thing to do (though perhaps not much longer). But I ask you: Do you place God first in all things? Ahead of the career you so diligently seek? Ahead of your wife and family? Ahead of the pride you guard so carefully? Ahead of the pleasures you find in life?

You say you do. Then test it by the principle of performance. Do your actions show it? Where are you on Sunday morning? Where are you on Saturday night? How do you use God's name? How do you treat your wife and children?

By their fruits you will know them.

Righteousness and Justice
Psalm 89:14-15

The Scriptures often draw us word-pictures of things indescribable to the human mind. This verse is such a picture.

Foundations are most important in any building, for all else rests on them. They are not to be moved. They are, as much as anything human can be, to be eternal. So it is fitting that righteousness and justice are the foundations of God's throne. These are attributes of his character, and he is eternal.

More than that, a foundation determines the shape and structure of a building. If you build an organization of any kind upon the principles of this world—what's in it for me, get away with as much as you can, take care of number one—the organization will crumble, sooner or later. If you think not, consider the trouble you have seen in any business. What happens when one person deserves a raise and another one gets it? What happens when a boss abuses his position for sexual favors? Can such a business last?

Foundations are to last; they are not to move. But buildings are built for a purpose. They are built to do something. From God's throne come love and faithfulness. Like righteousness and justice, these are eternal attributes of his character. Where righteousness and justice rest as solid foundations, love and faithfulness flow out from the throne of God to surround his people. Righteousness and justice may be appealed to; love and faithfulness come to us almost unbidden. His love and faithfulness will seek you out wherever you are.

So it is that those who acclaim God—those who proclaim his eternal character and praise Him—are indeed blessed. Note that this is something that must be learned. How do we learn to acclaim God? By walking in the light of his presence. This walk is made in the mind by the word of God; in the body by good works; in the heart by loving others and in the soul by prayer. Thus with our whole selves we acclaim God, and are blessed.

Blessed? Yes, for surely love and faithfulness are blessings, as are righteousness and justice. Righteousness and justice meet love and faithfulness at the Cross, and we are the ones blessed by it.

A Remarkable Gift

Luke 21:1-6

There is something intensely ordinary about this story. The Temple had a series of "trumpets" — receptacles for the offering that looked like trumpets placed mouthpiece up—into which the faithful could give their offerings. A widow, the picture of poverty in those times, comes to make her offering. It is interesting that she has two coins, for that means she could have withheld one of them. She did not. They are the smallest coins in circulation. It takes four of them to equal the next larger coin. She gave both. Even more interesting is what she did not do:

She did not compromise. Even these two coins are hardly enough to live on. She did not give in to the temptation to do something halfway.

She did not say, "What I have to give can make no difference." From the accountant's point of view this may be true. We may infer she took God's point of view, and did what she could, trusting God to honor and bless the gift.

This is an act of devotion: an act that costs the giver a great deal and can have no worldly effect. But what an effect on the heart of God! As with the woman who wet Jesus' feet with her tears, this woman gave everything—from the heart. It is not an act of calculation. It is not "an investment in the Kingdom." It is an extravagance.

Extravagance! The favorite concept of lovers. Have you ever brought home flowers "just because?" Have you ever reached down and plucked an ordinary flower out of the field and put it behind your love's ear? The monetary value is almost nothing; the value to the beloved is priceless. So it is with this widow's gift.

No doubt she had her trials. A widow was the symbol of poverty and misfortune in those times. It is clear, however, that she loved the Lord her God. Out of her trials welled up joy, and out of her joy came giving. We see poverty; Jesus saw devotion and love. Now the question is: what does he see in us?

A Psalm of Moses
Psalm 90

Ask most Christians who wrote the Psalms and they will tell you, "David." For the most part this is true, but here we have what just might be the oldest of Psalms, for it was written by Moses. Moses, who led the children through the plagues, the parting of the sea and the trials in the desert, saw God in the light of experiences you and I can only read about.

First, and most prominent, he saw an awesome God. In his experience, God was to be feared. Indeed, man should be in terror of Him. And why not? Consider the plagues and miracles, and see how this must be.

Next, He is the eternal God. We think a lifetime is a long time; he sees it as a breath. A day, a thousand years—the same to God, the Eternal One.

He is also the God of Life and Death. We often plan our lives as if we would live forever, but God pronounces differently.

God is compassionate. Even though man is wicked, God is forgiving.

Moses does more than praise God in this Psalm, however. He teaches his followers, and us, some things that this awesome God would have us know.

We need to recognize how short our lives are. We do not have any guarantee of waking up tomorrow morning. Have you put off that forgiveness? Did you delay that repentance? If God told you that you had only two weeks to live, would you change what you have done today? How do you know that you have longer than that?

We need to see and remember the deeds of God, his mighty works. Not just the works in the Scripture, but also the works in our lives. By recognizing these acts of God, we will recognize the splendor of God. This is a step in the path of knowing who God is. Knowing who God is—and acting in the light of that knowledge—is the path that gives a heart of wisdom.

Moses was known as a man of God. He saw the splendor of God and grew in wisdom. Has the Lord blessed you in your life today? Have you grown in wisdom for it?

Judges
Judges 2:16-23

A curious phase of Israel's history comes with the Judges. They are not judges as we think of them today, but deliverers.

First, note that they did not "arise" but rather that God raised them up.

God selects his men with care, and often picks one that we would overlook. Remember that King David's own father thought him least likely to be anointed.

God gives these men the power they need to save their people. This is one reason he selects them; so that we can see this isn't their own ability but God moving through them.

God does this so that his people might be saved—despite the fact that his people got themselves into the mess.

The people themselves are very much like us today. Over and over again, the pattern repeats itself:

When the deliverer first arises, they will not listen. Their hearts are hardened.

When this deliverer triumphs, they listen. But only as long as he is alive. His work dies with his memory.

And when he dies, the people quickly wander back. After all, the danger is gone - so why not repeat the mistake?

God, too, reacts again. This is one reason why the books of history are included in the Bible. We can see from the history of this people how God works.

It is not just their sinful nature, or their chasing after other gods— it is that they violated their covenant. They gave their word to be God's people, and they left him.

God uses the other nations to test them, just as today he uses the things of this world to test his people. It is tempting to ask God to eliminate these evils. Perhaps when we return to his covenant, He will.

But when they go astray, God gives them over to evil. This is so that the effects of evil may be clearly seen. Just as God allows us to suffer the consequences of our sin as individuals, so he does with a nation. This is so that we may see and repent.

Do the times look evil? Fear not. God will raise up his deliverer, time and again, until He returns.

Prayer in the Garden
Luke 22:39-44

Sometimes we can look at the Master and learn from the smallest details. Begin with this: He "went out." Most of us have used the excuse of "I can pray anywhere." Indeed we can; but our Lord commands, and sets the example of, prayer in a separate place. Set aside a quiet place for prayer, that you may better hear your Father.

Note also that He went out "as usual." In this he shows us the value of regular, persistent prayer.

Prayer is part of a personal relationship, in this instance a personal relationship with your Heavenly Father. The deepest of personal relationships are not sporadic meetings.

There is a sense in which practice makes perfect. You may ask, "How should I pray?" I answer, "regularly."

Persistent prayer becomes the Christian's first resource - not the last. Too many of us pray only for the fire department, and shun the fire inspector.

Jesus now shows us, in short language, the kind of prayer which suits a crisis.

He begins by acknowledging God the Father as supreme and omnipotent, for he begins with "if you are willing." If it is not God's will, Jesus does not want it. Nor should we.

He then makes a specific request. How often we meander about in our prayers, asking things like "God bless so-and-so" when what we really mean is, "Lord, straighten so-and-so out." Get to the point!

Then comes the word: "Yet." As he began his prayer by acknowledging that God's will is supreme, so he ends his prayer in the same way.

Even for so brief a prayer, the intensity is great. Notice that Jesus is persistent. He asks three times, with great feeling. It is clear that it is important to him, and therefore he persists.

God's answer is "no." But note that even in rejecting the request of His Only Begotten Son, God sends comfort. His will is perfect; His righteousness flawless; His mercy beyond our measure. He may, at His will, deny our request. But if we continue in sweet prayer with Him, He will send comfort along with the denial.

April 26

Go in the Strength You Have
Judges 6

One of the consistent facts of the Old Testament is that those chosen by God confront Him immediately with a series of excuses as to why they should not, or could not, do as he commands. Gideon is no exception

Faith only in the visible. The angel greets him as "mighty warrior" —and Gideon's only reply is that God sure has been slack about producing miraculous deliverance on a regular basis. Never mind that God did this or that in history; let's see the miraculous now.

Timidity. Gideon will do what God tells him (after a visible demonstration)—but only by night. Perhaps no one will notice that he has actually taken a stand for Jehovah? Indeed, it's his father who gets him out of the mess—and dad had nothing to do with it in the first place. How often God rescues us by the hands of those least expected!

Excuses. Usually these involve our human weaknesses. God has already told Gideon that he is a mighty warrior. Gideon then tells God that his clan is the smallest, and he's the weakest of his clan. So what? God perfects his strength through weakness; from his view, Gideon is just right.

Testing. Even after he sees the angel of the Lord bring fire from the rock, he still wavers. So he goes through the test with the fleece. His need for reassurance is not based on fact, but on the pressure of the moment.

Yet, with all of this, Gideon will triumph as a man of God. We can learn from this. It is not that we should have faith in only that which we see, or that we should be timid, or any of these failings. It is that God does not need a "super-saint" to do his work. He needs you and me, the weakest of the least. He will be patient with us in our doubts and fears, knowing we are but human. If we, like Gideon, will put our fears and doubts aside and do as the Lord commands us, then He will grant us victory in our lives.

Great faith is a great blessing. God can work wonders with just a little faith, in a little man—if the little man is willing to let God perfect his strength in that man's weakness.

Two Thieves
Luke 23:39-43

The Old Testament prophesied that the Messiah would be numbered among the transgressors. Indeed, Jesus was, for he was crucified between two thieves. We do not know their names, but in them we see the depravity of man and the hope of God.

The first thief joins the crowd. All around are mocking Jesus as King of the Jews. The taunt is this: if you really are who you say you are, then you should be able to save yourself. This, of course, is true. Jesus clearly stated that at his command the Father would have sent any number of angels to clear his way. But this would not have fulfilled the will of God. The power was there; God's will was otherwise; Jesus came to do God's will.

So this first thief, thinking that way, decides to join both sides of the "argument." He joins the crowd to provoke Jesus—but just in case Jesus is who he says he is, he makes it "save yourself—and us." "Me first" still rules in most hearts, and this is no exception.

The other thief, however, has a different view. He begins with the beginning of wisdom: the fear of God. It is not that he truly understands what Christ is doing. He does know that God is to be feared. He then shows us he recognizes three things:

He recognizes that he is a sinner. He has done wrong, and has sinned against God (as have we all).

He recognizes that what he is getting is not vengeance, not an accident of fate, but justice. What's happening to him is, in his mind, perfectly fair.

He also recognizes that what is happening to Jesus is not fair nor just. He is a sinner, but he knows righteousness when he sees it.

For such a man, with such a clear vision, how does he state his case for clemency? He doesn't. He makes no case for his own righteousness, he cites no history of "I know I've done wrong but..." Instead, he simply asks for mercy, no excuses provided.

His request for mercy is not "theologically sound." He has no idea when Jesus will come into his kingdom.

It doesn't matter. The request comes from a true heart, and therefore Jesus grants the intention.

Two ways. One of self-justification, telling God why he ought to be happy to save you. The other, a simple request for mercy. The answers to both have not changed in two thousand years.

The Universal Reaction
Luke 24:1-12

One of the finest proofs of the Resurrection is the undoubted fact that none of Jesus' followers were prepared for it. Every action, every word that came from them during the time from Good Friday to Easter was that of someone who was certain of one thing: Jesus of Nazareth was dead.

Joseph of Arimathea, a very minor figure in the Gospels, goes to Pilate to beg the body. This would be the act of a righteous Jew, in accordance with the Law. It is also an act of courage. But it shows that he thought Jesus was dead (as indeed He was) and did not hesitate to make his request to the Romans— who had every reason to make sure He was dead.

The women—considered second-class citizens in this time and place—follow Joseph to the tomb and mark the spot, for the Sabbath is coming. On Sunday they go to anoint the body, expecting for all the world to find it there. This too is an act of charity. Their reaction to the angels is typical —angels usually enter with the words, "Fear not"—and only when reminded do they recall the words of Christ. The Pharisees, suspecting deception, had excellent memory of those words. The women, knowing there was no deception, could not conceive of the Risen Lord.

The women tell the Eleven. The Eleven react just as logical men would react. They think the women are speaking nonsense. Perhaps in the excitement of many voices the message was not clear. One thing is clear: the eleven men closest to Jesus for over three years did not understand that He had risen.

But Peter—always the impetuous one—runs to see for himself. He examines the scene, and goes away "wondering to himself." We are told elsewhere that John believed at this point, but Peter does not. He is puzzled.

Not until they see the Risen Lord does this attitude change. These are people just like you and I. They are reliable witnesses, not so much by their words as by their actions. Until they saw, they would not believe. When they saw, they believed—and turned the world upside down. Their witness is still true today.

The Bodily Resurrection
Luke 24

"He is Risen" was the challenge. "He is Risen indeed" was the password. These were the watchwords of the ancient church. Hidden, persecuted, the church needed a way to recognize true believers from those who would betray them. So they devised various challenge and password combinations. Foremost among them were these. So it was that the ancient church would recognize its own true sons.

The method is much the same today. C. S. Lewis once remarked that Christianity could almost be reduced to one fact and one doctrine. The fact? The Resurrection. The doctrine? Redemption by grace. It is no wonder then that most heresies focus on either working your way into heaven, or the idea that Jesus did not rise in bodily form.

The testimony of the church from its earliest days is exactly the opposite. Jesus is clearly shown as having a physical body in many ways similar to our own. He can be touched, He has flesh and bones. He eats and drinks, He breaks bread with His disciples. Indeed, these two disciples cannot distinguish him from an ordinary man—until He permits it. Of this the Apostles were sure: Jesus, the Christ, crucified, dead, buried—rose again in the flesh.

To be sure, He seems to have powers beyond our mortal bodies today. We are told that we shall be like him at the resurrection of the dead. What, exactly, that body will be like is something which is yet hidden.

The disciples are not told these things. Indeed, they are chastised for being "foolish" and "slow to believe." They simply could not conceive of the Resurrection before it happened. Is this not the case today? How many Christians really believe that Jesus will return in triumph, in bodily form, accompanied by the risen saints? Yet this is the testimony of Christ Himself; we have the word of God on it.

The Apostles were told to remain in Jerusalem until power came upon them. We, in a sense, are "remaining" too. They waited for the Holy Spirit at Pentecost, as we wait for the resurrection. Let us wait as they did: praising God every day.

In the Beginning
John 1

John's Gospel is different. He knows you know the story told in the other Gospels, so he begins at a much deeper level. It is almost mystic how he commands thoughts to mind.

"In the beginning"—the words themselves conjure up the very foundations of the universe. When the worlds were formed, the Word was there. He was with God; He was God—and we see the statement of the Trinity as doctrine, and wonder. How can we understand the three in one? John does not say; he merely states that it is so.

"Through him all things were made"—this Word, then, is the agent of creation itself. What an awesome power this is! He who spoke and the worlds began is introduced to us.

"In him was life"—do you realize that you and I borrow the very *idea* of existence from him? The concept of life itself, of being an independent, self realizing spirit, is borrowed from the original creator. It is not just that we have life from him; he is its very source.

So we are introduced to this awesome person of the Godhead, the agent of creation—and then told that "the Word became flesh, and made his dwelling among us." Think of that! The one through whom all things were made walked on this planet as a man, just like one of us.

But did this world recognize its creator? No, indeed it did not. The very nation raised up for the purpose of bringing salvation to the world rejected its Savior.

But those who do recognize—and believe—have the right to become the children of God. Not by natural birth, but by the will of God Himself. The same will which caused the universe to be created will cause you and I to be his children.

Many of us have been Christians for decades. Sometimes we begin to take for granted the awesome nature of the gift of grace. This should not be! Before he came, we were just so many mortals doomed to die. Now we are the children of God who will be raised when the Lord returns, to reign with Him forever. The very thought is beyond our imaginations. It should not, however, be beyond our gratitude and praise.

Beyond Understanding
Judges 13:15-23

In the Old Testament we occasionally see glimpses of Christ before the Incarnation. This is just such an instance. We see him described as "the angel of the Lord" (not "an angel"). What really tells us that this is Christ is the question about his name. Manoah wants to honor this angel when his prophecy comes true, but the angel simply passes by the question. Or so it seems.

The phrase "beyond understanding" here is translated "wonderful" in Isaiah, in the list of names that are prophesied to be applied to the Messiah. So from this, and the character of events, we see here the Lord Jesus before his birth.

Manoah learns a lesson here. Note this: when he asks the angel what he is to do, the angel tells him clearly. But when he asks the angel his name he does not get a clear answer. It is as if our Lord is willing to tell the one but not the other. This is typical of our Christian experience. If we ask the Lord for the guidance we need to see our duty, he will give it to us. If we ask him for the courage to do it, he will give it to us. But if we ask him to reveal something not necessary for our right conduct or relationship with him–such as "what are you going to do with the other guy?"–our Lord is silent. If the hearing does not benefit us, we will not hear it from him.

Manoah teaches us another lesson: the fear of God. So often we are taught that God is love and we neglect the fact that God is righteous. Manoah knows himself to be a sinner; he fears to stand in the presence of the Holy One of Israel.

Manoah's wife teaches us a lesson too. She knows her husband's fear, and responds in faith. She trusts this angel; he has told her good things, and she knows that if the angel meant to kill, they'd be dead before the conversation started. Her faith balances nicely with her husband's fear.

In this little story we can see three keys to our relationship with Christ:

We do not need to know everything; we need to act on what we do know.

We need to remember that God is Holy, and that we are sinners in need of repentance.

We need to trust our Lord, and let our obedience give power to our faith.

The Radical Jesus
John 2:13-25

It is rather a shame that we have an image of Jesus as a meek, mild person. I suspect this is our attempt to put Jesus into our mold, since we so seldom want to fit into his. (Do I hear echoes of "out of my comfort zone"?) But, we need to read the Word and discover the real Jesus—and that includes the firebrand radical Jesus.

Zeal is now a "religious" word. It was not always so; in Jesus' time the Zealots were really a political party. We'd call them "radicals" today. Zeal is, in today's English, radicalism. Remember that radical does not necessarily mean "left wing." Remember Barry Goldwater? "Extremism in the defense of liberty is no vice; moderation in the defense of liberty no virtue"? That is the radicalism, or zeal, that is displayed here in the theological sense.

It is this extreme identification with God—what hurts him, hurts me; what helps him, blesses me—that is the characteristic of the zealot, the radical. What, then, drives a Christian to be so radical?

First, there is the absolute nature of truth. In an era that proclaims all truth relative (except this one) and all generalizations false (including this one), the Christian stands for absolute truth. You may have a right to your opinion—but that does not necessarily make it "just as true" as mine.

Christ drove the moneychangers out of the Temple—but didn't touch the local house of prostitution. Why? The struggle is not against flesh and blood; it's in the spirit.

There is a point of self-examination here. Why are you in church?

Is it just to "hedge your bets"? After all, it can't hurt to pay a little attention to God now and then. But look at the radical, all-or-nothing nature of the cause of Christ!

Is it something you are fervent about on Sunday (and forget on Monday) only because it's "safe"? What happens when (I did not say "if") it gets risky? Courage is still the foundation of virtue.

But courage and virtue are not enough; they must combine into action. Do they so combine in your life? Do you live for him? Are you ready to be radically kind, radically loving, radically righteous? Or are you trying to get halfway to heaven?

How Can This Be?

John 3

How can a man be born again, asks Nicodemus. Well he might. The phrase occurs only here, but it has become a part of our language. But some will ask, "How can I be sure that I am indeed born again?"

There is an outward sign, given here. Baptism is given both by commandment and example of Christ. But anyone can be immersed in water; how can we be sure? "By their fruits you shall know them," says our Lord, and here are some of the fruits of those who are born again:

First, there is faith. Not mere intellectual agreement over the facts, but genuine trust in Jesus Christ.

There is also the power over sin. Before we become the children of God there is no resisting sin, not over the long term. Now—whatever the struggle may be—we have the power to conquer.

Peace, too, comes to those who are born again. The peace of God. Not a confidence based upon worldly things, but the sure knowledge that God will provide.

Hope is another sign. Do you indeed look forward to the day when our Lord returns—or do you dread the possibility?

Obedience is another such sign. Do you seek our Lord's will in your life, and then follow it?

Finally, does your life flow with the love that comes from God himself? The unselfish love he showed us at the Cross?

The attack of Satan is subtle. "Surely you are not really saved. After all, shouldn't you be able by now to work miracles, speak in tongues, or at the very least be completely free from all temptation?" None of these things are promised to all of us; indeed, to be free from temptation comes to no man in this life. Consider the signs of your life. If these things are there, then you are indeed born again, for these are the signs of a child of God.

And if not? There is still time. Repent, and seek the Lord while his gracious mercy may still be found. You have no guaranty of tomorrow. Seek him today, and be sure of his mercy.

Only What Is Given
John 3:27-36

Americans in particular are entranced with the notion that anyone can become President. This may be fine for politics, but in the church we deal with reality.

A man can receive only what is given him from heaven. For us, we must see that this applies to our tasks in the Kingdom:

> What we are given in Christ is given from heaven, and is therefore exceedingly precious. Whatever our task, we should take it as if divinely appointed—because it is.

> We may not pick our task. We may find it, but we may not pick it—for God gives it, we do not choose. Remember that priests in the Old Testament had to be descendants of Aaron. Even Apostles were not allowed to choose their place of service. Why would we then be so presumptuous?

> We "can" receive it—but it will not be forced on us. We can reject it, at our peril, and compel God to seek another.

John the Baptist goes on to show us the right attitude of the servant of Christ. So many of us are concerned with our status! We seek the praise of others and recognition of the church. But John teaches us otherwise:

> He shows us, by the illustration of bride and bridegroom, that we must let the right people be in the right places. Our wants should not enter into it; God's will should decide.

> When the right ones are in those positions, things go as God intends. We should rejoice at that, no matter how small our part to play.

> Indeed, when the time comes (not "if") for our part to be reduced, we must accept the "less" with grace and joy.

So it would seem that God places great limits on us. But note well: these are not limits, these are directions and tasks. God puts no limit on how well we can do for his kingdom. He gives the Spirit without limit. Once given, any task he gives is within our power, for it is His power in us that works. This is one reason why the "unlikely" are so often chosen: so that God's power may be recognized through it. All this is done so that His ultimate purpose may be accomplished, that we might believe in His Only Son.

The Woman at the Well
John 4:4-42

"Sin" is an unpopular word these days. No one likes to be yelled at for their mistakes. Note the gentle way Jesus does this:

In the quietest way possible, yet with an unanswerable question, he points out to her that she is a sinner. She tries to duck and dodge ("I have no husband") but Jesus will not let her go from the point. She is a sinner.

It is also a reminder of the futility of denying it. Not only are we all sinners—God knows it. He knows what we have done. Why should we deny it?

We cannot "duck" the issue of personal sin—God knows it all anyway—but it must be handled with gentleness. Dare we say even with humor?

The woman tries a distraction. She acknowledges him as prophet (her understanding gets better as she learns) and asks about worship. Isn't it characteristic of most people that they want the "right answer?" So many of the people we meet have questions about eternal things, questions for which we should (and don't) have an answer. Here are two:

God does not want liturgy, formulas or rituals—he wants worship in spirit and truth. It sounds obvious today—but this question has as its background the idea that "so much empty ritual *can't* be what God really wants, can it?"

The worship is personal; Jesus is the "I AM".

It is most interesting to note the woman's actions after meeting Jesus. She brings others. There are some lessons here:

She does not wait until she is completely taught; she starts immediately. There is no "discipleship program," no study course. Her message is "come and see."

The basis of her appeal is fact: "come and see." She may know nothing about the theology, but she knows what she knows—and invites others to see it too.

Often when we meet our "woman at the well" we are too timid to deal with sin; too ignorant to deal with questions. But see what happens when courage yields action! Christ tells us to be ready with a defense of the faith. We should be ready at any time, even with those outside our own circle. They too were designed to be the children of God.

Under Whose Wings
Ruth 2-4

Ruth is a woman in serious trouble. To be a widow in those days was to be poor; to be a widow with no sons was to be destitute. So for her to abandon her family in Moab to go with her mother-in-law, Naomi, into Israel was a great leap of faith. Why ?

First, I think, for love. Something in Naomi drew her.

Next, because of the trust in God she must have learned from Naomi. Somehow, He would provide.

As Boaz predicted, she was richly rewarded. For what? For seeking shelter under the wings of the God of Israel! Not for her own virtue, but because she sought shelter in God. She trusted.

Boaz, too, is a man who shows much of God's character. He very correctly demonstrates his obedience to the Law of Moses in that he leaves grain in his fields for the alien to gather. But he goes beyond that! Again, why?

Perhaps he remembers the word of the Lord, how his people were "strangers in a strange land," and has compassion on this young woman.

It may be simply this: these commands in the Law of Moses often end with the statement, "I am the Lord." It is as if God were expecting the children to ask "why?"–and his answer is simply, "I am the Lord." One does not need so much to reason out why God commands as to obey his commands.

Boaz is a picture of the kinsman-redeemer. This is a picture of Christ, to us.

We too are children of God. But like Ruth, we have nothing with which to save ourselves. We are, spiritually, destitute.

In such circumstance, we can either snarl at our fate or take refuge under the wings of God. In trust, in love, we nest "under his wings." It is not a sign of our merit but his care.

By the character of God we are redeemed. As the closest redeemer could not afford the price, so the best of us cannot redeem even the worst of us. But God sent his son, Jesus, to redeem us—and He paid the price at Calvary. Of Ruth came Obed, whose son Jesse then raised David, the King. Jesus is often called "Son of David." God ties all things together - for those who will seek refuge under his wings.

Pick Up Your Mat
John 5:1-23

There is a certain comic element to this story. This poor fellow, waiting helplessly for 38 years, is finally cured. The man who cures him tells him to pick up his mat and move. So, in all innocence, he does it. The lawyers stop him; this is working on the Sabbath, strictly against the rules. That he has been cured excites no curiosity; the fact that he's carrying the mat is the problem.

It brings out the one point about Jesus that the Pharisees saw clearly and never could accept: he claimed, in the most casual but certain manner, to be God. Unique among the religions of history comes a man who says, to the one people in the world who would certainly understand what it meant, I am God.

> He said it here, directly, in commanding the man to pick up the mat. He is showing that he is superior to the Law.

> He says it every time he pronounces forgiveness of sins. For who can forgive, except the one offended? And who is offended at every sin committed, except God?

> He most clearly tells them that he is the Son of God, not just by title but by example. He calls God his Father; he proclaims that the things he is doing are given by example from his Father.

> Indeed, he claims that the Father has entrusted judgment to him— that he will be the one to judge the living and the dead.

The paralytic carries his mat. The Pharisees are burdened with a much greater burden: the system of rules and regulations of their own making. Like many such, they can see no virtue outside their own system. The system, for them, stands in the place of God. God is not a system; God is not a "force"; God is not just a set of rules and regulations. God is a person; indeed, three persons in one Godhead. Whenever we place our own views about God above his own call, we have denied Him.

Are you burdened with your own set of rules and regulations? Perhaps you learned them in your youth. You cannot go here or there; you cannot touch this or drink that; that kind of people are not to be spoken to. Christ went to anyone's house; ate and drank with the worst of sinners; and brought them all the good news of the kingdom. Are you bound by the rules, or are you the imitator of Christ?

Life and Judgment
John 5:24-47

In this passage Jesus makes specific reference to two key attributes which the Father has vested in him: life and judgment.

Life in Himself. The phrase is somewhat related to God's essence: I AM. Interestingly, the word in the Greek here is the word for biological life, not spiritual life. It is the same word which is used to describe God's creating power. The implication for us is clear: In our relationship to Jesus Christ lies our hope of the Resurrection.

Judgment to the Son. There is a point of justice in which the Father confides judgment to the Son. We in America believe that we must be convicted by "a jury of our peers." The phrase is originally from England and refers to social class, but there is a truth in it. Until you have suffered like I have, who are you to tell me what I should or should not have done? Think of all that happened to Christ; he became fit to judge through it.

Note that "judge" is used in the Scripture as we would use it in both the civil and criminal sense. To judge may also mean to reward, as an honest judge would give justice to that persistent widow. It also means that the criminal judge is there, most notably proclaimed in the parable of the sheep and the goats.

Interestingly, the Resurrection and the Judgment are tied together inseparably. At the Resurrection all will be raised—and then will come the judgment, by one who knows how.

To ensure that we do not miss the point, Christ cites the witnesses of his power. One is contemporary, John the Baptist. Another is recorded for us, the works he performed. A third precedes his birth, the prophetic record of the Old Testament. By these we can conclude that Jesus is who he claimed to be: God in the flesh, the very Son of the Living God. If He, then, tells you that he will return to judge the living and the dead, how can you ignore him without the gravest of peril? Yet so many of us do, thinking that we can put off the day of repentance. It is not so. We have the word of God on the subject.

Examine yourself, therefore, and ask—am I ready to meet the Judge? When I do, will he pronounce eternal life for me?

The Ark
1 Samuel 5-7

Much of the Old Testament is the history of God showing the nation of Israel what kind of God He truly is—and correcting the ideas that Israel obtained from the nations around them. We see such in this episode.

The Philistines, at first, see the Ark as a great triumph. They have captured something that has powerful magic, in their view. This is the view that many have of God: if I can just get the right things in my possession, all will be well. But God begins to deal with them severely. The first city gets a symbolic warning, as the idol is found face down before the Ark. The second city is plagued with tumors; by the time it reaches the third, the only question is how to get rid of it safely.

The next step is taken. Send it back where it belongs—but not without some sort of sacrifice. This too is a modern view. Many people feel that if they only give money to the right cause, or give up the right thing, that God will magically come to their aid. But it is not so. God does not desire sacrifice; God desires the love of his people.

Note the difference in Israel. They are God's people; they have a prophet. They are not sinless. So the prophet of God begins with the obvious. They must repent.

Repentance is not just the simple act of saying, "I'm sorry." Samuel tells them to put away the things that have snared them. In their case it is idolatry. But think: they worshiped a fertility goddess; we worship sexuality. They worshiped a god who was good for business; we worship materialism. They had an advantage over us: their false gods were staring them in the face. We have to look in a mirror to find ours.

But see the result. The great thing they sought, deliverance from the Philistines, was given to them without effort. It is His good pleasure to do so for his children when they are rightly related to Him.

So often we fret for the things we should not have or do not need. We cry to God and ask why we don't have them. The lesson is clear: we are asking for the wrong things. Begin with your relationship to God. Get that straightened out, and all else will flow to you. We do not even know what to ask for; but we should at least have sense enough to know *who* to ask.

Just What You Asked For
1 Samuel 8

Did you ever get just what you asked for—but not what you really wanted? That's what the Israelites got here.

Notice God's way of handling them. He uses the same methods on us when we ask for something which is wrong.

First, even before we ask for it, he has already told us not to ask. This business about a king was covered in the instructions given to Moses. So they should have known better—because God knew about it before it happened. For this reason we should examine the Scriptures daily.

Next, God gives them a messenger with his word. Whether this is a prophet or just a friend, God provides us with a warning—if we will listen.

He does not provide this warning in some mysterious oracle that cannot be understood by ordinary people. He makes it clear in the language of reason.

But the people persist. God does not prevent them or deny them, but uses the occasion that they might learn.

He teaches them that they should listen. He will remind us, too, that we need to listen to him. So often our pride stands between us and wisdom. God will use the lessons of our past so that our future will be brighter.

He teaches them that sin has consequences—consequences which must be borne. He rejects their plea for relief and lets them suffer so that they might know who is God.

Interestingly, in all this the messenger suffers too. How often have you tried to warn someone—a child, a friend, even your spouse—getting nothing but rejection?

If you are the messenger of God, then understand that rejecting the message is not rejecting the messenger—but the one who sent the messenger.

If you feel that this is "not fair," you're right. "Don't shoot the messenger," we say. But remember that the servant is not above the master. They crucified the Living Word; do you expect no rejection at all? God is just; God is love. In being both God must sometimes allow consequences to flow—even to his messengers.

His Love Endures Forever
Psalm 107

One of the great blessings of Scripture is that the Psalms speak to the heart. Poetry is the language that transcends translation, and this poetry speaks to us today.

He talks about those who are wanderers—and what is more characteristic today than those who wander in their lives? So many people lack a moral compass, asking, "Is there any meaning to this life?" God lets such people suffer—until they cry out to him. Those who are seeking the Lord will find him, and he will lead them "by a straight way" to a place of rest.

Some, however, have heard the word of God, and rejected it. Is there anything that brings more sorrow to a parent's heart than this? What does God do? He does not let them go entirely, but makes their lives full of "bitter labor"—they work, but they do not obtain satisfaction. Why? So that they too will cry out to him—and he will break the chains that bind them.

Others become fools not by method of thought but by actions. We see this constantly. How many people do you know who believe that if only they had more money, or the right spouse, or some other thing to be chased in this world, they would be happy? God lets them chase until they see the foolishness of this—even if this takes them near death. Then when they cry to him, he will save.

Others take a more mature view—or so they think. No fools, they think to use the world around them for their own gain. "Out on the sea in ships"—working the things of this world, commanding them for their own profit, they appear to ride high and serene. They are often admired. But the sea is still the sea; time and chance still happen to all. When the storm arises, they too can call to God, and He will still the storm.

Finally, there are those who have been blessed by God—and have forgotten who he is. They need but look back in history to see what God has done for them, but they choose to forget. God's response is to humble them—and then lift the needy out of their affliction.

> "Whoever is wise, let him heed these things
> and consider the great love of the Lord."

Who Do You Say That I Am?
John 7

Western civilization is largely founded on Jesus Christ. Therefore we cannot avoid the question: just who is this Jesus? This passage shows us that the answers we hear today are nothing new.

He's a good man

This is a popular attitude. After all, look at all the neat things he had to say! There are only two things wrong with it:

It's false. He never claimed to be a "good guy"; he claimed to be God in the flesh.

It ignores the consequences of ignorance. Just because I believe the bomb won't explode doesn't mean the bomb agrees with me.

He's leading the people astray

This is a theory that is returning in popularity. One of the great difficulties of modern humanism is the character of its opponents. If you were to read the popular press, the Christian (a.k.a. "right-wing fundamentalist"—to demonize you must label) is a raving lunatic. The theory is wonderful; the facts are to the contrary. Most Christians are, in fact, the "salt of the earth." If this is so, how can the humanist explain it? The only possible hypothesis is that while Christians are good people, they have been led astray.

This too falls on its face. What does it mean, "to lead astray?" Have you ever seen a group of people who were led astray and became *more* righteous? It is self-contradictory. How can this be?

He has a demon (in modern terms, he's nuts)

This theory at least has the virtue of simplicity. In its original version—the demon—it certainly explained Jesus' power. Again, however, it falls apart upon examination of the facts. If there is any one thing modern psychiatry tells us, it is that religion must be a neurosis—after all, these people are not facing reality. So then, what is the diagnosis of Jesus of Nazareth? Read his words; are they not the words of a man eminently sane, intelligent and shrewd? If he's a nutcase, why did he not go the way of all other nutcases—powerful in the flesh, forgotten when he's gone?

The theories fail because they are false. The Son of Man remains because He is Truth itself. The only question that counts has only one answer that works.

Living Water
John 7:30-53

Why do you want water? Because you are thirsty. Why do you want living water? Because you are thirsty. Remember, one can hunger and thirst after righteousness. We want water so that we will not thirst.

> We want water so we will not thirst in the mind. Desperately, we want the universe to "make sense." Is it really just a thrown-together collection of particles, or is there a purpose to it?

> We want water so we will not thirst in the heart. Each of us has been failed by someone, let down by someone, left longing for promised comfort and strength.

> We want water so we will not thirst in our strength. We chase security in every form. We invest, we save, we gamble, we build—all so that we may be secure against tomorrow. And at the end of tomorrow is death; and how are we to be secure against that?

> We want water so we will not thirst in our souls. Our time cries out for completeness, for integrity. "Something is missing in our lives"—and whole generations have set out to find it, and become lost.

In all these things Christ provides the answers. His Holy Spirit, the living water flowing from us, quenches these thirsts.

> The universe does make sense, for it was created from the mind of God by the hand of Christ. The author is at hand.

> Jesus never fails us; when all others retreat, he is with us still.

> Jesus is our security in this life and our promise of resurrection to come. No one else has come through what he has come through; no one else could make those promises and keep them.

> In Christ we find completeness, for He is righteousness, peace, love and justice; indeed, all things that are good flow from him. In him, we find perfection.

If you find yourself thirsting, ask yourself: is it because He does not provide living water? Or because you will not come to the fountain and drink?

Line Your Tiger Trap - With First Stones
John 8:1-11

Do you remember Wile E. Coyote? One of my favorite cartoons with Wile E. and the Road Runner starts with the old gag of Latin names. The Road Runner comes on (*velocitus incredibulus*) followed by the Coyote (*famishus vulgaris*). Later in the cartoon, Wile E. constructs a genuine Burmese tiger trap—which of course yields a genuine Burmese tiger (*surprisibus! surprisibus!*). A good part of the humor comes from the fact that the coyote constructed the trap himself. Here, the Pharisees construct a trap for themselves, and quite elaborately.

The trap as they intended it was for Jesus. It is a very subtle one, for it has three layers:

The most obvious one is that Jesus could advocate stoning (and wind up in trouble with the Roman government) or say that the Law of Moses is wrong.

More subtly, Jesus has the reputation of the friend of the sinner—and here is most certainly an appealing sinner, a damsel in distress. What will this do to his reputation?

But even more subtle is this: this is an invitation to join the system of rabbinical law. All Jesus has to do is to suggest that the Roman rule, which prevents the Law of Moses from being carried out, is God's just punishment on Israel—and he's now just another clever rabbi in the system.

Instead, Jesus stays true to the Father's calling: he is to seek and save the lost. Jesus did not come into this world to condemn the world, but rather to save it. Indeed, is it not just possible that his writing on the ground is nothing but a chance for the Pharisees to reconsider this judgment? For even the Pharisees are among those Jesus came to seek and save.

The failing of the Pharisees here is that of being judgmental. Jesus shows them the pit they are digging for themselves. We too can be judgmental; all of us have "first stones" to throw. Indeed, many of us have so many that we could line our pit with them. But--*surprisibus, surprisibus*—it's likely enough that we'll be the ones in the pit (and with the tiger, too). Consider well before you judge. You're likely to be the butt of the joke in this life, and a candidate for hell in the next.

Boast in the Lord
1 Samuel 17

God chooses those who will serve him in the most spectacular ways: he picks the unlikely person, in the most "coincidental" of ways, with the most unlikely method. Consider David:

David is the "runt of the litter." Jesse had eight sons; David is the youngest. In their time, that would make him the least. Indeed, his father esteems him so small that he left him with the sheep when Samuel came to anoint a king.

Why is David at this camp at this time? Because his father sent him up with some food from home for the three brothers who were with Saul. He's not even in the army; he's just visiting the camp!

By what method does David defeat Goliath? Not by the ways of the world, though Saul gave him the best he had, the king's own armor. David must use God's own method.

But God is not random; he picks those who are after his own heart. Consider David's preparation:

He has been faithful in the small matter of his father's sheep, even to the point of fighting a lion and a bear.

He does not neglect his preparations. We often remember the sling that defeated Goliath. We forget that David came armed with five stones, not just one.

David moved in faith. He does not taunt Goliath with his own prowess (which he used before Saul) but rather with the living God.

For us, there are certain lessons in this. God has provided many such instances of this, and in each of them we learn that God uses the foolish, the weak, the improbable of this world to astound the strong, the wise and the likely. He does this for one reason: that we may not boast of our own strength and wisdom, but rather of His. "Let him who boasts, boast in the Lord."

Why does God do this? No doubt the cure of our pride is difficult, and needs all the example we can get. But consider: if you want a real, personal relationship with the living God, you must know who He is. He is so much greater than any of us that our logical, natural reaction is worship. If we boast in ourselves, how can we worship? But if we boast in Him, how can we not worship?

Slavery and Freedom
John 8:34-36

Of all birthrights common to the American, none is so cherished as the word "freedom." In our time we have seen this word greatly abused. We need to understand the nature of freedom and slavery, for slavery has not left this world.

What is freedom?

Freedom is not simply liberty of action. If you take an eagle from the sky and submerge it deep in the sea, and then let it go, it is not free. It is drowned. If you release a man from the constraints of law and civilization, he is not free. He is a barbarian. Why? Because man was meant to live in company with others, and that means law and civilization.

Freedom, then, is the liberty to be what God intended you to be. For the eagle, this is flight—eagles were meant to fly. For man, this is to know God and serve him—for that is the designed purpose of man.

What is slavery?

It is easiest to describe slavery in terms of a slave master. You have a slave master if there is someone, or something, which you *must* obey. You can be a slave to drugs or drink, for example. The question is one of control: is there something or someone who prevents you from being free?

Ultimately, slavery is a visceral thing—a feeling in the gut. The drunkard may be happy under the barroom table, but as he sobers up he feels the intense despair of never being able to stay sober.

It is interesting to note that, despite all attempts at telling slaves how they should be happy to be slaves to a benevolent master, the desire for freedom seems unquenchable. It also seems unachievable at times too. But there is one Person who can set you free: Jesus Christ. Remember that freedom means being able to do what you were designed to do. You were designed to know God and serve Him. But no sinner can come before the righteous God of his own power—and thus we were slaves to sin. But by the power of Christ, deployed at the Cross, this slavery is broken. We are now able to be what we should be. The Son has made us free, indeed.

Suffering for the Glory of God
John 9

Why do we suffer? Of all philosophical problems this is perhaps the oldest and most difficult.

The theory most common in the time of the New Testament is displayed here. You suffer because someone sinned.

The most likely sinners were held to be the parents. Having a child born blind is certainly grievous. But this seems unfair; why should the child suffer for the sins of the parents?

A theory of the time was that the child had sinned, somehow, in the womb, before birth. This theory was the one the disciples wanted to know about.

The modern rationalist, of course, has a scientific explanation for the suffering. Here it would probably be a medical one. But that is not the answer to the question asked. Science can tell us what caused the suffering—but not why we (in particular) are the ones to suffer. The question is not, "Why?" but rather "Why Me?"

Christ gives us a different answer here: that the work of God might be displayed in his life. The phrase, "the work of God," is a curious one:

In the Old Testament this was a phrase of great power. For example, it was used to describe the writing by the finger of God on the tablets giving the Ten Commandments.

The Old Testament also teaches us that the "work of God" was beyond the comprehension of man, too high for him to understand.

The New Testament reveals a new thought: the work of God is that we believe in Jesus Christ.

Combining this, we see that this man suffered that he and others might come to believe in Jesus, the Christ, the Son of God. Suffering for the glory of God is an old thought, though not much preached in our day. We refuse to see that this could be the case. But consider Job: God never explained his suffering to him. His friends were so sure that he was a sinner they never considered anything else (judge not, my friends). But his suffering brought glory to God; the "patience of Job" is still a virtue in our day.

Suffer you shall. But all things can be done to the glory of God, and suffering most certainly can. The question is, will you give God the glory as you suffer? So that others might believe?

The Shepherd, The Watchman, The Sheep
John 10

Christ, the "good shepherd," is one of the enduring metaphors of the New Testament. In this passage he tells us what this really means - and in the process shows us how to detect religious fraud.

The Shepherd

The shepherd represents Christ, the legitimate authority over the sheep. We know this authority by the way it approaches us. Christ does not come to us in secret, by night, announcing that we are victims of a conspiracy. The word is preached openly—even in times of persecution. Christ is "upfront" with us.

The "thief by night"—who represents those who practice fraud in the name of God—shows himself in two ways. First, his appointment is his own; he is his own authority. Next, he "comes by night"—with tales of how some secret conspiracy has corrupted what the church teaches. The Bible is an open book; no wonder it must be attacked by "secret conspiracy" theories.

The Watchman

The watchman represents the faithful minister (or teacher, or elder, or deacon, or other leader) in the church. Note two things:

The watchman listens to Christ. He himself is repentant at Christ's command; he is open to the truth even if it means changing his preconceived ideas.

The watchman understands his task is not to be the shepherd but open the door to the shepherd. All he does is so that the sheep will hear Christ. His blessing comes not from how great people think he is but how much he blesses Christ.

The sheep

Most of us fit in this category. Most of us are not leaders in the church. But even here we may see our duty:

The sheep are to *listen*. Their ears are open, waiting to hear the word of the Lord.

The sheep are to *listen to Christ*. The skill of the orator is not important; the message from Christ is.

The sheep are to *listen only to Christ*. No matter what new theory comes along, they are to hear only their master's voice, and reject all others.

Life can be confusing; there are many who cry, "follow me." Know the good Shepherd; Know life eternal.

Nabal and Saul
1 Samuel 24-25

There is a curious comparison in these chapters. In the first instance, David spares Saul

Even though God places Saul in David's hand, all David will do is cut off a tiny corner of his robe.

When he does that, he is conscience-stricken. Even that seems too much to do.

Why? Because Saul is the Lord's Anointed, and David respects his life out of fear of the Lord.

This rebounds to David's great advantage. It is clear proof to Saul, and all those with him, that David is not seeking Saul's life. He is innocent. It is also clear proof to Saul that God's favor has left him and landed on David.

So, despite the encouragement of his men and the temptation of the opportunity, David leaves the most important matter of his life in God's hands. He is then greatly rewarded for it.

Not so with Nabal. The incident begins with Nabal's lack of courtesy. Custom would have obliged Nabal to invite David and his men to the feast that would accompany the shearing. David sends messengers requesting this. If this seems odd, recall that the servants see the justice of David's request. Nabal doesn't.

It is probable that Abigail, Nabal's wife, has gone behind his back before. She takes immediate action and remedies Nabal's discourtesy. In doing that, she points out the folly of what David was about to do: take vengeance. David sees the sense of it, proclaiming that God has sent her. Why the difference?

In the first instance David knew he was dealing with high and holy things—so he trusted God absolutely.

But in the second, he acted in anger—so he did not stop to think or to consult the Lord.

God, however, had other plans. He sent a remedy to prevent this sin from happening.

Is that not just like us? We are sure that in the high and holy things we will trust God—and Satan trips us up in the little things. But if we, like David, are men after God's heart, he will send the remedy to us to keep us from sin. Praise the Lord; He is merciful.

Jesus Wept
John 11

Often in my writing I have portrayed Jesus in the logical, thinking sense. This is so, but we must remember that he was completely man as well as completely God. He has feelings, and he displays them here.

In various translations Jesus is "deeply moved" or "groans inwardly." The Greek word is the almost unpronounceable *embrimaomai*, which carries with it the idea of a horse snorting in disgust, or a sigh of chagrin. Can you picture this of Jesus, that he was so upset with their lack of faith?

It is said that he wept. Mourners at a Jewish funeral (often paid mourners) wept aloud, but the word here is for silent weeping. Jesus is clearly upset at what is happening. The Jews see it as a sign of his sincere love for Lazarus; not the wail of the paid mourner, but the silent tears of a true friend.

The Christian should remember that he is to imitate our Lord, and here is a good set of actions to imitate.

First, he goes to the spot. How dishwater it sounds to say, "I'll pray for you!" How much more effective to go to the person, to visit the sick in the hospital instead of five seconds of prayer.

Next, he takes direct action ("take away the stone")—based upon faith. He does not do what common sense would tell him, but he relies instead upon the God He knows.

There is always some reasonable person—in this instance Martha—who knows why this won't work. Expect it.

He gives us the principle of such action: if you believe, you will see the glory of God. If you don't, you will see the glory of man, whatever that might be.

Our Lord provides us with a magnificent example. We may not be privileged to raise the dead, but we are still the children of God. It is not for us to be unmoved by the pain of others; we must weep with those who weep. But we must also go forward in the power of God, rendering such assistance as we can, trusting God for the result (whatever others think). If you believe—and obey—you will see the glory of God.

David, the Leader
1 Samuel 30

David spent seven years in the wilderness *after* Samuel anointed him as king. This is at the end of that period, just before the death of Saul. David is having a pretty hard time of it, and we can see from his example how the servant of God—the man after God's own heart—handles difficulties with others.

As David and the men return to camp—after being ejected from the service of the Philistine king—they discover that their families have been captured and enslaved. They weep; then the talk turns to stoning David! But note that David does not try to pacify them, or talk them out of it. Instead, he consults the Lord as to what to do next. God tells him to pursue the raiders.

It is fourteen long, hot miles across the desert from Ziklag to the ravine of Besor. No surprise, therefore, when many of his men are too tired to go on, especially as this followed three days of marching. Two hundred are left behind.

David next shows his character in dealing with the slave left behind. Many would have tortured the man, but David knows that God's mercy is superior. He treats the slave as if he were one of his own men—and is rewarded by being able to plunder the plunderers. His men come out of the affair richer than before it began.

But the trials are not over. Some of the four hundred who pursued now don't want to share the plunder. But David sees it differently. It is not the four hundred who gained the victory—after all, the escapees from the raiders numbered that many, so David's band was outnumbered—but God who delivered them. All six hundred are God's servants; all share in the plunder. It is a "lasting ordinance in Israel."

Here is the man after God's heart. He consults the Lord and does not listen to men. Even when "common sense" tells him to deal in evil, he delivers mercy. And like the Lord himself, he sees that all those who carry his name—even the grumblers and complainers—are included in the fruits of victory.

This is an example to us. Do you hear the Lord in prayer, or do you listen to the whispers and grumbles of the crowd? Are you merciful in triumph, leaving vengeance to God, or do you take it for yourself? And in victory—do you share and share alike, or reach for the largest share?

To the Rationalists
John 12:20-50

Throughout the New Testament there is a consistent theme, the power of paradox. Do things the world's way, in the best of the world's wisdom, and you will fail. Do things God's way, which seems like foolishness to the smart, and you will be blessed beyond imagination. How do we explain this to the scientific mind?

The Philosophy

Jesus begins with an analogy. St. Augustine remarked that God is so far above us that He can only be understood by analogy, and that is what Christ is doing here. He draws them the picture of a kernel of grain (the word here is a generic one for grain). They know (scientifically) that unless you bury it, it will not reproduce—but when you do it reproduces bountifully. So he establishes the principle of paradox in their minds as not something strange, but something already familiar—just unnoticed.

The principle is just this: if you love your life, you lose it. Despise it, and gain so much more. Like the hypochondriac who gets sicker with more attention to his health, our world chases after older whisky, younger women, faster cars and more money. The money fails, the whisky becomes cheap as the car breaks down. Of the women it is not polite to speak. The world's way is a failure, because it cannot satisfy. It is like giving salt water to a thirsty man—it just brings on more thirst.

Jesus gives us the application. He tells us to be like him, to follow him. We are to be his servants, and as such we are not above our master. Look at his life; one of service. He sought no worldly wealth nor honor; he had none of the trappings of success that we esteem. Yet who has greater honor?

The kingdom is still the pearl of great price. By giving all we gain all; the reward is eternal life. Like our Lord, we cannot remain as mere observers. He went to the cross, and "became obedient unto death." He paid the ultimate price for us, showing us that the Kingdom of God is worthy of all possible sacrifice, even the sacrifice of the sinless Son of God. How, then, can we refuse to be like him? We are not, in most instances, called on to sacrifice our lives in painful death. Rather, we are called to live for him. The world still says this is foolishness; chase the women, drink the whisky. But even the foolishness of God is greater than the wisdom of this world. The only real question is, to which voice will you listen?

Young Man, Pure Way
Psalm 119:9-16

The Psalmist asks, "How can a young man keep his way pure?"

Purity. The word is seldom used in our time, and almost no one considers it a good thing, except in soap or food. Even then the more common idea is "natural" or "organic." We value the process by which the food was produced, not the result. But purity is also a process. The word in the original carries the meaning of cleansing; the question might be phrased, "How can a young man keep clean?"

Verbs are action words, and the verbs here give us the answer to the question.

We are to "seek" — the word in the original carries with it the ideas of diligence and doing it frequently—God. In prayer, in reading, in thought, we are to seek Him.

We are to "hide" the word in our hearts. The original meaning is that of protecting the word in our hearts. Protect it by frequent reading and constant thought.

We are to praise God. If you know Him, then you know who He is, and his greatness. If you do, you cannot help but praise Him.

We are to rejoice in following his laws. Have you ever rewarded yourself for a job well done? Taken pleasure in your own accomplishments? Here is one accomplishment that is pleasing to God as well as man, and we should rejoice in it.

We are to meditate upon his precepts. Consider well the principles by which God orders His universe. Do you not see the moral order around you? Our generation has said that character does not count—and behold the result around you.

We are to delight in his decrees. The world declares that we ourselves create right and wrong. We know better than that. When you compare man's moral order to God's, is that not a cause to delight?

These are the causes of cleansing and the safeguards of purity in a man's heart. These actions are the soap that cleanses life itself. "How can a young man keep his way pure? By living according to your word."

Let Not Your Heart Be Troubled
John 14:1-14

It is easiest to see the import of Christ's words, I suspect, if we take it slowly.

"Let"—did you ever see it that you *let* your heart be troubled? You don't trouble it, but you allow it to happen. So many of us think there is nothing we can do about our circumstances (often true) so there is nothing we can do about our attitude (false!) I may not like the travel schedule I have—but I view it as something the Lord has given me, a chance to honor him in this very mild form of suffering, at the least. Perhaps it is a chance to bring glory to his name. Is it rain, or God's challenge to you to honor him? You allow the trouble, or not, as you choose.

"Your"—so many of us take our cue in life from others. If everyone else thinks this is a bad time, why, it must be, right? Not so for the Christian. The world listens to "everybody" when everybody thinks things are bad. The Christian listens to Somebody!

"Heart"—this is not just intellect, or emotions, but the will of man that we are dealing with. This is a decision, not acid indigestion.

"Troubled"—(really what is meant here) when we should rest calmly in the assurance of God! We let our minds rattle on when we should bring our thoughts to the throne of grace, there to be set at ease.

"Believe"—the word is often translated "trust"—and this is the core of things. The argument is simple. You trust in God; Jesus knows that. But God seems so distant; how could he care for one so little as me? Ah, but you also know the man Jesus. If you trust God, you should trust Jesus also—and He is the one who knows your troubles! Do not forget that God's strength is shown in our weakness. Trust Him, and see.

The matter is in our hearts. Do we trust our Lord? Really? Or do we say that we do (on Sunday) and run in panic on Monday? The matter is one of the will. We must choose to trust; we must choose to trust Him. The question is, will we?

A Wise Man's Prayer
Psalm 119:33-40

The 119th Psalm is quite long. It is, we are told, an acrostic in the original Hebrew. Each section, denoted by a Hebrew letter, may be taken separately. This section is a little gem, for it shows us clearly the attitude of a wise, worshipful man toward the Lord. In each step, he asks God to change him so that he might become more like the righteous one:

"Teach" he says, and I will keep. Many of us are too old to learn, or so we think. But the wise man asks, "teach."

"Give" he says. Give me what? Understanding! Do not let me rely on my own wisdom, but rather yours. Then I will obey with all my heart. Not "after I figure it all out" but "as you give me understanding."

"Direct" he says. Command my footsteps, so that I will go the right way. What will I find? Delight! How can this be?

It can be because God keeps me out of trouble—and I've been in enough trouble already to know the wrong things to do. He specifically asks God for this in two ways:

"Turn my heart" toward your laws and away from selfish gain. In other words, keep me from chasing money and the things it will buy.

"Turn my eyes"—keep even my desires under your control, so that I won't chase things that are worthless. Keep me from seeking the sins of the moment that seem so pleasant.

By doing this, he proclaims, God will be feared. And why not? A good example of a Godly man is hard to find —but powerful when seen.

The most poignant part is this: "take away the disgrace I dread." Who would dread disgrace more than a godly man? Remove the shame of sin from me Lord, so that it will not be a barrier to me.

God does remove that shame; He took it with him to the cross of Calvary. There he fulfilled all that is written here, giving us the power to follow the Law of Love taught by our Lord. Indeed, with the Psalmist we may say that his laws are good. Seek then his precepts; let him preserve you in righteousness of Jesus Christ himself. Seek his wisdom—by seeking his correction, that you may grow in Christ. "Lord, reform your world—beginning with me!"

The True Vine
John 15:1-8

Like the vine which draws moisture and nourishment from the ground through the hidden means of its internal structure, we draw spiritual nourishment from God through the mediation of Jesus Christ. He is the "bridge" between us and God – or, as Jesus expresses it here, he's the vine, we're the branches. Like all garden plants the vine has a purpose: to produce fruit. If it doesn't, the gardener gets rid of it. Indeed, the idea of a Christian who does nothing for God staying in the fellowship is rather absurd.

Sometimes this pruning appears as a disappointment. You work with someone for months, teaching them carefully, and then they go to another class, or another church. God is simply pruning your vine, and you may not know it. Why would he do that?

First is that any leader must not be given the temptation to pride. God does not need any particular leader.

It is also so that the "pruned" may grow! Can they learn from no one but you?

Most of all it is so that you will produce more fruit. A leader can only deal with so many at a time. Some must go on and be fruitful in themselves

How then, to be fruitful? It is quite simple: abide in Christ. Stay "in" Christ. This sounds so mystical that we sometimes miss the simplicity:

It is a mutual abiding. Whether by prayer, practice, repentance or study, we are in Him as He is in us.

We are to abide in "my words." In the Bible you will find the words of life, for there you will see revealed the author of life itself.

The result of this is that we shall be able to "ask whatever." If you are in God's will why would he *not* grant your prayers?

Indeed, Christ gives us three good reasons why we are to bear such fruit and live such a life:

It brings glory to God.

The fruit in and of itself is good—especially if you bring salvation to one who is lost.

It shows that you are his disciples—so that others will know.

Examine your life. Are you producing the fruit of God? Or will you compel him to prune you away?

God's Yardstick
2 Samuel 12

It was not easy to be a prophet of the Lord. Very often you didn't eat too well, and kings had a nasty habit of executing you for doing your job. Nathan, the prophet to David, has an extremely difficult message to deliver with regard to Bathsheba.

He does it in a way which reflects God's own thinking. He obliges David to use the yardstick of his own sense of right and wrong to condemn himself. It's a very convenient yardstick; each of us carries it around all the time. David's anger burns hot—until Nathan tells him who the culprit is. David now must face the consequences of sin:

Sin causes pain and suffering to others. We often like to pretend that our sin hurts no one but ourselves, but it is not so. Here the child dies, not for its own sin, but for David's.

Sin cannot be kept secret. We like to think that we can keep all things secret, living our lives in little compartments. We can appear pious on Sunday and vicious on Monday. But it is not so. If only at the day of judgment, it is not so.

We disgrace God when we sin. We are the people of God, and those who do not love Him are quick to spot hypocrisy and cover-up. One reason why repentance is public is so that the world will know. All sin is ultimately against God (who gave us righteousness from His own character). So it is that Nathan asks David, "Why did you despise the word of the Lord?"

After sin must come restoration. If we are to remain a child of God there must come a time of confession, then repentance but then restoration. God's wrath appears but a little while, then his goodness (see Psalm 119:65-72 also).

It is well for us to examine ourselves and bring about our own repentance. God provides amply for this in the study of His word. For if we are swift to repent, He is swift to forgive. When He is swift to forgive, He is swift to restore. His discipline for us has one purpose: to bring us back to a state of obedience and fellowship with Him. Examine your life with Him. Are you distant, or fearful? Not sure of what God might really want to say? If sin is in your life, it stands between you and God. Be swift to repent; He will be swift to forgive and restore.

Intercession
John 17

So many of us find ourselves frustrated at intercession. Why will God not hear our prayers, especially for others? (We can usually see our own selfishness).

Christ here paints a model of intercession as he pleads for his disciples (and for us—see verse 20):

The Intercessor and God. All depends upon our relationship with God, for he is the source of power.

> We must pray in God's time, not in ours. Pray without ceasing, not just when desperate.

> We must pray to glorify God. So often we ask that the doctors will appear so wise.

> We pray not from our own goodness, but from our standing as a royal priesthood. No mortal earns priesthood; it is given.

The Intercessor and Beneficiary. It may seem trite, but it is necessary for us to review why we are praying for someone. What is this person's relationship to us? Are we being honest with God in our motives of prayer?

We must also acknowledge their status before God. How often we pray for someone's healing knowing that they are not a Christian—when God's view is that this illness may give them the best chance of facing death and drawing closer to him.

Look at their history. What would God want for such a person? Do we pray that someone go unpunished merely because he is a friend of ours? Is that justice?

The Requests of the Intercessor. Let us tell God three simple things:

> What the situation is—at least, as far as we know it. If we know only a part, let us acknowledge our ignorance and submit the matter to his will, not ours.

> What we want—in plain language.

> What we, personally, are willing to do about it.

Christ prayed for his disciples here, and then went to the Cross to see that all these requests would be based in his sacred Atonement. He knew the cost; he paid it willingly. If you are willing to dare to pray to the ruler of All, then dare to commit all to him—including yourself.

Ittai, the Gittite
2 Samuel 15:17-22

The Old Testament is full of characters who come in and out of the various stories leaving little trace. Ittai the Gittite is such. We know him only from this story:

He is a Gittite, a resident of Gath. You will recall that this is the town from which Goliath came. Hence, Ittai and his 600 followers are actually Philistines!

For some reason lost to history, Ittai is a refugee. He and the 600 evidently have come to King David after being ejected from their homeland. Like many another before and since, he sought refuge in the house of the enemy of his enemies.

From his reaction, he must have known something about David. David is no longer the warrior of youth—but neither is he a tottering old man.

In David's reaction we can gain a sense of the courtesy required of kings. He is in distress, but that does not relieve him of the obligations of being a king. Those who are his followers are his sheep, and he is to care for them.

Evidently David is embarrassed about his inability to provide for this newcomer. Hospitality was an obligation in that culture, and still is in that area today.

So he suggests, strongly, to Ittai that better lodging might be found with Absalom. Note that this would mean that Ittai would now be obliged to support Absalom, not David. So this courtesy is an expensive one.

Ittai's reply returns loyalty for courtesy. Nothing will deter him. He came to offer his services to David, and with David he will stay. David gives in, and bids him march on and share the hard road ahead.

We have something to learn here. We are the children of the King of Kings, and royal hospitality is our obligation too. When someone comes to us for help, and finds us in our times of trouble, the obligation of hospitality is still there, and we must do the best we can with it.

God will reward that. Sometimes the "burden" unlooked for is really the blessing of God in disguise. Ittai was a refugee the day before; soon Ittai would command a third of David's forces. Do as God bids; he will see to your reward and comfort.

Shimei
2 Samuel 16:5-13

Shimei was a rash individual. David is fleeing from Absalom's rebellion, but he is fleeing with a band of armed men. Shimei seems to ignore this as he curses David.

This provides us a lesson. How do we deal with those who curse us? Perhaps we see those who sneer at us in our distress; perhaps it's just someone with a foul mouth.

There are two methods:

Abishai, one of David's commanders, has a simple solution. He'll just walk over and cut off this man's head. A simple if none too tidy solution. But David rejects it.

David's method is quite different. He sees three things that Abishai did not:

He sees that God may have commanded this. In his distress it is possible that Shimei is doing what God has commanded. It may be that God is using this man for his purposes, and therefore David will do nothing against it.

David also knows that Shimei's stones and curses cannot really harm him. He knows his standing with the living God, and he knows the mercy of the Lord.

Finally, David can separate the trivial from the important. His own son, Absalom, is in rebellion against him and is seeking to kill him. Compared to that, what's a foul mouth and a few stones?

David spares him. Later, Shimei dies at Solomon's command (his story is interesting; follow it through). But in this story we can learn much about the adversity we face in life.

Do we react to the anger of others with anger of our own? To do so is to use the weapons of Satan against Satan's child—and become for the while Satan's tool. Do not overcome evil with evil, but overcome evil with good.

Do we see the evils that come upon us as something from God? Is he teaching us something? Or is it perhaps that we should appreciate the honor of being cursed for Christ's sake?

Can we tell the difference between the trivial and the important? Is that idiot on the freeway really that significant? Or should we turn him, and our anger, over to God?

Lowly and Despised
Psalm 119:137-144

The 119th Psalm is the longest book in the Bible. It is an acrostic in Hebrew; each section belongs to a letter of the Hebrew alphabet. In this section, the Psalmist lays out some of the principles by which the righteous must live:

First, the word of the Lord is righteous because God is righteous. His word is a reflection of his character, which never changes.

Next, these statutes are "fully trustworthy." They hold water, they hang together. The righteous servant of God tests these promises. How? By living according to the word of God. Does it produce the results claimed? Indeed, he says, it does.

It is not sufficient for a righteous man to take these laws to himself for life. He experiences the frustration of seeing others who do not follow the law of the Lord, and it is a weariness. It wearies him that others will not obey. Have you ever experienced the frustration of counseling someone who just will not see that God's way is so much better?

The Psalmist now raises a most important point. Even though he is "lowly and despised" he continues in the law of God. It does not matter what our position in life might be. The power of God does not depend upon our social or economic status. The benefits of his righteousness are not limited to the rich and the powerful. It is easy to think so, for the poor and weak might ask, "Why has this happened to me?"

The truth of God does not depend upon the status of the person. Nor does it depend upon their situation in life, for trouble comes to all at one time or another. The righteous man looks to God in such times, and finds the word of God to be his delight. We find comfort in the word of God as well as guidance.

Indeed, the Psalmist ends this section with the idea that the law of God gives him understanding—that he may live. When you drive to a new destination, do you not consult a road map? Each day of your life is a new one. So consult the true road map of life, God's word. No matter how rich or poor, troubled or at ease, at the beginning of life or at the end, his word is your guide. It is a reflection of his character, and thus it shows you the path of righteousness and the love of your heavenly Father.

Doubting Thomas
John 20:24-29

Thomas, the twin, has come down in history to us as "Doubting Thomas." He's the man from Missouri; you have to show him.

In one sense this is not quite fair to Thomas. You must remember that all the other disciples had a similar reaction when the women returned from the tomb. Peter and John ran to the tomb. John believed; Peter wondered.

Indeed, Thomas' reaction is an entirely reasonable one, especially in the face of a completely unreasonable situation. The disciples expected Jesus to establish the earthly kingdom of Israel—not to go to the cross. This despite his many warnings of the cross! So what is the problem here?

It is simply this: the relationship between God and man is not one of physical laws. God is not "the Force;" God is a person, indeed three persons. If you want to deal with him at all you must first deal with him as a person. Personal relationships that work are founded on trust. Thomas did not trust what the Lord had said; ultimately, he had not trusted the Lord.

This is not to say he is faint-hearted. Far from it. (See John 11 for an example of this). He just does not know how to handle the situation.

Christ understands the Thomases of the world. He comes to Thomas and, echoing Thomas' own words, invites him to see and touch the evidence—and in so doing become evidence for us.

Thomas rises from the depths of doubt to the height of faith in one magnificent leap.

> "My Lord" - Thomas does not see this as a magic trick of no importance. Rather, it seals the relationship. He has Jesus as Lord, and obedience is implicit in that. Many want a savior; few understand He is Lord.

> "My God" - No other explanation for the Resurrection will do. Just as he was the hardest to convince, he will be the highest in his perception of Jesus the Christ.

Thomas knows that "believe" means to trust and obey. He saw; he believed—but our Lord says those who have not seen but yet have believed are blessed. Test yourself this day: are you still waiting to be bludgeoned with the certainty that will be revealed at his coming, or will you believe and be blessed?

Feed My Sheep
John 21

The Son of Man came to seek and save the lost—and he pursued that goal with his Father's will. Nothing shows that so well as the way he dealt with Peter after the Resurrection.

Jesus does not ignore the fact that Peter has denied him three times. He redeems those denials. Three times Peter denies him; three times he is restored.

Jesus does not just restore him to fellowship, but to his place as leader of the disciples. Indeed, we see in Acts that Peter is immediately the leader.

The man who said he would die before denying him, denied him three times in one night. You might think that beyond forgiving, beyond redemption. But no one is beyond forgiveness by the Christ.

Jesus looks beyond the sin of denial and sees the potential for greatness in this man. By his restoration he brings to the church its first great saint.

There are lessons here for us, too. So often we look at the sinner as beyond hope—or at least beyond any hope of restoration. But it is not so with Jesus.

We are not to ignore sin, we are to redeem it. Forgiveness is expensive (it cost Christ his life) but necessary. We must be like our Master, restoring the lost.

It is not sufficient to let the sinner back in the doors of the church. Restoration is just that; we must show that a person can climb back to where they were. Do not hide the repentant sinner in the closet. Put him on display for God.

No one is beyond repentance and forgiveness. No matter what you have done, the act of repentance claims the mercy of God. It should also claim the care of the church.

Great sinners make great saints. Often the one who is most defiant against God rises from his mire to glow radiantly from the hilltop.

Sometimes the lesson is in being forgiven; sometimes the lesson is in forgiving. Both are from the same source—the love of God shown at the Cross.

Time of Transition
Acts 1:1-11

The Ascension is a time of transition for the faith, and for the faithful.

> The disciples will change. No longer dependent upon the physical presence of Jesus, they will become bold beyond measure, and turn the world upside down.

> The geography of the faith will change. Jesus, in his ministry, never left the bounds of ancient Israel. He ministered almost exclusively to the Jews. Now the church will go to all nations.

> Indeed, the things that Jesus did, the church will now do. The church in fact will do greater things, as He prophesied. He came to seek and save the lost of Israel. The church will seek and save the lost of the world. The acts of mercy, charity and healing he performed, the church will repeat. He made twelve disciples; the church, millions.

> There is a change with the Holy Spirit as well. In times of the Old Testament, the Spirit came and went as He pleased. Now, the Spirit is within every believer.

> Access to God has changed, too. The High Priest is now Jesus, the Son of God and Son of Man.

The world will now see what Jesus has revealed to only a few at this time. For this reason Jesus must physically leave the disciples. He was raised in the flesh—He is not a ghost, and therefore he cannot just fade out. He must return to the Father. But as He does he sends out his disciples with instructions to change the world.

The disciples question him as to the time when he will restore the kingdom to Israel. His answer is that they are not to know. But one thing they are told. He is coming back. In the same manner in which he was taken up, he will return.

Things have changed. Things will change once more, when He returns. The question is, will we be ready for the change? When the Son of God returns in all his glory, to bring the world to judgment, will we be rejoicing? Or will we be wanting a little more time? Worse, will we be shocked that he really meant it? No one knows the day or hour. There is only one true course: be ready for his return at any time. Are you?

Peter's First Sermon
Acts 2

It is a curious fact: in the Book of Acts, the sermons have a common set of themes. Little is said of ethics or conduct; the listener is presumed to understand such things. The sermons tend to have three points:

Prophecies concerning the Crucifixion

The Crucifixion itself, and

The Resurrection.

Prophecy was common because the early church spoke to the Jews, to whom the Old Testament was indeed the Word of God. There is much to be learned in this:

It shows us the patience of God. For two thousand years God prepared the Jews for the Messiah. Will he not be patient with us, then?

It also shows that the Messiah was not an afterthought—but the firm purpose of God from the very beginning.

By any test of man, the Crucifixion should be the weak point of Christianity. It is a despicable death. Other religions have symbols of beauty. We have the old rugged cross. Why?

The cross is the sign of the atonement; our debts were paid, at great cost.

The cross is the sign of our reconciliation.

The cross is the measure of God's love.

The cross is our example of service.

Peter's third point is the Resurrection. This too is of central importance to us:

If there is no Resurrection, then we are fools and idiots to follow such a man.

But if there is, then we shall be raised at the last day when He returns.

Resurrection shows us the power of God—which lives in us by the Holy Spirit.

The sermon is a simple one. This is not clever argument, but the sweep of the greatest facts in history. The simple fishermen of Galilee took these facts to the known world and turned it upside down. If you will hear them, they will do the same for you.

Araunah
2 Samuel 24

Araunah is one of those minor characters of the Old Testament whose main distinction is that his name is difficult to pronounce. But he plays a part in a great lesson here.

Araunah is a Jebusite. The Jebusites were the inhabitants of Jerusalem when David conquered the city and renamed it "The City of David." He is evidently a man of property and means, but he is a second-class citizen, for David has turned the Jebusites into the manual laborers of the city. So when he sees the king coming towards him, he looks for a way to curry favor.

David has a problem. He has a plague on his hands, and the Lord has told him specifically to buy Araunah's threshing floor and erect an altar there. Many scholars believe this is the site where Abraham was told to sacrifice Isaac; it is also likely to be the site of the Temple. At this time it is a hard, flat rock, used for separating wheat from chaff.

David is in no position to bargain. God has told him this place, and no other. Araunah can name his price, as it were. But he has another idea: he will give it to the king, give it most generously, and thus put the king in his debt. You never know when you might need a royal favor. Indeed, he not only offers the land, but the ox for the sacrifice and the wood to light the fire.

David turns him down: "I will not offer a sacrifice to the Lord my God that cost me nothing." What a reflection of the man after God's own heart! The sacrifice that God made for us by sending his Son to die on Calvary is the measure of this principle. David understands that God does not want lip service, or following the regulations—he wants wholehearted worship. That worship never comes cheaply.

Is your worship cheap worship? Do you come on Sunday, sing the songs, put something in the offering (depending upon the quality of the sermon, of course) and leave God for another week? If you give him cheap worship, would you expect anything but cheap grace? God's grace is costly above price. He wants your heart, soul and mind in worship and service to him. If your prayers are unheard, perhaps it is because your worship is unreal.

Are you giving God the leftovers of your time, your talent, your finances? Or are you giving him the best you have? Never let your worship, your service, "cost you nothing."

Power, Words and Action
Acts 4

The Power of God

The early church shows us so much of the power of God:

Remember this fellow Peter? The one who on the night before the Crucifixion wouldn't even admit to knowing Jesus? Look at him now!

Power is shown here in the "nobodies" of this world. These men are country bumpkins—God's bumpkins.

Great power is shown in their attitude—they despise death, think it nothing, for they have seen the Resurrection power of God.

Noble Words

Peter here calls up great words from the Old Testament. In it, he expresses to the church (and to the world) three great themes:

The futility of what man does. What does it matter what man plans to do—if God has decided otherwise? Who can thwart what God has planned?

The power of God. Indeed, from the time of creation the power of the Resurrection was planned. It is now made public.

Because of this, Peter does not pray for safety or deliverance. He prays for boldness. He will not be less than the hour that has been given to him.

Noble Actions

Words alone may inspire us, but if they do not move us to action they are worse than useless.

The actions of the church flow from the Spirit, expressed so wonderfully here. We often forget that exhortation is necessary to provoke good works. Speak in the Spirit, then move in the Spirit.

Faith without works is dead—but faith with works increases bountifully.

The example of the early church is both clear and brilliant. They preached the Gospel; they fed the poor so that there were no needy among them. The power of God gives rise to noble words and then noble actions.

Ananias and Sapphira
Acts 5

This story provokes quite a commentary from some. It seems too harsh for the God of love. But, in fact, this is an act of love—the fiery love of the jealous God. Think of it this way: you love your wife; would you "share" her with another man? The church is the bride of Christ; how does He feel about her, then?

This story has its roots in ancient Israel. Land was a gift from God—a point familiar to Zionists in our day. That one would sell land and bring the proceeds to God was simply returning the gift. But a gift to God must be brought the right way.

Purity

We are taught today that evil is enlightening. We can be righteous on Sunday and "sophisticated" the rest of the week. This sounds good, but it won't work. God will have all of you—or none of you. Ananias and Sapphira thought that they could act pure in church; it does not work. God is not fooled. It is a sad fact: we demand purity in our foods, but not in our friends.

Hypocrisy

It is a common temptation to Christians to play the sophisticated "man of the world" on Saturday night. It feels so good to know on Saturday night that your Christian friends are just too naive to enjoy this—and then go to church on Sunday morning, knowing that your Saturday night friends could never understand the spiritual glow you get there. One thing is for certain: they'll never hear about it from you.

This has a name: hypocrisy. It is a deadly disease to the Christian. Like cancer, it eats you alive. Like cancer, self-examination is the best warning system.

Counting the cost

The church reacted to this display of God's jealous love with fear. Indeed, it is a good thing to fear the Lord. The elephant looks attractive, but his step is heavy—and should be respected. How much more his creator?

The Lord is a jealous God—he wants all of you or none of you. Beware of being lukewarm!

The Lord will weed out the impure—by their fruits.

We must count the cost of being a Christian. The benefits are eternal; the cost is our very lives.

A Deacon's Character
Acts 6:1-7

Much of the early church custom came from the synagogue. One such custom was the collection and distribution of food for the widows. Two methods were used. The first, a weekly collection on Friday ("The Basket"), was made to provide each widow with two meals a day for a week. Another, made daily ("The Tray"), was for day-to-day needs. It is this collection that the Greek Jews are complaining about.

It comes as a surprise to some that the Apostles did not consider it their function to oversee this. Our Lord is quite firm on the subject; it is a key test of faith that we feed the hungry. But the church is a body, and the Apostle's part is different:

They would give their attention to prayer first—so that in all things the church might move in God's will.

Then they would give their attention to the ministry of the Word—evangelism.

So therefore someone else was needed to handle this problem. Note what the Apostles did not ask for: business sense. They did not ask for professional waiters. Instead, they laid down two essential qualifications for those who will have financially and personally responsible positions in the church:

They must be full of the Spirit. This does not necessarily mean (though it does not exclude) speaking in tongues. The word "full" in the original carries a meaning of being complete. They are looking for a man who walks by faith.

They must be full of wisdom. Wisdom might be defined as applying God's way to men. God is gentle with us; if you know a truly wise man, you will know a truly gentle one too.

The character of a man counts, even if his task is simply to collect food and then redistribute it fairly among those in need. No matter how small the task that God has given you within his church, these are still the first qualifications.

Perhaps you are wondering why you have no task to perform in the church. Is it a lack of the Spirit? Ask God; he will give the Spirit to all who ask. Is it a lack of wisdom? Ask God; he will give wisdom liberally. Then go forward, seek out the part that God will ask you to play—and do it for the glory of God.

Temple for the Name
1 Kings 5:5

It is a curious fact, but quite important, that Solomon does not describe the Temple as being the "Temple of the Lord." He describes it as the "Temple of the Name of the Lord." This may sound strange to our ears, but consider:

> As Solomon notes in his dedication, all the universe could not contain God, much less this Temple.

> This was not an idle thought on David's part. From the time of the Exodus, God had told the people of Israel that they would make their sacrifices at a place where He would put his Name.

> The ark of the Covenant, which was placed in the Temple, was referred to as "called by the Name." In some sense the ark, therefore, was a representation of the Name of the Lord.

Now this may seem quite ancient to us. But there is a connection between the Temple being for the Name of the Lord and our actions today:

> If you will note, Solomon overlaid the entire interior of the Temple—one of the largest of ancient buildings—with gold. By one estimate, over 100 tons of gold were used to do this. Do you see what value is set upon the Name?

> The Temple was destroyed. God tells the Israelites that it was destroyed because they blasphemed his Name by setting up idols in the Temple. Do you see how God guards his Name?

It is sad, therefore, to see the ways in which many Christians today disregard the Name of the Lord:

> We usually think of this in terms of idle obscenity. This is evil enough.

> More often, it is not what we say but what we *fail* to say about the Name of the Lord which is saddening.

> Worst of all is when we put words in God's mouth—using the Name as an authority for our own opinions.

Do you not cherish your own family name and do all you can to keep it from disgrace? If you do that for your earthly family's name, how much more should you do for the name of the family of your Father in Heaven?

Ordinary Holiness
Psalm 128

Most of us will never be called to be missionaries in the jungles or deserts; nor to preach the Gospel to crowds of thrilled thousands; nor to minister to the poor in some exemplary way. In fact most of us will be those who walk in "ordinary holiness" —the fear of the Lord in a life that is otherwise undistinguished in the faith. The Psalmist here has such people in mind.

He begins by describing such blessed, ordinary people.

First, such a man fears the Lord. He knows who God is and knows quite well that God is awesome.

That knowledge is not just academic, however. He not only fears, he obeys and therefore walks in God's ways.

Does this seem rather obvious? It certainly is. But look about you—do you not see those who come to church on Sunday, saying that God is awesome, mighty and righteous, and then on Monday they live like the heathens?

The Psalmist then tells us how such a man is blessed. I ask you to consider it this way: count the number of men you know who are God-fearing, obedient Christian husbands and fathers. Of that number, tell me how many have problems in their marriages or family life. Indeed, I submit that the vast majority are the "ordinary holy" —

They work hard at an honest job. They are not rich by the world's standards, but they keep their families fed and still have money to give.

Such men have marriages that other men look at as "lucky." The wife may not be glamorous, but love abounds.

Their children are a blessing to them; you may have said to them, "You're lucky to have such children."

Lucky? No. Blessed? Yes. And what more could a man so blessed ask? That which the Psalmist makes his doxology; that God would continue to bless him in this way for the rest of his life; that his society around might be in peace and prosperity, and that he might live long enough to see his grandchildren too.

Such men do not appear in the papers. They are not heroes of the faith. They are the foot soldiers in the army of God. God is merciful and generous to such. In this life ordinary holiness brings extraordinary joy; in the life to come, even greater things.

Solomon's Prayer
1 Kings 8

It is one of the high points of the Old Testament: the dedication of the Temple. Solomon begins with an acknowledgement of who God really is:

First, that there is no God like him.

Next, that he is the God who keeps his promises, in this instance to David.

Finally, that even though this is the Temple of his Name, no place on earth or heaven above could contain God.

Could this be said of the God you worship? Or do you worship a God who means well—but feebly?

The Temple is a place—a place to come near to the Name of God. Human beings need something visible in their worship. This place was meant to be:

A place for justice to be done.

A place for healing to be performed.

A place where God is made known to all.

A place where forgiveness is found.

Could this be said of your church? Is justice done there? Are lives healed there? Is God Almighty proclaimed there? Can even the worst find forgiveness there?

Finally, Solomon asks God for the blessings appropriate to the occasion:

That God would be with the Jews as He was with their fathers of old.

That He would turn their hearts towards Him.

That He would uphold them, so that all who saw would know that the Lord is God.

Could this be said of your life? Think back to your father and grandfather; was God stronger in their lives than in yours? Does your heart go toward God, or would you rather he left you alone? Do all who see you know that the Lord is God because of your life, or do they even know you are a Christian?

Simon the Sorcerer
Acts 8:1-25

Simon—a man of such local reputation that he was called "The Great Power"—evidently was one of those oriental magicians who practiced sleight of hand and called it magic. When he saw the power of the Holy Spirit, he knew the real thing had arrived. It is interesting that Simon is a man of great wants—he doesn't want just the Holy Spirit, but the power to confer the Holy Spirit. He wants it for profit, for he offers the Apostles money for this gift.

The Apostles rebuke him—and in the process tell him his true trouble, that he is bitter and full of sin. Simon, to his credit, repents and humbles himself to the point of asking others to pray for him. The story has its applications to us today:

There is always the temptation for the church to ally itself with some local power—political, financial or otherwise. But the purity of the church should forbid this. The church is the church, not a political party.

There is also the temptation to peddle the grace of God at a price. The finances of the church are always inadequate—in the world's view. The power of God is always more than adequate. Which view should we choose? Is the grace of God, bought with the precious blood of Jesus, to be sold for the riches of this world?

The church will always have within her ranks great sinners who have repented, praise God. We must not condone the sin; we must not condemn the sinner. The repentant should be welcomed with open arms. Indeed, it is our privilege to do as Simon asked: pray that the just rewards of his evil deeds will not come upon him, but rather that God will be merciful to him.

So it is for the church—but wait, we are the church! These things apply to us personally as well. We as individual Christians will be tempted to compromise with the powers of this world, and so taint our witness. There is also the temptation to say to others that God will forgive—and forget that he will demand repentance before forgiveness. And when repentance comes, we must not be the Pharisees of Christendom; rather, we should welcome the worst of sinners with open arms, upholding them before Almighty God in prayer. God knows the heart, and we should accept what He has blessed.

The Conversion of Paul
Acts 9

The conversion of Paul is described three times in the book of Acts. Paul made it the center of his preaching and witness. Indeed, we often speak of "our witness for the Lord." What is a witness? One who can testify to what he has seen.

In this passage the Lord tells Ananias to go to Paul. In that instruction he is to tell Paul how much he will suffer for the name of Jesus. It brings us to a question: why does God allow the Christian to suffer?

Suppose the Christian did not suffer—but everyone else did. It would soon be apparent that becoming a Christian was a wise financial investment. Where then would faith be? And without faith it is impossible to please God. Since faith is required, risk of suffering is required.

It may also be thought that suffering is a Christian's way of earning a heavenly reward, for our Lord promises that those who suffer for the name will be richly rewarded.

We are imitators of our Lord, we are Christians. At the very least we should consider that he had the choice of whether or not he would suffer in his ministry on earth, and he chose to suffer. The servant is not above the master. In that sense, we should rejoice in suffering for Christ, for it means that we are worthy of the Name.

Paul himself learned these lessons well. He himself was to suffer greatly, but he knew how to deal with it. His secret? "My grace is sufficient for you, for my power is made perfect in weakness." Do you suffer? Consider the life of Paul, and learn how he dealt with great suffering and sorrow:

Begin by completely surrendering your life to Him. Do not complain that you don't deserve the suffering; rather, cast your pain on him and ask his grace through it.

Do you suffer at the hands of others? Imitate your Lord and King—who suffered to death, and forgave those who afflicted him.

Remember that you are a part of the family of God—ask that family for their prayer, support and help.

If we suffer with Him, we shall reign with Him.

Miracles
Acts 9:32-43

It is a constant of human behavior that people will see miracles and each react differently. The Israelites saw the parting of the Red Sea and the ten plagues, but still they wandered from God quite easily. We say, "If only I could see a miracle, then my faith would be so strong." History proves otherwise. We see in this story some of the reasons God provides miracles.

Authentication. Christ claimed the authority to forgive sins. Peter claimed to be an Apostle. Does God grant authority to perform miracles to a fraud? But even at that, Satan we know is permitted to counterfeit miracles.

Revelation. The Old Testament in particular uses miracles to reveal the character of God. The water becomes wine, as it does in nature. Stones do not become bread. God is ultimately consistent, and his miracles are consistent with his character as well as his purpose.

Faith. The miraculous does indeed strengthen the faith of some. But for most, one miracle is not sufficient. It seems they must happen regularly for us to continue believing. What then? If our faith is fueled only by constant miracles, is it really faith?

The Glory of God. Jesus delayed his trip to Bethany until Lazarus was dead—so that we might see the glory of God. The man born blind was not the sinner, nor his parents—but rather we might see the glory of God. If you see the glory of God, and compare it with your own, then is there room for your pride?

In this instance we see authentication, the credentials of Peter the Apostle. Ultimately, however, all miracles point to Christ. Some point to his first advent; some are associated with his ministry on earth; some help establish his church (as here) and others point to his return. It is not sufficient that we marvel at the miracles and wish that we had such power. God grants such power not to the wishful thinker, but rather to those he chooses for his purposes. His prerequisite is true faith; but even then the miraculous comes only at his bidding or permission.

Why then miracles at all? So that you and I will have sufficient evidence to believe. Evidence to believe not only that Jesus has come, not only that He is the Messiah, but also that we would clearly know that He will return!

Cornelius
Acts 10:1-23

God has a magnificent habit of taking unlikely people to do his greatest tasks. The church at this time is at a crossroads. It is entirely a Jewish church; but Christ has commanded the church to evangelize the world. The wall must be broken. God chooses Peter on the Jewish side of the wall—and Cornelius on the other. What sort of man was this Cornelius?

Like most military men, he would be a man of habit. A centurion is roughly equivalent to a sergeant today, and experience indicates that sergeants are not given to mental brilliance. They are men of habit, and one great habit of Cornelius is prayer. What an example for us! We can pray for hours in the crisis; can we pray for minutes each day?

He had another habit, too: giving. We see that he gave "regularly." As a "God-fearer" he was not bound by the ceremonial law for tithing, but he gave nonetheless. One can almost imagine that he had a budget for it.

Not only was he God-fearing, all his family were too. The leadership and example of this father was no doubt visible to his wife, children and servants.

In sharp contrast to Peter (who has to have the point made three times before he gets the message), Cornelius obeys the angelic vision instantly. We see here the lifetime habit of obedience, which is the lubricant of faith. Without faith it is impossible to please God, and without obedience it is impossible to keep faith.

So we see his character. It may be summed up in the phrase that his prayers and gifts to the poor had come up as a memorial offering before God. The phrasing comes from Leviticus 2:2 to describe an offering whose aroma arose to God. This kind of offering was frequently made by the poor—and it was called "most holy."

Of Cornelius we know nothing more than is given here. But God used this ordinary, devout man to bring the church to do extraordinary things. The power of God is shown in this man, who devoted himself to prayer, giving to the poor and obedience. Do you think you are nothing special in the church? See what God did with such an ordinary man.

Cover the Offense
Proverbs 17:9

There is a curious shift in the translation of the Old Testament from the time of the King James Version to those of today. The cover for the Ark of the Covenant was known in the King James as the "mercy seat." Today that same phrase is translated the "atonement cover." No new manuscripts have changed this, just the changing of words over time. There is a truth in the transition, however: the cover of atonement is indeed the seat of mercy.

Here we are told to cover over an offense, so as to promote love. How can this be?

First, for those directly involved, to cover over an offense against oneself is to forgive. When you forgive, and mention the offense no more, that is love from the offended one to the sinner.

It is also an example to the rest of us. How noble an example for one offended: to forgive, and not to allow the matter to be raked up again! Such things are rare—but prized.

Some might object to the second half of this proverb. After all, if I am telling the truth, what possible objection could there be? None—if you are telling the truth in love, as our Lord commands. But there is some truth which cannot be told in love, and therefore cannot be repeated without breaking fellowship.

Sometimes the truth repeated will break up friends, particularly those who are not mature in the faith.

More often, however, repeating such a truth is like pulling the scabs off an old wound. It may heal again, but the pain returns when the scab goes. Is it not more loving to let the wound heal completely?

Sometimes repeating the truth brings the church into disgrace. We should never be afraid to admit our sins; but we need not trumpet the sins of others.

Sometimes repeating old offenses stirs up dissension in the church. If there is no need, why should we cause this trouble?

The small snake is sometimes the most poisonous. We should not justify raking up old sins by calling it truth, for we should speak the truth in love.

Handling Conflict in Love
Acts 11

There is a myth in the church that real Christians never argue. This is absurd, of course. Real Christians argue. It's how they argue (and over what) that counts. I suggest that Peter gives us a great example here:

> He handles the dispute with courtesy. He does not remind them of his authority in the church; rather, he begins with the facts, respectfully.

> He does so in love—for his response is not a defense of his actions so much as it is a statement about the Gentiles and God.

Both sides here show great sense in that the matter is taken up not in court nor in gossip but face-to-face.

We must remember that this is a dispute more than church discipline. Peter could, if the matter were one of opinion or of taste, decline the argument. Indeed, we are taught that we should prefer one another in honor, as the King James had it. In this instance, however, the dispute is unavoidable. The other disciples consider themselves devout Jews who follow Jesus. The dietary laws and separation from the Gentiles are commandments—until God changes them. How then to handle so serious a dispute?

> Note that Peter does not stand alone. He brings six brothers as witnesses. That makes a total (with Peter) of seven witnesses, which in Roman law was considered to be sufficient to make a document binding. Peter is providing a basis in fact which is beyond dispute.

> The facts alone are not sufficient. They must be tied to the will of God. In short, he points out that his choices were clear: disobey God or eat with the Gentiles.

> His opponents concede gracefully, and accept joyously what God has done. They are not concerned with winning the argument; they too are concerned first with God's will.

Conduct your arguments with love and courtesy, face to face. Be willing to concede graciously. Remember that victory in the argument is not the same as victory for God's will. It is not your pride which must triumph, but his church.

Still Small Voice
1 Kings 19

It is one of the most amazing changes in the Bible. Elijah has just come from Mount Carmel. There he opposed 850 prophets of the false gods. In doing so he has called down fire from heaven. Perhaps you feel that if you had that experience your faith would know no bounds. Bounded or no, Elijah knows God—but he also knows Jezebel. He knows she means it when she threatens him with death.

How is it that such fear comes after such a triumph? We think that triumph makes faith strong. Satan knows that after the triumph there is a chance to attack. After Jesus was baptized by John in the Jordan—with the Father's voice and the Spirit coming down—he went into the wilderness, and was tempted there. This is Elijah's wilderness experience. Satan waits until the moment of triumph is over, then attacks. He wants to wipe out the memory of victory and replace it with despondency and defeat.

The Lord has an interesting cure for this. Elijah is depressed and ready to die. The Lord sends an angel to him —with a recipe book. No great advice, only a few calories. We often forget that we are spirits in animal form. What affects our bodies affects our spirits. More than that, it shows how God plans to deal with what Elijah thinks is a major problem.

He begins with what might be seen as grandeur. First there is the wind. Then there is the earthquake; then there is the fire. Each goes by, and the solemn cadence rings: "but the Lord was not in the ..." (earthquake, wind or fire). Then comes—in the exquisite phrasing of the King James—the "still small voice." God needs no wind, earthquake or fire; the smallest whisper from him is quite sufficient.

You know the still, small voice. But quickly, without looking, what did God say to Elijah? Do the words match the grandeur? No! The instructions are quite practical. Go here, anoint so-and-so, then do this. It is God's laundry list.

There is the cure for the attack of Satan after the moment on the mountain top. After we have called down our own equivalent of fire from heaven, Satan is sure to attack. Fear not. God will not take you back to Mount Carmel. He will tell you to get some lunch and get on with his work. Do the things at hand! Do not wait for wind, earthquake and fire, but listen to the still, small voice—and then get to work.

The Call of the Missionary
Acts 13:1-15

In a very real sense no one ever volunteers to be a missionary—he is called by the Spirit. But note the way in which the church handled the matter: they were fasting and praying when the Spirit revealed his choice. Barnabas and Paul had either to follow or disobey. See also how the church sent them out. You might think that—since the Spirit has chosen them—nothing the church could do would add to that. But they fasted, prayed and laid hands on them, to add the blessing of the church to the selection of God.

A missionary's personality is also seen here. There is a common thread to great missionaries: it is their personal devotion to Jesus Christ. Paul frequently described himself as a slave of Jesus Christ. The thought would have been a common one to the Christians of his time. The joy of being the slave of Christ comes from his authority, the perfect authority. This leads the missionary to the great key of faith: obedience. It is not obedience to a code of conduct or set of rules, but to the person—Jesus.

> This devotion to Jesus, this obedience of Jesus, this faith in Jesus is the root of the power of the missionary soul.

> Paul tells Elymas that he is the enemy of God—and in God's name triumphs. The power is not in Paul—but in Jesus.

> Likewise, the authority is in Jesus. Paul is not just expressing an interesting opinion when he preaches the good news. He is delivering a message from the Lord. Paul you may ignore; Jesus you ignore at your peril.

> The power and authority are in Jesus because the redemption is in Jesus. He is the one who made atonement for us. His appeal to us is not wisdom (though he is its source); it is not power (though none exists without his consent); it is not joy (though he is a fountain of it); it is redemption. By grace we are saved, through faith.

The missionary is not his own person. He has been purchased at a very high price—the cross. By the call of God he becomes a channel through which the Living Water flows. Each and every one of us who claim the name of Jesus has been purchased at that price. Do you let the Living Water flow through you so that others may believe? Does the call of Christ come through you?

The Evidence of History
Acts 13:16-41

Christianity, almost alone among the major religions, asks you to consider the evidence. Its critics say that Christians have nothing but faith. Consider, then, the nature of faith.

Faith is built on evidence

Faith is not sight—that is to say, it is not proof. It is a logical conclusion from the evidence, on which one commits oneself. So then we must ask what evidence Paul brings forward here:

First, he cites the facts that God has been dealing with a particular people—the Jews—for thousands of years, preparing them for the coming of the Holy One.

In the course of doing this, he has stated in various places, in various ways, prophecies concerning the coming of this Christ.

These prophecies are fulfilled in Jesus Christ.

Faith precludes absolute proof

God could have made faith a result of absolute proof. He could have made mankind incapable of doubt. He did neither. He wants neither the calculating man who sees the profitability of being a Christian (though its profits are eternal) nor the man who has reduced him to mathematical certainty (though he is more certain than mathematics). He wants, and loves, those who believe, and who commit themselves to him.

This is in the nature of personal relationships. You cannot prove, by science, that your wife is faithful to you. You dare not assume it, either. But you look at the evidence and (I hope) have faith in her faithfulness to you. God simply asks that you do the same with Him.

Faith is reproduced in faithful lives

Paul is a witness, an eyewitness, to Jesus Christ. The eyewitness testimony of many is recorded in the Gospels. This too is evidence for faith. But more evidence is before our eyes: the effect that Jesus has on his followers.

You are powerful evidence that Jesus lives. The effect he has on your life can be seen by those around you. They too can reach such conclusions. The challenge is this: do they see anything about you which would cause them to ask, "What caused that?" Help them believe. Be the evidence that Jesus lives.

Elijah's Mantle
2 Kings 2

The cloak (or mantle in the King James) is the badge of the prophet from the time of Moses and Samuel. It is the symbol of the prophet's authority from God. Elijah uses it in just such a way:

> When he goes to recruit Elisha, his action is to throw his cloak around him. It is the sign that Elisha is to be his successor.

> As we see in both these men, as they strike the Jordan with it, it is not only the symbol of prophecy but also the sign of the power of God. The Jordan parts for the Ark of the Covenant—and Elijah's cloak.

In this passage Elijah knows that he is to be taken up to heaven this day. So he spends his last hours on earth going from one group of prophets to another. Each of these groups tells Elisha what is to come. Elisha is not alarmed—he is a man armed with virtue, and he will persist.

> He has the virtue of persistent friendship. Many are fair-weather friends; Elisha is one who does not know what is coming but stays with his mentor no matter what.

> He has the virtue of finishing the race before him. Many there are who start well, but fail to finish the course God has set before them. They seem to believe that God will honor a good start. Not so Elisha; nothing deters him from the finish line.

> He has the virtue of asking, seeking and knocking. Elijah tries to send him away, but Elisha has his eyes on the prize.

That prize is the "double portion" of Elijah's spirit. The double portion is the right of the firstborn child, and Elisha, spiritually, is Elijah's firstborn. For this, Elisha's ministry is triumphant.

There is a parallel in this for us. The Jordan is often the symbol of death, and Elijah crosses the Jordan before going to heaven. But before he goes he (by God's command) appoints Elisha his successor. If you are now old enough, do you have a successor in the church? One who is appointed to carry on after you?

Elijah had Elisha, and Elisha carried on the work of prophecy. The church needs each of us to bring an Elisha with us across the Jordan, so that the work of faith will go on in double portions.

The Perils of the Missionary
Acts 14:8-28

Paul and Barnabas in this passage experience one of the temptations that comes to Christians in position of leadership. It is so easy for the unknowing to worship the speaker they see rather than the God they do not. The peril has not left us. Have you ever had anyone praise you for what a fine Christian you are?

It produces a wonderful feeling. The temptation is in believing it is true. You may appear to someone to be an awesome Christian, but you should know how you stand before God. If you give in to the temptation, there are two immediate problems:

It inflates your pride, which is the deadliest of sins.

It blinds the person who is praising you. They need to know that you are a sinner too, that no one is good except God.

When you are praised for your Christ-likeness, you have a choice. You can take credit as a copy, or you can point to the original.

Paul and Barnabas take the right way here. There is no thought of enlightening these heathen later, after the party. Rather, they are dismayed at such misplaced worship, and try to enlighten them. The process proves quite difficult.

Ultimately, however, the city rejects them. Why is the Christian, the bearer of Good News, so often rejected?

First, because the Christian is (or should be) a reminder of righteousness in a world which wants to forget it.

Such righteousness should be admired. But Satan will twist admiration into envy if he can.

When a time of wrath comes, the Christian looks for forgiveness. The Christian is then a cause of shame.

Paul and Barnabas are soundly rejected here in Lystra. Indeed, Paul is stoned to the point where they think he is dead. Note what he did next. He left.

This doesn't seem like a very courageous thing to do. Bravado would have Paul stay. But our Lord was quite explicit about it. When we are rejected, we are not to waste time and courage butting the wall. We are to "shake dust." The message of the Gospel is so urgent, the call of Christ so pressing, that we are not to waste time with those who reject Him. The life of the servant of Christ is indeed a very difficult one. It is also a very exalted one. Are you willing to walk this "road less traveled?"

Testing the Lord
Acts 15:1-35

In verse 10 we see an unusual phrase, about testing God. The thought is somewhat foreign to most Christians. Perhaps a homely example would do.

Let us suppose that you are happily married and decidedly lacking in wisdom. You decide to perform an experiment to see if your wife (or husband, as may be) is faithful to you. You hire an actor to pretend to be a would-be lover, and await the results.

You are an idiot if you do this. If it "succeeds" you have an unfaithful spouse, and it's your own doing. If you "fail" you have treated her as a laboratory rat. You have tested her love as if it were a tube of chemicals. You have treated her with contempt. She will (quite rightly) feel utterly betrayed by your callousness.

The same sense of betrayal of a love relationship is the root of testing the Lord. Why would we do such a thing?

Sometimes it is presumption. We think ourselves so wise, so learned, that God could not possibly disagree with us.

Sometimes it is pride. God would certainly take direction from us, right?

Sometimes it is familiarity! We think of Jesus our Friend, and forget the holy, awesome, sovereign God.

Do we as Christians test the Lord? It may surprise you how often we do. Do you recognize any of these?

Do you test him by *not* asking forgiveness—but presuming that he will grant it without asking?

Do you test him by giving counsel to others, knowing that they will think it godly counsel, without taking counsel of the Lord first?

Do you promise the blessings of the Lord without teaching the Word?

Do we test him by saying, "Thus saith the Lord" at the end of our own thoughts?

All of these tests begin with the same idea. I, personally, am strong; I am wise; I am worthy. God's strength is not perfected in our strength, but our weakness. Acknowledge your weakness and his perfection. Do not test him, but rather lean upon his grace.

Failure
Acts 15:36-40

Mark, the author of the Gospel, was a failure. That's how Paul saw it. Barnabas—the son of encouragement, as his name tells us—saw it differently. They could not agree and parted.

Let's suppose Paul was right. Later on he changed his mind, but for now suppose that Mark is indeed a failure. What can we say to such a man?

Failure is inevitable

This is a sinful, fallen world. We are sinners. We will all fail at one time or another. But as often as we fail the love of God, in His great mercy, is waiting for us. Jesus told Peter to forgive seven times seventy; will not God do even more than that?

Bring your failures to God

How often we try and conceal our failures from God! We have the image that God has somehow placed a limit on our failures. After that, no repentance can avail. It is not so! You are to love the Lord your God with all your heart, soul, mind and strength—in other words, with your whole human self. That includes your failures.

Dealing with failure

When we fail, we must follow our Lord's instructions for dealing with failure. His picture is that of cleansing, like washing your hands before dinner. Remember how he washed the feet of the disciples at the Lord's Supper? It is this cleansing we need.

This is done by confession. You may think that since God knows your every sin, you need not admit them. His knowledge is not the point. Your admission of sin—that is what He desires. He wants you to admit it—to confess.

Is this hard for you? So it seems, and often we make it worse because we do not follow our Lord's instructions. He tells us to confess our sins one to another. If you do this, surely you are to seek help from your fellow Christians! Christianity is not a solo flight.

Walk in the light

Once confession and cleansing are there, it is important to turn around and go in the way Jesus directs. If you want to see where you're going, you need a light. He is that light! Come close to Him, and He will light up your road—and lighten your load.

Suffering
Acts 16:16-24

The oldest question in the Bible is simply this: Why does God allow his children to suffer? This is too deep a subject for so short a writing. I have no answers, but perhaps a few questions will shed a little light on suffering.

Why did God allow Jesus to suffer?

Jesus, after all, is his son. Of all his children, his only begotten should seem the last to be made to suffer.

But in suffering our Lord is better able to help us in our suffering (see Hebrews 2:18). Just as those who have suffered a particular illness are better able to sympathize with others who have it, our Lord knows our trials.

Sometimes God shapes an instrument to a task by suffering, as Jesus was shaped to his task (Hebrews 2:10). We too can be shaped into a person capable of great things—by suffering.

So we see that even Jesus suffered at God's command, for his purposes.

What should the Christian's reaction be to suffering?

First, we should *not* retaliate. Violence and hatred are Satan's weapons. Jesus did not retaliate, even as he went to the Cross.

Next, we should not suffer alone, if possible. God has given us the church. When one part of the body suffers, the whole body suffers—or should. When suffering, we should reach out to the church, and the church should reach out to us.

We should not compromise. Paul and Silas had but to cooperate to avoid prison. Instead, they turned a jail cell into a concert hall for Christ. Their eyes were on God's glory, not their pain.

How will God reward the sufferer?

In this life, suffering produces perseverance. Just as Jesus was shaped to God's purpose by suffering, so we may be made fit for his cause and kingdom.

In the times to come, we shall be joint heirs with Jesus to the kingdom of God. If we suffer with him, we shall reign with him, and we shall share in the glory to come.

Approaching the Intellectuals
Acts 17

Paul entered the intellectual center of the Roman world, Athens, and there met the test of the thinkers of his time. Many Christians are of the opinion that faith and intellect are contradictory. It is not so; Paul shows it here.

God is Revealed

There is a natural mistake in the Greek mind shown here. The picture is one of the "great minds" studying God, just as one might study gardening, or snails. But "to study" in this sense implies that you are superior, just as our minds are superior to the brains of snails. The matter becomes more difficult with a person. After many years of marriage, and much "study," there is still much to learn about my wife. If it is so difficult with another human person, how much more so with the person, God?

Fortunately, God reveals himself. So our study becomes instead our search for the revelation of the one true God.

The Approach of the Child

Paul then continues his thought: we are the children of God. Therefore, God cares deeply for us. Indeed, this also implies that we are all brothers and sisters. More than that: it also clearly means that He has authority over us, as a father should over his family. The Fatherhood of God and the Brotherhood of Man are the roots of western civilization. No wonder our Founding Fathers proclaimed all men are *created* equal!

The Evidence

The inquiring mind cannot be turned by logic alone. There must be evidence. It is sad indeed that the prime evidence is the prime stumbling block for the intellectual (the "Greek.") It is the Resurrection. The center of Christian doctrine is redemption by grace. The center of Christian evidence is the Resurrection. No wonder Satan attacks both so strongly.

Preference for the Unknown God

So many of us prefer the unknown God. For the Unknown God is whatever we make of him—merciful without demanding repentance, accepting of sincerity without truth. The Unknown God would not condemn a "romantic" adultery; the Living God demands fidelity. The Unknown God demands nothing of us. The Living God must be sought; must be heard; must be worshiped. Which God do you serve?

The Coincidences of God
Acts 18:1-22

Consider the series of facts which seem so unrelated in this passage, and how God has orchestrated them for the kingdom.

The Emperor Claudius evicts the Jews from Rome

Claudius, like several other Caesars, was not above finding a scapegoat for his troubles. In this instance, the Jews were chosen. So it is that a God-fearing couple, Aquila and Priscilla, come to Corinth. They could have met Paul at the synagogue, but God had a deeper relationship planned. Paul is a tentmaker by trade, and he is earning his living at it. As would have been both customary and charitable, he works with these fellow Jews who share his trade. It is an opportunity to witness to them. They see him not just as a speaker in the synagogue, but their fellow worker.

The result: Aquila and Priscilla become missionaries to the city of Ephesus.

Silas and Timothy come to Corinth

The result of this is that Paul may now step up his ministry. He does so—and the result must have seemed disastrous. The Jews completely reject the word of Christ. Is this the disaster it seemed? No indeed; for it brings Paul to minister to the Gentiles in this most wicked of cities—for a year and a half.

The Roman governor is indifferent

Gallio was a noted man, but in this instance it seems he just did not care what happened. Perhaps he had experience in such matters. Whatever the facts, Paul is protected—as God said he would be—by the complete indifference of the officials.

Tentmaking as a lifestyle

Tentmaking—the preaching or teaching of Christ by those who are also employed full-time outside the ministry—is not much taught these days. But see its power! The tentmaker can learn much from Paul here:

Accept God's providence in your life. If you are fired, the next job will be where he wants you.

Do not complain of your work. By it God has been pleased to let you earn your bread, and that is honorable enough.

Use the providence of God for his kingdom. Wherever you are, in whatever circumstances, remember that you are a servant of the King of Kings.

The Teacher's Burden
Acts 18:23-28

In this short passage we meet Apollos, the teacher. Other than what is recorded here, we know only that he was a Jew from Alexandria—a center of intellectual and mystical Judaism—and that he unwittingly caused factionalism in Corinth.

Here we see his teaching ability. Luke gives us three clues about this:

First, he was a man with a thorough knowledge of the Scriptures. If you wish to teach the word of the Lord, there is no substitute for this.

Next, he himself was very teachable. There is a subtle point in Luke's writing. Writers of this time listed people in importance. Note that Priscilla is listed here before her husband. Apollos was taught by this woman, which in his day would have been considered humbling indeed.

Finally, we see that he had courage. You cannot teach the Gospel without offending people, for Christ is the "Stumbling Stone" and the "Rock of Offense." You must not offend just to give offense or puff yourself up; but you must not fail to offend where the Scripture calls for it. Apollos spoke boldly.

More of his character can be seen in later in Corinth. Paul records that the Corinthians had formed factions, some after Paul, some after Apollos, some in other ways. Paul refutes this factionalism. But we find at the end of this letter that Apollos had refused to return to that church, despite Paul's urging. It is not too much of a stretch to surmise that he left Corinth to prevent the body of Christ from being split apart. In so doing he gave God the glory and sacrificed his own pride at being such a good teacher.

There is another tender point in this story. Apollos is bold, but he is not yet instructed fully. Note how Priscilla and Aquila take him into their home and explain the way more adequately. This is a mark of respect and also a sign of humility on their part. They do not challenge him publicly, but instead they take him aside, in private, and teach him the truth. Since he is a student of the Scriptures, he immediately recognizes this truth.

Who teaches the teacher? Christ, and many others. But most of all the teacher learns from the patient hands of friends.

Magic
Acts 19:13-41

Magic, in the sense of the sorcerers here, no longer exists in Western civilization. But its descendants are still with us.

The Counterfeit Principle

Let us begin at the beginning. There is nothing in this universe, seen or unseen, which God did not create through Christ. Satan is a created being; he creates nothing. All that he does to deceive us is by way of counterfeiting. The counterfeit is the worthless substitute for the valuable, such as:

Adultery and fornication, the counterfeits of Christian marriage.

Greed, the counterfeit of honest labor.

Pride, the counterfeit of "Well done, good and faithful servant."

Magic is the counterfeit of science. Science relies upon the unchanging nature of God in his creation. Science is hard work. Magic is the cheap and easy counterfeit. So how does Satan sell us this fraud?

The desire for knowledge

All of us desire knowledge, and the power it brings. But true knowledge is hard work, hence the appeal of those who say, "I have studied the great mystics, and (for a price, of course) you can have their wisdom." The appeal is secret knowledge.

Dealing with Guilt

As all of us desire knowledge, so we all desire release from guilt. This too is hard; it cost Christ the Cross. Whether by the modern magic of psychology or the mystic magic of the East, man is promised relief from guilt. Counterfeit relief.

Partial Gods

As we desire knowledge and freedom from guilt, we desire power. Magic promises power; it promises a god you can control. By placating the spirits, by chanting your mantra, you can have power—without the price of your whole being. So promises magic.

God delivers—knowledge, forgiveness and true power. Magic sells the counterfeit, even today. Magic asks part of your life, and delivers fraud. God asks all of your life, and delivers true life. Are you willing to pay for the real thing?

Preparing an Apostle
Acts 20

A glance at a map will reveal something interesting here. Paul has taken a shortcut (verse 13) while his friends sailed. It is a walk of some twenty miles. Why did he take this walk alone? Perhaps he needed to be alone with the Lord, to prepare for his final missionary journey, which would end in martyrdom.

Preparation

How does God prepare a saint for such a fate?

Service—warning them with humility and tears

Testing—through many trials.

Caring—shown here in Paul's tender words for the church and people he loves.

Attitude

Paul shows us the attitude of a saint prepared to die:

His life is nothing; the challenge before him, everything.

His life is lived in innocence and purity.

His life is founded on courage. He is not afraid of death; more to the point, he is not afraid of life.

His life is founded on giving from the riches God has given him.

See the stewardship of this man, especially in the time God has given him. He calls the elders to him rather than return to Ephesus, and delay.

The Inner Life

We have seen how Paul has taken time to be alone with his Lord. We see also that the Holy Spirit is his constant guide—and the one who warns him of what is to come. These show the inner life of the saint.

For us there remains an example. Consider Paul's life, and ask yourself this:

Am I living the inner life of prayer, study and meditation?

Is my attitude that of a courageous servant of God?

Do I serve my Lord with humility and loving care?

These were the keys of a saint in the time of Paul. These keys still unlock the door of saintliness today.

Hezekiah
2 Kings 18-19

The anger of God can indeed be awesome. Consider this: of all the thieves, prostitutes, murderers and other sinners in Israel in the time of Christ, the only ones whom Jesus physically attacked were those in the Temple. It is said that He is zealous for the name of the Lord.

Here too we see the zeal for the name of the Lord. This is one of the most destructive miracles ever recorded. The angel of the Lord, in whom some see the preincarnate Christ, strikes down 185,000 men in a single night. Why?

It is not for Hezekiah's righteousness. Indeed, early on he admits that he has done wrong, and sues for mercy at the hands of the Assyrians. But it is worth noting that Hezekiah, one of the most spiritual of Judah's kings, does not put his trust in armies or fortifications, but in the Lord.

Those who slander the name of the Lord—and they are many in our day—can be seen in this Assyrian commander. He makes two contradictory statements:

First, he says that God has told him to attack and destroy this land.

Then he tells Hezekiah that this same God cannot deliver Judah from his military power.

The slander of the name of the Lord is like that today. We have many who tell us that anyone who opposes (for example) abortion or homosexuality is morally wrong! We have gone from the days of "necessary evil" to moral goodness for such things. Like this commander, they claim the mantle of righteousness in proclaiming abortion—and then deny the Author of Righteousness any part in their lives or the life of their nation.

You cannot have it both ways. You cannot deny the Living God with one breath and claim Him with another. To do so is to slander the name of God. This is not the only example of God's reaction to those who slander his name.

Each of us must be on our guard against such things. Do you say, "God is so loving, surely he won't mind if I ..." and then condemn someone else for his sins? You slander his name if you do. You do that at your peril. God is zealous for his name. Would that his children were too.

The Vow
Acts 21:17-36

The word "vow" is not much used in the English language in our time. Its last common use is "wedding vows," the exchange of promises between husband and wife during the marriage ceremony. The concept has been neglected, which is a pity.

The vow taken here is one given in the ritual law. It required the Jew to abstain from wine and meat for 30 days, to worship daily in the Temple the last seven days, and to present certain ritually pure (and therefore expensive) sacrifices. As most men were day laborers, they could not fulfill such a vow without starving. But a benefactor, such as Paul, could pay for these men to eat and for their sacrifices. This would have the effect of certifying that Paul was a devout Jew. There is a lesson in this, even for those who know the vow only in marriage.

The appearance of the vow

A vow is intended to be taken publicly. We go to great lengths to arrange a marriage ceremony, inviting all we can. We seek others to witness our vows. Why? There is one satisfactory answer for the Christian: we are calling upon the church to assist us in keeping that vow. Marriage is imperiled in our time; we are right to call on the church to aid us.

An act of devotion

The world says, "why would you bother to keep your wedding vows? Isn't that an extravagant thing?" Yes it is. It is an extravagant act of worship. It is not only the church we call to witness, but also our Lord. Keeping your wedding vows in purity is worshiping your Lord.

The peril of failure

Solomon said it best: "When you make a vow to God, do not delay in fulfilling it. He has no pleasure in fools; fulfill your vow."

Vows at another's expense

Keeping your marriage vows pure is not easy. There is one other lesson for us in this story. Sometimes we feel we just can't do it—we are just not strong enough to carry on. Marriage can be rough sometimes. In our own strength we may fail. But the vow is to the Lord; it is a vow which is acceptable to him, pure and holy. We can therefore call upon him for strength and wisdom, for the aid of friends and counselors—and keep that vow at his expense. No pleasure in fools—but a heritage of righteousness.

True Courage
Acts 21-22

It is a sad thing, but courage has lost its meaning for our time. We recognize braggadocio and bravado and call them courage, but we forget that courage is not only a virtue, but the bedrock on which all other virtues rest.

True Courage is Morally Righteous

Paul could simply have made his explanations to the commander at a later time—but he would have missed the chance to set things to rights. He feels the compulsion to let the crowd know that he is not evil, but indeed possessed of the righteousness of God. There is a reason why our mythical heroes had this sense of righteousness; without it, they are nothing but swaggering children.

True Courage Gives No Thought to Self Gain

The prudent thing to do in this circumstance is to escape the mob. Paul does not think so—he sees them as those who need Jesus so desperately. He is thinking of their salvation, not his safety.

True Courage Acts in the Face of Adversity

This is typical of Paul. Often beaten, chased out of town, stoned, shipwrecked—the life of adventure that our cinematic heroes could not stomach. Courage is not for applause; the applause cannot be heard for the adversity ahead.

True Courage Is Based on Hope

Only those who can see that their actions further the kingdom of God—and therefore are to be rewarded by their Lord—would take such courage. No matter what happens to me, I know that God will triumph—that is the central hope.

How can I obtain such courage?

Defiance is not courage; defiance in our time brings applause, not consequences. Bravado is not courage; it is without hope. These are the imitations of courage we generate ourselves. True courage comes from one thought: God is with us. He is our strength and shield. But understand that courage does not come to the defiant, but to the obedient. If you will march to his call, he will tax the uttermost limits of the universe to support you. Be strong in your faith! If you will be obedient to his commands, if you will view those opposed with love and not hatred, then He will provide you with courage more than sufficient to his commands.

Resurrection of the Dead
Acts 22:17-23:10

From the oldest books of the Old Testament it is clear that a time will come when the dead shall rise. Job prophesied it, and longed for it. Isaiah saw it; Ezekiel saw it pictured in the valley of the dry bones. Daniel prophesied that it was not just resurrection, but resurrection to judgment—some to reward, some to condemnation.

C. S. Lewis once remarked that Christianity could almost be reduced to a single fact and a single doctrine. The doctrine would be redemption by grace; the fact, the resurrection. As such, the fact of the resurrection of Christ is the central fact of our faith.

We know too, from the writings of the New Testament and the example of Jesus after the resurrection, that the body in which we rise will be of a new form. What this might be cannot be told, but it is likely enough beyond our imaginations.

For most of us this is a very pleasant doctrine, and yet it has surprisingly little power in our lives. This should not be. We need to remember what this fact means in our daily lives:

It is not sufficient for some. For some people the fact that Jesus rose is not adequate evidence of the truth of Christianity. They weren't there to see it. But they are there to see you. If the power of the resurrection is alive in your life, they should be able do see it. Do they?

The Resurrection is proof that Jesus is the Son of God. Others were raised from the grave; only Jesus prophesied his own resurrection, both in the Old Testament and in person. This alone should give him the preeminent place in our thinking and actions.

The Resurrection is our spur to imitate Him. If we are to share in that resurrection to glorious life, if we are to reign with him, then surely we must be willing to suffer with him. To do that we need only imitate him.

It is quite the case here that Paul is on trial for the resurrection. He has made the argument in terms which his audience will understand, but the central fact remains. He has seen the risen Lord. That is the central fact of his life, and he must testify to it. So I ask you: have you met the risen Lord? Is he the central fact and person of your life? Are you living the resurrection life?

Testimony
Acts 23:11-35

It is a maxim of English law that legal memory begins with the reign of Richard the Lionheart. The law was passed, with some technical reasoning, during the reign of Edward I. But it is highly appropriate, not for Richard but for his father, Henry II. Henry was the man who brought to the English system of justice the idea of the jury. Our concept of a jury is different than his. In his day, a jury consisted not only of the disinterested, but also the witnesses. The witnesses would tell their story to the others, and all together would decide the case. The key point for us is that men must be willing to testify, if justice and righteousness are to prevail.

The concept of "testimony" runs throughout the Old Testament. The Ark of the Covenant was also called the Tabernacle (tent, or dwelling place) of the Testimony, for in it was the evidence of the events shown in the time of Moses.

Testimony comes in many forms. Preaching is one, for it tells the story of the Gospel to another generation. Our actions are a testimony, for the world sees them without setting foot in a church building. Indeed, our entire lives are a testimony to what we believe—Jesus, or not.

Christians often feel that they cannot testify. They think themselves too weak, or lacking in eloquence. Sometimes they feel that religion must be a private thing. But it is not so; silence is a testimony too—a testimony that what you say you believe is not important enough to speak out loud.

If you would but realize the power of testimony, perhaps it would not scare you so. The original word for testimony is the same word from which we get "martyr." A martyr is one who testifies. So indeed it is dangerous. But by the testimony of the saints Satan is defeated.

So you ask: to what should I testify? I have no great miracles in my life. There are these things to which Christians must testify:

That He is risen indeed. If you do not believe in the resurrection, you are a fool to be in church. If you do, then testify to it.

That Christ has given eternal life—and is coming again.

The time is now. The question is—are you willing to testify?

Felix
Acts 24

For two years Felix keeps Paul in prison. Behind this, there lies a story.

Felix is a very unusual ruler. He was born a slave. Tacitus, the Roman writer, tells us about him: "He exercised the prerogatives of a king with the spirit of a slave." Felix was a king, but his spirit was that of a slave—a slave to lust, anger and fear.

Lust? He was on his third wife—whom he seduced from her prior husband (also a king). The writers of the time concluded that he enlisted a magician to help him in this. Drusilla, his wife, controlled him by her beauty.

Anger? Roman justice was supposed to be impartial. When a Jewish riot broke out in Caesarea, he didn't just suppress the riot—he sent the soldiers in to slaughter the Jews.

Fear? You can see that in the lawyer's speech. He is appealing to the fear of a governor: rebellion must be suppressed at all costs.

The charges and defense you may read. What is interesting is this: Paul seeks to defend himself in his first speech. Once the initial debate is over, however, his next message is on the subject of righteousness, self-control and judgment to come. See the courage of Paul the Apostle of Christ! No lawyer's flattery, but the fire of the word of God. Felix can't handle it. He stops Paul—but then sends for him often. No moth was ever drawn to the flame like that.

Interestingly, this is the only recorded sermon on the subject in the book of Acts. Paul knows that Felix is still a slave—a slave to his lusts, anger and fear. To break the chains of that slavery he must accept righteousness, practice self-control or face the judgment to come.

Each of us must face the same decision. It is perfectly human to be a slave to lust; to be in bondage to anger; to live in fear. As with Felix, we long for a way out of our bondage. That way is Jesus Christ. Not a system; not a rulebook—but a person, God in the flesh. His sacrifice on Calvary, and his loving care for his children, enable us to break these chains. But it is not sufficient for us to flutter around the beacon of God's light. We must go in, and become the children of light—or face the judgment.

I Appeal to Caesar
Acts 25

God seems to take some delight in bringing about his purposes in ways never expected by his servants. In this passage we see some of the principles by which God works his providence.

The principle of the unexpected

Most of us are quite good at telling God how to arrange things to suit us. Paul is of the opinion that he will take ship from Judea and sail to Rome. This, however, is not quite the method he had in mind. What enables God to use the unexpected method? Paul's obedience. Had Paul made a deal with the Romans—a bribe—he could have been released. As it is, he's about to get an all-expenses-paid trip to Rome. Second class, to be sure—but paid. This principle certainly keeps life from getting dull.

The principle of moral judo

It is clear that Satan is possessed of much power. All the power of the state may be said to be his. Students of judo know that the key to success in judo is to use your opponent's strength as his weakness. The law provides Paul the option of appeal to Caesar. To Caesar he will go.

The principle of working together

Some Christians feel that God works only by miracle; we forget that he weaves all things together for the good of them that love him. There is no such thing as luck—there is only God's providential care. Paul certainly could not have seen that providence in the two years he spent in jail. When an honest governor finally shows up, he still can't get justice. Instead, he will go to Rome—carrying the flame of the Gospel to the center of the known world.

Not by might, nor by power, but by my Spirit

Felix, like most governors, assumes that power is sovereign. It is not. He has all the power he needs—soldiers, court, local residents clamoring for Paul's blood. The result? Felix is worried about Paul; Paul is not worried about Felix. Who's in charge? The answer to that is quite clear.

If you're struggling with circumstance, remember Paul's two years in jail. God had his faithful servant waiting —to do great things. Be faithful; wait on the Lord, and in his good time He will prevail.

Persecution
Acts 26

It amazes Christians in America today when they are persecuted. How can we be the butt of all those jokes; how is it that Christians can be denied employment because of their faith; how is it that we, in a "Christian" nation, can be so persecuted?

All Christians are persecuted, in one way or another.

Persecution is promised to the Christian (see 2 Timothy 3:12)

Indeed, we are told that as the end approaches, we will be persecuted even more.

This persecution is not for our sake, but for our Lord's sake. The servant is not above the Master.

The Christian walk alone will bring persecution. Cockroaches hate the light.

But we are not to react to persecution with the attitudes that the world shows to us. Indeed, our Lord is quite specific that we are to respond to persecution as He did.

We are to bless those who persecute us (see Romans 12:14).

We are not to fight them, but we are to flee them (see Matthew 10:23). This is not cowardice but obedience.

Indeed, we are to consider our persecution a blessing.

This seems a very strange attitude towards our persecutors—until you see Paul's remark here. He would like everyone who hears him to be just like him, except for the chains. The world tells us to persecute our enemies—to put them to death. Christ tells us to put them to life. We are to bring them into the family, making the ones who persecute us friends and brothers. Indeed, we must make every effort to do so— for we are sinners as they are. Christ's love triumphed for us; it can triumph for them. Mercy triumphs over justice.

By the power of our suffering in his strength, the strength of our forgiving in his love, Christ triumphs over his persecutors—our persecutors—and changes them into brothers and joint heirs of the kingdom. The battle is over when your enemy is defeated. The battle, but not the war. The war is over when your enemy becomes your friend and brother. Christ seeks to end the war between God and man by turning men into children of God. Is there any greater possible triumph?

A Good Thing
Proverbs 18:22

Providence—the idea that God weaves the events of life together in such a way as to bless his children—is not much spoken of these days. This passage explains the nature of the providence of God in the simplest and deepest terms.

He who finds...

In this part of the proverb it would appear that the man who finds a wife did just that: find. It would seem that it is entirely up to him to search for such a woman as he might search for buried treasure.

Receives favor...

But in the next phrase it appears that God himself has risen up and pronounced a blessing upon the man, given him a gift, treated him with royal kindness.

Both ideas are correct. We must do what we can to further God's purposes (and marriage is held sacred) —and rely on God to do what only he can do, looking ahead where we cannot see.

For those who have "found what is good" (and I am one) this is a paradox like no other. When I was married, it was not possible for me to imagine the joy and love my wife would bring to me. Even though I was utterly convinced of the rightness of the marriage, I am much happier today than I imagined possible. Was I the one who wooed and won the girl? Or was God the one who turned my small blessing into a magnificent one? Both are true.

There is one thing more. When you receive a gift, you should say "thank you." Gratitude is both socially acceptable and morally right. Sometimes, however, the fact that we did our part (we "found") conceals from us the fact that God has done so much more (when we "receive favor.") In such a circumstance, we forget to say "thank you" to the Almighty God who has so richly blessed us. So I ask you: have you thanked the Lord for the favor you have received from him? Have you gone to your knees in prayer and blessed his holy name because he has shown his favor to you? Does the sight of your wife (or husband, as may be) cause you to reflect how kind the Lord has been to you?

Do not delay. Thank him this very night that you have "received favor from the Lord."

Character of a Christian Leader
Acts 27:21-44

The passage here is the stuff of which movies are made. The hero of the story is Paul, and in his heroism we can see the character of a Christian leader.

Hope

Without hope a leader can lead us only to destruction. In the Christian leader, hope is unconditional. Even if our heart's desire is not accomplished in our lifetime, we know that God is eternal, and his purposes will prevail. Have you ever considered how it is that movie heroes can stand so much excitement? It's easy; they've read the script. They know how the movie turns out. So does the Christian.

From hope such as this we draw strength. From God's eternal view we draw patience. But the greatest blessing is this: even though we do not understand how things will work, we know how things will turn out. Things over my head are under His feet.

Practical Help

There is no sense being so heavenly minded that you are of no earthly use. Sometimes we are paralyzed by uncertainty. Thomas à Kempis gives us some practical advice. Suppose you knew the end result with certainty. Would it change what you would do? Usually, the answer is no.

Practical assistance is an imitation of our Lord, who fed the five thousand, healed the sick and raised the dead. Sometimes we just need to get on with it.

Swift to cut the ropes

There is a sense of urgency to true Christianity. The Passover was to be eaten in haste, sandals on the feet and staff in hand. The New Testament Passover—the Lord's Supper—should be a call to action.

One reason to cut the ropes: you may be in the Lord's way. Even the Apostles did not choose the place of their own serving; perhaps God is telling you to cut the ropes and move on.

One last reason for haste is this: you do not know the hour of your death. But die you will, unless the Lord returns first. Your time is limited; should you not make the best use of it? The King James spoke of this as "redeeming the time." Indeed, should we not live in hope; work as our Lord worked—and be swift about it?

Hospitality
Acts 28

In the midst of this story of adventure there is a simple act of hospitality—a neglected virtue. In those days the traveler depended very much upon the hospitality of strangers. We need to examine this virtue more closely.

Hospitality – a form of sacrifice

Most of us don't think of hospitality as a sacrifice. If it were not, hotels would not charge for it. But consider:

It is a sacrifice of the *pleasant*. Each of us arranges our home in such fashion as to please us. But for a guest, beds are rearranged and rooms upset. Even the meals may be special, for an honored guest.

It is a sacrifice of the *present*. Most of us think that "my time is my own to spend." Spending time with a guest may be an imposition, but hospitality requires that it be done cheerfully.

It is a sacrifice of the *private*. My home is my castle; if you enter it, you enter my life. You see what I hold valuable, and what I consider cheap. On my bathroom counter you see the prescriptions that tell you my illnesses. You see what I might not wish to display. You might even hear the thoughts I do not wish heard!

The Scripture enjoins us clearly: we need to practice hospitality. It does not matter that my home is not a magnificent palace. But for some, the size of their home imposes such an obligation. Does the visiting missionary have a place to stay?

The guest of every Christian

There is one guest to whom every Christian gives hospitality. That guest is the Holy Spirit. So permit some questions, o host:

Do you sacrifice what is pleasant for the Holy Spirit? Can you abstain from pleasure for the sake of a weaker brother?

Do you sacrifice the present for the Holy Spirit? You had counted on the time for pleasure; a sister in need calls. Will you sacrifice your time for this?

Do you sacrifice the private for the Holy Spirit? Do you share your inmost thoughts in prayer, or just those things acceptable in public?

Last of all: do you do so *cheerfully?*

The Just Shall Live by Faith
Romans 1:1-17

Of all the letters of Paul this one comes closest to being a textbook on theology. He did not know the Romans personally, but he knew that they were at the center of the known world, a place from which the Gospel could explode. In this brief section he lays out the key to his life: the Gospel.

First, he says he is "not ashamed" of the Gospel. It is a curious phrasing, for elsewhere he glories in the Cross. But he was writing to those who lived in a city of spectacle and glory, and by his turn of phrase he points them to true glory.

He tells us the nature of this Gospel. It is the very power of God. Consider it: if you had a live artillery shell, would you use it as a doorstop? No! You would handle it with all care and respect. So it is with the Gospel. It is not a light thing, but rather the power of God in our world. Since it is from God, it is holy; it is righteous; it is exceedingly powerful.

He tells us the aim of this Gospel. In one word: salvation. Salvation despite all the sins you may have committed (did I not say it is powerful?); salvation purer than all the filth in your life (did I not say it is holy?); salvation capable of turning you into a saint (did I not say it is righteous?)

He tells us the scope of this Gospel. It is for everyone, all who believe. There is no entrance requirement for the kingdom of God save this: you must be a sinner first. If you believe in Him, you can be saved by this Gospel. It is the very nature of God not to play favorites, and here is the greatest evidence of that.

Finally, he will tell us the content of this Gospel, summed up here as "righteousness by faith." Righteousness? Beyond the purest of the pure, for this righteousness comes from the shed blood of the only sinless man to walk the planet—a man who was sacrificed for all of us. None of us can be worthy of this; we cannot earn it. But we can receive it—by faith, as a gift.

This was God's intention "from first to last" —that the just shall live by faith. The just shall live by faith on this earth, for without faith justice will soon crumble. The just shall live by faith when our Lord comes again, for without faith there is no salvation.

The Wrath of God
Romans 1:18-32

In this era when the very concept of Hell is considered taboo by so many who preach, the idea that God would even be mildly upset seems out of place. What then to think of the Wrath of God? But there it is in the Scripture.

We have arrived at this situation because of a misconception which has been cherished for over two hundred years. It goes by the name of the Noble Savage, or Original Innocence. The theory is that if people were unspoiled by civilization (read: Christianity) they would be noble people, righteous and true. The truth is quite different. The painter Paul Gaugin believed in this myth. He went to Tahiti to paint these noble savages—and came back convinced that they were just as wicked as the rest of us. There is no original innocence—there is only sin.

Today this idea is often expressed in terms of how "bigoted" and "prejudiced" those "right-wing fundamentalists" (read: Christians) must be. After all, doesn't everyone know:

It doesn't matter what you believe, as long as you're sincere.

A loving God would never send anyone to hell.

Does it matter that you believe the earth is flat (as long as you're sincere?) From whom did we learn of Hell, if not from Jesus Himself? The truth is that God is righteous and just. That requires his Wrath.

But even in his wrath God reveals himself to be the God who is love. See verse 26; God shows his wrath by turning people over to their sins! Why? Because sin has consequences, and those consequences are designed to cause people to repent.

Such is God's loving choice (consider that the alternative is to toast the planet.) The result is that people become deeply depraved. Read the list of sins given here; does it not seem to be a list that could be used today without revision?

There is one test that Paul gives so that we may know that we have reached the extremity of sin. It is not just that we tolerate such things; nor even that we do such things; but that we approve of those who do them. Sin is now righteousness.

But take heart, Christians! God still reigns. It may be that we can do nothing more than live a godly life, but we can do that. Do not be discouraged. God is merciful and patient—not dead.

Judgment by What You Know
Romans 2:1-24

In this passage Paul establishes a crucial principle of God's justice and righteousness: he will judge you on the basis of what you know.

You know you are a sinner. How can I say that? It's easy; every time you condemn sin in any way, you pass judgment on sin. You don't like cheaters, you disapprove of liars, you think murder and rape outrageous. In so doing you accept the idea that there is such a thing as right and wrong. If you accept that, then you must also accept the idea that at some time you have done wrong.

But—you might reply—I have also done right. That may be the case. Remember the thermometer principle: just because the thermometer says you have a fever doesn't mean you really have one. It may be that you have a hot water bottle and a test at school that day.

If you have an active, working faith, your life will produce good works. You should be able to see the fruit of your spiritual life.

But just because you do good works does not mean you have a real spiritual life—because you could be using works to cover your lack of faith.

Those "in the know"

You see how this makes it worse for those of us who know what the Lord wants. Those in the know:

May brag about the relationship ("I don't see how non-Christians get through a crisis like this.")

Approve of the right ("No sex and violence on my TiVo")

See themselves as guides for the blind ("Some people just don't know when to listen to good advice.")

But don't you see that doing such things means that God now must expect greater things from you? You say you know him—do you act like it daily? Do your works fit the state of your knowledge, or are you sticking the thermometer in the hot water bottle?

You teach others; do you teach yourself? You think you have come a long way in Christ—and likely enough you have. If so, then should you not see that you have a long way yet to go? And only by the grace of God can you get there?

Arguments Against the Faith
Romans 3:1-8

Paul in this section deals with some arguments against the faith. Some of them sound rather silly today (and they did in his day too, as his reply points out).

<u>Argument:</u> There are so many hypocrites in the church, how can there be anything real about it?

<u>Answer:</u> There would be no hypocrites if there were no truth; and where the truth is, the hypocrites are most closely clustered around it—in the hope that some of the credit will rub off. It's just like money: if there were no real twenty-dollar bills, there would be no counterfeit ones.

<u>Argument:</u> People in this church have such puny faith. How could anyone think that this is for real?

<u>Answer:</u> It's not their faith that counts—it's God's faithfulness in keeping his promises that counts. You may believe completely that the gun is not loaded—but shouldn't you check the magazine?

<u>Argument:</u> My sinfulness is a great way of showing God's goodness (nothing is ever a total loss; it can always be used as a bad example). Since I'm doing him such a favor, how can He condemn me?

<u>Answer:</u> (You've got to be kidding!) Haven't you heard that judgment is coming? Just who did you think He had in mind? Would your mother take that argument from a five-year-old?

<u>Argument:</u> My evil lets God bring good out of it. Every time I sin, God gets the chance to bring good from it. How can that be wrong?

<u>Answer:</u> Your own mouth has just condemned you. "My evil" tells God all that needs be known.

Two things are very clear:

We are extremely clever at justifying our sins, and

in the process of justifying, we condemn ourselves.

This also disposes of willful ignorance (what if I choose to remain ignorant of Christ?) To ask the question is to admit the answer: I chose to remain ignorant of the one who could save. Could there be any greater condemnation?

The Just Shall Live by Faith
Romans 3:9-31

Paul now lays out the three great thoughts of his letter—which are fundamental to the faith:

We are all sinners

There is a way back to God—by faith, not works

That this was the culmination of the Old Testament

That we are all sinners

Being a "sinner" is now an unpopular concept. We have so many good excuses! But take them all against the man Adam:

"My heredity is imperfect—I was born with a genetic impulse to do it." He was created perfect.

"My parents didn't raise me well. I had a terrible childhood." Adam was created adult.

"It's my environment." He lived in the Garden of Eden.

"The rules are too complex." He had one rule.

"They need to make the penalties more severe." He faced the death penalty.

The result: the original sinner. Just like us.

Justification by faith

So what are we to do? Some rely on keeping a code of rules and regulations, as in the Jewish Law. But this does not work; all of us violate at least one of them. The more complicated the code, the more common the violations. So should we do without a code? That leaves us with no guide at all. The solution is radical, and simple: we cannot be justified by the code. We can only be justified by faith.

Old Testament fulfillment

How can this be? Look back at the Old Testament. The constant theme is that of animal sacrifice. Why? The word "atonement" appears regularly. But we know that animal sacrifices cannot possibly provide real atonement. They are just a picture of the sacrifice that was to come—the sacrifice of Christ upon the Cross. What animals could not do, the perfect sacrifice could.

The picture is complete. The Law is not nullified, it is completed. The sacrifice is made; there remains only the faith needed to participate in it. From the beginning of time God planned it so. There remains for us now the life of faith in Him. True in the Old Testament; true now—the just shall live by faith.

Abraham Discovered
Romans 4:1-12

Verbs are the action words of the English language. In this section notice: "Abraham discovered." For indeed Abraham discovered how faith works by putting it into practice; it was not by instruction but by practical discovery that his faith was developed. There are three prime examples:

He emigrated to the land of Palestine at God's order. I wonder how many of us would go to, say, Chile at God's command.

He trusted God that a son would be born to him and Sarah—at a time of life when most of us would be telling God that Medicare doesn't cover pregnancy.

At God's command he tried to sacrifice his only son. This was God's great test of his faith.

Such an example of faith seems beyond reach. One reason for this is that we do learn from our experience. We look at other people around us, see their failings and conclude that God somehow must have the same failings. Of course, the conclusion is an unconscious one. Look at it this way:

People cannot be trusted like that because they change their minds. But God is eternal; His purposes never change.

People cannot be trusted because they do not have the power to carry out their intentions; but God is omnipotent.

One reason God allows such failings in others is to drive us to trust in Him alone.

Our reaction to such a world is to "hedge our bets." We'll trust God—to a reasonable point, of course. We'll also rely on our good deeds to build up brownie points which God "owes us." Paul points out the fallacy of such a hedge:

If you work, you get wages. Wages are proportionate to the value of the work. If you have faith, what you get is totally disproportionate. It is a gift. How do you "work" to obtain a "gift?" The two are mutually exclusive.

They are also mutually exclusive because righteousness can only reside on one side of you—the inside or the outside. Either you are confident of your inner righteousness (and are outside a hypocrite) or you are confident of your inner sinfulness (and therefore a repentant sinner on the outside, and thus justified).

Is it just possible this is why our faith is so weak?

Faith and Works
Romans 4:13-5:5

Suppose you encounter (as you stand in the bread line at the Union Rescue Mission) two men. One, a thorough legalist whose pride is the spur to his legalism, pours the soup. The other, a man who loves Christ and therefore helps his brothers, hands out the bread. Can you really tell which is which? It is almost impossible to distinguish in others between works as the cause of righteousness (i.e., self-righteousness) and the effect of love. Paul gives us the distinction here in terms of the process of each:

Start with the law; it yields transgressions (you can't run a stop sign that isn't there). Transgression yields punishment, the wrath of God.

Start with faith; it yields repentance. Repentance yields grace.

Many Christians have the idea that they must learn "the rules of the game." It's as if they expected the church to be a locker room. They walk in thinking, "If I see pads and helmets, it's probably football. Look for a bat—that means baseball. The thing then is to choose the right game." In fact, you walk in and see pads and helmets on one side—and an artist's palette, brushes and canvas on the other. The choice is not "which game" (i.e., which set of rules) but choosing between "playing the game" (legalism) and creating a work of art—a life pleasing to God.

Paul talks much here of "the promise." The word is interesting in the Greek: *Epaggeliaia*. It means a promise which is unconditional. God does not change; his promises are unconditional. For us to "claim the promises" is to take God at His word. In short, we are to say "yes God, I believe you will do what you say you will do -- and I'm going to act upon that belief." I propose to you three simple tests of this in your life:

What do you say about God's promises? "God can do so little with me; I'm such a sinner" sounds so humble. It really says, "I don't believe God's promise that he can make me great in the kingdom—it's just too tough for Him."

Do our actions show such confidence in Him—or are we hedging our bets?

Do our worries show a lack of confidence in Him?

Reconciliation
Romans 5:6-11

Christ, by taking on the form of man while remaining God, reconciled God to man and man to God. The war caused by sin can now end. In our passage here we see some important points:

...at just the right time... God selected this time carefully. He prepared Israel for it by the words of the prophets so that all would know approximately when. More than that, the world situation was so set that an explosion in the size of the church would happen. This was due to the sense of sin in most men, and to the fact that the Roman Empire provided a society in which the Prince of Peace might spread His reign.

... when we were still powerless... This recalls Paul's earlier argument about the Law. Since those who knew God were under the yoke of the Law, they were sinners with no escape—powerless to effect reconciliation.

...God demonstrates his own love for us... This is a very strong argument for the nature of God. Death is universally feared (or was, before Christ). To die for someone else is the pinnacle of love. It is also the "why" of the Cross.

Justification and Sanctification

Justification is a change of status. It is instantaneous, and comes at the acceptance of Jesus Christ as Lord and Savior. Justification requires faith.

Sanctification is a change of state; i.e. a change of character. Sanctification requires obedience.

Perhaps an example would serve us better. We have some friends who adopted twin boys. These boys lived with them for many months, learning from "mom" and "dad." One day, all of them went before the judge. He pronounced the adoption final. At that instant (like justification) the children's last names were changed to Smith (really). The process of growing up in that family, however, had already started and would continue (like sanctification).

By analogy then, God justifies (adopts) us by faith in an instant; He sanctifies (and saves us from His wrath) by obedience over time.

God has performed our adoption; we are heirs of the kingdom. The question now is, will we grow up in his family, or will we reject his name? Will we be sanctified by obedience in the faith?

Slavery

Romans 6:1-23

Have you ever heard, "He's a slave to that ..." garden, woman, motorcycle, hobby, job, etc." Paul is using a similar metaphor (see verse 19) in this passage:

(Note that we are not speaking of slavery in the negative sense which is common in America. Slavery was a very common economic status in this day, and it did not carry with it the connotations we have today).

Paul here is countering a weak (but very pervasive today) form of Antinomianism: "Hey, let's be cool about this Christianity thing. God will forgive; and I'm not out to be a spectacular sinner; what's the problem?" The argument is, in essence, "why should I try to be righteous? It doesn't make any difference." Yes indeed it does:

You're a slave to whatever masters you. If sin masters you, then you are a slave to sin. Which would you rather be slave to? God, or sin?

Consider the fruits of each. When you're a sinner, what do you get for your troubles?

Even more, note that sin *earns* death; but grace *gives* life.

The issue is one of lordship. Who's in charge of us? If we answer "me," we answer in pride—and we answer in sin. Note how Paul puts it to the Romans when he tells them they have done the right thing:

"Thanks be to God"—not "congratulations on being so righteous."

Note the words "form of teaching"—it implies a visible impression in the Greek. It's as if we have been pressed into God's mold.

and the form is "to which you have been entrusted." Again, it is not what the Romans have done, but have been done "to."

In a real sense, we have the "hard and easy" of Christianity. We are freed from sin; we are the slaves of righteousness. Righteousness is very hard, indeed impossible—except by the grace of God. The practical question is, will we accept it and act upon it?

Dead to the Law
Romans 7:1-13

In Chapter 6 Paul says we are dead to sin; here (verse 4) he says we are dead to the law. There are three simple points to this:

We are "dead" by the principle of identification.

The result of being alive to the law was that we are controlled by our sinful nature. The law arouses "sinful passion" (more on this later) and produced "fruit for death."

Being dead to the law means being alive to the Spirit, and the fruit of the Spirit is in our lives.

For many Christians this would seem to imply a complete, radical change of character. It does not. It implies a complete, radical change of direction.

Take an example. Try to walk from California to Washington DC—by going westward. You'll soon run into the ocean. The other direction will get you there after a long walk—but the important thing is the direction. Similarly, we as Christians are headed in the right direction, but we must not mistake that for having arrived. Someday heaven will be our home; someday. Ultimately we are headed for heaven or hell; we make the choice. Indeed, it can be said that God condemns no one to hell; those in hell have condemned themselves. The law was put there to lead us to Christ, not away from him.

This is a very personal passage. The words "I" and "me" occur no less than ten times in this little passage. Paul reaches to his core and talks about the love of his youth—the Law. In so doing, he brings out the central paradox of the law:

The law itself is holy, righteous and good

It also produces sin!

How can this be? There are two ways:

First, by defining sin, it produces sin

More important is the concept of "forbidden fruit." Who among us has not had the temptation to sin just because it feels so good?

We were designed to be free. We chafe at the rules. Satan offers us a counterfeit freedom in breaking the rules. God offers us real freedom in Christ, who fulfilled the rules and offers us freedom in eternal life. We must decide: break the law in counterfeit freedom, or surpass it in the freedom of Christ.

Wretched Man

Romans 7:14-25

The awareness of sin is a sign of spiritual maturity. Paul here outlines the conflict of mind and flesh (not strictly the body). In his mind, he knows what is right, but somehow he sins anyway. I find this strangely comforting. Paul is not a plaster saint, completely ignorant of temptation and sin, but a man like me struggling against the conflict between the spiritual and carnal natures of man. This struggle will continue. There are three things I would say about this:

First, this passage demonstrates the uselessness of human knowledge. Just because I know what is right doesn't mean that I have the will to do it. Knowledge is in the indicative (I know what to do); righteousness is in the imperative (I have the will to do it); there is no link between.

Next, there is the New Year's Resolution problem: no matter how strongly I intend not to sin, I sin.

Finally, even knowing the first two is not enough. Diagnosis is not to be confused with cure.

Is it any wonder that Paul cries out, "What a wretched man I am! Who will rescue me from this body of death?" No sooner is the cry raised than Paul gives the answer: "Thanks be to God—through Jesus Christ our Lord."

The answer is and always will be the person of Jesus Christ. We all are, to some extent, carnal Christians. The issue is not whether or not we are carnal, but what we are to do about it. Will you take the problem to your Lord?

If you do, He will send his Spirit within you to expose the problem—and bring you to the point of decision. You must decide: will you repent, or will you continue in your ways? As you think on these things, remember the Pharisee and the tax collector at the Temple. One praised himself in the sight of God; the other could not even look up to God, but begged, "God be merciful to me, the sinner."

Humble yourself in the sight of the Lord, and He will lift you up. The war may be long or short, but the victory is won. It was won on the Cross of Calvary. Will you not march with the Victor?

Obligation
Romans 8:12-17

Obligation. The word has a number of meanings, because we can be obligated in a number of ways:

There is the legal obligation—a debt under a contract.

There is social obligation—other people expect certain behavior from you.

There is moral obligation—not just other people, but we ourselves, set up a moral requirement to do something.

Finally, there is the obligation of self-consistency. This is the Popeye principle: "I am what I am, and that's all what I am." And I am a child of God!

We are the children of God! If you are led by the Spirit, you are the child of God. This means that

we are protected by our father, just as we protect our small children. As they grow, we loosen the "apron strings." God will provide us with just the right protection.

we share his Spirit; it is a constant companion to us. Our correction, our encouragement are always with us.

Paul says that we are adopted sons. Being a Jew of Roman citizenship, he could have referred to either model of adoption.

The Roman model revolved around the legal system. If a person was adopted, he was literally considered a new person. His debts were canceled. The Roman model also involved the idea that the father had absolute power over the son, even when the son was fully grown. Our father in heaven can be seen to have such authority over us.

The Jewish model is found in Esther. Mordecai adopted her. That meant that he assumed all obligation for her daily needs—including those for family affection. Where the Roman model was in law, the Jewish model is in love.

What, then, is the result of this adoption?

First, our relationship to God has changed. From the Old Testament times when everything went through a priest we have come to the point where we are children of God

We are co-heirs with Christ.

As he suffered in this world, so shall we.

As He was raised from the dead, so shall we be.

Therefore, "set your mind on things above."

What Should We Pray For?
Romans 8:26-28

Our Weakness Most of us don't think of ourselves as "weak." But indeed we are. The question is not whether or not we are weak but rather what God is going to do about it:

He may take our weakness and turn it into his strength, as he did for Paul:

We need to remember that Jesus understands our weakness, for— after all—he is human too:

His dealing with our weakness sets us an example in dealing with the weaknesses of others:

What should we pray for? There are many people who are very reluctant to pray in public. One reason is that they're not sure just what they should pray for!

Maybe we don't know what to pray for!

It is also true that we cannot see the future; sometimes we might be praying for a disaster unknown.

Often we need a model; thus we have the Lord's Prayer.

James tells us that sometimes our prayers are not answered because our motives are not pure.

Sometimes the reason we don't get what ask for is that He *is* listening.

The Spirit Intercedes... We have chosen to have the Spirit of Christ in us. The Spirit "translates" for us. For we pray with mere words; the Spirit groans for us—a picture of the completeness of the Spirit in prayer.

In accordance with God's will... What does it mean to intercede "according to God's will?" I submit the following:

You must do so in the name of Christ. Not just using the words as a formula, but praying *just as if you were Christ.*

You must do so without doubt.

You must do so in obedience to God's commands.

In all things God works for the good of those who love him... There are a two points that might be brought forward with profit:

God's will prevails, in all things. That being so,

We should acknowledge that in all our prayers.

The word translated "together" is the root of our word synergy. He weaves our prayers and lives together for good – for those who love Him.

A Sudden Transition
Psalm 19

There is a modern literary device in Psalm 19. It's in verses 6-7:

> {6} It rises at one end of the heavens and makes its circuit to the other; nothing is hidden from its heat. {7} The law of the LORD is perfect, reviving the soul. The statutes of the LORD are trustworthy, making wise the simple. -- Psalms 19:6-7 (NIV)

Do you see the sudden transition? The modern poet uses this too. It's as if David said, "I left out the connection between these two verses—because it's so obvious." The connection is obvious; as the heat of the day (in Palestine—where it gets really hot) sears every bit of the desert, heating everything, nothing hiding from it—so the Law of the Lord searches out every corner of the soul.   So it is that the Lord defends his children against sin. But the passage is not a negative, "thou shalt not" verse. Indeed, it promises us four blessings:

"reviving the soul"—do you know what "soul weary" is? If you do, then you know the refreshment that the Word of God alone can bring.

"making wise the simple"—wisdom is not for the high IQ alone. It is for everyone, by the grace of God. John Bunyan was

'A Tinker out of Bedford,
 A vagrant oft in quod
A private under Fairfax
 A minister of God
Two hundred years and thirty
 Ere Armageddon came
His single hand portrayed it
 And Bunyan was his name!'

(Rudyard Kipling) ["quod" = jail] John Bunyan was a vagrant tinker, often in jail—and wrote Pilgrim's Progress and The Holy War. His education? The Scriptures alone.

"joy to the heart"—the original quote is lost to my memory (but bet on Max Lucado) but I recall reading that "A Christian is never afraid, always joyful—and constantly in trouble."

"light to the eyes"—is there anything like the Bible to make sense of our senseless world?

Compare this to the existentialism and nihilism (its child) of our time.   Would you base your life on "a foundation of unyielding despair"? (Bergson) - or the light of the Lord?

Zealous
Romans 10:1-4

The beginning of the this passage is touching: "Brothers." Paul still has a heart yearning for his people. That yearning translates into prayer and self-examination – which showed him the problem of the Jews of his day.

He begins by testifying that they are zealous for God. Zeal is often mistaken for truth. This brings about problems:

First, there is the "Linus" problem. You remember Linus, from Peanuts: "It doesn't matter what you believe, as long as you're sincere." We may take that statement in two senses:

It may mean that our mortal minds will make mistakes in interpreting the Scripture; but that as long as our hearts were pure, God will forgive. This is liberty.

It may mean that we don't have to try to interpret the Scripture; just that we have to hold our beliefs sincerely. This is license.

Zeal without inspiration is a terrible thing; as Goethe put it, "nothing is so frightening as a bustling ignorance."

Zeal can be maintained for the sake of zeal—it feels good! An ideology is stronger than a theology. Ideology says, "You are wrong, I am right and therefore I have the right to ...." Theology says, "God is right; you are wrong, and God ..."

Such a zeal instills in a person a sense of self-righteousness. If I seek out my righteousness, I must reject the idea of submitting to God's righteousness. We sometimes assume that our acts of repentance and subsequent good deeds have placed God in our debt. But once we assume that God *owes* us something for our efforts, we have abandoned grace, and are depending on our works. We must not mistake his generosity for our merit.

If I want to be righteous, there must be a standard to meet. I can either create one of my own or accept true righteousness, Jesus Christ. This is one reason why so many will not believe. They are not willing to give up the idea that they are already righteous.

Paul describes Christ as the "end" of the law. God spent two millennia pounding into the heads of the Jews just what He is like, so that they would recognize him when he came -- and then they missed it. They missed it because they captured the feet of the Law, but not the head. Let the lesson be learned: we are saved by grace, not by works or self-righteousness.

The Remnant
Romans 11:1-10

Throughout the Scripture God makes clear the principle of the remnant: he is not going to get everyone to follow him. He does not expect it; rather, he expects that a remnant of the faithful will remain.

The example here is given as that of Elijah. A man easily discouraged, that Elijah (remember the aftermath of Mt. Carmel?) —but God tells him he is not alone, there are others.

Sometimes the number saved is very small (Noah); sometimes beyond counting. Always there is the remnant.

The call is issued in the broadest sense; the number responding is obviously much smaller. (Mat 22:14 NIV) "For many are invited, but few are chosen."

Those who respond do so of their own choice: (Luke 13:23-24 NIV) Someone asked him, "Lord, are only a few people going to be saved?" He said to them, {24} "Make every effort to enter through the narrow door, because many, I tell you, will try to enter and will not be able to.

And finally, as this passage makes clear, these are the elect, the chosen—chosen by grace, the unmerited favor of God. These have chosen God, therefore God has chosen them.

One cardinal principle of the remnant must be remembered. God forces the division; He tolerates no one on the fence:

(Mark 9:38-40 NIV) "Teacher," said John, "we saw a man driving out demons in your name and we told him to stop, because he was not one of us." {39} "Do not stop him," Jesus said. "No one who does a miracle in my name can in the next moment say anything bad about me, {40} for whoever is not against us is for us.

It is discouraging at times to see the way in which our society is crumbling—crumbling for its lack of wisdom. The secular world declares that Christianity is on its last lap. But God is faithful; he preserves a remnant to worship him. Being a part of this remnant is never a popular thing. It is often a dangerous and painful choice. But does truth really depend on popularity? Those in whom still waters run deep will recognize that the decision must be made. Those who will be saved will choose to be with the remnant of God.

What Can God Do With Evil?
Romans 11:13-36

Again we see much to learn about the character of God. The word "hopeless" cannot be applied with God. Even though the Jews have rejected the Messiah, Paul utterly rejects the idea that God is through with them. To reject the Messiah is evil, and in this passage we see how God deals with evil:

First, God does not give up—He still waits. Sometimes we mistake this for a lack of concern, or a slowness which is inexplicable. But every moment is "his time"; he will act when he chooses.

Even on the evil God brings his blessings. Indeed, this is such a part of his character that we are commanded to do likewise. Even to those who have turned from him his call remains "irrevocable."

And when He permits evil, He will bring an even greater good out of it (St. Augustine's solution to the problem of pain). In this instance the rejection of the Messiah by the Jews brought about the spread of the Gospel to the rest of the world.

Here, in the metaphor of "branches," (a common one in the Scripture), he makes clear both the basis of our spiritual life and the consequences of ignoring it:

If you are disobedient he will prune you right off. Our Lord said much the same thing when he told the branches to abide in the vine.

If he prunes you, you will be replaced with someone else. Not one of us is indispensable; and all of us are sinners.

But if you remain in fellowship, you will be very fruitful indeed.

Finally, note that there is only one olive tree. Whatever the grouping in the faith, there is only one church -- for there is only one God. Hear, O Israel, the Lord your God is One.

God is not the author of evil, except in the same sense that light can be said to be the author of darkness. Wherever the light shines, the darkness flees. When darkness flees, hope arises. Hope is not disappointed with God, for he counts it a virtue and rewards it.

Are you "abiding in the vine?" Are you looking to the light?

A Variety of Gifts
Romans 12:4-8

Paul frequently uses the metaphor of the church as a body—one united thing, composed of many parts. For a body to function well, each part must perform its proper function. Therefore, if you construct a "body" you must find out the proper function of each part. So it is with us.

We must remember the rule of "right use." Is there anything that so irritates you as when some amateur tries to "help" you do your job? The same is true in the church. One reason we are encouraged to look at our gifts is so that we won't irritate others by butting in where God has not put us. We need neither to overstate nor ignore our gifts; rather, we need to examine ourselves carefully and prayerfully.

> Gifts are not just those of ability, but also those of a call. Many of us have a lot of talent; determining the gift of God means not only a talent inventory but a listing of the calls God has made upon you.

> Sometimes we "select" our gifts on the basis of the prestige we see in them. But is one service to our Lord greater than another? Even the Apostles were not permitted to choose their place of service.

Gifts; too often the subject is preached when there is a campaign going to recruit workers. This can be (and should be) an exhortation for us to examine ourselves. If we do so honestly, we may discover some interesting facts:

> Knowing our gifts is a way to know ourselves. Some of us have hardly been introduced to ourselves; we're afraid of what we might find. The life unexamined is not worth living.

> This is also one reason God forbids us to judge others. How can we know what their gifts are?

> We must remember that they are gifts from God. They are not what we have given God, but what He has given to us.

> As they are gifts from God, we should use them for His glory—not ours.

Finally, note the phrasing: "let him (teach, encourage, whatever)." If a person's gift is apparent, we should not stand in the way. Each should do his part; each should let each other do theirs as well. Do not let the committee prevent the body.

Daylight Behavior
Romans 13:13-14

A frequent metaphor in the Scripture is to compare light to goodness and night to evil. I suspect that (in the absence of neon lights) Paul had every good reason to make the comparison.

Some sin is performed "at night" simply to hide the act. We don't want people to know what we did, or who did it. Except for criminals, this is seldom the reason today, for we have lost all sense of shame.

Some sins -- particularly the sexual variety—actually are more attractive in secret. There is a certain "tang" to the forbidden fruit. Is it pride? Defiance? Who can say?

More common among Christians is hypocrisy—it's "amen" on Sunday morning and "oh boy" on Sunday night.

Paul gives us a list of "midnight sins." Sex and drunkenness are obvious; more surprising are dissension and jealousy. Is the evening meal a drunken orgy—or roast preacher?

Paul ends with the command to be clothed with Christ.

We put on Christ—and so when God looks at us, he sees as we see, looking at the outside. He sees Christ.

Clothes often define a man, especially the old and familiar ones. Do your spiritual clothes define your spiritual man, or are they like a tuxedo—for special occasions only?

If you wear them long enough, people come to expect them. If you wear Him long enough, the world will not let you take Him off—they know better.

Little children can have a lot of fun dressing up in their parents clothes. It is a charming sight. But to the children it is very serious—they are learning what it is to dress like an adult. We, the children of God, are learning to dress too. We are putting on Christ, who is God in human form. Sometimes this may seem like hypocrisy—especially when we fail. But judge not; what might appear to be hypocrisy may just be a step in growing up in Christ. The key is to continue to imitate your Lord; to put on Christ.

Do you "put on Christ?" Do you study his attitudes and his words, and then put those attitudes into your life and those words into your mouth? It's a very comfortable garb—and it lasts forever.

The Faith That Is Weak
Romans 14

This passage is often taken to describe someone with a besetting sin. It is not so. It is about the one who adds rules to the faith—for what appear to be good reasons. Paul describes *this* man as one whose "faith is weak." We often see it as strong, but in fact it is weak.

We must distinguish between liberty—freedom to do as I please, with the responsibility for the results—and license (which takes no responsibility at all). It is Christian liberty we have. To that end, Paul gives us instruction.

We are not to condemn the weaker brother. It is a curious reversal of form. We usually think of the person with all the rules condemning the liberal one. Paul prohibits condemnation on these grounds:

First, God has accepted this person as His child. Who are we to say to God, "You made a mistake on that one?"

Next, in doing so we exceed our authority of judgment. We can only judge ourselves, and then only to bring repentance (Godly sorrow). We cannot pass judgment on someone else's servant; not in this world nor the next.

Finally, to pass such judgment is itself a lack of faith!

It says, "God, you could never make anything decent out of ....." Is it ever proper to deny the power of God?

We sometimes get into this habit because of our misunderstanding of humility. We say, "Oh, I'm so rotten, God could never make anything out me!" This is completely presumptuous (and rather blasphemous) talk, masquerading as humility. True humility says, "I can't make myself into greatness -- but He can." And if He can do it to me, why not my weaker brother?

We are commanded to accept them. Not to tolerate and look down on, but accept them. It is fitting both for our humility and our service that we do this. Humility, in that we are sinners too; service, in that they are the children of Christ also, and as we receive them, we receive Him.

Christ has made us into a family. In a family we are not all exactly alike—but we are together eternally. Thus we must accept and love each other.

Unity
Romans 15

There are three interesting "unities" in this passage.

Endurance and encouragement. Endurance represents our experience and encouragement the words of others, including the Scriptures.

Heart and mouth. The heart represents the "inside" of a person— the thoughts and emotions. The mouth represents, of course, what we say. We recognize hypocrisy as having these two not united.

God and Father. We have a central mystery of the church in this unity. We have the "God ... of our Lord Jesus Christ" (the human side of Jesus, acknowledging God as divine) and "Father of our Lord Jesus Christ" (which emphasizes His divinity). God and Christ are one; and Christ prayed that we too should be one.

The "Why?" of Unity. If you want to motivate an American, you have to tell him not only what to do but why. Paul takes that same principle here; he gives us the "why."

The internal side: to glorify God. This is essential to keeping us in a right relationship with God.

The external side: to bring praise to God. Wisdom is proved right by all her children. Do we, the children of God, bring praise to God? If we glorify Him in the church, should we not bring praise to him outside the church?

The "How?" of Unity. The basic instruction for the "how" of unity is to accept one another.

We must accept that each of us has different gifts. We are explicitly told this; yet sometimes we expect more of others than their gifts will allow. This is yet another reason we are told "judge not."

We are all possessed of the same Spirit, and that Spirit gives us peace with each other:

Over all this, the love that God commands of us binds us together:

There is one overriding aspect of unity in the church: we are to be united, in imitation of our Lord, that the world may know that He is God, and that He loves us.

Asking For Help
Romans 15:30-33

There is no greater indicator of struggle than the cry for help. When we face difficult situations we often call upon those who love us to "pray for us" because we are afraid of what might happen. To ask for prayer in such circumstances is to admit fear -- in the hope of overcoming it.

Paul here asks for the Romans aid in prayer. Note carefully just what he requests:

> He asks them to "struggle" alongside him. The prayer of a genuine "prayer warrior" is just that: a struggle. We must feel the heat of combat with those for whom we pray. Pain with their pain, joy with their joy, we must put our hearts with those for whom we pray.

> He asks them to pray for his deliverance. Note that Paul is not asking them to pray for his strength when handed over; he's asking to get out of the situation. "Lead us not into temptation" is still good advice.

> He asks that the results be acceptable. It is not altogether clear what the problem might be, but it has been speculated that Paul might be delivering an offering from Gentiles who sacrificed for Jews who wanted nothing to do with them. Sometimes pride will tell you that the food basket should go to someone else.

Finally, Paul closes this section of the letter with the hope that he will soon see them. He invokes the God of peace, again reminding us of the unity of the church, and then anticipates his arrival:

> He wants to come to them with joy. It is not his wish to come to reprimand them (though the letter often sounds that tone) but rather that his coming would be a joyous time. The Man of God comes in joy and peace; a glimmering on the horizon of the time when the Son of God shall return, bringing us joy and peace.

> He wants to be "refreshed together" with them. In this he reminds us that Christianity is not a solo flight. The Man of God needs to be among the people of God.

In all our troubles we need to seek the help and prayers of our fellow Christians. God intended this, so that we might be one body. Do not let pride interfere with His purpose.

Josiah
2 Chronicles 34

Josiah is one of those seemingly endless kings of Judah—but with a difference. The history of the kings past Solomon is usually ended with the words, "and he did evil in the sight of the Lord." Not so with Josiah. He took the throne as an eight-year-old child—after the murder of his father—but at sixteen he "began to seek" the Lord. It was a seeking that would bless him all his life.

Ten years after he began to seek the Lord, he commanded the rebuilding of the Temple. In the process of this reconstruction, a copy of the Law of Moses (probably the first five books of the Bible) was found, and brought to him. His reaction shows the character of a man of God:

> He could have said, "Hey, I didn't know anything about this. Surely God will forgive my ignorance." But he didn't. Ten years of seeking God had taught him better than that.

> Instead, he tore his robes—a sign of deep distress in that culture— to show his sorrow and repentance.

> Then, instead of letting a show of repentance be the end of it, he inquired of God: what shall I do? He followed his show of repentance with action.

This is all the more important because he was the king. As king, as leader of his people, he had the privilege of standing in the gap for them. By his repentance he turned God's wrath away from that generation. He stood in the gap for his people—and raised himself to greatness as a king.

The Wrath of God is not a popular subject, but it is found all through the Bible. God is just; he cannot tolerate our wickedness. He had already pronounced judgment upon Israel. He could not go back on his word. Wrath (or justice, if you will) could not be denied—but it could be deferred.

Josiah's reaction to God's deferral of wrath is another indication of his closeness to God.

> First, in solemn ceremony, he renews the covenant. In the way most likely to impress, he tells the people who is God.

> Then, in joy, he celebrates the Passover (next chapter).

Josiah was not perfect—but he showed us how a leader's repentance can move God to bless rather than destroy. A pure and contrite heart is still precious to God.

Unity of the Church
1 Corinthians 1:1-17

One of the saddest aspects of the modern church is its myriad of divisions and sects. There are major divisions of the church (Protestant, Catholic and Orthodox) and within these divisions other divisions. To those within the church, it seems unlikely that Christ's prayer in the Garden, "that they may be one," will be fulfilled any time soon.

Worse, despite the best efforts of those who would unite the church, new denominations and sects seem to arrive every day. It seems as if any person dissatisfied with his present organization within the church universal is obliged to go out and start a new one. Often that new one proclaims itself as the only true church, the only way. Upon what grounds? Frequently the differences are so small as to be utterly trivial. There are two groups now discussing their doctrines with each other whose major difference is this: one believes in the rite of foot washing (as Christ did at the Last Supper); the other does not. Unity is, however, a long way off, even for such a small difference.

How do such things spring up? Is it not first a question of a strong personality, willful and proud, proclaiming that the current situation is intolerable? Gathering followers around, he strikes out alone, and another division is born.

The church is a body. It is not designed to function in fragments. We are to partake of "one loaf." One Lord, one faith, one birth are our heritage. The divisions of Christendom are a sorrow to man and God alike. But what can we do?

Consider this passage here. The problem is an old one. The great leader, Paul, tells us plainly that he is not to be worshiped, nor to be the founder of a sect. He preaches the Gospel of Jesus Christ, and it is Jesus who is to be honored and praised. Here is our first defense against sectarianism: Jesus alone is worthy of honor.

Call everyone who honors Christ as Lord, Savior and God your brother or sister. Do not ask about the label on the door of the building, but about the Spirit inside the people. Seek those who worship the Father in spirit and in truth. As Paul commands here, agree with one another. Seek unity with your brothers as far as it is possible within you. Let us be those who build the walls of the church—not those who carry the bricks away.

The Paradox of the Cross
1 Corinthians 1:18 – 2:5

Throughout the New Testament there is a common theme: the Gospel appears to men as a paradox. By dying on the Cross Christ gives us eternal life. By submitting to this shameful death he triumphs over all the forces of the world. By coming as a baby in the manger he arrives greater than any king ever to reign. God, it seems, has a sense that only through weakness and what seems to be foolishness can his cause triumph. Why does he show his power this way?

That no one may boast

How often have you thought of it this way: I have done something wonderful, or difficult, for the Lord. Surely he owes me now! Surely he owes me great things! But it is not so. You are greatly in his debt for the Cross; his pure, sinless and perfect life was given so that your sinful one would not pay the penalty of that sin. What service would you claim to offset such a thing? So he triumphs in foolishness, that we may see how great he is.

That we may learn his great wisdom

We think ourselves so wise that we give advice to God. Does he ever follow it? Or does he not perform the desired end in a way in which you never dreamed? Have you ever told him exactly how to arrange matters to get the result you know he wants—and discover that he has a much better plan? Learn well who is God!

That He may treat us with gentleness

Consider the opposite possibility. Suppose God decided not to deal with us in such foolishness. Have you ever seen a father playing with a baby? His talk is childish; the laughter is at the most childish things—and the father loves it. If he spoke to the baby as if he were an adult, we would consider him harsh and demanding. So God deals with us, that we may not be in terror of the God who loves us. Rather, knowing his awesome power, we also know his infinite love.

As you go to prayer this evening, consider that he already knows your needs; he already knows how best to meet them. But he cherishes the conversation with you, and is willing to talk with you in the foolishness of men rather than in the power of his almighty nature. Praise him for his foolishness, for the foolishness of God is greater than all the wisdom of this world.

Tests of Spirituality
1 Corinthians 2:6 – 3:4

Most Christians consider themselves "too modest" to claim to be "spiritual" people. They think themselves too insignificant in the eyes of God to make such a claim. The modesty is ill-placed. God will grant great spirituality to anyone who will ask him for it. Here Paul tells us how to discern true spirituality.

The Spirit searches all things

One of the reasons for this modesty is a sense that, over and over again, one keeps discovering sin in oneself. This is a sign of true spirituality! The Spirit is exposing your sins to you—sins you would not have had strength to handle earlier, but now the time is ripe. The Spirit is to convict the world of sin and judgment. So when the Spirit causes this conviction in you, you have two choices: develop a spiritual callus—or bring that sin to Jesus, asking for help. If you will ask for help, the Lord will graciously give you all you need. It may seem that you've discovered another weakness—but in fact this is a sign of the Spirit working within you.

The spiritual man understands the things that God has given us

Have you read through a passage in the Bible that you've seen many times before, only to discover a completely new meaning? The old meaning is not now false; your understanding is now deeper. That is a sign of being spiritual. Similarly, if the man you used to think of as "too pious" or "too sanctimonious" now appears in your eyes as a blessed saint, the Spirit is opening your eyes—praise Him for it! Does prayer grow sweeter each day? Has it grown from a growling duty to a time of pleasure and deep meaning? The Spirit is moving within you.

The carnal man

The man who is not spiritual, the carnal man as described in this letter, does not accept spiritual things. Because these things are discerned with the Spirit, they cannot be discerned in the flesh. The sign of this is shown here: jealousy and quarreling. The man who chases the world's way sees the peace of the spiritual man as inexplicable.

Do you lack the spiritual life? Then go to God in prayer; surrender to Him. Ask him for the Spirit in your life. It will take some time. Children do not grow to adulthood overnight, physically or spiritually. So start now, do not delay it.

Each His Task
1 Corinthians 3:5-23

One of the key discoveries Christians must make—early on, one hopes—is that God assigns to each Christian his or her particular task in the church. One reason for this is to prevent our pride from taking hold. If we "achieve a position," that is one thing. It is entirely different to be assigned a task. We are what we are in the church as God determines.

God assigns. God determines where you are best to serve. It may, or it may not, be along the lines of your natural ability. He considers not only the obvious facts of character and talent, but the unknowable facts such as, "what would such an assignment do to him?" Therefore, we should be content with our work.

God is responsible. It is a great comfort to the Christian worker who is called to a work of patience to know that God is responsible for the assignment, and therefore for the result. We are responsible for the work—but "God gives the increase." Again, so that we may not boast—but also that we may not despair!

God will reward. If God assigns, and God is responsible for the result, then he will reward the diligence of our efforts. Since he alone can justly weigh our opportunities and efforts, he alone is capable of giving just reward. So do not be discouraged if your efforts seem to have produced little. Be diligent; God is not deceived. Someone must do the hard things of the faith; someone must have the patience to carry on a work which may not be finished in their lifetime. Perhaps that someone is you.

Quality counts. God will not reward us at random, nor entirely on the basis of results. But he will reward us on the quality of our work. Do you give him your best, or do you give him what you have left over? Your reward depends upon that answer.

The assignment for all. Each of us is responsible for our own selves, in the body. To the extent we can, we need to become wise in the ways of God. Study to show yourself approved; continue in prayer; practice hospitality—these are things that each and all of us can do. Forgiving others is a task for every Christian. Doing those things which reflect the Spirit of God within us, without respect to our individual tasks, will bring us reward for this at least. Whatever other assignments God has given you, he has put you in charge of you. Take good care of the saint he has entrusted into your hands.

On Pride
1 Corinthians 4

Paul is correcting the people he loves. Like many others, he uses himself as an example of what to do about pride – for his pride was conquered on the Damascus road.

He tells them to regard him (and others) as servants of Christ. The word "servant" prevents pride.

He forbids judgment—for judgment may bring about a feeling of superiority.

He then punctures their pride in a few key points:

Look at what they are taking pride in! Not what they have done—that at least could be understood—but which teacher they follow. (The feeling is familiar, is it not, to every fan who has cheered his team to victory).

Paul rightly points out that they are no different from anyone else. There is only one qualification for becoming a Christian: you have to be a sinner first.

Are you rich? Are you intelligent? Are you strong? Are you beautiful? If you are, are any of these things entirely yours to boast of—or are they the gifts of God? Did you choose the family into which you were born, for example? You have these things not because you are worthy but because they are gifts from God.

Indeed, we are all rich—and kings! The Christian is a member of a royal priesthood. But rich? Yes! The rich man is not the one who has much but needs less than he has. Your God supplies your needs (and beyond).

But, you say, my needs are one thing—but I also have my wants. It is foolishness. To say, "I want" to God of anything which is not in His will is to defy him. It is arrogance, and as Paul tells us, the kingdom of God is not a matter of talk but of power. In whom is power—you, or God?

Pride—the competitive, "I'm better than you are" arrogance so prized by our society today—is the source of much that is evil. It is through pride that Satan fell. If you want a personal relationship with anyone, it must begin with knowing who that person is. If you want that relationship with God, you must know who He is. That excludes our pride—and opens the door to His love.

Inside and Outside
1 Corinthians 5:9-13

The Corinthian church existed in the midst of one of the most depraved cities of the Roman Empire. Even for that time, Corinth was known for its immorality. Paul brings to their minds a question which has been with the church ever since: what is a Christian to do with those who are immoral—and unsaved?

He begins by telling us what to do with the unrepentant sinner inside the church. We are to refuse to associate with such a person. There are two reasons for this:

The church must maintain the reputation for righteousness she needs to be the body of Christ on earth.

More important, perhaps, such treatment may bring that sinner to his senses—and cause repentance.

Unfortunately, some Christians have concluded from this idea that we are not to associate with the wicked of this world. If we carried this idea to its logical conclusion we would arrive at Paul's statement here: we'd have to leave the planet. This could get expensive.

What we usually do is to refuse to associate with *some* of the wicked of this world. There are socially acceptable sins (for example greed, when you label it thriftiness or enterprise) and sins which are not socially acceptable. So we pick and choose which of the worldly will be allowed our company. It should not be so.

"What business is it of mine to judge those outside the church?" In that sentence Paul banishes this attitude from Christian conduct.

To judge those outside the church is to steal from God – for that is his right.

Rather, our attitude should be this: they—like the rest of us—need Jesus Christ as Savior.

Is there anyone so vile, so wretched, so sinful that we cannot touch them? Are we like the Pharisees of old, avoiding the sinful so that we might not become unclean? Surely we should avoid those who tempt us where we are weak. But that is a confession of our weakness—not a display of Christ's strength. In any other case we should not fear to associate with anyone—for out of such an association may come salvation. It might even clear us of the accusation of being judgmental—who can tell?

Disputes in Court
1 Corinthians 6:1-6

One of the saddest signs of our church age is also one of the oldest. We see one Christian sue another one in court. Paul was outraged at the Corinthians when they did that. Today we consider it normal. But why?

First, we have lost the sense of community that the church must have. We see our churches as large institutions; we "go to church." The truth is we do *not* "go to church"; we *are* the church. The church is the body of Christ. It is to be united as Christ and the Father are united. So when we go to court against each other, we not only display our lack of unity, but we display it to the world at large, to our shame. It says to the world that we cannot get along even with our fellow Christians.

It carries another message as well. This tells the world of our lack of wisdom. Think about it: if there was a man of wisdom and discernment in the church, what fool would go to court? Would not a wise man seek out this man of wisdom and have him decide between two Christian brothers?

Consider it: suppose your tree crashes down upon your neighbor's storage shed, ruining it. Are you responsible for the damage, or is it his loss? You could run to your lawyers and go to court (and spend prolifically), or you could go to the church and ask for wisdom and mediation. Which is cheaper?

But suppose your brother refuses this. Should you go to court? If you do you bring the church into shame. Is the price of his storage shed worth that to you? Even if you are sure you are in the right, does that really matter? Is not God able to give you a thousand times the price of that shed? Do what honors him, and trust him for the finances.

We are ambassadors of reconciliation between God and man. We can surely spare a little time to reconcile man and man as well. When disputes come, do not think of "How can I win this argument?" Rather, think of how you can end the argument by bringing honor to your Lord. It is better for you to lose the argument, it is better for you to be cheated out of the money, than it is for your brother to turn his back on Jesus Christ and be condemned. The court case is now; salvation is for eternity. Do not insist upon your rights; rather, act so that God is glorified and your brother is blessed—and the church strengthened.

What Counts
1 Corinthians 7:1-24

Paul's commandments on marriage sometimes confuse or anger Christians of our time. This chapter contains some of the more detailed instructions on marriage—and it also contains the basic principle by which God, through Paul, has instructed us. It is found in verse 17:

"Nevertheless, each one should retain the place in life that the Lord assigned to him and to which God has called him."

For those who fervently believe in our own bootstraps, this seems a strange statement. There is great wisdom in it.

We often confuse a good thing with the best thing. It is a good thing to be married; a loving Christian spouse is a great gift from God. It is a better thing to have the self-control such that you do not need to be married. Not many of us have it.

Throughout this passage is a theme. In whatever circumstance or condition we find ourselves, we are to do our best to bring honor and glory to God. Are you married to someone who is not a Christian? Bring glory to God by your patient endurance, and so sanctify your children. Indeed, such behavior may win your spouse to Christ. Are you poor? It would be good to become rich—and better to learn to control your desires. A man is not rich when he has an abundance of things; he is rich when his possessions exceed his needs. If you pursue this with the idea of pleasing God he will reward you with true riches.

Even to the slave Paul says, "Don't let it trouble you—although if you can gain your freedom, do so." These things are temporary; they will last only the rest of your life, at most. You were designed to live forever in the presence of God. What is seventy years compared to eternity?

From such a view of things comes contentment. More than that, however, such a view produces a deep desire to please God. It also produces a much clearer view of the world. Have you ever watched our youth chase after the latest fashions? How much better to see through the advertisements to the things which really last.

Examine yourself. Do you chase after money, power or fame? These things are fleeting. Instead, set your mind on things above. You can have your power to earn reward, or God's power to give grace—but not both.

Avoid the Reproach
Nehemiah 5:1-13

Nehemiah had a most frustrating situation on his hands. He is trying to rebuild the walls of Jerusalem, fearing attack any moment, and this domestic difficulty comes up.

It seems that many of the people had become very poor. Either they had so many children that their land could not support them, or they had mortgaged the property during a famine, or they had borrowed money to pay taxes. They could not repay, and in the custom of the time they were selling their sons and daughters as slaves to pay their debts.

Meanwhile, Nehemiah and his company of men had been raising money—to buy back Jews from the Gentiles, releasing them from slavery. No wonder he was angry!

In his stinging rebuke, Nehemiah makes two points that we should heed today:

We should "walk in the fear of our God." For so long we have been told that God loves us that we forget that he is both awesome and righteous. A father loves his children; he therefore disciplines them. If God loves us, will he not discipline us? Should we not fear the one who holds the keys of heaven and hell? Indeed, the fear of the Lord is the beginning of wisdom.

We do so not only because God is righteous and powerful, but also to "avoid the reproach" of our enemies. Have you ever heard someone say that the church is full of hypocrites? Have you ever given them reason to say it? No matter how you rationalize it, the enemies of Christ will be quick to point out hypocrisy. In so doing, some will be prevented from hearing the Gospel.

Nehemiah calls a meeting and condemns those who did this. In short order they repent. Nehemiah then gives them a visual lesson: he shakes the folds of his robe. He tells them that as he has shaken his robe (as if to get rid of some crumbs) so God will shake them out if they fail to keep their promise.

It is well for us to remember that. God is patient, ever willing to forgive, but there comes a time when he says that such a man must be shaken out if there is to be justice. Do your actions cause reproach on the church? Do not try God's patience!

Learned Man's Burden
1 Corinthians 8

Paul deals in this chapter with a problem which has not confronted most Christians for over 1500 years—food sacrificed to idols. In doing this he lays down three principles which particularly apply to the intelligent, educated Christian.

First, my freedom should not become your downfall. In Christ there are no rules and regulations of the type found in the Old Testament's levitical law. Dietary regulations, in particular, find no place in the Christian's life. This is not a command to eat everything; rather, it is permission to eat anything. But any freedom carries with it responsibility. In this instance, Christian freedom is to be used in such a way that it does not cause others to fall away from the faith.

We are particularly warned to beware of our brother's conscience. Paul tells us to "be careful." It is a needed warning. Often we forget that others do not enjoy the same sense of freedom, but may still be under the burden of rules and regulations which they think are needed for the faith. This may seem foolish to us. But there is a difference between the rule being foolish— and the conscience. To keep your brother's conscience from becoming weakened, do nothing to damage it. Even if that means giving up our Christian freedom.

What may be most surprising is this: a Christian brother could be destroyed by our knowledge. The point is simple enough: there are certain things you would not tell a young child. The child does not have the maturity to handle the information, so you keep that information from them. We shield them, for example, from scenes of horrible violence (or at least we should). If we do this for a child in the flesh, should we not likewise do it for a child in the faith?

Like Cain, we sometimes resent being our brother's keeper. It cannot be avoided. The educated, knowledgeable Christian has a duty to share that knowledge with other Christians as well as possible. That includes keeping the brothers and sisters in the faith from stumbling over things for which they are not yet prepared.

Do you love your fellow Christians, as Christ commands? Then keep them from sin and trouble. Do not give them any reason to defile their conscience.

At His Own Expense
1 Corinthians 9:1-18

Paul, in a vigorous passage, proclaims something which is not pleasant to most of us. We would cheerfully acknowledge that the man who mows our grass, the woman who serves our meal in a restaurant, or any other worker, is worthy of a living wage. Except a preacher. Why?

Perhaps it is this. There are among us the hirelings, those who use the office of preacher solely to obtain their living. It is a temptation to some. After all, in the right denominations, a minister of the Gospel is very well respected. He is listened to, and his opinions on a variety of subjects command respect. With a little diligence and effort, he can rise from church to church until he obtains a position as a minister in a well-to-do congregation that will support him appropriately. Indeed, there is often a subtle exchange of winks: you don't trouble us in our wealth, and we'll pay you to preach against sins we don't commit. It should not be so.

Paul, to his credit, is of another type. He has suffered for the Gospel. He is a living example of one who does what he must do for Christ, for Christ will provide for those who do. Such people are more numerous than those who preach for money—but much less public. They can be told by their newsletters asking for a contribution; not so that the ministry may be expanded, but so that it might be continued. The glossy photographs are not there; this kind of ministry lives in black and white.

The quarters are seldom elegant, and the hours are often long. Those to whom they minister are sometimes ungrateful—and often move on shortly. Paul's own ministry was such; beaten, arrested, half drowned, he was not the kind of candidate an upscale church would be looking for.

Yet—despite his problems and poverty, his working for a living while preaching the Gospel—he turned the world upside down for Jesus Christ. How? Simply this: his preaching was an offering to God. It was an act of devotion, and as such it was accepted by God as a sweet sacrifice. God honors such men, not with worldly fame but with heavenly results. One man preaches, another teaches, but God gives the results.

Christian, have you made such an offering to your Lord? Or do you complain of your living? Sacrifice brings honor.

The Chameleon
1 Corinthians 9:19-27

The chameleon, we are told, is capable of changing its coloring to blend in with its surroundings. There is an interesting parallel to the chameleon in this passage.

Freedom—and purpose

Evidently the chameleon can be whatever color it pleases, within the limits God has set for it. But such changes of color are not at random; rather, they are done for a purpose: to blend in with the surroundings while lying in wait for insects. Likewise, we have the freedom to "blend in" as well. Paul tells us here about his liberty in Christ—but he also tells us the purpose he has. That purpose is to win as many as possible to Jesus Christ. Therefore, his freedom is a tool to become like those around him—it is not a casual change of clothes.

Freedom—and others

Paul makes these changes quite deliberately. Note that he does not become strong to impress the weak. He stays under the Jewish law when dealing with the Jews. It is not his intention to demonstrate his freedom, to show it off. Rather, he is using that freedom for their benefit. He is bringing Christ to them, and them to Christ. It is not for his own pride that he changes, but rather for their salvation.

Freedom—and preparation

Such a use of freedom is a noble and good thing—but there is a danger in it. Is it your call to go into the bars to preach the Gospel? There are those who have such a call. It is their special duty to make sure that they do not fall prey to drunkenness. To do this, they must prepare themselves for what they must face. Whatever our task we must use our freedom in such a way that we prepare for it. This is discipline; the denial of our freedom in order to prepare for our task.

Christian, ask yourself:

Do you use your freedom in Christ to serve his purposes, or to please yourself?

Do you know the task to which Christ has called you, and do you use that freedom to perform it?

Do you prepare yourself for the task given to you, giving up your freedom to discipline yourself?

We Are One
1 Corinthians 10:14-33

Many of us view the word "member" as meaning one more interchangeable person, having no particular task or duty, but somehow a part of the society in question. The New Testament church has members, but none in that sense. The illustration Paul uses here is that of a body. As such, the "members" of a body, if you can recall the older sense of that word, are not interchangeable. Each member has a specific task to perform and a role to play.

Much can be made of that, but I would ask you to step behind the thought. Why is it that we are such members? Paul tell us here that it is because of the Lord's Supper. By that he certainly does not mean that any mindless person who participates is a member. Rather, he means that we share in the death of Christ. And because we share together, we are one body. It is not the emblem, but rather the sacrifice for which it stands, which makes us one.

We can understand that readily in our time. Many of us work in large offices with many people—but our friends are those who join us in our homes. When you have "broken bread" with someone, sharing a meal, they are much closer to you. If that is true for any ordinary meal, how much more true should it be of those who share the most sacred of meals? We are one in the body.

> We are one in geography. It does not matter where you live; if you take the body and blood of Jesus Christ, you are one with me.

> We are one in time. The monk of the Middle Ages, the writer of the early ages of the Church, they are one with us too. When "the trumpet of the Lord shall sound and time shall be no more," they shall join us at that final roll call. Our oneness will be apparent.

> We are one in the winds of doctrine. The church is not based upon careful understanding of church councils and decrees but on the body and blood of Jesus Christ. Even our own divisions cannot prevail against Him. If you name the name of Jesus, call Him Lord and Savior, and break bread at His table, we are one.

We are one in the Spirit, too. We often think ourselves so weak and the world so strong. It is not so. He who spoke and the worlds began calls us His own—and we are one with Him.

Everything Comes From God
1 Corinthians 11:3-16

No concept in the Bible so infuriates the "liberated woman" as much as the idea that woman should be in submission to man—particularly in marriage. Hidden in this passage—which is full of commands which made a great deal of sense to the first-century Christian, and puzzle us—is the key to understanding the relationship of submission.

"In the Lord, however, woman is not independent of man, nor is man independent of woman. For as woman came from man, so also man is born of woman. But everything comes from God."

Submission, in the Biblical sense, is simply the idea of being in right relationship—peer to peer, superior to inferior, mankind to God. It does not matter what the relationship is; God commands it be put right. So it is that we are commanded to be obedient to the civil authorities. We might (as Christians) argue that we are free; we are citizens of the Kingdom of God—so who is the local sheriff? But God tells us to be in submission to such authority.

Consider first that God has ordered the universe. In creating man and woman (a temporary division which will be abolished at Christ's return) he has set up not only a biological method of reproduction, but a social order. Our society denies the validity of that order; you may judge for yourself the effects of that denial.

It is also most necessary that *all* Christians are in submission—and not just to God. If the husband is head of the house, he is also in submission to his wife, for his body is not his own, but hers as well—they are one flesh. If he claims authority, he does so by Christ's authority—to which (logically) he must submit.

Why is submission so necessary? What is the great sin of the practicing Christian? If Satan cannot turn you by the flesh or by the world, there is always the deadly sin of pride. By practicing submission you keep yourself from pride, the sin of Satan himself.

Everything comes from God. If you will take good things from his hand, will you not take his instruction as well? Will you not accept the submission he gives you as a blessing from the Father who loves you?

Let a Man Examine Himself
1 Corinthians 11:17-34

When the early church celebrated the Lord's Supper, it seems it was much more physically nourishing than the symbolic method we use today. I suspect that the Passover feast materials were used, and so it was that people were fed there in a physical as well as a spiritual sense. Imagine Paul's outrage, then, when this most sacred of feasts was abused by such flagrant bad manners. From the accusations, one might conclude that the wealthy were the first in line. Those first in line pigged out, leaving nothing for those who came later. If you were first to the wine, you got drunk. No wonder Paul was upset!

Note, however, the retort Paul throws at them: "...do you despise the church of God...?" The terror of this behavior is not simply bad manners. Bad manners are usually a form of lack of respect. In this case, the lack was directed at the church itself. The church, however, is not the building—indeed, in those days, they had no buildings but met in homes. The church is composed of its members. In other words, the rich (in this instance) were despising the poor, and in despising them, despised the church. Could such a thing happen with us today?

I regret to admit it could. I'm not speaking about accusations like "old so-and-so is an elder only because he contributes so much" (you see, the poor can despise the rich too; they call it *envy*), but rather this. When you take communion, do you look around and think, "Look at old so-and-so, that hypocrite! How he can dare to take communion without fear of the roof falling in on him...." You see the point, I hope. Whether it's outright condemnation or the more subtle "I'll have to remember to pray for so-and-so's repentance..." we tend to look around and see the sins and failings of others, rather than examining ourselves.

Make no mistake about it: this is judging others (as in "judge not, that ye be not judged.") Just because it comes under the pious cloak of self-examination makes it no less judgment. Examining myself does not mean comparing myself to others. It means comparing myself to what God wants me to be. When I judge others at the Lord's Table, I'm saying they're not good enough to partake—and I'm despising the church of God.

The command is simple: Let a man examine *himself*—and no one else.

One Spirit
1 Corinthians 12:1-26

Much is made of this passage, and (sadly) much division has come out of it. There are those who insist that if you cannot speak in tongues you must not be a Christian; there are those who say that if you do, you are a fraud. What pain this must be to God, who by Paul's hand here proclaims the fundamental unity of the church. The point is enforced by Paul; please note:

The Common Good

The Spirit (verse 7) is not given for our individual amusement but for the common good. How often we forget that! Whether we speak in tongues or not, we forget that it is not for our glory that the Spirit gives gifts such as wisdom and knowledge. Nor is it because of my selfishness in prayer that the Spirit would grant me faith. Certainly it is not my righteousness that would bring the gift of prophecy. Rather, the Spirit decides these things for the common good of the church. We are one; the Spirit blesses that one.

As he determines

The Spirit gives these gifts as he determines (verse 11). It is not for us to ask for a particular gift; rather ("thy will be done") is it not better to ask the Spirit to determine the gift I should have? Who are we to decide such things? Indeed, for the miraculous gifts of prophecy and healing, for example, the Old Testament teaches us how often they fall on the least likely! This is as the Spirit determines. Man proposes; God disposes.

One honored, all honored

Have you ever banged your thumb with a hammer? Then you know it is of no use saying, "Well, I have nine other digits that aren't throbbing with pain—on balance, I'm pretty well off." Your body won't let you do that. The thumb hurts; you hurt. It is the same with the church. It is also true, though, that if some of us are honored for Christ's sake, all of us are. If we are one in pain we should be one in glory—for we are one in the Spirit.

Christian, consider well: do you ask God for spiritual things for your own ego and gratification, or are you content to let him decide these things? When you get them, do you use them for the Spirit's purpose—the common good of the church? Perhaps the motivation for asking forbids the granting.

No Record of Wrongs
1 Corinthians 12:27-13:13

The corporation, as an institution, has been a major source of employment for a little over a century. Companies are often compared to feudal kingdoms, but there are two key differences. There are two things kingdoms had that corporations lack.

The first is a court jester. Corporate life is very sober and serious, giving the impression that it is of supreme importance. It is not; it lasts but a few years—but we are designed to live forever.

The other and more serious lack is that of a court priest. It is not so much the ritual that is missing as the key function of the priest of that time: dispensing forgiveness. It is a saying in corporations that "you advance until your first mistake." Hence so many are so anxious to avoid even the appearance of a mistake. But in our ruthless pursuit of "perfection" in corporate life, do we not throw away many able human beings along the way?

The failure is this: in corporate life, we keep a record of wrongs. Everything you do that is not successful is recorded carefully, for your competitors will want that ammunition. There is no forgiveness.

Suppose God operated that way! As the Psalmist says, "If you, O Lord, kept a record of sins, O Lord, who could stand?" But God in his mercy keeps no record of sin for those who are forgiven in the blood of Jesus Christ.

How is it that God sees the wisdom of keeping no record of wrongs—and we see it just the opposite way? It is because the world operates on the principles of hate, fear and greed—but God is love. Corporate life will eventually fade away, but the word of the Lord is forever.

Christians, who are the earthly picture of Christ, the imitation of God, filled with the Holy Spirit, should indeed use the same principles. We too should keep no record of wrongs. Sadly, so many of us keep detailed, exact records of wrongs against ourselves. Why? Because we do not love our brothers. We may appreciate their efforts, enjoy their company, sympathize with them in times of trouble—but still keep the books open.

This should not be. Does the name of your Christian brother and enemy spring to mind? Go to God; forgive that brother and ask forgiveness yourself. Then go to your brother and begin again—this time in love.

Job, Suffering
Job 1-3

Some scholars regard this as the oldest book in the Bible. If so, it is fitting: it speaks about suffering. No problem so besets the Christian as that of the suffering of those who are innocent. In these opening chapters, however, we can see some guidance for those who suffer.

Do not accuse God

"Job did not sin by charging God with wrongdoing." Those who do not believe in God often accuse us of "creating God in our own image." The charge is false, and here is the evidence of it. If God is "just like us" then it would be reasonable to accuse him of our own failings. But God is holy. Therefore, to accuse him of wrongdoing is to place a false accusation against him, which is, of course, sinful.

Do you want comfort? Where do you seek it, from strangers or from friends? From friends? The first step of friendship is to get to know someone. To know God is to know he is holy.

Do not lose your integrity

There is a curious thought from Job's wife: to curse God is to lose your integrity. How is this? Job is a man who did not deserve to suffer. His integrity (the word can be translated innocence) is based upon this. If calamity comes, does he turn from being a righteous man into a sinner? If so, he has lost his integrity, his "oneness" —and his relationship to God.

Do not expect to know "WHY"

Job suffers (quite eloquently) for many chapters. At the end, he still never knows why he suffered such terrible things. We know the result, by revelation; he did not. It is entirely characteristic of God that he does not reveal his reasoning to us. It may be simple, or it may be beyond our understanding—but it certainly is something that belongs to God. Job never learns "why." Most of us never do.

Christian, take a lesson from this righteous man of so many years ago. Are you suffering? Do not accuse God as if he were a human being. Do you suffer unjustly? Keep your integrity; don't blame God. Are you puzzled as to why you are suffering? Job did not know either; but even our Lord Jesus suffered. Should we expect less? Suffering is a great mystery; but God is greater still.

Blessed is the Man
Job 4-7

In the surpassing poetry that is the Book of Job we find much in the way of wisdom. Eliphaz, one of Job's three comforters (from whom Job seems to draw little comfort) shows us such here.

Can a mortal be more righteous than God?

The question needs but to be stated to see the answer. How strange, then, that we so often presume to give advice to God. So often our prayers are not the requests of children to their heavenly Father, but a laundry list and set of directions for fixing our part of the world. It is not strange at all, then, that God does not hear. Eliphaz hears the hushed voice asking, and his hair stands on end. The ghostly terror of knowing that he is in the presence of the awesome righteousness of God does this. It is an emotion we would do well to cultivate, for it would show that we have some idea of the righteousness of God, and of our own sinfulness.

I would lay my case before him.

Do you feel that events, people or even God himself have treated you unjustly? Then take your case to God. Does this seem strange to you? Read the Psalms; over and again the psalmists complain to God of the injustice of things. How the wicked prosper; how the righteous are neglected—and yet always with the hope of God's redemption. Is justice denied you? He is the God of justice. Are your pains great? He is the God of comfort. Bring your troubles to him; he cares for you and loves you so greatly.

Blessed is the man whom God corrects.

As you bring your troubles before him, understand this: he loves you, and therefore will discipline you. This is not a sign of his anger; it is a sign of his love. Indeed, the very troubles of which you complain may be his correction. Do not complain of his correction; rather, accept it and do as he asks. Give him the joy of your repentance.

All of this is good advice. But there is one bit more. When a man is suffering, good advice is no substitute for a good friend. If your friend is suffering, do not come with advice only. Come with a warm heart, a hug and a listening ear. Be the comfort that you would have in similar circumstances. Who knows? You may be the living image of Christ this very day.

One Fact, One Doctrine
1 Corinthians 15:1-28

C. S. Lewis once remarked that Christianity could almost be reduced to one fact and one doctrine. The fact would be the Resurrection; the doctrine redemption by grace. We see both of them proclaimed in this passage.

"Of first importance" —the Resurrection

Paul does not lightly pass on the good news of the Resurrection; he calls it "of first importance." So it is! But see how his argument is made:

First, that this death, burial and resurrection are in accordance with the Scriptures—in this instance meaning the Old Testament prophecies. This was not a random event but the plan of God from the very beginning.

Next, this was not some vague event in the distant past, but something well known to many witnesses. Those witnesses saw him die. Their actions at his death show us clearly that they did not think he could rise from the grave. *But he did.*

"By the grace of God I am what I am"

Paul was a man who knew what he deserved. His first reception in the church after his conversion shows clearly that the church did not trust him. They had good reason for this; he was one who had vigorously persecuted the church. If we were the ones in judgment on Paul I suspect we would have been much harsher with him. But see how God treats one who persecuted the church:

He grants to him grace—unmerited forgiveness. Paul had no chance to make amends when God called him. He wanted Paul (and us) to know that he is merciful.

He did not confine him to the basement of the church, but rather appointed him to a place of high honor—which is to say, a place of great service. For honor in the church comes not with position but with service.

There it is. The power that raised Christ from the grave, the power that triumphed over the deadliest enemy we have, death itself, proclaims to all the doctrine of grace. Those who believe are forgiven; they are saved to serve others. Those who were his enemies are now his children. Amazing, grace.

If a Man Dies...
Job 12-15

"If a man dies, will he live again?" It is the question among questions, for all men die.

Job puts it before us in his lament. But we may not take it out of the context:

Job begins by telling us of the might of God; so strong, so powerful that nothing he purposes to do can be foiled. He is Lord of all living things; he can turn the wisest of counselors into fools and the most powerful of kings into madmen. Nations rise and fall at his desire.

In the presence of the Almighty, then, what is man? Job knows what he is: a man with grave troubles, but one who is anxious to state his case to his God. Why, he asks, does God pursue and torment one so insignificant as Job?

For indeed he knows that any man is insignificant before the God who created all things. Our lifetimes are short; he is eternal. We are sinners; he is righteous.

In the face of such futility, Job asks: "If a man dies, will he live again?" The question is often repeated. But Job also gives the answer here, though it is seldom remembered. For a time man will be concealed in the grave. Then, those who love the Lord will be called by God. God will "count my steps" but "not keep track of my sin." For those who love the Lord, the resurrection is sure.

Job is, by some scholars' accounts, the oldest book in the Bible. If this is so, then no other revelation to man has been recorded before this one. How, then, is Job so sure that God will call him out of the grave?

"You will long for the creature your hands have made." In that one statement is the resurrection of the dead. We are creatures made by the hand of God, formed in our mothers through his power, which upholds all things physical. He will long for us; that is, he loves us and wants us. Therefore, out of his love he will call us forth. That this implies the Cross to come, Job did not see. He did not need to see the Cross in the dim future; the love of God in the clear present was sufficient. For all whom God loves, his love is sufficient to triumph, even over death.

My Redeemer Lives
Job 16-19

If this is the oldest book in the Bible, as some say, then not only was the advent of our Lord planned from the very beginning, it was announced in the first writings. Job clearly shows us that he has seen some vision of the Holy One of Israel, the Christ.

My advocate is on high

Poor Job! He is in utter sadness for his loss, and his three friends—who supposedly came to comfort him—have spent most of their words explaining that (obviously) Job is suffering for his sins. As his suffering is great, they reason, so must his sins, however well hidden they might be. But Job knows better. He knows his own conduct; and he knows that such an accusation will be defended against in the courts of heaven. But by whom? Job names him:

"My witness" —the one who has seen what I have done, and testifies to God about it.

"My advocate"—the one who pleads my case before the Judge, the Almighty.

"My intercessor"—the one who stands between me and the Judge, taking upon Himself my sins and penalties.

"My friend"—not a hired attorney, bought with sacrifices, but one who is Love Himself.

These four terms are a powerful description of Jesus Christ, thousands of years before he came. Job sees clearly, because Job knows the character of God.

His vision extends further still. He sees beyond the first advent of our Lord to the second.

"My Redeemer lives" —not, "will come" but lives; the everliving one is my redeemer.

In the end, Job knows, he will stand upon the earth. Not some ghostly presence, nor a faceless god announced by a prophet; no, this Redeemer will stand.

When will Job see this? After the destruction of his body—and Job will see him with his own eyes. His foresight has seen the resurrection of the saints.

See clearly, like Job. Believe steadfastly, like Job. The time is coming. Your Redeemer lives—and is coming again.

Affliction and Comfort
2 Corinthians 1:1-11

It is a fact: affliction and comfort go together in the life of a mature Christian. It is a form of Newton's Third Law: for every action there is an equal and opposite reaction. For every affliction, there is an equal and opposite comfort from God.

Why does God allow us to go through affliction? The Apostle brings up some very good reasons here:

First, so that we will see what God can do. Is your affliction great? Then the comfort of God will be great, too. Those who are mature Christians sometimes look back and say, "I don't know how I got through that—and I would have bet that I couldn't get through it." We think we could not bear this or that, but God shows us his power in what he raises up to be able to bear.

Having done that, a second purpose is revealed: that we might comfort others. There is no use in hearing "I know how you feel" from one who plainly does not know how you feel. But to hear it from one who has been through the same thing means this: if my Christian brother could get through it then, with God's help, so can I. We are to encourage one another.

More than encouragement: we are to share. One of the wisest women I know once asked, "How will they learn to give if you will not receive?" And how can I learn to receive what others will give if not in affliction? Affliction welds the body of Christ together most strongly.

Finally, affliction turns us from thoughts of our own strength to complete reliance on God's strength. The Apostle tells us here that he and his friends were under such pressure that they despaired of living. No doubt they asked why. God gives the answer: so that they might learn to rely entirely upon Him.

There is one last thing. As God takes us through afflictions (note the plurals) we gradually develop that sure and certain hope that says, "He has taken me through so much; he will take me through all that is ahead of me; then he will take me home to be with him." By affliction God builds his saints. Rely on him in all your troubles, and show the world his handiwork.

The Conclusion of Discipline
2 Corinthians 2:1-11

Piecing together Paul's comments we can see what has happened. Paul has been obliged to write and visit the Corinthians in an effort to produce church discipline. The object of that discipline is always the restoration of a fallen Christian. Paul shows us the last part of that process—one that is often neglected.

First, he reminds the Corinthians that if this man has caused Paul grief, it is just a part of the grief given to the church. In this he shows the unity of the church, for if one part of the body hurts, the body hurts. So he establishes that "we" have been grieved, not just "me."

Then he reminds them that punishment has been inflicted. This implies that no more is due; we should not continue to afflict those who have repented. Indeed, he says the punishment is sufficient.

Rather than continuing to punish, we should first forgive and then comfort the one who has repented. The purpose of such discipline is to produce restoration, not depression. To prevent that "overwhelming sorrow" we are to comfort the one punished. This is the way we say, "We still love you."

Not by command but by example Paul tells them to forgive. Indeed, his forgiveness is such that he is willing to be bound by their forgiveness. If the Corinthians forgive, Paul forgives, and so Paul shows his unity with the Corinthian church.

Just to make certain that they understand this, he tells them that this is no "private" forgiveness. He has "registered" that forgiveness with Christ, so that it may not be revoked. By this method he reassures the sinner that forgiveness is not on a trial basis, but a completed act.

So by these steps the repentant sinner is welcomed back into the family of God. Why? Wouldn't it be more polite just to drop the matter out of conversation? Let bygones be bygones? No indeed! We must not forget that Satan is looking for an opportunity. Will that sinner hear, "How do you know they have *really* forgiven you?" The answer must be plain; you are forgiven and you know it by the love we showed in welcoming you back home. Don't tie a yellow ribbon; tie a thousand.

August 28

My Soul Thirsts for God
Psalm 42

The Psalmist here is suffering. The words have often been put into a song of joy, but the Psalmist is suffering here. So often, however, we do not know joy from sorrow. Are we persecuted? Then we long for God, and often we are closest to him at such a time. Here the Psalmist thirsts for God.

It seems bleak. "Where is your God?" his friends ask him. He remembers with tears the processions of joy.

But up from the soul wells the hope of the servant of God. Why are you upset? Why is there a frown? Do you not know whom you serve? This is no ordinary prince, a man like other mortals, whom you call Lord. No, this is the King of Kings, the Lord of Lords, the ruler of heaven and earth—He who spoke, and the worlds began. Put your hope in Him, and in no one else. Fear God; dread naught.

My soul is downcast? I will look to the past, when I praised Him with great joy. Has he changed? Not at all. I praised him with joy before; I will praise him again.

Do I lack evidence of his care? Consider well: "deep calls to deep"—the roar of nature attests to nature's creator, the God who cares for all creation will care for those who love him.

What is God doing? He is growing the virtue of *hope*. Hope is "the evidence of things not seen." Hope is the certainty that the unchanging God who loved me yesterday continues to love me today and will do so through all my days.

The song writers have cast these words of despair and grasping for the living God into one of triumph. The realist says, "I am in despair, how can I hope?" But the song writer, the artist, says, "I am in despair, how can I not hope?" For when things are at their worst God is at his best. In our weakness he is made strong. In our deficiencies is his perfection shown. Will he abandon his children? It cannot be; he is from age to age the same. His children are his love, to the point of the Cross.

Christian, are you in despair tonight? Does the burden seem impossible? Hear the words of one who carried such a burden thousands of years ago. "Put your hope in God, for I will yet praise Him, my Savior and my God."

Craftsmanship
2 Corinthians 3

In some way lost to history there was a dispute referenced here about letters of recommendation. Paul disdains such, for an obvious reason: the craftsman is known by his work, not by the letters people write.

There is a point there for every mature Christian. Do you want to know how you are doing? Would you like to know what kind of Christian you really are? You are sending out your letters of recommendation in those you teach.

Consider first your children. Have you ever been to a restaurant in which someone has brought an ill-behaved little child? You don't say, "How unfortunate for her; the child was born ill-behaved." Instead, you think, "I could tell you a lot about how to raise that kid—can you spell the word *discipline*?" Turn the question around. If someone encountered your children, what kind of letter of recommendation would they be for you?

It is a difficult question. Our children, whether we admit it or not, are sinners just as we are. So we may think, "How can this sinner hope to bring forth children who are godly?" Paul gives us the answer here. In our own strength we will produce children who are no better than we are. In God's strength we can produce those who are indeed much better. (Indeed, ask a grandfather; it seems that if you give this a couple of generations they are magnificent indeed.)

Teachers face the same problem. Teachers are not pure and completely righteous—but by the power of God their students may excel in righteousness. A teacher is not known by his own righteousness, but by the power in his students. If he conveys the power of God, he has done well for them.

If left to our own devices we will sink; if we reach to God we will rise. Now then, as this is so, what limit can be placed upon us? If God works through us, then our children, our students and all those we touch may surpass us in holiness, righteousness and blessing by God. This is not our own work, but God working through us.

If we look backward and say, "my teacher was great," then we decline. Look forward, saying, "God is awesome and great." Then your teacher will be a starting point, and your students be your recommendation letters to God.

Jars of Clay
2 Corinthians 4:1-12

God, it seems, does not understand the first thing about advertising.

The way of the advertising world is this: if you want to sell a machine to make your body strong, you hire a strong man to advertise it. Who would buy one from a pot-bellied spokesman? If you want to sell perfume, show it going on beautiful women. Cars are shown racing, not at a stop sign.

God takes the opposite way. He packages up the truth in "jars of clay" as Paul puts it. His apostle describes himself as one battered in every way—but defeated not at all. It would seem not much of an advertisement for the Gospel that its spokesman could be so persecuted.

Why is this? So that we might see that God's word is the truth. In the advertising world man seeks to put the best possible appearance on the product. We see the products of this world at their best; we see the product of God at its worst. This is because God not only tells the truth, he does so in the truth—because his Word is truth.

This has an effect which no advertising of our age can match. We look at this and say, "It must be the truth; no one would do that for a lie." Or at least that is what God desires.

Paul subtly hints at a problem in this. It is possible that a man would be willing to suffer persecution not for the truth but for the message he himself has invented. The desires of the flesh and the world can be barred with persecution; pride will go on. So Paul gives us another test of the true minister of God. He does not preach himself, that is, he does not glorify himself. He preaches (and glorifies) Jesus Christ.

It is a fact: whoever would preach Jesus Christ will "carry around" the death of Jesus—for in that death is life in Jesus. As he was persecuted, so shall his followers be, until he comes again. But as he was triumphant, so shall his followers be. Even to the point of death, his followers must show his life in themselves.

This is a life of sacrifice. To the world it appears to be a hard life, and one which is unprofitable. To those who love the Lord, the burden is light, for this is the triumphant life. It is a test for each of us: do we show the truth in truth, in our daily lives?

Where Were You?
Job 38-39

Over thirty chapters in the book of Job are devoted to Job's complaint and the explanations of his friends. The matter of his intense suffering is examined by wise men, each seeking to explain the agony of Job. Out of the storm God answers Job.

And does not answer him at all. Job has pleaded his case; Job has declared his innocence; Job has declared his trust in God. His friends have accused him of being a secret sinner; his friends have justified God. Now God replies—on God's terms.

The point, made in magnificent poetry, is simple. All the pleading of man, all the wisdom we store up, all the explanations we concoct, are insignificant in the sight of God. For us to say to God, "Why did you do that?" is akin to telling God that he has made a mistake. He reminds Job of this: he is not talking to an equal. He is talking to God.

This is a puzzle to us. We ask, like the disciples, "why was this man born blind?" Sometimes the answer comes back, "So that you might see the glory of God." That is true in this passage.

Suppose Job did get an explanation of his suffering (as we did, early in the book). Suppose God explained to him, in painful detail, how his suffering was required as a part of God's divine plan for the universe. Job would still need to suffer; the pain would be no less from the loss of his children. His disease would be no easier to bear. Indeed, it is possible it might be worse. Think of your own sufferings. Had you known beforehand, what would you have felt?

That we will suffer is guaranteed. The only questions are how, how much, and when. God knows the answers to those questions too, but in mercy declines to tell us. In other words, in his great mercy he declines to reveal our futures to us. Is it not therefore likely that it is his mercy which causes him to conceal the reasons for our sufferings in the past?

One thing is certain. God is wise beyond our understanding. We are told that his way is perfect, flawless. Like many others, I have had times when it does not appear perfect to me. I have asked, "Why me?" I have said, "Lord, your way may be perfect, but this is one intelligent man who just doesn't understand it."

He never said I would understand how his way is perfect. He just said it is. "Where were you when I laid the earth's foundation?"

Reconciliation
2 Corinthians 5:11-21

Reconciliation has become a "church word." It was not always so. Reconciliation still has meaning, however. We can speak of fathers and sons being reconciled to each other, meaning that they no longer stand apart, but return to love each other.

The ultimate meaning of reconciliation is in Jesus Christ. Paul here tells us the secret of spreading this reconciliation.

First, we must view everyone from God's point of view. Is the man a wicked sinner? He is one for whom Christ died. Is he a cynic? It is but the symptom of his blindness. Does he appear rich and charitable? It means nothing without the Cross.

We must not judge by human standards; indeed, judgment is extremely risky. Rather, we should view all as fallen children of God—and deliver the message of reconciliation to them.

Note that this ministry called "reconciliation" is entrusted to "us." Paul keeps using those plural pronouns! It is our ministry, not the ministry reserved for the few. It is not evangelism or preaching, but reconciliation.

Note that ours is the message. It is entrusted to us, and we must handle it with care. We did not create the message, and so must not tamper with it—just deliver it.

But we are not just messenger boys. We are ambassadors of Christ; we are in authority. As long as you follow your instructions, ambassador, you may commit the one who sent you. Is forgiveness needed? Offer it, in Jesus name. He has the power to forgive sins; you have the authority to convey that power.

The reconciliation is not by our own power. It is in Christ that we find out righteousness, not ourselves. So we can safely say that we understand the sinner—for we are sinners too. Only in the power of Christ can we reconcile men to God.

We are ambassadors of reconciliation—to the whole world. God has reconciled the world to Himself through Christ. We are those who represent that Gospel; let us not forget that "Gospel" means "good news." Ambassadors of Good News—that's us.

The Paradox of Christian Living
2 Corinthians 6:1-13

Paul has a gift for listing the things that happen to a worker for God—probably because so many of those things happened to him. Here is one of those lists; see how much of this you recognize as your Christian experience:

Glory and dishonor. The church sees you as one who strives for Christ, and therefore worthy. The world sees you as a fanatic for some strange religion—probably a nutcase.

Bad report and good report. The newspapers of our time see Christians as fools and villains. Those who see real Christians know their love.

Genuine, seen as imposters. You struggle with the call to holiness, knowing that you are a sinner and imperfect. You call on God for mercy. The world sees you as a pious fraud, a hypocrite, for no one could be serious about righteousness.

Known, yet unknown. The doctrine of the church is plain and aboveboard, posted on the wall and written in the Scripture. The world says that there must be more to it—some hidden agenda, some secret cause.

Dying, yet we live on. For some this is literally true. For others, it seems that we "don't know how to live." We seem to just exist, faithful to one spouse, not seeking the next thrill.

Sorrowful, yet always rejoicing. How can these Christians be so sour about the state of the world, calling sin what the world calls freedom, and yet be so joyous?

Poor, yet making many rich. Counted by money, we are often the poor. Counted by true riches, the wealthiest of all mankind are we.

Having nothing, yet everything. All the things that do not really matter seem to escape us. All the things that do, are ours. How can this be, asks the world?

Is this a description of your life? The world wonders how someone with so little in the way of worldly wealth, thrills and pride can be so completely joyous about life. Perhaps it is that we understand true life. After all, we've met Him.

My Big Mouth
Ecclesiastes 5:1-7

Of all the methods for getting into trouble, the mouth is usually the quickest. This is no less true in the house of God than anywhere else.

Some of us approach the house of God with a light heart. It seems warm and friendly, as it often has been designed to be. The warmth sometimes distracts us from the nature of God—the awesome creator of the universe. Solomon gives us wisdom here. We should not enter the house of God casually, but with a great sense of purpose. When we arrive, we should be prepared to listen.

Prepared to listen? Have you ever watched a congregation during a sermon? After the first two minutes you will notice a great deal of activity which is anything but listening. Why? Because we did not come to listen; we came to "participate." Listening is hard work; it means that we are taking in the preacher's words and applying them to our lives. It is much easier to "tune out" for a while and pick it up again later. As long as we say, "Amen" at the right time, we feel we have done well. But we haven't.

It can be worse. Sometimes we do listen—and decide to act. Whether or not we speak our intentions out loud, we sometimes make a promise to God—a vow—that we will do something. We will apologize to our spouse, we will not get so angry, or any number of other things.

Then we leave the house of God—and somehow the promise gets left behind as well. But do not be deceived. God was listening the first time; he is eternal; he will expect you to live up to your word. If you do not, what then? You have lied to God—even though you "didn't mean to." Do you expect he will ignore the point?

Approach the house of God with humility. Remember that we are all sinners, in need of God's grace. Do not go to tell him how wonderful you are; sing his praises instead. Do not go to tell him of the great things you will do; thank him for his great deeds instead. Above all, do not take God lightly. He did not take your sins lightly; he sent his Son to the Cross so that you might have the privilege of entering the house of God forever. That is no light thing. Therefore, be glad—be thankful—and be serious about it.

Quiet Words
Ecclesiastes 9:17

My mother never yelled at me. She did not have to.

My mother has a way with the still, small voice. It is sometimes frustrating to argue with her, for she does not argue. She merely states what she believes to be the truth, and states it in a calm, low voice. Such is the way of wisdom.

Truth must be told in a truthful way. If it is wisdom you are telling, then it must be told in a wise way. The way of wisdom is in the quietness of the soul which is completely under God's control. Therefore, if you look for wisdom, do not expect to hear it being trumpeted. Do not expect it in the blare of advertising, or the pious pomp of political campaigning. Listen for it in the still, small voice.

Solomon had great wisdom, and sought it all the more. From him we get most of the book of Proverbs. Like many since, he pondered the folly of life, wondering whether or not it really had any meaning. Not until the end of this book does he pronounce judgment on that, but along the way he gives us this advice. Consider that he had plenty of opportunities to hear the shouts of the rulers of fools! Such men are still with us; their speeches still fill the daily news. Some people still believe that this political party, or that politician, or this movement, or that philosophy will become an all-conquering bandwagon. Remember when communism was the irresistible wave of the future?

Do not seek the shout of the moment. Each new year brings us another announcement that science has finally triumphed, putting all knowledge and power within our reach. Strangely, next year this thought will be "obsolete." Truth is never obsolete, though often out of fashion. Wisdom is always worth hearing—though sometimes you must listen carefully through the noise of fools.

"I am the Way, the Truth, the Life," said Jesus. In him Solomon's quest for ultimate wisdom is satisfied. In him is the source of all wisdom. Indeed, the very foolishness of God is greater than the wisdom of man—so the wisdom of God must be very great indeed, far beyond our own ability to think through and debate. But it is not beyond our ability to hear, and to heed. We do not need to know *how* God's wisdom can be so great. We only need to know that it is.

September 5

First to the Lord
2 Corinthians 8:1-15

Paul was not shy about his criticisms, nor about his praise. Here he has reason to praise the Macedonian churches for their generosity. Giving during a time of wealth is good; giving during a time of poverty is indeed Godly.

There is in this passage the secret of giving. Have you ever, in your daydreams, said, "If I ever inherited a million dollars, I'd..."? Of course; but most of us never inherit the million dollars. God is not concerned with what you *would do*; he is greatly concerned with what you *will do*. Here the Macedonians give us the secret of giving which is pleasing to God.

They gave themselves first to the Lord. Above all else, they sought to serve the Lord God Almighty. This is the secret of devotion. By so doing, they placed themselves at the service of God, and he made use of them as he saw best—much to their benefit and joy. Consider this: though poor—and by our standards "exempt" from giving—they pleaded with Paul for the privilege of sharing.

Have you ever been left out of the game? Have you ever been the one who was always left sitting on the bench? That's how the Macedonian churches must have felt. Poor, and therefore never asked to help others, they had to plead with Paul for the privilege of giving! Only those who have given themselves in devotion to God would do such a thing.

The Macedonians set an example. We learn a little from our books, a bit more from our speakers—but volumes from the examples in front of us. These Christians set the example of giving, and here Paul urges the Corinthians to do likewise. God is not concerned with what he has given you (though no doubt he has given careful attention to the matter) but rather what you do with it. Are you faithful in the little with which he has trusted you? If not, how do you expect to gain the riches of the kingdom of God?

Christian, consider it this way: you are a steward of whatever wealth and possessions you have. Do you hold them tightly in your hands? If so, your hand is closed; God can put no more in it. A pond holds a little water; a canal can transfer much water. Are you the pond holding a little of God's blessing, or the channel through which his grace is poured? You decide; his grace flows in the way you have decided.

All Night Long
Song of Songs 3:1-4

Of all the books of the Old Testament none is less familiar to the average Christian than Canticles, or the Song of Solomon. This is no surprise, for when we open it we find in it poetry (a lost art to most of us); love poetry at that. It seems, somehow, out of place in the Holy Bible. It is not. The God who created heaven and earth, the God who is Love, created love between man and woman. He created it, and named it a picture of the love between Christ and his church—and with that picture to guide us, we can see the Spirit in the Song.

All night long

There may be Christians whose life never shows the slightest variation in the intensity of their spiritual condition. They may go from one spiritual peak leaping to the next, with no valley between. I am not one of those, nor do I know any. There are long nights in the Christian experience. But note the first condition of the long nights: they are spent "on my bed." It is when I will not move to Him that I cannot see or find him.

Get up now

It is only when I get up and begin to search again for the lover of my soul that things change. Even then, the result is not immediate. In the searching I learn again just how much I love Him. In his absence my heart aches; in that pain I measure my love for him. The search sometimes seems long, but never fruitless.

The watchmen

The search is not a lone one. There are those around me—watchmen, appointed by God—of whom I may inquire. So many of us think our spiritual life to be a solo flight, when our Lord tells us (nowhere less than here) that it is a group effort. How this lover is accompanied! She by her friends; Solomon by his sixty warriors. Ask those who are watchmen in your life—"where is He?"

I found the one my heart loves

He who seeks, finds. He who asks, receives. Knock; it will be opened. Jesus is anxious that you ask, seek and knock so that he may come in to you. Look for him, Christian—you will surely find him. Just as the night is darkest before the dawn, it may appear black to you now. But at the dawning you will see Jesus turning towards you; your heart will leap with joy again. He never fails.

September 7

The Cheerful Giver
2 Corinthians 9

Sometimes it is unfortunate that we have chapters and verses in the Bible, for it is tempting to quote the verse and leave the surrounding words alone. The passage about the "cheerful giver" is frequently quoted in the church—usually as part of an offertory message—but the rest of the section is usually ignored.

Principle: sowing and reaping

No one need tell a farmer that the more acreage you sow, the more harvest you reap. But like any financial investor today, the farmer would plan his sowing carefully. So it is with our giving to God. We need to plan ahead in doing it. Consider the opposite: suppose we only gave when someone made an emotional, last-minute appeal. Giving would be chaos tinged with more than a little cynicism.

Principle: plan on God

The farmer looks to the land and the rain; the investor to the state of the business—and the Christian to God. God asks him to give not in fear or compulsion, but gladly—joy is the hallmark of a true Christian; if you feel compelled to give or afraid of being found out, then you are giving out of the wrong motives. How then do I receive such joy? It starts with knowing that God will supply my needs. That he may do so by taking from me the money I have to supply my wants and whims is also the case.

Principle: God provides for the kingdom

Some would view this as a crude investment: I give generously to the church, God takes care of me and I get richer, and the cycle continues. For those who have the right spirit, this in fact happens— because they expect God to provide that which is necessary for righteousness. As they take on more financial responsibility (whether in the offering plate or in personal charity) they know that God will provide for their needs.

Principle: Shared Thanksgiving

If you indeed give with this in mind, God will indeed provide. There is an interesting effect to this. Your needs are met; you are blessed; you thank God. But your giving also meets the needs of others—who give thanks to God. So God is praised twice: once in your giving, once in their receiving. Indeed, it is a wonderful thing: that God is praised in your giving. Are you rich in this world? Provoke the poor to praise God for your generosity.

Weapons
2 Corinthians 10

The mark of a warrior is his weaponry. If you were to go to a hobby shop that sells toy soldiers you could see little distinction between the faces of the soldiers. The distinction between a Roman legionnaire and a French soldier of World War I would be in the weapons, not in the faces.

We too can be told by our weaponry. The weapons of Satan are many; hatred, greed, pride, to name a few. The weapons of the Christian are completely different. They have some interesting characteristics:

They are completely distinct from the weapons of the world. You can tell who is a Christian very quickly by the weapons he chooses. Does he quickly decide to use his tongue to slice and dice a slower foe? It is Satan's weapon, and no good will come from it.

The weapons are those of peace and love. Their effects may include sorrow, but this is godly sorrow, which produces repentance.

These weapons are not based entirely (or even primarily) upon emotion. They are based upon God's own power. So it may appear to the world that they are not "logical" (in the world's use of that word) because they do not accept the restrictions of the world. But they are powerful weapons.

They are powerful weapons in so far as they reflect the power of their creator. As the one who wields them reflects the life of Christ within himself, they grow in power, even as the soldier of the cross appears to become less and less significant. This is because these weapons bring honor to Christ – not to the Christian who wields them.

These weapons do not obey the world's limits. Indeed, they are the weapons of God, and as such they cannot be limited by the world's devices. Those who wield them may appear to be weak and small, but the one behind those weapons is omnipotent.

Christian, whose weapons do you wield? Yours? The world's? Or those of God? Perhaps the lack of power you feel in combat with the world comes from the choice of weapons you have made.

"Woe to Those"
Isaiah 3-5

In the midst of a passage which is clearly prophetic of the Lord's return Isaiah gives us a series of "Woe to Those." It is instructive. Such laments are usually passed over quickly—but see the things that God hates, the things which bring God's wrath to those who practice them:

Those who live only to drink (those who are "heroes at drinking wine")—no surprise in that!

Those who say to God, "Hurry up! Return as you promised!" Some of these are among us, saying that since God has yet to return, he never will.

Those who take evil—and call it good. In our day we have seen abortion called "choice"; homosexuality is "an alternate lifestyle" and those who believe in God are, of course, "right-wing fundamentalist fanatics."

Those who consider themselves wise—in our day, those who believe that man, not God, is the ultimate authority on right and wrong.

The list is by no means complete, but it is sufficient to show us two things: first, that Isaiah in his time saw such things—we are not unique or new in any way. Second, that such things are a characteristic of those times when God sends mighty deliverance to the righteous and punishment to the wicked.

God is patient. It is not his desire that any of us should perish—not even those who mock his name, deny his existence and presume to tell him what right and wrong now ought to be. God is so truly pure love that even these are to be rescued, if possible. But there comes a time when it is clear that further decline is the only possible direction, and God must intervene.

We pride ourselves on our military might. We are sure that we are untouchable. So thought many empires of the past, and their corrupted remains are still with us. Sometimes God sends one to bring the message of repentance; sometimes, later, he sends one to bring the message of justice—and destruction.

Christian, it is not too late. Ask your God to send out those who will reform our civilization, those who will bring it to repentance. But beware: you are not asking for this in a vacuum. As one Christian put it, "Lord, reform thy world—beginning with me."

A Man of Unclean Lips
Isaiah 6

There is a sense of awe that surrounds the living God. Unfortunately for us, we have lost this sense. Isaiah shows it here: "I am a man of unclean lips, and I live among a people of unclean lips, and my eyes have seen the King, the Lord Almighty." It is the sense of Peter, begging the Lord to leave him after he stills the waves—I am too much the sinner to stand in the presence of pure holiness; I court my own destruction merely by standing in the presence of the Holy God.

We understand the sensation only dimly. A few times in my life I have been in the presence of those who were utterly saintly. My immediate reaction was split: should I stay in the presence of one who is so human and yet so close to divine—or should I leave immediately, for I do not belong here? Men are sometimes stunned into silence by the presence of a beautiful woman; how much greater the silence caused by the awesome God.

God understands that in us. We spend much of our lives trying to ignore the fact that we are sinners—but when confronted with holiness and purity, the facts are too obvious and the shame too much. We cannot stand in his presence; indeed, to fall flat on our faces and worship is impudence. But God here sends an angel to Isaiah, to purge him of sin, so that he might—by God's grace and not by his own work—be counted worthy to be in the presence of the Holy God.

Thus forgiven, Isaiah hears the words of the Living God. Evidently he has been forgiven for a purpose: God needs a messenger. God does not ask Isaiah; he merely states the need. There is no compulsion except the awesome presence of God—and that is enough to produce unlimited commitment. "Here am I. Send me!"

God the Father has been merciful enough to each and every Christian to purge him of sin by the blood of Christ. We are called into his presence by the work of the Cross; we are admitted into the very throne of God by the kinship of our Redeemer. We are in the presence of the holy, awesome God. He asks of us no service; he demands of us no sacrifice; he merely states what must be done. By asking and demanding nothing, he impels the Christian to offer everything. Shall we, like the prophet Isaiah, say, "Here am I. Send me?"

September 11

Sufficient
2 Corinthians 12:1-10

It is the way of the world that great men are arrogant, conceited and worshiped. It is the way of God that great men are humble, knowing their own sins, and pointing other men only to the one true God. Why is it that God has so arranged things?

"to keep me from becoming conceited"—the great enemy of the great saint is pride. God must, at whatever price, prevent those he loves from becoming arrogant and conceited, for this state of mind looks down on others—and therefore cannot look up to God..

"my grace is sufficient for you" —that we might recognize not only the power of God, but that this power is all-sufficient. We respect power, but at the back of the mind is the suspicion, "what if?" God intends that we know that there are no "ifs" with his power.

"my power is made perfect in weakness" —were the power of God displayed as it truly is (have you looked into a clear desert night sky lately?) you would see his awesome nature. But would you repent? Power displayed is one thing; power in perfect use is another. God's power is often used to cause repentance, and that may indeed require my weakness.

"For when I am weak, I am strong." —in my own strength I must match myself against others of similar strength. In his strength there is no match. But his strength requires my weakness, it seems. I must proclaim myself disabled—so that he will be enabled. For as long as I say, "I can do all things" I will not be able to show that "he can do all things."

Christian, do you struggle with your life? Do you wonder why God has given you your difficulties, whether those be spiritual, intellectual, physical or emotional? He knows you. He knows what you will become if you are left to yourself—and the picture is not very pretty. So he comes to you, knocking down your pride, destroying what you see as your strength, showing you his own so that you might show his strength in your life to those around you. You are his witness, his ambassador—the one who testifies to him. How can you be such if you have never felt his power? Thank him for your humbling; praise him that he has made you weak—for in your weakness he displays his strength.

256

Where Will You Leave Your Riches?
Isaiah 10

It is a curious but clear fact: in all the Gospels, Jesus has words of woe for only one group: "woe to you, Scribes and Pharisees." It is the pious hypocrite for whom Jesus pronounces his woes. This is all the more biting because of the words in the "Fifth Gospel" —Isaiah.

Here God pronounces his woe upon those in authority in Israel. He begins with those who make "unjust laws." In our day such a thing is often treated as a contradiction in terms. After all, if it's legal, it's moral, right? God says quite the opposite. He lays upon those who make the laws the responsibility of making those laws reflect his righteousness.

What! Do you mean he expects us to "legislate morality"? Indeed, we do this frequently. Bank robbery is considered immoral, not because it is against the law but because we know it to be wrong; we legislate morality and send the robber to prison. If this is the normal duty of those who legislate, how angry will God be with those who pervert justice in the making of law?

Does such occur? It is the history of the human race that our legislators care little for the powerless—the poor and the oppressed, the widow and the orphan. But before we pronounce too heavily upon those in the halls of the legislature, let us remember that we too have responsibilities in this matter:

We are citizens of a democracy. As such, we share the responsibility of such legislation. It is not the pretty speech that should move us, but the record of action.

In our own little ways, we too are legislators. Do you manage a department? Do you preside over a household? Are you one who sets the rules in your classroom? Then justice must be your guide.

God considers not just the opportunity but the motive. Is your failure to oppress the fatherless and seize the property of the widow merely an accident of your helplessness? You would if you could? God is not deceived.

There is no substitute for a sense of justice. Even those who sit on a jury must weigh the evidence and render true verdict. In our daily lives we face many chances to line our own pockets at the expense of the helpless. God is not deceived; beware!

September 13

The Day of the Lord
Isaiah 13-14

In the mysterious language of the prophet, Isaiah lays out for us a vision. It begins with a vision of "Babylon" —a name in prophecy that stands for evil in the world. For this evil Isaiah reveals that the Day of the Lord is coming—a day of wrath.

Wrath? Is not this the loving God? How can a loving God come in wrath? Consider what the phrase "loving God" really means:

Have you ever poured your heart and soul into a work you cherish – and seen it ruined? Wrath rises with the destruction of the thing you truly love. God loves his creation; evil is the rebellious destruction of that creation. Should he not rise in wrath?

Is there a person you love dearly? How would you react if that person betrayed you? Is not the wickedness of the world a betrayal of the God that loves us dearly?

Only the perfect God can love perfectly. But the perfect God is perfect in righteousness as well; can one who is perfect in righteousness let evil exist forever?

The rebellion of the wicked is a tragedy. We sometimes imagine that the evil in this world are truly that: evil. Remember that all God has created he has created "good." Evil is not the opposite of righteousness—it is the corruption of righteousness.

"How you have fallen from heaven, O morning star, son of the dawn!" The words apply to Satan, who began existence as an angel of the highest order. He fell through pride, the desire to exalt himself above God. Pride is the vilest form of rebellion against God; so it is that Isaiah shows God's desire to "put an end to the arrogance of the haughty."

Christian, you may think this of no application to you. Satan seems something discussed in church, or the comic figure in red tights. That is why Isaiah tells you of the Day of the Lord: the day applies not only to Satan but to you. The day is coming when the Lord "will make the heavens tremble, and the earth will shake from its place at the wrath of the Lord Almighty." Are you ready for that day? Have you looked at yourself and asked, "Am I living as he would have me live?" Have you asked his forgiveness? The matter is the most serious one in your life. Perhaps it deserves your attention beyond the time to read these words.

Do Not Consult With Any Man
Galatians 1

Paul repeats his story of his conversion several times in Acts and in his letters. It is the defining event of his life.

Before he met his Lord on the road to Damascus, he was a zealous Jew. Indeed, he might have been the young genius of the Jewish thinkers of his day. He went to the right schools—Gamaliel is famous among the Jews to this day. He was well advanced in his understanding of the traditions of the elders at a young age. He was a man who had a great future ahead of him.

Then he met the risen Lord. Instead of a life of comfort and great respect, of being greeted in public with the admiration which the ordinary man has for the true man of God, he is suddenly cast into a role which he could never have expected. From the first he is warned how much he will suffer—indeed, he will die for the faith.

Most of us would think long and hard before making such a change in our lives. We would certainly consult with those we respect and with those we love. But Paul tells us here that he consulted with no one. God had arrived in his life; no one else was of sufficient importance or wisdom to even merit a passing question.

There is a deep lesson in this for us. Sometimes we hear the voice of God calling us to go, to do, to be. If we stop and form a committee to discuss it, the voice of God will be drowned in the babble of talk. If once God speaks to you about where you are to go, go there. Do not ask others if God has spoken to them like this—did anyone else get Paul's vision? If the Spirit convicts you of your sin, turn from it, and do not worry what the world will say about it. What's the worst they can do? Paul saw the worst ahead of him and still continued on. Man can abuse and kill the body; God has all of eternity to deal with the soul. Whom, then, should you fear? To whom should you listen?

This is most true when you hear him in the call from the Scripture. With the Word in front of you, things may jump from the page; I must do this; I must say that. Do not hesitate! Don't ask anyone else; rather, hear the word of the Lord and obey it, immediately. Your reward is in his hand; do not fail to reach out for it. Take counsel of no man, once God has revealed something to you. His word is flawless; whose would you add to it?

Some of Us Are in a Hurry
Galatians 2:1-16

In the rush to reveal the story of his setting out to convert the Gentiles of the world Paul drops us a few hints as to how God prepared him for his task.

Fourteen years

Twice the Old Testament number of perfection, seven, does Paul wait for the Lord to reveal how he is to serve. Remember that at the beginning of his conversion Jesus revealed to Paul that he would suffer much in this cause. Now for fourteen years he has remained in Damascus, preaching, studying—and waiting upon the Lord. Were there times when he wondered if it was all a dream, or that God had forgotten him?

I took Titus along

To go to "headquarters" —in this instance, the apostles in Jerusalem—he takes a friend. And what a friend to take to the land of the Jews: a Gentile. No wonder he worried if the race was in vain. God, however, was gracious, and the hints of the universal church were made all the more plain.

We did not give in...

The instant he arrives, the opposition begins. After such a wait you might think that things would be easy, but it was not so. God allowed opposition—perhaps to give Paul the perspective that opposition was to be his constant companion, and therefore develop in him a firmer devotion.

Common ground

Of all the debates that might have developed, one between the apostles would seem the worst. It is clear that the Jewish apostles had no clear idea of what Paul was really going to have to do—that, after all, was God's affair. Truly in the faith, they were seeking only what God would have them do. So they sought common ground between Jew and Gentile—and found it in loving charity.

In our lives we often feel that God has forgotten us, that our preparations seem lost, our time forgotten, our trials of faith daunting. It is not so. He is preparing each of us for his tasks, working all things together for the good of those that love him. Trust him in this; surrender to his call. Be ever ready to go—or to wait, even for those fourteen years. Those who will wait upon the Lord will bring him glory—in his time.

"Hypocrites"
Galatians 2:17-21

One of the more common accusations against the church is this: "You Christians are all hypocrites. You claim to be righteous but I can clearly see that all kinds of sinners are in the church. Obviously, then, you must be lying hypocrites."

Indeed, as it is obvious that there are all kinds of sinners in the church, the charge must be true—if we claim we are righteous, at least in ourselves. But that is precisely the opposite of what we do claim, as Paul points out in this passage.

His point is rather simple. Suppose you catch me in the act of doing something righteous—namely, rebuilding something that I have destroyed. It is good that I rebuild. It indeed is righteous. But the very word "rebuild" means that I tore something down in the first place. Christians are not those who create or possess righteousness; rather, they are the ones who are given righteousness by Christ. Since they accept that righteousness, we may safely conclude that they needed it. In short, righteous (in and of ourselves) we are not.

Does this dispose of the accusation? Perhaps. If we live as those whose righteousness is a gift, we claim no righteousness of our own—and therefore we are not hypocrites. How can we do that? We are taught to pursue righteousness and to live morally upright lives. Would it not seem that if righteousness is a gift then our conduct is irrelevant?

No indeed! That righteousness comes through our living in Christ. In glorious words Paul tells us: "I no longer live, but Christ lives in me." *That* is how we are given righteousness—we are given Righteousness Himself. If that righteousness—in the person of the Holy Spirit—lives in us, how then can we go on living in sin?

We cannot attain righteousness by our own efforts; we become hypocrites if we depend upon them. We can only be righteous in that Christ is righteous and died for us. If we accept that gift of righteousness, we do so by the indwelling of the Holy Spirit. It is not so much a place as a journey—a journey that does not end in this life. Listen to the promptings of the Spirit; consider if there is some area of your life that needs the cleansing of repentance and forgiveness. Let the living Spirit within you bring you home to God in the righteousness of Jesus Christ.

Hear My Cry
Psalm 61

It is true of most of us that we cry to God only when in trouble. But it is also true that the deepest and most eloquent cries of the Scripture come from the hearts of God's saints—when they are in trouble. Christ in the garden, and here, David in his pain.

"Hear my cry, O God; listen to my prayer." It is as if David is afraid that somehow God will not hear him. This is not the calm, mannered prayer of the King of Israel, but the heart wrenching appeal of a man who is overwhelmed with his problems.

"From the ends of the earth" —have you ever felt that God was very far from you? That you were alone, in an isolated place, and that—somehow—God was not able to reach you? Perhaps it is being homesick; perhaps it is being pursued—but the agony is very real. This is a man who yearns for the comfort of God.

"My heart grows faint" —the King James has "overwhelmed" — that heartsick feeling that says, "I just can't win. I'm at the end of my rope. No one but God could save me now." It is a deep emotion.

"Lead me" —not, "Let me come in, give me permission." Not "show me the way." Rather, it is "take me by the hand and lead me." I am so spent, so down, that I cannot find the way—God, you must take my hand and lead me as if I were blind.

"to the rock that is higher than I"—in my own strength I cannot resist what the enemy is doing. I need a refuge, not just a shield. A place where I can hide and be safe. There is only one such place—the rock that is my God.

It is the cry of a man who has emptied himself before God. No more pride, no more royal pomp, no more self-sufficiency. All that is left is the man who is seeking refuge, the man in desperate trouble who has but one place to go.

But blessed are the poor in spirit, for theirs is the kingdom of heaven! It is in such circumstances that we see most clearly our own weakness and the awesome strength of God. At such a moment we are pushed ever closer to God, hiding in him—and in hiding, discovering his wonderful secret ways.

Christian, are you pursued or in pain? Perhaps God is pushing you to the shelter of his wings. Do not resist; rather, run to him and rejoice. The kingdom of heaven is yours; embrace it with open arms.

Rest in God Alone
Psalm 62

Rest—it is something that at one time or another all of us have sought. It may be rest from physical weariness; often it is rest from the stresses of life. Do those around you seek your downfall? You want to hide somewhere, crawl into a fortress and there be safe—and let the tension fall from your shoulders. You want rest, as the Bible would describe it.

Perhaps it is the office; perhaps it is your family; perhaps—well, anything in life which pains and stresses you. It is difficult to escape from some of these, for they are often so near that we cannot escape. We often seek rest in false escapes—the new thrill of a new sport; a vacation in some distant land; a new job; even a new wife. These do not satisfy for long. There is only one true rest for mankind, and that is found in God alone.

God alone? Yes. Consider what you desire from this concept called "rest":

You want safety from those who pursue you. But what if the problems are within yourself? If you flee to a foreign land, the first person you know there is yourself.

You want the calm assurance that nothing new will bother you— that you will not be shaken. Who else but the Almighty could say such a thing?

You want freedom from the system this world produces—the important people whose egos need feeding, the lowly whose envy cannot be argued, those who cheat around the system in little ways—all these things are spider webs to drag you down. To free yourself from their sticky cling, to whom could you turn but God?

It comes down to this. You and I do not have the power within ourselves to protect ourselves from all things. We dream of retiring to the country, away from crime and job—only to find that humanity is still with us. Only God can deliver salvation and refuge. Why? Because only God has the two characteristics necessary: he is powerful to save (indeed omnipotent) and he is willing to save (indeed completely loving).

Christian, if you have been holding back from your commitment to Him, ask yourself this: can you *really* do everything yourself? Trust in Him, and let him be your rock and salvation.

Seeking and Singing
Psalm 63

The Psalms express the heart of the servant of God. This Psalm is one of the most emotional expressions of that heart, for in it we see the heart of the Christian laid out:

Seeking

Look at the verbs in the first section: "seek," "thirst," "long." These are not the pale emotions of "want" or "desire." These are the passions of a soul which must be satisfied. Have you ever been genuinely hungry? Or incredibly thirsty? Or tired beyond all recognition? The experience is beyond description, and that is what the Psalmist expresses here. They are the words of one who has walked the desert of Palestine, agonizing in the heat, seeking water— and yet he uses the same words for his God. Can we?

Remembering

Seeking looks forward; remembering looks back. In looking back the Psalmist declares the glories of the sanctuary—his "mountaintop experience" —and tells us that God's love is better than life itself. This adoration, this devotion, shows itself in one thing: praise. "I know but two things: what a sinner I am, and what a Savior he is." It is in this praise that the very innermost part of a man, the soul, is satisfied.

Singing and clinging

Athanasius held that in chanting the Psalms man came closest to God—for only in song does the human being commit all of the heart, soul, body and mind to the praise of God. The picture is one greater than that: it is in the shelter of God—"under his wings"—that I sing. Free from fear, my heart is released to praise the Lord who protects me.

Righteous and wicked

We so often forget that we are all mortal, but that God is eternal. In his eyes the wicked of today are but passing through—he knows their fate, and has shared it with us. By his power he will see that they obtain what they deserve. By his grace he will see that we do not. Is this not a cause for rejoicing? Is this not a reason to remember the goodness of God? Is this not something which should drive us to seek him more closely?

"O God, you are my God, earnestly I seek you; my soul thirsts for you, my body longs for you, in a dry and weary land where there is no water."

Love God – And Do As You Please
Galatians 5:13-26

"Freedom" is a word most precious to Americans. It has been purchased in blood for us many times in many ways. The times have arisen, however, where we have lost the true meaning of the word. Freedom is not license nor is it anarchy. With freedom comes responsibility.

The problem for those in authority, then, comes down to this: how do we permit freedom and still require responsibility in using it? You are free to drive the roadways—on the right side. It is difficult enough to write a traffic code; imagine how tough it must be to write a moral code for living.

Paul gives us here the "law" of freedom" "Love your neighbor as yourself." It is the second commandment, of course, the first being to love God. But in these two come all the law the Christian needs.

If you love God, and you love your neighbor, what will be the result? Paul gives us his famous list: love, joy, peace, patience, kindness, goodness, faithfulness, gentleness and self-control. Have you ever wished for these things? They are the natural fruit of living in the Spirit.

And if you don't? Such a life has its natural fruit also. We see some of the signs given here: jealousy, fits of rage, factions and envy—the list is long enough. This is the result of freedom gone astray, turning from freedom into license and anarchy. Note one thing: the effects are not just "personal" —in the sense that they harm only one person. We often hear, "if it doesn't hurt anyone else ...." It does. The same spirit that produces sexual immorality produces rage and jealousy.

Look around you. Those who abuse the royal law of freedom wind up as Paul warned: "If you keep on biting and devouring each other, watch out or you will be destroyed by each other." This comes of loving yourself rather than loving God and those God loves, your neighbors.

Rules and regulations do not produce a good man; they keep a bad one in check. A truly good man, in God's service, is one who follows St. Augustine's rule: "Love God—and do as you please." This is why the devotional life is so important, for in prayer, reading the Scripture and other devotions the heart is changed. God looks upon the heart; what does he see in you?

Restoration
Galatians 6

In this passage Paul lays out one of the more neglected responsibilities of the Christian: church discipline. Discipline in the church is not the same thing as punishment; if you will think of discipline in the phrase "disciplined athlete" you will have a better picture of the word. In fact, the root word, *disciple*, tells you what it really means: to bring someone to being a disciple—of Christ.

How are we to do this?

Restore. First, we must recognize that we all sin. If this becomes persistent in someone, those who are spiritually mature – not a job for the new Christian, wait for the timing of the Lord – are to do the work of restoration. They are to bring this person back to the faith.

Gently. This is to be done with all gentleness. It is not a time for fire and brimstone, but for the love of Christ to be displayed, firmly – but gently.

Watch yourself. If it happened to him, it could happen to you. Take care that you do not fall into the same temptation; indeed, if you are prone to it, ask others for help in this.

Carrying the burden

Paul then finishes the thought with what appears to be a contradiction:

We are to carry each other's burden.

Each one should carry his own load.

How can this be? There is only one logical way: my load is to carry my brother's burdens. This is the law of Christ: to love your neighbor as yourself. If you carry your own burdens, and love your neighbor as yourself, would you not carry his? There is to be no slacking—but also none should carry his own burdens alone.

This can be a wearing experience, so Paul encourages us not to give up doing good. Remember, the Lord is coming and at his return he will reward such righteousness. Is there really a choice here? If we are not bearing each other's burdens, correcting each other and restoring each other, then are we not tearing down the church? And what will our Lord say about that? Bear each other's burdens, and fulfill the law of love.

Thanksgiving in Intercession
Ephesians 1:15-23

Intercessory prayer often seems difficult to us. Perhaps we just don't know where to begin. Paul gives us the example: begin with thanksgiving.

Thanks for the person

When you intercede for someone, do you realize what privileges you have?

First, there is the privilege of intercession itself. Most of us would consider it a privilege to be allowed to speak to Congress; how much more a privilege to speak to God?

Next you have the privilege of sharing in the work of God. He allows you this so that you might draw closer to him.

Beyond that, you have been entrusted with someone who is, or could be, a child of God. Does not God expect you to pray for him?

Had this person not had such trouble, you would not have such a privilege. You would be reduced to begging for yourself, with no work for God and no responsibility from him. Give thanks, then, for how God has placed such a work in your hands.

Thanks for their faith

It is so much easier to pray for a Christian, isn't it? First, you know that their ultimate security is perfect, as is your own. Even if the one you are praying for dies, they are with the Lord. How difficult it is to pray for one who is not a Christian, for there is always the fear that they may die before they accept Christ.

Thanks for their love

Love can be seen in action, and Paul here commends those actions towards other saints. This provides us motive for intercession:

There is a sense that we are "returning the favor." They have done good for the body of Christ, and we are trying to do good in return by interceding for them.

It is not a case of saying, "He is worthy." None of us is worthy before God. We are saying, "He is worthy before us."

In a sense, we are praying for a "friend of a friend." These are the ones who are the friends of Jesus Christ, and he is a friend of ours.

Intercede, then, for your brothers and sisters—and begin by giving thanks.

Reconciliation
Ephesians 2:15-22

Our reconciliation to God can be seen here in three tenses: past, present and prevention (future).

Past. Christ is our sacrifice, our atonement.

In the sense that he has set right our debts, our sins past.

He did that in the sense of fulfilling the requirements of the Old Testament Law.

In doing this, Christ became the bridge between God and man. We see here the mediator who bridges the gap.

Present. Christ still breaks down the "wall of hostility." In other words, he is constantly removing the causes of this hostility between us and God.

In the sense that he removes the curse of sin, God no longer need look at us as "automatic" sinners.

In keeping us from sin he removes the next cause of hostility on the part of God. As we do not sin, God does not need to deal with our sin.

But when we do sin he forgives us when we repent. He cleanses us through life, keeping us acceptable to God.

Prevention (future). He is our "peace." The Christians of medieval times understood this better. Each man had his "peace." It was a crime to break that peace ("breach of the peace").

Think of a bunch of bickering nobles. The king walks in. The bickering dies down, for fear of offending the king.

We also have peace *with* God. By his constant presence and our conscience, we are kept from sin. In this we have peace.

The process of reconciliation is not easy. It cost Jesus his life on the Cross; as his ambassadors, it will cost us too.

First, the innocent party must take the first step in reconciliation. God approached us; the innocent one moved first.

It is costly. It may cost us the delicious sensation of anger remembered; it may cost us vengeance. It is expensive, but necessary.

But there is joy in reconciliation. What was lost can be found; what was weak can be made strong again

We are the ambassadors of Christ, his imitators, his body. Let us do as he does, reconciling ourselves to each other and those outside the faith to him.

The Servant of God
Ephesians 3

There does not seem to be an employment office to become a servant of God. Indeed, Paul makes it quite clear that he is a servant by the grace of God, God's free gift. Why is this so?

So that we might see an example of God's mercy. In seeing that God has showered grace upon Paul we learn something about God: that he is merciful to perfection.

So that we might imitate one who imitates God. God the Father is invisible. Paul the Apostle whom we see showing mercy gives us a living example to imitate.

So that we might not despair. If God forgave and then used one who persecuted his own church, is there any sin we can commit and say, "I am too wicked to be forgiven?"

Such servanthood does not come with a Bible and a map with directions. You become a servant of God through the power of God.

We achieve things through his power, not our weakness, and therefore we can achieve so much more.

It is so that our faith might be increased. If we will look back and see what God has done—despite our unfitness for the task— then we can see his power and have faith in it.

Finally, it is so that we might not doubt the possibility of *anything*. When he gives us a task, we should not look to our means but his power.

God does not use what he has at hand; he shapes what he has at hand into what he wants. When he does, we see three things:

First, we see humility. Once the servant of God appreciates that the power of God at work, there is no room for pride.

Next, there is the unlikeliness of the servants of God. Nothing is so remarkable about God's servants as the remarkable fact that they were "least likely to succeed." The devout Pharisee, Saul of Tarsus, would never consort with the Gentiles. Paul, the Apostle, is sent to these same Gentiles. They are one and the same man.

How is this possible? Because God equips, or better said, gifts, his servants with what they will need. The servant says, "I can't see how I could do that." God says, "I didn't say you'd see it—I said you can do it through my power."

Live a Life Worthy...
Ephesians 4:1-16

Paul begins his second exhortation to the Ephesians urging them to a life worthy of the calling they have received. How?

First, we must be completely humble. The King James Version uses the word "lowliness," and I think that expresses the meaning very well. It is the basic virtue, for it is the virtue set against the basic sin, which is pride. Note well, too, that we are to be "completely" humble. Can you see that we must be humble in:

Words—do our words sound the call of our own glory, or do they praise our Lord Jesus Christ?

Actions—are we always concerned with our own status, or do we care more that others have what is theirs?

Bearing—even in the way we carry ourselves, we can either be strutting in the world's way or walking gently like Christ.

This is all the more important when we consider ourselves in the light of the sins of others. If we are called on to correct the sins of others, our ministry will not be received if we are judgmental. But we must pass judgment on the sin. How can this be? Only if we are clothed in humility, so that the sinner knows that it is not our judgment he faces, but God's.

We must be gentle. The King James word was "meekness," and it means someone who is not easy to provoke. It does not, as some think, mean weakness; it means powerful but under control. As Wesley said, it is "our passions in due proportion."

We must be patient, or as the King James so expressively puts it, longsuffering. We need to be able to suffer the faults and irritations of others for a long time if we are to please God in this.

We are to bear with one another in the bond of love. The word for "bearing" here carries with it a sense of using your body to hold something up. We are to use ourselves to hold our brothers and sisters up.

It is an intensely personal requirement. This is not something acquired sitting in the pew, but in times of prayer and meditation, followed by patient and gentle action of a saint in the world.

Deception
Ephesians 4:17-32

There is an enduring myth in Western civilization, since the time of the French Revolution. It is this: living a "passionate" life – a sinful life, in Christian terms—is the path to sharpening your intellect. Paul tells us here that this is not so. The meaning is clearer in the translation known as the Jerusalem Bible:

(v19) Intellectually they are in the dark, and they are estranged from the life of God, without knowledge because they have shut their hearts to it.

Timothy Leary in the 1960s gave us the modern version of this. Use drugs, expand your mind. The temptation is by no means original. Sin is supposed to be enlightening. How is it that the serpent tempted Eve? That she would be like God, knowing good and evil! This is the modern myth: that evil is enlightening. Satan, in the person of Mephistopheles, is a man about town, clad in top hat and tails, sophisticated, debonair. Surely this is the life to live!

The hardening is gradual

It is not the life to live. The reason this deception keeps working is that the effects are slow to be realized. The word Paul uses for "harden" is *porosis*, from which we take our medical term *osteoporosis*. It means a gradual hardening of the bones. C. S. Lewis had his demon, Screwtape, express it this way:

"The safest road to Hell is the gradual one—the gentle slope, soft underfoot, without sudden turnings, without milestones, without signposts."

The slow but sure hardening can be seen in history as well. In the early days of America even men in the South considered slavery to be an evil. It was a necessary evil, but still an evil. Gradually, it became less and less evil and more and more necessary, until finally it was proclaimed that slavery was righteousness itself, ordained by God for the black man, beneficial to both black and white. (The parallel to abortion, by the way, infuriates feminists whenever mentioned.)

Examine your heart today; has it become slowly hardened to the truth of God? Do not delay; go to God in prayer and ask him for your forgiveness. He will soften that heart; he will forgive; he is merciful. Let him crack the shell, and pour his Spirit into the broken heart, mending it to be like new.

September 27

Be Imitators of God
Ephesians 5

If there is any one principle of conduct for the Christian, it is this: What would Christ do? Jesus Christ, God in the flesh, is our role model as well as our teacher and Savior.

We are to be imitators, as "dearly loved children." The word in the Greek is *agapetos*, a diminutive form of *agape*, the love of God. Consider it for a moment: how do children who are dearly loved behave?

> Perhaps the best way to see it is to look at children whose parents do not love them dearly. Those parents just "going through the motions" or who put their careers ahead of their families—what kind of children do they have? Are they not children who are always "acting up?"

But children who are genuinely loved by their parents show two key characteristics:

> First, they are well disciplined children—for loving parents discipline their children.

> More than that, you can see that they imitate their parents—sometimes with great comic effect. Not just in biology, but in manner and habit, our children are mirrors of ourselves. So, therefore, we should be mirrors of God.

The word translated here as "live a life" really means "to walk." It is a life in which one "walks the talk." We are to be sincere in our profession of the faith. And—in imitation of Christ—we are to live, if you will, two lives:

> The life of sacrifice—that which I give up. I am to give up sexual immorality, greed and pride, and all uncleanness which keeps me from God.

> The life of offering—that which I offer up. I am to offer up to God those things that are pleasing to him—virtues such as kindness, goodness and charity. Praise in word and song are his, as are thanksgiving and music in the heart.

We are the children of God. The question is, what kind of children are we? Are we the disobedient ones who must be punished frequently, or are we the ones who truly imitate our Heavenly Father? It is a choice that we must make, and indeed have made. Which we have chosen is shown in what we give up, and in what we live up to. *September 28*

The Least Favorite of Virtues
Ephesians 6

Humility is the least favorite of virtues. If we are courageous, we may be rewarded in this life. If we are generous, we may feel good about it. But if we are humble, we are certain to discover that this world does not place any value upon it. To the world, pride is the source of power for virtue. To the Christian, God is the source of power. So it is that we must choose: are we to be virtuous because we are proud of ourselves, or because God strengthens us to do so? Consider what Paul commands:

The wife is to "fear" her husband; the slave is to obey with "respect and fear". Is this just because of slavery? Or is it the fact that our world demands lip service of the servant, but God will demand integrity?

The slave is to serve with "sincerity of heart." This means that we must forsake secret cheating and petty revenge. How often have you desired to "get even" with the company? Yet our Lord commands exactly the opposite attitude.

There is most definitely an aspect of "turn the other cheek" in this. Are you a slave? Then bear with it, turning the other cheek, so that your Father in heaven will reward you. Are you oppressed on your job? Bear with it in the name of Christ, and Christ will reward you for it.

We are to serve "wholeheartedly." This is not sullen oppression, nor stoic acceptance, nor mystic resignation—but the complete enthusiasm of one who enjoys the day's work.

The situation is transitory. They are our masters "according to the flesh." That means two things:

First, that God recognizes no such distinction by right. It is something that man has done. It is therefore trivial.

Second, it is something which can last no more than a lifetime. We are meant to be eternal. It is a trivial thing; but if we are not faithful in trivial things, who will trust us with eternal things?

Do you need an example of the virtue of being a good servant? One should suffice. Christ, on the night before the Cross, washed the feet of the disciples. If your Lord and Savior was willing to do that (and the servant is not above the master) then tell me what you must not tolerate.

The High and Lofty One Says
Isaiah 57

In magnificent words the prophet Isaiah brings us the word of the Lord. He who lives "in a high and holy place" speaks:

The lowly in spirit

Throughout the Scriptures this theme occurs: God will humble those who raise themselves up in pride, but those who are lowly in spirit (blessed are the meek) will be raised up by God. In those hearts God will work; in those hearts he will dwell.

Not accusing forever

Sometimes it seems to us that God is pointing the finger at us all day long. It is not so; his purpose is our repentance. When we turn from our evil ways, he rushes to us, to welcome us home. How did the father greet the Prodigal Son? By running to him from a long distance away. This is God, running to meet the repentant heart.

God tells us that he is enraged by our sins—and that we keep on in our sinful ways. Despite this—and God has taken notice of it—he will heal us, says the prophet. He does not say how at this point, but the answer to that is clear: at the Cross.

Guide him and restore him

Forgiveness and redemption are the beginning of God's mercies, not the end. For after forgiveness and redemption come the steps of God's guiding us in his ways. He does not want miserable, mourning sinners who repent only; he wants them to grow in grace to become those on whose lips he has created praise. We are to praise him forever, and that is a joyous, not a mournful, thing.

Peace, peace

To those far and near, God proclaims peace. Not just the absence of war, not just the absence of conflict between God and man, but the resolution of that conflict at the Cross. To those who will repent and grow in righteousness, the war between God and man is over.

To the wicked it is not so—my mother used to quote this verse: "There is no peace for the wicked." It is still true today. Those who oppose the righteousness of God find only restless turmoil and endless self-justification. But for those of us who accept the sacrifice of Calvary, there is peace—peace on this earth, and peace forevermore.

Work Out
Philippians 2:12-13

The verses referenced here seem to contain a complete contradiction in one sentence.

Work out your salvation

From that command—it is a command, as you can see—we might conclude that our salvation depends upon what we do. This is utterly at variance to the rest of the New Testament. So we might ask, what can this mean?

The phrase is "work out" —and as many have noticed, we are merely working out what God has worked in. It is the outward sign of inward transformation, the transformation made by the Holy Spirit.

We are to do this "in fear and trembling." If salvation depends upon us, why the fear? But if salvation is a precious thing, holy and sacred, then it should be treated with awe and respect.

There is another sense to this. Each of us is given certain spiritual gifts; each of us is given a particular calling. We are not to ignore these but rather to give them their fullest possible expression—to work them out, as one might work out a problem in mathematics. We are to "solve" the mystery of our own gifts and calling— through hard work.

It is God who works in you

We must never forget that the Holy Spirit lives within us—and like Christ, He did not come to be served but to serve. Since He lives within us, we too are to serve rather than be served. So the Spirit moves us to good works, not only in intention (the will) but in action.

This action is not random, nor is it isolated to any given purpose. It is made by the will of God for the benefit of his people, the church. It is "according to his good purpose." So we are to work, for God works in us, not for our own benefit (though we will benefit greatly) but for the purposes of God.

There is no contradiction here. The soul that loves God will work for him; this is the expression of salvation. It is the hymn of joy sung by the working Christian; its notes are good deeds, its melody the will of God; its orchestra the church. Its result is a symphony of praise to our Lord Jesus Christ.

October 1

God is Good
Psalm 73

You can almost picture the Psalmist: he is just *so close* to slipping into sin. Why? He envied the arrogant for their prosperity.

The picture is familiar to us; we've seen it in motion pictures and literature. The character is one of a rich man, strutting across the stage of life, letting the world know how great he truly is. It is so common as to be a caricature. What is not so common is to recognize our own reaction to it: the mixture of envy and hatred. Hatred, because of the arrogance; envy, because we wish we could be like that person. Pride need not be expressed to be real; it can also be found in the imagination. "Someday I'm going to show them all."

We imagine that God does not notice (if we pay any attention to the idea at all). He does. It is not our outward state of wealth for which he cares—what would the creator of the universe care for our *wealth?* —but the state of the heart. One can be poor, envious—and proud.

When this state comes upon us, virtue becomes weariness. Every temptation to cheat just a little shows up as a major issue in our lives. We say, "If only I could get just a little ahead, then someday I'll be able to tell them all exactly what I think." Pride in our poverty is a desperate state.

There is a cure: the Psalmist goes into the sanctuary of God and sees. For us, this may be a time of prayer, or a time of worship, or just one of those moments where God gives clarity. We see that "today" is a very short time—especially when compared with eternity. In eternity those who take pride in their wealth and position, those who lord it over others—they're gone. Today's wealthy and powerful will go the way of all before them. God reigns and rules; this is still his universe.

It is a matter of proportion. If this world is all that matters, and this life the only one we can ever have, then claw your way to the top, step on anyone you need to, and be arrogant for the little while you remain there. If there is a God, and he says there is eternity, then put this life in proportion—and live it in a way pleasing to him who holds the keys to heaven and hell. Do not envy the arrogant; do not desire their position. Take your refuge in God instead; he will prevail.

Press On
Philippians 3:7-16

Here is the secret of Paul the Apostle. In this little passage he describes greatness in a Christian.

Consider everything a loss

Have a sense of proportion. The kingdom is like the Pearl of Great Price. It is worth giving up everything you have or hold dear to obtain entrance into the kingdom of God. The world sees this as "out of proportion." God sees it in true proportion.

To gain Christ

It is not a system of rules and regulations through which we hope for heaven—it is by the indwelling of the Spirit, the sacrifice of the Son and the provision of the Father, the three in one. The knowing of Jesus Christ is the entrance door of the kingdom.

Righteousness from God

It is essential to see it: we are not the source of our own righteousness. Nothing we could ever do would attain such a righteousness; we must have God's own righteousness through Christ.

Righteousness by faith

We seize hold of this righteousness not by worship or action but by faith—which results in worship and action.

Sharing his sufferings

If you are his child, you share his nature. If you share his nature, the world will react to you as it did to him.

The Resurrection

This is the great prize: that when he returns we will rise from the grave and live eternally, reigning with him.

Paul does not consider this something past tense. It is in the future. He gives us the proper perspective of that future:

He forgets what is behind. Is there sin in the past? It is forgiven by God. Is there failure? Today is another chance.

He strains for what is ahead. This is not just coasting along, bouncing from point to point, going with the flow. Rather it is the vigorous attempt to become like Christ.

He presses on. Troubles come; press on. Failures happen; press on. Whatever the world throws at you, however Satan lies to you—press on.

The example is set; the race is before us. Press on.

Whatever Is True
Philippians 4

Our civilization has forgotten the concept of nobility. The idea that something in and of itself might be a noble thing is now foreign to us (perhaps because nobility itself is now regarded as only an accident of birth).

It was not always so. Men in former times recognized that certain things—tangible and intangible—were intrinsically worthy of our praise. The sensation is not entirely lost; look up at the stars some night should you happen to be deep in the desert.

Whatever is true

God is truth; whatever is true comes from him. It may seem to be in a strange costume, but welcome the truth wherever you find it, and ponder it.

Whatever is noble

Does the thing (or person) you see command respect because of character? Is this someone who is self-sacrificing? Is it something which inspires you to reach to heaven? Ponder these things.

Whatever is right

Despite all odds, is it right? Is this thought, thing, or person—whatever—standing against the tide of opinion, a rock of righteousness on which the waves of fashion dash? Ponder it well.

Whatever is pure

Is this someone whose life tells you that honesty and faithfulness are altogether admirable—because you admire that person? Ponder well the purity that is admirable.

Whatever is lovely

Beauty proceeds from within; whether art or human. If it is lovely, is it lovely only in form or lovely in fact? If in fact, ponder it well, and ask, "who made it so lovely?"

Whatever is admirable

Does the saint before you stand tall? Why? Is it eloquence of voice, or eloquence of living? If the latter, ponder it well—and follow the example.

All that is lovely, pure and admirable is from God—every good and perfect gift. If you have received such, praise God for it. If you see such, consider it well. God puts the admirable and pure before you so that you might see more clearly what he longs for you to be. Do not fail to look at what he asks you to ponder.

The Firstborn Over All Creation
Colossians 1:15-20

Have you ever asked yourself why the "laws of Nature" are just that – laws? Why doesn't gravity change from day to day? It is because the universe was created by the eternal God – it is his work, and it reflects his eternal qualities.

More than that, this work was made by the one we know as Jesus, the Christ. It seems that in all matters relating to the physical universe, he has the supremacy. His supremacy is clear:

All things—whether in heaven or on earth, visible or invisible, spiritual or physical—were created by him.

He is "before" all things. That is, before any created thing existed, He Is.

In Him all things hold together. He is the glue that makes the universe run consistently

This alone would make him supreme. But supremacy to him is something which is of his character. He is supreme in all good things, including love.

He is supreme over the church, his body on earth, the agent of his love.

He is supreme in the resurrection, being the first of those who will rise with new bodies.

What an awesome God we serve! But for us the greatest of his works is this: that in his own body he reconciled us to God. God, the holy and awesome, who can tolerate no sin, has been reconciled to us, the sinners of this world, by the body and blood of Jesus, the Christ.

Some things by their very nature excite our admiration and wonder: the stars on a clear desert night, the majesty of the Rocky Mountains, the beauty of autumn in New England. These things are merely his works. How much more, then, should we admire and wonder at the glorious beauty of God as revealed in Jesus. We see the works of his hand, and we are awestruck. Some day we shall see the Author of those works, face to face. Words cannot express the feelings we shall have on that day.

That day is coming; no one knows when. "Soon" he said—and he who created time calls all time "soon." So Christian prepare your heart to greet the Lord of Creation, coming in power and might—to gather his own to himself.

First Things
Colossians 1:21-28

Amazing as it sounds, it is true: some Christians still cannot state the essence of the Gospel. If for no other reason, you should know this passage. Just what is "the Gospel?"

Once you were enemies

All of us start out as sinners—those who rebel against what God commands. That shows itself in our behavior. Since we are all sinners, none of us is privileged to pronounce judgment on anyone else—only ourselves. We're sinners.

He has reconciled...

Note two things: first, the "He" in this passage is God. He is the one doing the reconciling. It is not something we have discovered or done; it is something he has done and revealed to us.

What has he done? He has reconciled us to himself. He has made us right with him—the debts paid, the sins atoned for. It is as if I had a rich uncle who cleared away my debts. I'm broke (a sinner) but he is rich enough to cover it (reconciliation).

By Christ's physical body

How did he do this reconciling? By the death of Jesus Christ, the sinless man, on the Cross. The penalty of sin is death; that penalty had to be paid. To reconcile, however, required the death of an "unblemished" (sinless) sacrifice—Jesus.

Holy in his sight

The point is not that I am now sinless; I still am a sinner. In God's eyes, however, my debts for sin are paid and therefore he sees me as having the holiness of Christ.

If you continue

It would be absurd to imagine that once I have been saved I can continue to go on as I did before. I am not perfect—but I am going in that direction. (It's a long, long trip). So it is that the Gospel includes walking in the direction God points you. Righteousness must be practiced.

Not moved from the hope

A great part of that Gospel is hope: the hope of the resurrection of the dead; the hope of his return. We look forward to the day when Christ comes again to judge the living and the dead. This hope moves us to prayer and good deeds, for we seek the approval of our Lord—the "well done, good and faithful servant."

The Gospel—the good news of Jesus Christ!

Rules and Regulations
Colossians 2:8-23

One of the great difficulties of the faith is the concept of rules and regulations. Despite the proclamation of the law of liberty, many of us seek a clear set of rules and regulations which we can follow—and thus earn our way into heaven.

It is not to be. God has already produced such a set of regulations; they are found in the Old Testament. They no longer apply—as rules. They apply as lessons.

Paul had the problem somewhat more explicitly than we do. People in his time were piously proud of celebrating festivals, the Sabbath, New Moon festivals, and all sorts of things. These people then looked upon others who did not do such things as inferior Christians. If we worship anything less than God we are indulging in a false worship, a false humility—no matter how pious it might appear to others.

Why? "After all, it doesn't matter what you believe—as long as you're sincere." So we think—but the Scripture is quite to the contrary. Reality pays no attention to what you believe—only what you do. God must be worshiped in spirit and in truth. He is the ultimate reality.

Such worship is, in fact, completely worldly. The world says, "Play the game. Manipulate things according to the rules, and if you're better at it than the next fellow, things will come out better for you. If magic works, use magic. If science, science." This is the world's way: substitute the partial obedience to the rules for the complete obedience to God.

God's way is opposed to this. He asks of us everything we have—and when he does, the petty things of rules and regulations fade into insignificance. We have died to the world—that is the measure of the commitment we need for Christ—and so these things should have no effect upon us. We must remember: the good is often the enemy of the best. The Law was good—the Law of Love is the best.

Consider it in your life. Are there things you will not do because of tradition? Or fear? Some of these things your Lord will continue to command to you; the alcoholic should not take the first drink. In others he will command you to the most radical of things. The question is not whether or not he will command; the question is, will you obey?

Set Your Mind on Things Above
Colossians 3:1-17

The hardest physical task in all of the major sports is hitting a baseball. A 50% shooter in basketball needs a lot of work. A 50% passer in football is soon looking for another line of work. A 30% hitter in baseball can make a lot of money. Over and over again, Little League (and other) coaches tell their players: "Keep your eye on the ball." Over and again the players look where they want the ball to be—not where the ball actually is.

It's like that in life too. Our Lord clearly tells us here to "set your mind on things above." Pay attention to the kingdom of heaven! Do that first! Everything else will follow in its proper course if you do. And, of course, we don't. We look to where our desires lead us—not to where God calls us.

The things we look after—lust, greed, pride, and all the rest—are listed for us here. These we are to put to death; their effects—anger, malice, slander and the like we are to get rid of. This is just the first step, however. To truly turn our minds to the kingdom of heaven we must exceed the "thou shalt nots" —we must go on to the good things of the kingdom.

> On the outside we must place the right attitudes: compassion, kindness, humility, gentleness and patience. These should be the signs others see of our mindset.

> Between ourselves, we must be the ones who forgive, the ones who bear the burdens for each other. Always caring for the other one, looking first to serve.

All this must be glued together with love.

This is not easy to do alone—but Christianity is not an individual sport. It is a team effort. Paul tells us that we are to "admonish one another in all wisdom" —like the kid on the bench in the baseball game who keeps shouting out encouragement to all his teammates. We are to keep each other's vision on things above.

Aim low and get what you aim at. Aim high, and the low things are caught in the same net. "Seek first the kingdom" said our Lord, and it is just possible that he meant it. The paradox of the faith is this: if you seek the world's way, you will find it and achieve your goals—and be disappointed. If you seek God's way you will never reach the ultimate goal this side of heaven—and you'll be supremely glad of it.

See To It
Colossians 4:17-18

We know almost nothing about Archippus, the man. Besides this injunction, we know that he was a friend of Philemon whom Paul called his "fellow soldier." So we may conclude that he too was some sort of evangelist, perhaps to the area around Colosse. More than that, Paul evidently considered him a good friend – since his comment is at the end of the letter.

Paul's injunction has three points:

See to it. The work of the Lord is sometimes imagined to be a carefree existence, requiring no diligence but rather a prayerful spirit. It is not so. The word here means "to look after" —it is the word that applies to the diligent.

Complete the work. So often in the church we see a work begun and never finished. It is no disgrace if the work takes longer than your lifetime—but complete the task you are given. Patience and endurance are still virtues.

You have received in the Lord. We must remember that the tasks we have in the church—whether in the church building or on the streets around—are given to us by the Lord. Are you called to teach? Teach at the Lord's command. Are you called to sweep? Sweep as if he were to walk on your floors this very day.

Paul then emphasizes his command: "Remember my chains." There is no greater honor than disgrace for Jesus Christ's sake. Paul points out that he is in chains for the Gospel—what then, friend Archippus, do you find so hindering in the completion of your task? If I can continue to preach the Gospel from a jail cell then surely you can complete the task God has assigned to you.

For indeed, God does not match us with tasks without giving us the strength to perform them. Such things require faith and prayer, but remember that God often chooses the unlikely to accomplish the impossible.

Perhaps he has set you a task which you think is too heavy. Do not compel God to find another to carry this load. Go to him in prayer and ask for his strength. Then, remembering that this task came from our Lord, complete your task with diligence and hard work. He is mindful of you; persevere so that you may hear the words, "Well done, good and faithful servant."

Our Lives As Well
1 Thessalonians 1:1 – 2:9

Paul begins his letter with something of a defense of his stewardship of the Gospel. He points out his honesty; he points out that he earned his own living while preaching to them. All this might be seen as a defense against a sniping congregation—except for one little phrase: "our lives as well."

Here is the measure of the evangelist's love. It is one thing to preach the Gospel. The evangelist is entitled to be supported, that is clear—but it is a noble thing if he works for his own support, for this produces an even better example. Some are called to do this; most are not. That an evangelist would be strictly honest is to be expected; that he would not seek praise is a severe trial of human nature. But we can imagine an evangelist so committed to the cause of Christ that he sees his hearers not as brothers but as—you will forgive the term, I trust— *targets.*

That is not Paul's way, nor should it be ours. He shared not only the Gospel with them, but also his very life. This is a sign that these Thessalonians had indeed become very dear to him. It is one thing to preach on the street corner or in a rented hall. It is entirely another to invite the crowd to join in your life, and turn them from crowd to dear friends.

It is likely enough the secret of his success. Eloquence will draw a crowd; love will keep and make friends. Which would you have—the eloquent speaker or the dear friend?

This was not easy; Paul speaks of "toil and hardship." But is any good thing brought about easily or cheaply? See the results of what he did. Instead of mild approval he produced Christians—Christians who would endure "severe suffering" for the name of Christ. They welcomed the message with joy—and became examples to others in the area of what a true believer was like. Paul's example was reproduced a hundred fold in this community.

This is a key ingredient in our evangelism—that has been missing lately. It is not sufficient to be an example (which we should be). It is necessary to share our lives with those around us, so that they can see what is in our inmost being—the Holy Spirit. Preaching may be reviled; an example may be ignored; but a Christian who shares his life with others stands as an irrefutable witness to the Gospel of Christ.

Stand It No Longer
1 Thessalonians 2:10-3:13

My mother tells me that I never wrote her while I was in college. The facts that the college was forty miles away from home, and I came home frequently, are not relevant to the point. Mother was upset that I did not write.

Parents are like that. We raise our children with the full intention of turning them into adults who are mature and responsible—and then are shocked to discover that they don't need us every other minute. Why the surprise? Because we care; we love our children and long to know how they are doing.

Paul is like that here. The Thessalonians are his children in the faith; he has been separated from them. So first he tries to return to them; then he sends Timothy. At long last the good news comes to him: they have been faithful! His labors were not in vain; his children are strong in the faith.

Now, does God see you in the same way? Perhaps it has been some time since he has heard from you. Has he sent someone special to look in on you, to encourage you in the faith? Someone you respect and even love? This just might be a sign of how much he cares for you.

Like Paul, our Lord Jesus longs to return, waiting only for the moment selected by the Father. In the meanwhile, he sends to us those like Timothy, to encourage us and to lead us. These may be great orators, or simple Christians. What will he find?

The Thessalonians had been through trials, as Paul had told them they would. They had been persecuted by their own countrymen. This will happen with us as well, for the world will always seek to drive out the church. Paul had prepared them for this; they met the test. But just to make sure, he sent Timothy to strengthen them. God will do the same for us.

In each age and generation the trials will come. They differ in form and intensity, but they are there. These are God's ways of refining the church. Those who withstand the trials come out stronger for them. God is seeking such. Those who have overcome serve to pass the faith along to the next generation.

There remains the question: "when the Son of Man returns, will he find faith upon the earth?" He will—if we will remain faithful in time of trial. Let us therefore encourage one another, for the time is short—and eternity is long.

A Christian's Funeral
1 Thessalonians 4

There is a great difference between the funeral of a believer and the funeral of a non-Christian. The non-Christian funeral may be a time of anger at death; or a time of sadness at loss; and very often it is a time of stifling formality—all present relying on politeness to replace the words they do not have.

The Christian funeral is a time of mingled joy and sadness. Sadness, at the separation of a loved one—but joy also, because our brother or sister is now with Christ. More than that: it is not a forever separation, for the Lord is coming again—and with him the resurrection of the dead.

Paul states the simple facts here: Jesus rose from the dead. This changes everything; the fact of the resurrection alters our view of death completely. The dead in Christ are described as those who have "fallen asleep."

When our Lord returns he will bring these dear brothers and sisters with him, by the power of God. What a reunion for those who believe! Indeed, Paul is quite explicit about the order of events here, starting with God's command and ending with us being with the Lord forever. The matter is evidently something that God has planned in advance!

It makes a difference at the funeral; it should make a difference in our lives. God is not deceived by us; he also does not deceive us. We should therefore live such lives that on the day He returns we will hear, "Well done."

What kind of lives shall we live? Some few are called to great things in the faith, but most of us are described here. Three major items Paul brings to mind:

Sexual immorality should be rejected; self-control should be practiced. We are called to be holy.

Brotherly love should abound more and more as we grow more mature in Christ.

Surprisingly to some, we should try to lead quiet lives. Why? So that the faith will be respected by all who see you.

Christians should be different from other people; they should be the people God intends them to be. In that way others will see what God designed for us. Who knows? You may be the quiet life which leads another to Christ.

Respect
1 Thessalonians 5:12-13

A featured main course for Sunday dinner in many households is that famous dish, roast preacher. If a preacher talks about stewardship, he's begging for money. If he talks about self-control, he's meddling. If he talks about the theology evident in Second Hezekiah, chapter 3, he's obscure. (If this is your first time through the Bible, please note: there is neither First nor Second Hezekiah. But do keep that a secret.)

Paul admonishes us to the contrary. He tells us here that we should respect those who are over us in the Lord. There is a qualification to that; he starts with those who work hard at it. If your pastor is typical of most, being sure of working long hard hours is the least of his difficulties. That comes with the job.

Interestingly, the one thing that really qualifies them for our respect is that they admonish us. That is, they tell us what we are doing wrong and how to fix it. Consider: if your tooth hurts, you go to the dentist. If he says it needs a filling, do you argue? You may groan, but you do it his way—he's the dentist. If your stomach hurts and you see the doctor, you take the prescription he gives you. Each of us goes to considerable expense and trouble—not to mention pain—to seek out this unpleasant advice and follow it. So then, when the person charged with your spiritual welfare gives you a prescription, what should you do with that?

Moreover, consider how respected are the dentist and the doctor. Their professions generally pay well, but even without the money they are regarded as "professionals." It is a term of respect in our society. Surely we should accord at least the same degree of respect to the one who is charged with our eternal welfare? After all, which is more important: the question of heaven and hell, or your teeth?

If all that—hard work, long hours and great responsibility (and a fair amount of experience and learning thrown in) are not sufficient for respect, then this should be: God has appointed the man to the task. Whether he fills it well or poorly, God alone must judge. Most do the best they can with what they have. They have earned the respect due hard work; they should also have the respect due a difficult job. Beyond that, they are those who are most visibly God's servants. For that reason alone, they are worthy of all respect.

What It Is To Know Me
Jeremiah 22:13-17

The name of Shallum is little known to us. Indeed, if it were not for this prophecy by Jeremiah, he would be but a name in a list of descendants of Josiah. Josiah was one of the greatest of Judah's kings; his sons and grandsons seem to have missed the cause of his greatness.

The sins of Shallum are common enough in the history of those in power. He oppressed his people, conscripting them to build his palace and paying them nothing. He committed extortion; in the course of his reign he caused the innocent to be murdered. What would cause a man to do such a thing, especially after growing up in the palace of an honest king?

Greed and pride explain it. The little we know about Shallum is this: he had a desire for a two-story palace, decorated in red and paneled in cedar. He wanted the pomp and pride that goes with being a king. He was a little man in a big chair, and it was his downfall.

"Does it make you a king to have more and more cedar?" This is Jeremiah's stinging question. Just what does make a man a great leader? Is it brilliant oratory or great generalship? No. Great leaders have this in common: they do what is right. Josiah defended the cause of the poor and needy, delivering them from their oppressors. His son delivered them to their oppressors for his own personal pomp and prestige.

He was a little man far away and long ago. But his like is with us today. Consider this: if someone is unfairly treated in your place of employment, what do you do? Especially if you're the boss? It does not take a kingdom to create unrighteousness. Are there those around you who are the "poor and needy" —and do you neglect their cause? Do you say, "Well, they deserve what they get." It sounds righteous to say that, but consider well: do you always want to get what you deserve? God, the righteous judge, is merciful to those who will be merciful.

You may not have the power of a king. God knows what power you do have, however, and will ask of you what you have done for the poor and needy. "As often as you have done it for the least of these, my brothers, you have done it for me." We are to reign with Christ when he comes. Are we paneling the place in cedar—or are we defending the cause of the poor and the needy?

A Doorkeeper
Psalm 84

John Milton—who certainly knew better—put words in Satan's mouth: "Better a ruler in hell than a servant in heaven." Satan is not the ruler of hell; hell, rather, is his place of torment and punishment. To that end he shall surely go.

But Milton's character puts the point to us clearly. Most of us would rather be a proud character in a small part than a humble one in a large part. We would rather rule in our own hell than serve in God's heaven. This is because of our pride; we know best, and therefore we must rule—at least something.

The temptation is to be the biggest of frogs in the smallest of ponds. But that's what it is: temptation. The Psalmist has it right: it is better to be a doorkeeper in the house of God than anything in the "tents of the wicked." The choice is ours, however.

We can create the small pond, the personal hell—we can pitch the tents of the wicked on our own land. Perhaps it is in our family; perhaps on the job; maybe we even own the company that provides the job. It does not matter what the material is; the question is, what do we make of it? Do we use our place as a chance to rule, or to serve?

For there is the difference. This world is not our home, but we are certainly passing through it. If we choose to be proud rulers of whatever domain we happen to possess, we have created our own hell to rule. If we choose to serve God—in whatever circumstances—we choose to be a "doorkeeper." One who serves his fellow men, particularly one who points them to Jesus Christ, is a doorkeeper—the man who opens the door to the Temple of God.

Will God honor such a man? Certainly he will—through trial, at times. The trials may be difficult, but they will not be anything which cannot be overcome. God seeks such men.

The question is not one of your status in life. It does not revolve around your job, or your wealth, or your political station. It does not concern itself with your education. It is entirely a question of this: whom do you serve? Do you create your own kingdom in which to rule, a little pond for such a big frog—your own hell? Or do you seek first the kingdom of God, so that he may add all things to you? One way is tempting; the other is true. Do not choose by absence of mind; choose wisely and well.

On Idleness
2 Thessalonians 3

Most of us dream of the day when we shall be wealthy enough to cease being employees and join what we consider the ultimate in privilege: the idle rich. It matters little to us that most of the rich are not idle, but very much driven to work.

What is more important is this: God designed man to work; without work, a man is not complete. Paul brings that point to a more specific case here. There were evidently those who were idle in the church and expected the church to feed them.

Paul deals with this problem in these ways:

First, he begins by pointing out himself and his comrades as examples. They were entitled to be supported by the church, for they devoted themselves to the *work* of the church. This is an undeniable principle. However, in order to set an example to such people, Paul and his companions worked to earn their own living—so that all might see God's purpose clearly fulfilled.

Next, he recalls to their mind his specific rule: "If a man will not work, he shall not eat." This is not about those who *can not* work, but those who *will not*. This makes it clear!

Some, however, hoped to cover their idleness with busy-ness. Paul identifies this correctly too: they are busybodies. They flit from house to house, chatting—and hoping you will mistake this for ministry. Just because your calendar is full does not mean you are busy.

For such people there is an effective cure. We are not to associate with them. The object is that they will feel the proper shame—and get to work. As always, the objective of church discipline is restoration. They are still our brothers.

For us there is a lesson beyond the words on the page. We should not seek to become idle; that is profitless in spiritual as well as financial terms. Rather, we should seek out the work to which God calls us. Some few are wealthy enough that matters such as salary are not significant in the decision. Even they should choose work which is pleasing to God. As for the rest of us, we should not view work as a burden, but as the means by which God has allowed us to provide for the needs of others—instead of the others providing for us.

Of Whom I Am the Worst
1 Timothy 1

Paul never lost the sense that he was a sinner. Great sinners, it is said, make great saints—and this was never so true as with Paul. Consider this: here was a man who had persecuted the church from his youngest days. He zealously sought out the opportunity to jail Christians and even put them to death. It would test the love of even the greatest of disciples to forgive such a man; but Jesus would not be denied. Despite his evil, Christ chose him to be the apostle to the Gentiles.

So it is that Paul sees the entire point of Christ's coming: to save sinners. John's Gospel tells us that Jesus did not come to condemn the world, but that through him the world might be saved. Even a man like this, not knowing whom he was really persecuting, was forgiven.

Forgiven? Not just that, but raised to high position in the church. It is a lesson for all of us. Many of us are perfectly willing to take those we consider the worst of sinners and allow them the privilege of repentance. But afterwards, they are to sit in the back of the church and be invisible. That is man's way with things. God's way is different. He takes the vilest of sinners and turns them into glorious saints.

There are many reasons God does this—but Paul does not hesitate to tell us the one of most importance to the evangelist. It is to be an example to the world. If God can take a man like Paul and turn him into an apostle to the world, what sin have we committed which is so vile as to keep us from the love of God? What can we have possibly done that he cannot forgive? God forgave a man who slaughtered his children, and raised him to be an apostle; what will he do for us?

The love of God does not change. It does not matter if you are one thinking of becoming a Christian – or one who's been a Christian for fifty years. Whatever you have done, however horrible it might seem, he can forgive. He will forgive if you will turn to him and ask him, turning from your sin to his way of righteousness. You may think that no human being could possibly understand or forgive; you may be right. But God forgives. You only need to ask him in true repentance.

Paul's persecution was a great evil; his ministry a greater good. Sometimes God allows the worst to show his best.

All Those in Authority
1 Timothy 2:1-15

There is a consistent theme throughout the New Testament concerning those in authority: they are to be given all respect, and to be prayed for. For many American Christians this seems unusual, for we are taught to distrust authority. The issue is not trust; the issue is the spread of the Gospel.

Make no mistake: the purpose of Christ's coming was to seek and save the lost. To that end, therefore, God ordained a time of peace throughout the Roman Empire that the Gospel might spread quickly. How is this so?

God ordains authority

We must remember that man proposes, but God disposes. The authorities that exist do so by God's consent—either that good things will abound or that out of their evil greater good will be brought forth. In either event, we should praise the grace of God for providing them. And why not? The faith is one which preaches peace to all men—something greatly welcome to the civil authorities. Most of the laws we have reflect the righteousness of God, however imperfectly. Therefore, as we would welcome any act of God, we should pray for those in authority over us.

In peace the Gospel spreads

In time of conflict many see an opportunity for the Gospel. This is indeed the case. We must remember, however, that Christianity alone among the major religions of the world invites examination of the facts of its founding. The fact of the Resurrection is central to the faith. Such examination comes best in times of peace. In war men look to their immortality; in peace they can be led to look for the truth.

In peace the reputation of the church is glorious

In war men value that which is destructive. In peace, they value that which is good. The church is the ultimate good thing among men, for it is the body of Christ. By our conduct we may win others to Christ in time of peace.

Therefore, pray for those in authority over us. Pray that there may be peace in our time. Pray that those in authority will see in the church the gentle correction of their sins, and the staunch support of their righteousness—so that all men may see Christ in us.

The Overseer
1 Timothy 3:1-16

The role of "overseer" (elder, bishop and presbyter are other terms for the same word) is one which dates to the earliest days of the church. The qualifications for this task start with one thing: desire. The man who wants this job must desire a "noble work." "Noble" is often a synonym for "self-sacrificing" —and all who would succeed at such a task must indeed be that.

Such a man seems a bit tame by the world's standards. By our thought today, a man who is the husband of but one wife (loosely, not a man who goes through wives like calendars) seems a bit stuffy. Indeed, all these virtues have something in common: they represent a man who is greatly under control. "Flamboyant" or "notorious" do not come to mind as adjectives for this man.

Why does this seem so odd to us? Is it because our culture portrays such a man as one who has "missed all the fun in life?" Perhaps it is; for this is the oldest lie in history—that evil is enlightening, fun and altogether to be desired while righteousness is stale and boring.

We try to have it both ways. We want the sensation of doing something which is bold, daring and especially risqué, but at the same time we like to think of ourselves as trustworthy, honest and someone who can be counted upon—in short, faithful. The former is usually tied up with sin; the latter with righteousness. It is like asking for a brightly lit darkness.

The man to be admired for his progress as a Christian—an elder, if you will—is one who has mastered his bodily desires (sex, alcohol and temperance); his emotions (anger); his desires (money) and his pride. Such a man is mature—in the very best sense of that word. We see "mature" as a negative word today ("old and gray") —but substitute the phrase "old pro." One who has mastered the art of living the Christian life.

Such people are required to be "apt to teach." The phrase does not mean so much good at speaking as it does one who has mastered the subject. It might better be said that such a man is one from whom we can learn much. Most of us learn best by example, and such examples are sorely needed today.

More than that, such examples should serve for the rest of us as guiding lights. The Christ I cannot see may be portrayed in the elder I can.

October 19

A Young Man's Gift
1 Timothy 4:11-14

Timothy was at the time of this writing a young man—with a great responsibility. Responsibility affects different people in differing ways; Paul counsels his young man not to let anyone look down on him (in those days the aged were respected, not scorned) but rather *to set an example.*

We learn by example. We expect Christian maturity in the older Christian. How powerful the example is, then, when found in the young Christian. What example should the young man be?

Speech

It is the first thing we notice about a person's character: their speech. Not just how they say things (or their use of offensive language) but what they talk about! Is your speech idle chatter, or do the things of God occupy your conversations?

Life

Talk will take you some distance, but the life lived must match up to it. Do you practice what you preach?

Love

No virtue so graces a young man as the selfless love described in the Scriptures. Kindness is almost synonymous with grandma; generosity with grandpa—but love is beautiful at any age.

Faith

In whom do you trust? Are you constantly scheming to get rich, or are you trusting God for the things you need? Do you look to him to guide your steps, and do you call on his name for sustenance even though all around think it foolish?

Purity

Purity is not innocence—it is knowing sin and refusing it. Purity is not just in sexual matters (though that is important for the young) but also in business dealings and personal relationships. Are you honest? Do you keep your word? Do you behave yourself?

These are matters which do not need a description of age. They are usually found in older Christians—who have learned by experience. The young may have them too, if they will look to the examples around them and imitate those who imitate Christ. You reach your goal faster if you take aim on it first.

Practical Workings
1 Timothy 5

There is a common misconception about the Bible that it is concerned with the dreamy and impractical side of life. Simple examination should reveal this for a myth—and nowhere better than this passage. It says much to indict our times for their lack of family care.

In the days when this was written an elderly widow of a poor man was quite literally subject to starvation. The church, following the custom of the synagogue, took up a collection of food for these widows. The difficulty with this is abuse: those who did not really need such help might be tempted to take it anyway. Paul lays out certain practical steps:

The widow who is genuinely in need should be known for her good deeds.

She should also be over sixty years of age, so that it is certain that she is not capable (in that time) of supporting herself.

The younger widows are specifically exempted from this distribution of food

Families are to be the first source of care for a widow.

Note that this "list" is more or less a permanent one; to be on it means that you are not capable of supporting yourself for the rest of your life. Temporary charity is not affected here; this is an instance of life-long support.

There is a key point in here, one which is often missed in our society. The family is to care for the needy first. Only if the family is absent or unable to care for the widow is the church to step in. In this way the church, by *not* feeding the widow, strengthens the family. The test is not the beggar on the street corner but the elderly in your own family—who feeds them? We may mollify our feelings of charity by giving money to the corner beggar—but caring for our own can be much more costly.

The point is simple: God has a plan for our family and social lives as well as for us personally. We are, in the words of the Old Testament, to "honor our father and mother." Our children should see that in our care of our parents we honor those who gave us life, and the God who teaches us to care for those in our own family. Who knows? Perhaps the whirligig of time will bring the lesson back—to your own children.

On Wealth
1 Timothy 6

Wealth, in the times of the Old Testament, was looked upon as a sign of God's favor (remember how rich Job was? And Abraham?) The ancients reasoned that since God rules and reigns, anyone who became rich must have done so at least by God's consent. Whether this is a blessing or a trial is still a question today.

In one sense wealth is a blessing: "I can solve that problem with one check!" It is clear that poverty has its drawbacks as well.

But wealth can also be a trial. Paul makes it clear to us: those who chase riches first have fallen into a trap. They have placed the things that cannot bring eternal happiness before the things that can.

But what about the one who has already attained wealth? This is a question that applies to most Americans, the wealthiest people on the planet. Paul gives us these commands:

First, do not be arrogant. "First class is a style, not a seat on the airplane," one passenger told me. It may be elegant, it may be refined—but it is not arrogant. Rather it is gracious. A wealthy man who is kind and gracious is not resented but admired.

Next, do not trust your money to be your salvation. It is a useful tool, but it cannot cure death.

Instead, the rich are to do good with their wealth. This may take many forms; but there is one constant factor: the willingness to share. Wealth donated ostentatiously receives its reward in applause; wealth shared generously receives its reward from the Lord.

Rightly used, wealth is not only a sign of God's favor but also the method of passing that favor along. For the rich man, such sharing lays up the treasure in heaven so many will long for on judgment day. It was best expressed in a song:

> He is no fool
>> If he should choose
> To give the things he cannot keep
>> to buy what he can never lose.

That which you have, share. Are there those poorer than you? Do not look down on them but be their benefactor. Are there those richer than you? Do not envy them, but be their example.

Do Not Be Ashamed
2 Timothy 1

God provides the Spirit for the Christian—and the Christian spends much time and effort holding back the Spirit.

Why? The Spirit of God within us is, as Paul describes him here, a spirit of power, of love and self-discipline.

Power. In us lives the Spirit of God, the Almighty. How often have we heard described the mighty things done by the least likely of souls—and then said, "But it cannot happen with me."

Love. Power without motive is aimless; the aim of the Spirit is to show the world the love of God, displayed at the Cross. In so doing, we should be the examples of love.

Self-discipline. Power may be aimed, but it must also be controlled. To this end we are given self-discipline.

With all this, so often we are silent when we should speak—or worse. We are too often ashamed even to mention the name of Christ, particularly when it would make the greatest impact. This should not be.

The circumstances of Paul's writing are such that most of us would be embarrassed. He is in prison. Those who have a friend in prison often neglect that friend, or ignore him completely. Paul puts it in quite the opposite sense. He has met opposition because of the Gospel—as we will, if we will not be timid—and that opposition has him in chains. Just where God can use him best!

Many have deserted him. No doubt they were embarrassed to mention that their teacher was in jail. But note that Paul is not ashamed. Prison is what men confer upon us; it is an honor to be in prison for the Gospel.

Remember this: if you are ashamed of the Gospel of Christ, if you avoid mentioning that you are a Christian and hope that no one will notice, then on the day of his return Christ will be ashamed of you. Rather, you should consider the Gospel the most precious of your treasures, to be spoken about readily. Who knows what you might accomplish? God does not always use the eloquent or the mighty; he has a habit of taking the least likely of people in the least likely of circumstances and—if they are not ashamed of him—turning them into great saints.

Broken Symmetry
2 Timothy 2

If we died with him

We shall also live with him. Make no mistake; the resurrection of the dead is intrinsic to the Christian faith, for Christ is risen indeed from the dead. We believe that all shall rise from the dead, some to judgment, some to glory, depending upon their relationship to Jesus Christ. What evidence of this is there? Only this: that Jesus is risen from the grave.

If we endure

We will also reign with him. It is no small matter. We were taken from the depths of sin and redeemed by grace. Even to be a servant of the Lord God Almighty forever would be a great privilege and honor, exceeding anything this world has to offer. But this is not will happen to us. We will not only serve him, we will reign with him. How this shall be no mind knows and no tongue can tell—but the Lord has promised it.

If we disown him

He will also disown us. The essence of the matter is your personal relationship with Jesus Christ. Nothing else is of any importance in comparison. If we say to the world that we do not know him, he will say to the Father that he does not know us. The matter is that serious. Consider your words carefully, for the time may soon come when it is more than a matter of life and death—much more.

If we are faithless

He still remains as he is—faithful. Faithfulness is one of his attributes, and God is his attributes. He can no more be faithless than the sun could turn to pink lemonade. No matter what we do, he is still faithful.

This is a great comfort, for it means that no matter how great our sin, he is willing and able to forgive it. We may turn our backs on him, but he never turns his back on us. Softly and tenderly he pleads with us to return to him. When we do, like the Prodigal's father, he runs to us with open arms and welcomes us home.

Christian, count your blessings. They may be disguised as pain and death, but through them we will reign with our Lord Jesus. If you cannot say that, then go to him in repentant prayer—and see that he is faithful; he will forgive. He must be true to himself, and He is Love.

Inspired
2 Timothy 3:16-17

There is much debate over the exact meaning of this passage. It is a pity that so much of the debate is so acid. For the result of inspiration—whatever the word might really mean—is quite clear in this passage.

Useful for teaching

The primary purpose of the Scripture is to teach us about Jesus the Christ. If it did nothing else, it would be worthy of all the attention given to it. For in Christ, and no one else, is salvation. So the book of books that teaches us how he died for our sins—and is coming again— is clearly to be taught, again and again.

Rebuking

The matter is relatively simple. Each of us, at one time or another, is in need of rebuke. Rebuke is the blunt, simple answer that brings home the conviction of the Spirit. Sometimes nothing but this will do.

Correcting

More commonly (one hopes) the rebuke is not called for; rather, the sinner must be corrected in a loving fashion. The gentle whisper from your wife that tells you that, perhaps, you were a little too emphatic in your opinions; the sudden conviction by the Spirit when listening to a sermon—this too is the function of the Scripture.

Training in righteousness

We must not only be rebuked and corrected from our wrongs but encouraged and taught to do what is right. One can be hit with "thou shalt not" until spiritual timidity sets in. Rather, our Lord tells us to do what is right—and we must be trained for it.

The purpose

Note that the purpose of this is not the performance of good works. The Scripture does not see good works as an end; they are merely the indicator of the holiness within a person. The purpose of all this teaching and correction is to produce someone who is *thoroughly equipped* for every good work. That such a person will do these works is obvious. God, however, does not look upon the works but the heart that brought them about. So then, we must diligently study the Scripture—so that we too may become those who are equipped for good works. God "breathed" it for our use; let us use it frequently and well.

Time for Departure
2 Timothy 4

This letter is written at end of Paul's life; apparently he could see that he was about to be martyred for the faith. Despite that, it is full of hope for the future. But Paul faces his death calmly, for he can look back over his accomplishments for the Lord.

I have fought the good fight

Paul says nothing about "winning." We often make the mistake of confusing results seen for hearts unseen—but God does not. He knows that Paul has struggled earnestly for the Gospel. Did he have failures? Surely he did; but God can take our failures and turn them into his successes. Sometimes we must fail so that another Christian can succeed much more than we could imagine.

I have finished the race

Many people make great beginnings. When a new baby is born, we are all excited; we are enthused by beginnings. But beginnings lead to other things, and the cheering is long gone as the runner paces through the middle of the race. Many people find that Christianity soon becomes a source of resistance by the world—and they quit. Paul here points out his finish: he made it to the end line. There are those who run marathons not to be the fastest—it is beyond their capabilities—but just to say, "I did it." We too must finish the race before us.

I have kept the faith

This can be seen in a number of ways:

It may mean that Paul has received the faith from Christ, and he has kept it, not adding or subtracting.

It may mean that he has personally been faithful to Christ, never denying him.

It may mean that despite all his trials, he has never lost sight of the fact that Jesus is Lord, and put his trust in him.

All these, and more, can be seen in this little phrase.

Reward

Our Lord is just. If we labor for him, he will reward us. He will reward us in accordance with the riches of his mercy, so Paul looked forward to the crown of righteousness. That crown is available to all who will fight the good fight, finish the race and keep the faith. Christian, that crown is waiting for you—so persevere! Keep on keeping on!

You Cannot Cheat an Honest Man
Titus 1

Swindlers are an amiable lot, by and large. In eighteenth-century London one such set up shop advertising a marvelous investment opportunity—but one so secret "that no one may know what it is." He promised magnificent returns on the money, however, and managed to collect several thousand pounds before happily absconding with the money.

How do swindlers get away with it? They are swindling those who want to get rich quickly. Those who want to get rich quickly are often not too careful as to the ethics of their methods—they know that the honest method of hard work takes too long for their taste. So they are perfectly willing to let someone else take their money and engage in the shady dealing. P. T. Barnum had it right: you cannot cheat an honest man.

This is the negative version of Paul's word to Titus: to the pure, all things are pure. Those who are pure in heart cannot conceive the desire to swindle—therefore, they cannot be swindled.

Purity and innocence

Purity is not the same as innocence. Innocence does not know the sin; purity knows it and rejects it. The word "purity" when applied to people sounds so much like "Puritanical" that we often reject it. But consider: which man would you rather do business with—the one who cheats on his wife and his taxes, or the faithful man? Then which one should you be?

Purity and God

"Blessed are the pure in heart, for they shall see God." Indeed, it is quite correct to say that the pure heart is the only instrument capable of focusing on God. For only the pure in heart can understand his will, and know him intimately. God is holy; if we are to know him, we must be holy and pure.

Becoming pure in heart

Many of us desire to be worldly and sophisticated on Saturday night—and then get up early on Sunday to be pure and holy. This only produces a permanent hypocrisy. If you wish to be pure and see God you must (as Peter tells us) purify yourself by obeying the truth. Sorrow for sin is good; sorrow for sin which produces repentance is better; sorrow which produces repentance and obedience is God's desire—the best. Do not let the good be the enemy of the best. Purify yourself; obey the truth.

Older Women
Titus 2

There is a sense of community found in the early church which seems to be lacking today. One example of this is in the instructions Paul gives to Titus with regard to older women teaching the younger ones.

In our culture today it is almost unimaginable that a younger woman would ever ask advice of an older one. After all, our culture teaches us that youth alone has skill. The slightest observation of the world, however, denies this. Experience still counts. Here, however, is an even more extreme statement to our ears: the older women should actually *teach* the younger ones!

To do this, these women must be worthy of the title, "teacher." To this end Paul commands that they be reverent, not slanderers or drunkards. If you are to teach, you must first be able.

What, then, are they to teach? The words seem incredible to our modern ears; what would the feminists think if our older women were to teach the younger ones this:

Love for their husbands and children—rather than self-fulfillment.

Self-control—rather than self-assertion.

Purity—rather than "open marriage."

To be busy at home—rather than too busy to be at home.

To be kind—instead of strident.

And worst of all, to be subject to their husbands!

Why would Paul command such utterly radical things? "So that no one will malign the word of God."

It seems radical, but consider: how does one malign the word of God? By representing it to say something it does not. If we say that God's word makes men and women interchangeable parts, we are maligning the word.

Each era has its characteristic mistakes. Those living in those eras look at the word of God and say, "What an error!" But the eras pass, and the word of God remains. The "errors" of God remain with us, because even the foolishness of God is greater than the wisdom of man (or woman). We make a mistake when we attempt to change God's word to fit the times; much better to fit the times to God's word. He, after all, created time—and He will have the last Word.

Be Careful
Titus 3

Paul, in magnificent words, sums up the Gospel of grace in this chapter. He stresses that we are saved by God's mercy, not our righteous actions, and are the heirs of eternal life. He ends this noble eloquence by telling Titus to "stress these things." To what end?

"That those who have trusted God may be careful to devote themselves to doing good." It seems a little trite to bring forth the glories of God's grace only to have them serve as a motive for doing good. The next paragraph gives us the reason by comparison.

Evidently those on Crete (where Titus was ministering) were given to argument and controversy. So Paul tells them to avoid such things—like arguing over genealogies, or quarrels about tiny points of the Old Testament. He knew that such arguments produced nothing of good fruit. Tempers flare and pride is raised when men argue about ordinary things; how much more when they argue about the things of God?

It is not sufficient to say, "don't do that." Paul knew that you cannot just drive out an evil; you must also replace it with something which is good. So he tells them to "be careful" to devote themselves to doing good. Don't just cease from argument; replace it with good works. If you are busy doing the good works of the body of Christ, will you have time to debate? The serious nature of this offense is clear from Paul's instruction to shun a man who has been twice warned for this.

Paul's letters often end with a section of personal requests. It is interesting here that he asks Titus to help some friends of his—the very practical acts of doing good he has just commended. He adds another reason for this: so that they may live productive lives, not being a burden.

One fascinating note comes from this. Look at the list of those Paul has asked Titus to help. Included is the name of one Zenas—who is a lawyer. A man whose profession is argument and debate, Paul asks that he be given everything he needs. If the professional arguer can become one who is worthy of such care, no doubt for his good works, then which of us would not be ashamed to continue as a "Christian" who debates the words rather than obey the Word?

A Letter Debated
Philemon

This little letter seems so personal, so devoted to one little incident, that many have debated its place in the Scripture. It is seldom the subject of a sermon. This is a pity, for it is filled with instruction by example:

No human being is insignificant to God

In this time a slave was nothing but a living tool. For Paul to take such time to write to a wealthy man like Philemon shows the care he had in God's name. To do so with the courtesy and gentleness he used marks him as one who loves deeply. But to send the slave, Onesimus, back with the letter—that signals Paul's love in the most visible way.

Good may come of evil

We often ask why there is evil in the world. No doubt Philemon thought Onesimus' departure a loss, an evil thing. He lost a slave; he gained a brother. One reason God permits evil is so that greater good may come of it in this sinful world.

The call upon the rich

See how Paul refuses to presume upon Philemon's goodness! Even though the man is rich—he owns slaves and his house is large enough for the church's meeting—Paul asks a favor. This from Paul, the man who brought Philemon to Christ. That the rich are commanded to be generous is clear; that others should not presume upon them is now also clear.

The price of reconciliation

The price of reconciliation is always this: that the pain of the sinner falls upon the shoulders of the reconciler. It is so with Christ, reconciling us to God at the Cross. Here Paul gives us an example of it in daily living: if Onesimus owes Philemon anything, Paul will pay. Are we so devoted to the cause of Christ that we would pay to reconcile one brother to another? This lesson alone justifies the one small page this book occupies in the Bible.

It is a letter of one chapter, of twenty-five verses. We find no memory verses for our children in it. Yet it gives us great lessons. Are there some you do not consider as worth your time? Do you curse the evil done to you, and not praise the good that comes from it later? Are you courteous to rich and poor? Are you willing to pay the price of your brothers' reconciliation? These are lessons worth a page of reading.

Exact Representation
Hebrews 1

This passage may just be the closest thing the New Testament ever gives in the way of an explanation of the Trinity—at least as far as the Christ is concerned. We often see Jesus as the gentle lamb of God; he is far more than that.

He is the Word of God—the ultimate message of God to man. In former times God used prophets, ordinary men, to speak to us. Now, the Word is Christ.

He is the "heir of all things" —that is, all authority in heaven and on earth is given to him. He is the one to whom all things belong; he is their natural master, by right.

Through him the universe was made. We know that God created the universe; now we know that God created it through Jesus Christ. He is the one who "did the work," so to speak.

He is the radiance of God's glory—that part of God's glory which we can see, for in him God was seen in the flesh.

He is the exact representation of God's being. As a perfect photograph would portray me, Jesus is the perfect representation in the flesh of God the Father.

He sustains all things by his word. Why do the laws of the universe remain unchanging? Because he says so.

He provided purification for our sins. It is one thing to be awesome; it is entirely another to be awesome and yet one who loves to the point of the Cross.

He *sits* at the Father's right hand. Not only is he God's "right hand man," he is God's equal—for a subordinate would be required to stand.

This, then, is the Jesus of Nazareth who seems so reachable to so many. We sometimes forget the sense of awe which is his due; the sense which causes us to see ourselves as unclean sinners in the presence of a holy God. This is the wonder of the ages: that God, the sovereign of all things, became a man like us, even to the point of death; and in dying gave us eternal life. Our sense of wonder at this must begin by knowing who Jesus truly is. As you go to him in prayer tonight, remember to whom you are speaking. The one who is the Friend—and the Awesome God.

Praise the Lord
Psalm 103

The Psalms were originally meant to be sung, evidently. As such, we see much repetition in them. One curious feature is this: very often the praise of the Lord consists of the Psalmist telling us to praise the Lord. In this Psalm we see why.

His Benefits

The first cause for praise is perhaps the simplest. It concerns what God does for those who love him. Forgiveness is first; as it should be. But we see healing next, and then the "crown" of love and compassion. It is an interesting picture; as a symbol of the honor God has showered upon us we have his love and compassion.

His benefits are those things that satisfy our desires. Note that our desires are satisfied with "good things." God does not ask us to desire and not be satisfied. He wants to satisfy our desires with good things.

His Character

The writer knows that character is shown in action. The Lord's actions begin with righteousness, as portrayed in the ministry of Moses, the Law Giver. But He is not just a stern judge; he is slow to anger and quick to forgive—we might say gracious. Because of his great love for us he removes our sins from us; it is the love a father has for his little children.

His Compassion

Compassion begins with knowledge. Did you ever meet one of your school teachers several years after you graduated—and discover that they were actually human? The ogre turns out to be an ordinary person. God knows our frailties and the shortness of our days, and thus has compassion for us. He does this for those who love him. How can we recognize those who love him? They are those who obey him.

Praise the Lord for what he has done for us. Praise the Lord for who he is; his character is beyond comparison. Praise the Lord for the compassion and love he showers upon those who are his children. Is it any wonder that the Psalmist commands all that God has made— including us—to praise the Lord of Creation?

Hold On
Hebrews 3

The house of God: did you think of yourself as a part of that? You know that we are called the Temple of his Spirit; here we are called the very house of God.

There is a condition, however. We must hold on—hold on to our courage and to our hope.

Courage, for it is through fear that Satan attempts to pry us away from God's house. In this world we will have trials and tribulations, and for this we must have courage.

But it is not a courage of a grim nature. This is not the courage of those doomed to defeat, but defiant still. This is the courage of those who know that victory is sure. It was gained at the Cross, and Satan cannot overturn it.

As an example, the writer tells us of the Israelites in the desert. They abandoned their courage and hope, and as a result never entered the Promised Land. They gave up. This, despite all that God had shown them, was their hardness of heart showing.

The message is clear: it is possible to falter at the end. This is not the infirmity of old age, nor the change in role that comes with the wisdom old age often brings. It is the abandonment of the hope and courage of youth. That hope, that courage, should not be abandoned but polished and perfected into maturity.

How do we "polish" and "perfect" such hope and courage? Our writer tells us plainly: we do it for each other. There is a spot on your back that you cannot scratch, no matter how you contort your body. So you ask for help; we "scratch each other's backs." We do this literally; we do this figuratively. When we do it spiritually, we do it by encouraging one another on a daily basis.

Are there those around you who are suffering trials? Of course there are. You may not be able to help them in any physical way, but you can provide encouragement. You can remind them of the hope we share in Jesus Christ. Do you remember the times in your life when you needed encouragement, and someone came with a friendly arm around the shoulder? As you have received these things from others, you should pass them along.

Suffering is certain along the way; unless the Lord returns first, death is our common lot. But the hope of the Resurrection and the courage of Christ will sustain us along the way.

The Word is Sharper
Hebrews 4:12-13

The word of God is living and active, the writer tells us. Indeed, when we hear the phrase, "the word of God," we can think of three things:

We may think of it in terms of direct revelation, as to one of the prophets. "The word of God came to me..." In such circumstances, as God speaks directly, the prophet must obey. It is the direct command of the Lord, and carries his full authority.

We may think of it most commonly as the Scripture itself, the Bible. This is indeed a correct sense, and it is the one most often used when this passage is quoted.

Or we may think of it as Jesus himself, the Word of God, as he is proclaimed in John's Gospel.

All of these three senses are correct in referring to this passage. Consider it this way:

Should God speak directly to you, in unmistakable terms and words which are for your ears alone, would you dare resist him? Would you say to him, "Are you sure?" Indeed, you would not. But it would be a dividing point in your life: Obey, or know that you are one who has taken himself out of fellowship with God. It is a terrible peril.

The Scripture carries with it the same sense. For though it is not directed at each of us specifically, its truth is such that it carries the same penetrating power—and authority. When the Scripture convicts you, do you dare disobey?

Then there is the sense in which your divine Companion can convict you. No revelation from on high, no quotation of chapter and verse, but the still, small voice that says, "This you must do." Indeed, the most perilous of voices to disobey.

Christian, has he spoken to you directly? Has he spoken to you through the Scriptures? Or perhaps the still small voice of Christ himself is upon you. Do not ignore the promptings of the Lord. Give to him the honor that is his due. Heed his words, and do not slink away like a skunk. Stand up in courage. If you do not feel strong enough to obey, tell him so—and ask for his strength. Faith, strength and courage are in his hand—to give to those who will hear the Word of God.

Priesthood
Hebrews 5

It is a common expression among Christians: we are a royal priesthood. Have you ever considered what that really means? Here the author explains the priesthood as God might see it.

The priest represents men to God. We of course understand that we are to represent God to all men—such is the great commission—but do we understand that we are to intercede with God on behalf of others? Indeed, even those others who persecute us?

Because we too are sinners, and we have been ignorant of the grace of God, we can deal gently with sinners ourselves. We should never look down on those for whom we intercede; rather, we should go to God on their behalf with all humility and kindness.

To do this we must offer sacrifices for our own sins. The only acceptable sacrifice is Christ on the Cross; therefore, our own repentance and contrition must precede our intercession for others.

We did not "volunteer" for this; God has proclaimed it. Only God can make a priesthood. Not one of us is worthy of the calling.

Our High Priest, Jesus, is the eternal high priest. He is the one who is closest to God for us, as we stand close to God on behalf of others.

So then, knowing our own weaknesses and dealing gently with others, called but not volunteering, we stand before God, pleading for others. We plead for our fellow Christians, we plead for those whom God loved so much that his Son went to the Cross. Each of us who claims the name of Christ is such a priest, whether we wanted the job or not.

So then, Christian, do you stand before God Almighty, pleading for the lives, health and most of all souls of those you know? It is not yours to choose for whom you must pray; if God lays them upon your heart, to Him you must go with their name on your lips. Do you beg God's mercy upon those who persecute you, that they might learn who He is and join his family?

Stand in the gap for those around you. Go before God, interceding for them. Be what he has called you to be.

Confident of Better Things
Hebrews 6

The author begins with a dangerous introduction in verse 9: "dear friends." It is usually more dangerous to give advice to friends rather than strangers. When giving advice to strangers it is usually the case that they have asked you for it. Friends usually have not.

What advice does he give? It is the warning about a lack of perseverance to the end. He tells them a simple truth. If once you were fertile for Christ, but now you are sterile, then God must eventually take action. It is not that warning, however, that is the concern. It is the correction of poor habits. How do we encourage those who have been faithful for many years to continue to be so?

God is not unjust

Have you worked hard for the kingdom of God? God is not unjust; in due time he will reward that hard work. Have you sacrificed? He is not unjust; the sacrifice will bring blessing beyond measure as God deals with you.

Diligent to the end

It is one thing to begin well. It is entirely another to continue to be diligent. Many of us get lazy and decide that we no longer need to work with the same care and enthusiasm we did at first. We become bored; we go through the motions. This is often because our view is so short. God tells us to take the longer view—the view with hope. To make sure that our hope will come to pass, we must be diligent to the very end.

Faith and Patience

Each mature Christian understands the need for faith. But often we do not understand the need for the combination of faith and patience. It is one thing to say, "Someday God will..." It is entirely another to say, "Someday God will... and in the meanwhile, until my dying day, I will patiently and faithfully work for him." The length of time between our first enthusiasm and the day of his reward sometimes dampens our spirit. We are to be long distance runners, moving at a pace such that no matter how long the race (do any of us know the day of our death?) we still have strength to finish. How long did Abraham wait for Isaac? We must have the same patience. Do not be discouraged; do not give up hope. God is just, and his reward is sure.

A Rebellious People
Ezekiel 12-14

Ezekiel, like most of the prophets, was dealing with a rebellious people. It is the duty of the prophet to bring unwelcome news, and Ezekiel was no exception.

Why is this so common? It is because the people have eyes, but do not see, and have ears, but do not hear. Have you ever tried to explain something to your teen age son, only to walk away with the feeling that he understood every word you said, and no thought that you conveyed? Ezekiel knew exactly that feeling—with the entire house of Israel.

So the Lord commands him to do something unusual. He is to dig through the wall of his house; cover his face so he cannot see his homeland, and set out for a foreign place. The action was prophetic, but it had no effect on Israel. They refused to listen.

Why are the people so hard-hearted? One reason is given; it is that things go on from day to day just as they have before. We are like the man jumping from a tall building. Each floor on the way down he was heard to say, "So far, so good; so far, so good." The street is rushing up quickly towards us, but so far, so good—so things look like they will never change.

Another reason is that there is no shortage of prophets—of good news! The nation may be mired in sin; its evil a complete reproach, and its sinfulness plain to all—but there will be a chorus of voices telling us that we have now achieved a state of "sexual honesty" and "liberation." By applying a label to sin we think we cover it over. We call adultery "having an affair" or "expanding our sexual horizons"; greed is "the entrepreneurial spirit"; arrogance is nothing but "self-respect" and a "positive self-esteem." The labels sound good, but sin is still sin, and it is still a reproach.

"This is what the Sovereign Lord says: 'Repent'"—or so the prophet records. God's demand is simple and constant, that we turn from our ways and return to him. The demand never changes, for he never changes. Our rebellion is disguised by new forms and the fading memory of older versions, but it remains always the same. God's wrath—and his mercy—do not change either. For those who will not repent, his wrath. For those who will, the tender mercy of a Father who loves his children. For those who love him—the duty to proclaim his words.

A Friend in High Places
Hebrews 10:18-39

The look on the sergeant's face was priceless. He was all set to chew out this new recruit. After all, that recruit had barely made it to sign in just in time. But just before the sergeant let out his tirade, the older gentleman next to the recruit calmly spoke. "I'm Colonel Macy," the man said. "The young man has been a guest in my home, and I was a bit late getting him here. I hope that hasn't caused you any trouble, Sergeant."

The sergeant assured him that it was no trouble at all. The recruit (me) reflected upon the value of having friends in high places.

So it is with all Christians: we have a friend in the highest of places. Like that recruit, we can deal with things a bit differently. Where once we would have stayed back, hiding in the shadows lest the Lord God notice us, now we can come near "in full assurance of faith." Our behavior is changed because we have a friend in high places.

> We begin to act like one in the know. Our knowledge of things exceeds that of other people—not because we are smarter, but because God has revealed his purposes to us. Not by our wisdom, but by his, our lives are filled with peace that passes understanding.

> Our behavior changes too. If we have friends in high places, we discover that we are expected to act like that friend would have us act. He did not achieve that place by indolence, and we are expected to behave in a similar way.

> We soon can become a go-between for our friends. The religious word for this is "priest." It means simply one who uses his friendship to assist his friends in their needs. Did you ever do a friend a favor by asking another friend for one?

That's us. We are the friends of God, the children of the kingdom. We are no longer condemned; we have influence in heaven. We are in the know, having had revealed the wisdom of God. Therefore, we begin to behave like those in the know—those who know what God wants (and expects). We go to our "person of influence" (Christ) on behalf of our friends.

Now you know what a kingdom of priests is: it's a circle of people with friends in high places.

Give Thanks to the Lord
Psalm 107

His love endures forever—this is the promise of the Psalmist, one who should know. Consider how this is:

Some of us were lost—just plain wandering around in life. Our Lord reaches out to us, and shows us the way.

Some, however, were in active rebellion against God. "I want to sleep with my girlfriend," one said, "therefore there is no God." Did God utterly reject that one? No! He subjected him to suffering—but when he cried to him he was quick to answer and return him to fellowship.

Some were just foolish—paying no attention to God. Did he pay no attention to them? No, he afflicted them, so that by their suffering they might return to him.

Some sought the things of this world—wealth, fame and power. They were riding above the storm—until the storm rose above them. Did God abandon them? No, he rescued them so that they might know who is God.

Some—does this sound familiar? —descended into wickedness. They started out as righteous people, but soon declined into the most wicked. Even these, who could be seen as those who had denied him, God did not abandon. Did Christ abandon Peter? No, he restored him! So God restores all who will turn to him

But, you say, I am none of these things. I study the Word; I pray; I worship. Hear the words of the Psalmist:

"Whoever is wise, let him heed these things and consider the great love of the Lord."

If God will reach out to the lost, the rebellious, the foolish, the worldly and even the wicked, is there anyone to whom he will not reach? If you are his child, and one who imitates him (however poorly) then there is no one on earth to whom you will not reach in God's name. In my own strength I can do very little, but in his strength I am mighty. Are you then mighty for the weak? Are you a guide to the lost, a counsel to the fool, a mediator to the rebellious and a priest to the wicked? Such is your Lord's command. Reach out to the lost as he did. He causes his rain to fall on the just and the unjust; surely then you can cause his mercy to fall upon both as well.

"Yet You Say"
Ezekiel 18

How often we hear it: God does not exist—and the atheist is mad at him for it. It is an ancient mistake.

"The way of the Lord is not just." That is the lament of ancient Israel, and God deals with it here.

Our perception. If a man is wicked—no matter what he does after his sin—he should be severely punished. That is the intent of the law. But understand God's point of view: if it were just a matter of punishing the wicked, the planet would have been a cinder long ago. Perhaps God has something else in mind; if it were just a matter of punishment for sins, does not God have plenty of evidence to destroy us all?

God's view. God's objective is different. We see sin as belonging to others; we are the offended. But in every sin against us there are two who are offended: the one on earth (who is also a sinner, having offended as well) and God (the innocent one, who does not sin, for it is impossible for him to sin). Which of us is more qualified and justified in pronouncing judgment?

But God does not pronounce judgment. His object is not the punishment of the sinner (if that were so, we would all be suffering in hell this minute) but rather the repentance of those who have sinned. If a man turns away from his sin, repents and follows what God desires, God spares him—now and eternally.

And we complain this is unfair! But if we, the sinners who are offended, complain—that is one thing. God, the innocent, forgives. If the innocent one forgives, how can the guilty complain?

Even if we do complain, do we not condemn ourselves? How often have you complained of someone else doing something which—if your secret thoughts could be read—you have done yourself? We are sinners. We recognize the justice of righteousness; out of self-interest we complain about others but justify ourselves. God is not fooled.

Neither is he merciless. If the wicked man—even the wicked man who judges others according to his own sins—turns away from his foolishness, God will forgive. God's will is that mercy triumph over judgment—but that depends upon each and every one of us. Will we repent? Will we turn from our ways and follow him? On such matters turn the fate of nations—and more important, heaven and hell for each of us.

Be Wise, My Son
Proverbs 27:11

Most of us will never play in major league baseball. Not many of us will be among the "beautiful people," nor will most of us have our "fifteen minutes of fame." The norm of the human race is to go from birth to death unnoticed by history—but well known to those around us.

There comes a time when we must ask: "what is life all about? How do I know I've done a good job? Why should a man try so hard to do well?" The search for meaning in life has occupied the philosophers for ages—but most of us are not philosophers either.

There is one point that is clear to most of us. If you want to know what kind of a man someone is, you can usually tell by the way he does his work. By his works you know the craftsman, it is said. It is true, too.

But what are the works of life? How can I say, "I led a successful life?" For most of us this cannot be measured by wealth—there are many who have as much; nor by fame—we are known to our friends and anonymous to the world; nor by the brilliance of our minds. If we are to measure ourselves as human beings, I submit that there are these criteria:

Whatever you use to measure me, it must be something that I hold to be very important.

Whatever you use to measure me, it must be something that I have spent long months on – not just a day's occupation.

Whatever you use to measure me, it must be something which can honestly be said to reflect the whole of whatever makes me who I truly am.

One measurement fits these things: my children. I hold them very dear; of course they take a long time, and as they see me in day to day life much more than others, they reflect who I truly am.

Is it any wonder, that Solomon commanded wisdom for his son— so that his son might bring joy to his heart? When your children are truly wise, you feel that you have succeeded in raising them— something very important. So then, children of your parents, do they have reason to bless the wisdom you show? And do you pass this wisdom on to your children? How do you measure up?

November 10

Only a Shadow
Hebrews 10:1-17

Fashions change. Should you be clearing out your attic you might find a picture frame with an oval in it. In the oval, entirely in black with raised accents, there you would find a silhouette of someone you once knew. These silhouettes have passed from fashion but it is surprising how clearly they can portray someone. So it is that we can look into the past.

A silhouette might also allow us to look into the future too. Christians sometimes ask why the Old Testament is still in print. There are many reasons, but one of them is that the Old Testament is the silhouette of the New Testament. In the silhouette of the Old Testament sacrifices we can see the image of the sacrifice of the New Testament—Christ upon the Cross.

Those sacrifices had to be from animals "without blemish" —and Christ was our sinless sacrifice.

Those sacrifices had to be presented in a particular fashion, on a particular day—as He was.

It was the blood of those sacrifices which was considered to be cleansing—just as the blood of Christ cleanses us from all sin.

A shadow, or silhouette, is not the real thing. The animal sacrifices of the Old Testament were not really effective. They were, however, the picture of what was to come. A picture is often useful in describing things, and the Old Testament picture is very useful in describing Jesus Christ.

He is our High Priest—the one who has direct access to God. We can picture him going into the holiest place of the Temple of God to plead for us. It never hurts to have friends; sometimes it can really help—and in this instance it is eternally vital. By his sacrifice on the Cross Jesus has opened wide the doors of heaven, allowing us access to the Living God. So much of the Old Testament is devoted to describing this sacrifice—in silhouette—because it is so important when it arrives in reality.

God painted a silhouette of the Cross into the sacrifices of the Old Testament. He paints another silhouette today: we are the picture of Christ to the world. The world looks at us and sees the silhouette of the living Christ. The question is, would they recognize Him by looking at us?

It is Mine to Avenge
Hebrews 10:18-39

The writer of Hebrews is anonymous—but not unaware of the truth. Here is one of the most terrifying passages in the entire Bible.

We will occasionally be subjected to the "pygmy in Africa" argument—namely, what happens to the pygmy in Africa who never heard of Jesus Christ? Heaven or hell for him? (The correct answer is to inquire *why* that pygmy has never heard; it usually means someone is constructing arguments instead of going with the Gospel). But there is an opposite case which is seldom mentioned. What about the man who hears the Gospel, responds to it, acknowledges the truth of it, claims Jesus as his Savior—and goes on sinning as if nothing had happened? What happens to him?

We know the answer instinctively. Such a man deserves the hell he gets. But we want so much for the opposite to be true; there are those whom we would like to *wish* into heaven. Our writer in this passage says no.

The sacrifice of Christ on the Cross is once for all. If you despise that sacrifice by continuing to sin, what hope is there for you?

Such an act treats the blood of Christ as if it were an ordinary rag, to be used and thrown away. A man who does such a thing grievously insults the Spirit of God.

God is the God of vengeance, for only God can judge justly. He alone is righteous; therefore he alone should judge. And judge he will, repaying evil with vengeance.

It is "a dreadful thing to fall into the hands of the living God." For if he is angry with you, who can save you? How then do we escape such a thing?

By being faithful. The Christians of this time were persecuted in ways we can only imagine. They did not "throw away their confidence" —which is to say, they did not abandon their faith—but rather stuck it out to the end. Sometimes that end was bitter indeed, resulting in horrible death for calling Jesus Lord. When the test comes, who do you say that Jesus is? Lord—or someone whose name seems an idle obscenity? The answer may make all the difference for all of eternity.

On Faith
Hebrews 11:1-16

"Now faith is..." what? The word runs through the Christian experience, and yet many Christians still do not understand its meaning.

Sure and certain

The words imply action. It is not sufficient merely to have an intellectual notion of the truth—you must act upon it. A simple example is sufficient. You say you have faith in your wife; do you check up on her, asking her whereabouts? Your actions betray your doubts. If you genuinely have faith, then your actions will be those of a man whose understanding is certain.

What we hope for, what we do not see

It is not faith if it is mathematically certain. Faith involves the possibility of doubt. But it also involves evidence. The result of this faith is something very desirable—that God will sustain you, or whatever has been promised. But there is always the possibility in your mind—and often in the whispers and complaints of your friends—that this cannot be. Faith overcomes this, and puts its confidence in what God has promised.

The examples

Noah building his flood insurance in the desert; Abraham buying pregnancy coverage for a woman in her nineties—these seem comic to the modern mind. But when God speaks and promises, it will be so. These men did not so much depend upon the power of God ("God can do anything he wants...") as they did the character of God— "He is faithful." What he promises, he will perform. They knew God, and therefore they had faith.

The Christian experience today

The examples of the patriarchs seem far away and long ago, but God never changes. That which he promises, that he will perform. We often think that these promises were delivered just because they were so extraordinary. It is not so; God is not like a man, being inconsistent. The slightest of his promises are as guaranteed as the greatest. The problem is not with *him*. The problem is with us. He is still faithful—and the things for which we ask are trivial in comparison—but we just don't want to believe them. Wake up! The God of Abraham is the God of the church today. If we will have faith, then he will deliver on his promises—just as he did then.

The Fear of the Lord
Psalm 111:10

The "fear of the Lord" is a topic not much used in sermons in our day. It seems out of place in speaking of the loving God. But one must examine the Scriptures as they are found; and they are found to contain many references to the fear of the Lord. So then, why fear?

Fear may serve as motivation. I grew up in the military. One particular post had a large amount of unexploded ordnance on the grounds. I was given the chance to watch a very small canister of explosive being set off at a very great distance—with a very, very large bang. I became exceedingly cautious in dealing with explosives. One does not wish to anger the Lord God Jehovah.

Fear God, fear nothing else. Is it not usually the case that we would like to do what's right—but we're afraid of what our friends might think? We're afraid of what it might do to our career? Fear God—and dread naught.

Fear—to obtain a "good understanding." I learned to drive a car at a young age—when most of us think we are immortal. Immortality (at sixteen) does not extend to losing control of the car. In order to control the car you must understand how the steering works. So fear can lead to understanding, just as it should with us. We should fear God, and study to show ourselves as his children.

This passage is preceded by verses which tell of the glory and great works of God. It is not a Psalm of God's wrath; it is a Psalm of his great works. It is not a Psalm of terror and pain, but one of grace and compassion. It is not a Psalm of misery in captivity, but of triumph for his people. In this context it is said that the fear of the Lord is the beginning of wisdom. Here is the greatest reason to fear the Lord: to fear him is to obey him, and to obey him is to bring glory, honor and eternal praise to his name.

Christian, do you live your life without the fear of the Lord? Do you feel that, after all, he will forgive without the slightest discipline in your life? Perhaps you are not paying attention to the minor discipline he gives those he loves. Fear him, and do not provoke him to sterner measures.

All Commended, None Received
Hebrews 11:32-12:13

The writer of Hebrews—alas, anonymous—gives us quite a point at the end of the eleventh chapter. All these heroes of the faith were commended for their faith—but none of them received the promise of the Holy One of Israel. They were made perfect only when Christ came.

It is a discouragement to most of us when things of which we dream are shown to be impossible in our own lifetime. Indeed, we feel that if something cannot be done in our own lifetime, then it cannot be done. This comes of our worldly view. If we were to take God's view— that these matters will happen in his time, as he pleases—then perhaps our perspective would be better sited. What does it matter that God's purpose is fulfilled a hundred or a thousand years from now? That is his concern. Our concern is that we do what he commands. He will not ask us, "Did you achieve in your own strength that which I desired?" He will ask us, "Were you a good and faithful servant?" If it cannot be done in our lifetimes, then we must remember that God is eternal. It most certainly will be done in his.

What, then, should we do? Our writer gives us our orders:

We are to throw off entanglements. Anything which distracts us from the cause of Christ is to be jettisoned.

We are to run with perseverance. It is a long distance race— perhaps longer than our own life. If so, it is a relay race, but whatever the race, God has marked it out for us. Ours is but to run it.

We are to keep our eyes—our minds—fixed on the objective. For us, that is the same thing as fixing our minds on Christ, asking, "What would Jesus want me to do?"

We are to endure hardship—but we are to look at it as discipline, not pain. God is shaping us to his ends.

We are to do what we can with what we have—"Make level paths for your feet." In all things we are to heal rather than wound, for this is how Christ came to us.

Is it so hard? Perhaps. We like to see results, not just efforts. But the results are not ours, only the efforts. God commends the servant for his efforts, and provides the results as he himself pleases. Be content—and give his cause your best effort.

Make Every Effort
Hebrews 12:14-29

"Make every effort" says our author. It is comforting to know that God judges by the heart, not by the result. It is also a warning that he does so.

What efforts shall we make?

To live in peace. It is a simple concept, yet one of the most difficult. Does the dog bark in the neighbor's yard? Do you threaten, bully or bluster—or do you calmly talk it out? The first feeds your ego; the second feeds your soul.

To be holy. Remember that you are a people set apart. You are not set apart for your merits, nor for your works—you are set apart because God has chosen you in Christ. It is a gift. If someone gives you a great gift, are you casual about it, or do you work to preserve it? This is the message of Esau—that he treated the gift of God as something to be traded for a simple meal.

Do not miss the grace of God—and see that others don't either. Do you speak to those who do not know the Lord, or do you assume someone else will do it?

See that no one is sexually immoral. Adultery is casually praised in our day; this should not be. A Christian should stand apart by his faithfulness to his marriage partner.

Why is this so commanded? Is God being unreasonable in this? Think back to the ancient Israelites. They were terrified by God on the mountain—hemmed in by strict codes of law. We, on the other hand, have a friend at the right hand of this God the Father—none other than Jesus the Christ. If they were condemned for rejecting so stern a vision, what will be our fate if we reject so kindly a vision?

This brings us then to worship the God who has so favored us.

We are to be thankful—do your prayers consist entirely of requests, or do they contain more thanksgiving?

We are to worship in reverence and awe—for God is a consuming fire. Do we perceive the Lord God Jehovah?

Christian, you have been afforded the greatest privilege the world has ever known—salvation by grace. Do not despise so great a salvation. Worship God in truth, thankfulness, reverence and awe—for God is a consuming fire.

Crucible, Furnace – and Praise
Proverbs 27:21

It is a fact: a man is tested by the praise he receives. Indeed, it is one of the greatest tests for a Christian, for in it he meets the temptation of pride.

What do you do when you are praised? Do you point the one praising you to the true source of all good things, or do you know that you have accomplished this of your own strength? One of the things that has helped me in this (besides having a wife who is not fooled for a moment) is this thought: If you were conducting a Sunday class on nuclear physics, would anyone come? Ah, but the Gospel? He who teaches the truth of Christ never lacks for an audience, no matter how poorly he speaks.

There is, of course, the more excruciating moment. Suppose you work long and hard for the cause of Christ. You have labored many years, often silently and with no real recognition, and then fortune smiles. Your name is on every lip, you are a hero of the faith, everyone wants you to speak at their church and autograph your book. This is trial enough—but consider what happens when someone else arises in the kingdom to even greater honor. How do you feel about them? What is it like to be in "second place?" Saul knew, and fell to, such a temptation. "Saul has slain his thousands, and David his tens of thousands." From that moment David's life was in danger.

Saul failed the test. He forgot that he (and David) were nothing in God's eyes—the recipients of grace, as are we all. We have not earned grace; nor can we really earn fame in the kingdom. We must remember that we are not the source of such greatness—it is the gift of God.

We do not see it as such, but praise is one means by which the Lord tests the heart of a man (see Proverbs 17:3 for a striking parallel passage). His object is not to destroy, nor to tear down—but to refine. We are to learn from our failures and from our successes. Our failures scream lessons; our successes whisper them. But in the whisper there may be wisdom. He is preparing us as a refiner would prepare silver or gold—by putting us in the crucible. The heat is in the praise of others. We will either burn off like so much slag, or become refined, and therefore resistant to the heat of praise. Thus we will be better prepared to serve him—for indeed, to Him belongs all the glory.

Count It All Joy
James 1:1-18

The point James makes is one which is quite startling: the Christian must make *joy* the standard, habitual response to trials. This is Christian maturity indeed.

Consider this first: when you go to a party, you tell stories about yourself as a way of introducing yourself, so that others might get to know you. What kind of stories do you tell? Are they not the stories of the trials of your life?

If you consider yourself a Christian you must certainly recognize that your Lord and Master, Jesus Christ, suffered greatly. Did you expect to be greater than he is? So then, when you suffer, you are sharing in the experiences of Christ; you are counted worthy.

If we suffer, then our brothers in Christ will too. In that time, we should come along side them and bring them such joy.

Testing

Such trials are said to be a "testing" of our faith. We need to consider just what "testing" means:

Some testing is morally neutral: we test-drive a car. We want to know what it can and can't do.

Some testing is self-imposed—have you stepped on a scale lately? We do this for our own good. We should also test ourselves in the matter of sin—by self-examination, not by bar hopping—especially before prayer. It is always good to know what you need to repent for.

There is also divine testing. Generally, God does not permit us to test him (for such would be a lack of faith, and blasphemy) but there are exceptions. But he does test us, as He did Abraham. This is to prove to us what we really are. God also permits Satan to test us—but never beyond the limits which we can endure.

All this results in "perseverance" —a word difficult to translate. It might be rendered "toughness" —the attitude of a veteran towards combat. The veteran does not desire combat, but knows how to handle it. The Christian never asks for testing and trial, but knows that God will provide the strength to endure it. This is the goal: that we may be tough, persevering warriors for Christ. Are you in training, or on leave?

The Wishful Christian
James 1:19-27

Suppose your long lost uncle in Australia dies and leaves you a fortune. Do you see yourself as the beneficent Christian, handing out money to good causes? But you may say, "That would be great, but right now money's tight..." If you do, you are a dream giver—and probably a dream Christian, a Wishful Christian.

Many of us are at our best in our dreams. If we only had money, we'd be so generous. If our acquaintances were just better people, we'd be so kind. If my wife was a trophy wife, I'd be so loving. The truth is that many of us get our MDR (minimum daily requirement) of holiness by going to church every now and then. If you're a Christian only in your dreams that's exactly where God will bless you.

Hope

But there is hope! James tells us what to do. We must get out of our dreams and into our lives, being those who do what we are called to do.

We have the "perfect law." Any system of rules and regulations will ultimately fall into paradox, for we are human. But the Christian is Spirit-led. This confuses people, for it seems that we are not consistent to some set of rules they imagine we must follow. We must be consistently led by the Spirit, consistently following our Lord Jesus Christ. In all else, we must be as inconsistent as he demands.

This law gives freedom. To understand this, we must know what freedom is. Suppose you capture an eagle. You bind it, take it into a submarine, and at six thousand feet below the waves you shoot it from a torpedo tube. The eagle is now "free." Really? It no longer is bound, but it is not capable of being an eagle. Freedom means "able to be what God designed you to be." God designed you to be in fellowship with him. That is the freedom this law gives.

To live in this law of freedom we must "look intently" at what God gives us. The phrase originally meant the action of a man who looked deeply into a well, shading the surface so he could see all the way to the bottom. In other words, it's hard work. But is not this true of all forms of freedom?

If you do this, you will be blessed by God. In short, stop dreaming and start doing—get to work.

The Thermometer of Faith
James 2:18-3:18

Do you believe that the earth is round? Of course you do. Does it make a difference to you? Other than marking you as someone who doesn't want to be singled out for believing in a flat earth, no, it doesn't. You can go through your entire life without worrying about the shape of the planet.

Do you believe your wife (or husband) is faithful to you? I hope you can answer yes to that. Does it make a difference to you? It certainly does!

Faith, in the Christian sense, is believing as defined in the second paragraph. It is not just intellectual assent to the facts; it is placing deep reliance upon them. So when someone says, "I have faith," you might ask just which kind they have! Indeed, it is a very important question. Here's how to tell the answer:

The first paragraph defines "dead faith." You believe, but you don't do anything about it. The second defines "living faith." You believe—and depend upon it. Since you depend upon it, you do something about it. As James would say, faith without deeds is dead.

You must remember that deeds are a symptom of living faith. They are the thermometer of your belief. Like the thermometer, they can be deceiving. (Give me a few minutes in the bathroom, an ice cube and hot water and I can make it tell you anything I want). A hypocrite may tell you about his thermometer; a legalist may manipulate his thermometer, but a true Christian's thermometer shows normal body temperature—living faith. His life is full of the practical good deeds of one who loves the Lord.

The beginning Christian often looks for a list of rules and regulations. James is not sending us back to the Law of the Old Testament for such; rather, he is repeating what his Lord taught. It does no good to wish someone well and not help them. Far from tasking us to go back to rules and regulations, James is teaching us to be mature. The experienced, mature Christian does good deeds because this is a natural result of living in the Spirit.

This is the faith that God honors and blesses. James gives us the example of Abraham, whose faith was great—and whose blessings were even greater. He had no book of rules to guide him; only the Spirit. Perhaps Augustine was right: "Love God—and do as you please."

Perspective
James 4

We do not know how to die. This is not surprising, as most of us only get one chance at it—no practice runs. Is it any surprise then that most of us act as if we were going to live indefinitely?

This has a very unfortunate set of side effects.

We make plans on the basis that we are in charge of our own lives. James reminds us that we should preface our plans with, "If it is the Lord's will,...."

We make plans on the basis that we will have time to complete them. James reminds us that we should preface our plans with, "If it is the Lord's will, we will live, and..."

In fact, we have neither the ability to guarantee our plans will produce the results we desire nor the certainty of lifespan to see them through. We are mortal.

But this is not all. Thinking ourselves to be "immortal", we act like it. We fall in love with the things of this world—after all, this is where we're going to be living forever, right? But see what this does to our relationship to God! He knows better—and has mentioned the point to us.

The popular phrase has it, "this is the first day of the rest of your life." It may be, but it is also the first day of the rest of eternity. We are designed to live forever, in fellowship with God. Do we act like it?

Do we seek the desires of this world, or the desires of God? Which of these will last forever?

Do we ask God for the things that are eternal, or the things which are temporary? If temporary, are they the things which build us up, or tear us down?

Do we choose to take life in our own strength, or in God's strength? Which of these will last forever?

The matter is one of perspective. If you see yourself as a great person on earth (or at least one entitled to a little respect) then you are not seeing with the eyes of eternity. If you see things as God sees them, you realize how trivial the things of this world really are. You also see how important the things of eternity must be.

"Humble yourselves before the Lord, and he will lift you up."

A Man Like Us
James 5

At first blush it seems ridiculous to say that Elijah was "a man like us." Most of us have yet to call down fire from heaven. Most of us are not prophets of God. The usual reaction is to consider Elijah as the consummate prophet of the Old Testament—remember how Moses and Elijah came to Jesus on the Mount of Transfiguration? But Elijah was not all supreme confidence and fire from heaven.

Consider a few things you might not have known:

Elijah prophesied that there would be no rain until he commanded it. Sounds like power? He spent those years in the wilderness at first, then in the house of a poor widow. Evidently God was taking no chances with Elijah and the issue of humility.

The defining act of his ministry is calling down fire from heaven on Mt. Carmel. The scene is dramatic and well known. What you might have forgotten is that Jezebel let him know she would have his head for it—and he ran as fast as he could to get away. This is faith?

We remember the earthquake, wind and fire, and then the still small voice. Do we remember the fact that God then told him to anoint his replacement, Elisha?

The fact is that Elijah did his great works at the command of God—but at heart he was a man very much afraid of those in authority, most of whom were his enemies for God's sake. This man was not a bold man, nor a learned man, nor a man of great and powerful faith. He was a man who heard what God told him—and trusted. He trusted no further than the words he had heard, evidently—but that was enough.

James tells us that the prayer of a righteous man is powerful and effective. His example is Elijah. Not a man of great courage, nor of great skill in war, but a man who trusted God and did as God commanded. He was obedient; this is the key to righteousness. He trusted what God told him. He was not one who denied fear, but one who experienced it fully. He did not ignore it or deny it, but he overcame it by the command of God.

A man like us? Yes, I think so. The real question is whether or not we will be men like Elijah—obedient and trusting God.

November 22

Living Hope
1 Peter 1

Of Faith, Hope and Love, the most misunderstood is Hope.

We speak much of faith, and love runs throughout the New Testament, but of hope we hear little. Peter, in this short passage, points out our Living Hope, the salvation which will be clearly seen at the coming of our Lord.

First, it is a hope rooted in the mercy of God. This is most essential for us, because if our hope were rooted in our own righteousness it would be a fool's hope. Our own righteousness does not impress God Almighty, who is righteousness itself. Nor is our hope rooted in our own good works, however noble and plentiful these might be. What would our good works be compared to His?

Next, our hope is founded squarely upon the Resurrection. If there is no resurrection of the dead, then we are surely fools. But Christ is risen from the dead, and he promises to all who believe in him that they too shall someday rise, at his return. The apostles understood that the resurrection of Jesus changed everything—the view of death is now completely different, and so is our hope.

Then too our hope is based upon the character of God. This is seen in Peter's description of our inheritance: it cannot perish, spoil or fade. This is simply a reflection of the eternal character of God, who does not change. God is not like us, prone to change our minds. What he has promised, he will deliver.

Our hope is shielded by the power of God. He who spoke and the universe came into existence uses that same power to guard our inheritance of salvation. Though we may suffer in this life, the inheritance of salvation is sure, for the power of God guarantees it.

The world looks at the Christian and sees a pilgrim, an alien just passing through. The world sees one who is not at home in this world, and somehow just can't adjust to reality. The Christian knows that God's view is different. God sees the elect, the church, on their pilgrimage through life. Suffering and sadness for a little while; then the welcome home to await the renewal of all things, the living hope of salvation.

Be Holy, Because I Am Holy
1 Peter 1:13-25

Holiness is a concept which has left the English language. It is now a "church word." It has no meaning to anyone outside the church, and very little meaning to those inside. It should not be so, for the word is simple to understand and extremely powerful.

It means "to be set apart." A simple illustration should make it clearer. When I was young, my mother kept two sets of dishes. One was for everyday use. The other, referred to as "china" rather than "dishes", was kept for special occasions such as the visit of someone of importance. In a very real sense, the "china" was "holy." It was kept apart.

We are to be holy, because God is holy. How is God holy? He is completely apart from sin and unrighteousness—and we should be too. Peter here tells us how we are to accomplish this:

We are to prepare our minds for action. How often we neglect this simple precaution against Satan! Are there going to be idiots on the freeway? Of course. Are you prepared to forgive them and forego your anger? You know they will be there; are you prepared for them *spiritually?*

We are to be self-controlled. Our society says to let our feelings be displayed without limit; if we don't, we're repressed. God says that self-control is still a virtue. Your doctor weighs you when you come in; does he think self-control is good for you? If physically, even more spiritually.

Set your hope on grace. Do not presume that your righteous acts— however praiseworthy these might be—are a substitute for grace. Depend upon Him, not upon yourself.

Do not conform to the world, but transform your minds. You tell your children not to follow the crowd; there is wisdom in that. Do you abide by that wisdom too? Only if you replace the world's desires with the transforming mind of God.

Live as strangers (aliens) in this world. Are you so attached to the things of this world—physical pleasures, wealth, prestige and power—that you could not give them up? Or are these things trifles to one who is a child of the King of Kings?

Be holy, because your Lord and God is holy.

The Christian Weapon
1 Peter 2:11-3:7

One of the great temptations to the Christian is to seize the weapons of Satan to try to defeat Satan. This never succeeds. Our Lord is quite clear that we are to overcome evil with good.

Peter gives us an example of this here. Please recall that the king of whom he is speaking is the Roman Caesar, who frequently persecuted the church. How is the Christian to deal with this situation? He is to do good, so that those who are ignorant of what Christians are really like will be silenced by example.

This is an example of the power of submission. It seems that Christ would have us perform spiritual judo. In judo, one key principle is to use your opponent's strength in attack against him. Here is the same idea. Are you persecuted by the authorities? Show them proper respect, not defiance. Leave them in stunned silence how someone so utterly out of step with the world around them could possibly be so respectful of authority. Let them deal with the contradiction—for the Christian does not see one. God commands respect for the authorities instituted by man; the Christian must be obedient to his Lord.

Indeed, this goes so far as to submit to unjust punishment. Many a Christian of this time was beaten merely for the fact that he was a Christian. In later years just being a Christian was a capital crime, punishable by crucifixion. Hundreds of thousands of Christians went to their deaths—obedient to their Lord, not rebellious against authority. In these deaths the church provided a great witness; as Tertullian said, "The blood of martyrs is the seed of the church."

In the English speaking world the Christian is seldom martyred for his faith these days. Often ridiculed, but seldom martyred—and the principle of obedient submission still applies. We have something the mockers do not—and our Lord wants it clear to them that we do. Do you need anything further than your Lord's command? Then consider his example. When he was tried and taken to the Cross for our sins, did he trade insult for insult? Or did he go to his death in obedient submission to his Father?

The result was seen in the centurion: "Surely this was the Son of God." "If I be lifted up," Jesus said, "I will draw all men to me." We are the imitators of Christ. If called upon, we must follow his example in obedient submission. In this, we lift Him up.

Finally, All of You...
1 Peter 3:8-4:6

Have you ever given anyone that "one last word of advice?" Peter is doing that here. He is speaking to Christians, telling them how to get along with other Christians.

Live in harmony

It is worth noting that harmony is not the same thing as unison. We are not all to sing the same note—but the notes must blend together. There is no thought here of a line of robots all acting in the same way, but rather the blending of actions of an experienced choir. We need to sing along, each with his own part.

Be sympathetic

It sounds like we are just to be in emotional support of one another, but there is more to it than that. If you are sympathetic, you are not judgmental. Your brother may be in this predicament because of his own actions; that does not lessen the predicament nor should it lessen your sympathy.

Love as brothers

At the least, see this as a command to share. See it also as the command to reach out to your fellow Christians in every way they need, caring for them like family.

Be compassionate

Do not be one who calculates in giving. Do not ask, "How little can I get away with?" Do not ask, "What is expected of me?" Ask, "What would I want in that situation?" Then be compassionate, and give to your brother.

Be humble

The King James Version uses the word, "courteous." It is a good translation, for the arrogant are so often rude, but the humble are always polite. Politeness springs from the desire to have smooth relationships. Politeness overlooks the tiny wrongs which create such friction in life. Politeness is humility in action.

Return blessing for evil

Always good advice; at the least it confuses those who mean you evil. More importantly, it marks you as one who is doing what the Apostle commands: you are one who imitates the Lord Jesus. He gave his very life for those who took him to the cross, for the sinners of this world. He returned blessing, infinite blessing, for the evil he suffered. We are his followers; we should imitate Him as best we are able.

Administering God's Grace
1 Peter 4:10-11

It is an awesome thought: we are those who minister the grace of God. Peter here instructs us in humble simplicity how we should do this.

First, whatever grace we have received, it is a gift. It is not something we earned, but something God has given us.

The gift was not given so that we may be idle and enjoy it, but rather that we may serve others. Indeed, this may be the test of true grace, that it serves.

We must do so faithfully—as one who has been given an important trust, no matter how small it appears in the eyes of the world. God has given it; he gives no insignificant graces.

It comes in various forms; we should be content with that. Do not envy the eloquent but rather be content knowing that your own grace comes from the same God.

Peter gives us two examples. These were selected, perhaps, because they are so visible in the church. The principles given, however, apply to all.

Has God given you the grace of speaking in public? Perhaps you are the preacher; more likely a teacher, as these are more numerous. No matter how young (or old) your students might be, you are to speak as if you were speaking the very words of God. Indeed, for those who teach the very young, this may be quite literally the case.

Does your ministry require unusual strength? Perhaps you are a counselor to those who are afflicted; or one who cares for the sick; perhaps one who works solely with his hands. It does not matter whether the strength is physical or spiritual; it should come from God and be used for him.

Those precepts may not seem too general. Not many are called to speak; but many are called to serve. When called to serve, do you serve as if you were called by God for his particular service? You are so called; therefore, take your calling seriously. You may not sweep the floors, but you can give your calling all your strength, asking God to strengthen you. Love the Lord your God with all your heart, soul, mind and strength—and serve him likewise.

The Eightfold Way
2 Peter 1

Peter, the fiery disciple, in his maturity lays out for us the progression of virtues necessary for us. Note, please, that there is an order to these things. Note also that we are to possess these qualities in increasing measure. So let us run up the notes of the scale with Peter:

Faith—the assurance of that which you do not see; the root relationship of Christ. Trust in the Lord with all your heart.

Goodness—the common morality recognized by all men as the sign of good character. These are things like honesty and trustworthiness.

Knowledge—not just knowledge from the books, but knowledge of spiritual things. It most especially would include knowledge of ourselves; it would certainly include our knowledge of Christ. Study, to show yourself approved.

Self-control—the sense of self discipline that makes a person capable of being trusted because he will not betray his Lord or himself.

Perseverance—that blend of toughness, persistence, patience and steadfastness that makes a person undefeatable.

Godliness—the quality of being an imitator of God himself; one who treats all with compassion, no matter how sinful they may be.

Brotherly kindness—that superb virtue which makes a person the most valued of friends, the one that sticks closer than a brother.

Love—the pure, unselfish love displayed by Christ on the Cross, the love that sacrifices for the unworthy.

It is a stairway. You begin with faith, for only the faithful obey. But you must not stop there. The steps may seem hard to the beginner. That's normal; the beginner is a child in Christ. But those who are mature must pursue these virtues, so that they will be effective and productive for Christ.

Consider it well, Christian. Look upon yourself five years ago. Do you see a change? Have you climbed these steps a little higher in those five years? If not, it is not because our Lord has moved the ladder.

Judgment by Knowledge
2 Peter 2

This is one of the stormiest passages of the New Testament, full of bleak condemnation. You will recall that Christ forgave the worst of sinners—but condemned the Pharisees for their sins. It is profitable for us to ask, "Why?"

We are judged by who we claim to be

Suppose you have a cold. If your friends tell you to take Vitamin C—and it doesn't help—well, they tried to help. If your doctor prescribes a drug, and it makes things worse? You are much more upset, because your doctor claims to know medicine. Your friends don't. You judge the doctor more severely because of what he claims to be. So it is with the hypocrites.

We are judged by what we have seen

If you have seen miracles, and still will not repent, then judgment is more severe. If you have seen lives transformed by Christ, and still you remain lukewarm, what will you expect?

We are judged by what we have heard

Do you claim to be a Christian? Have you sat through a thousand sermons and two thousand Sunday School lessons? Then you have heard. God's standard is that you should have been listening.

We are judged by what we know

"What about the pygmy in Africa? How does God deal with him?" I have no idea—but you're not the pygmy. You are the one who has heard the word of God. You know what He expects. Therefore, you will be treated as one who knows what to do. The question is, do you do it?

We are judged by how we handle holy things

A man's reputation is made—or broken—by how he handles his responsibilities. We, as Christians, are entrusted with the sacred word of God. We may neither add to it, nor subtract from it—in teaching or in action.

The passage sounds harsh. Christ was harsh with the Pharisees. But even this was merciful; nothing but such an attack could shake their self-righteousness. Sometimes radical surgery is required. Take warning, Christian: according to your knowledge and responsibilities you will be judged—by the one who knows you best.

Wholesome Thinking
2 Peter 3

Peter ends his second letter by encouraging his readers to engage in "wholesome thinking." The word for wholesome is an interesting one in this context: it means something judged in the light of the sun, and found to be genuine. Peter is hinting at the Day of the Lord, when everything will be held up to divine light and judged for what it is.

What, then, should be found to be "wholesome?" The word translated "thinking" is also translated as "the mind." It can mean the imagination or the understanding. Both of these are important. Is your imagination something that could be held up to the light of God? Is your understanding that which would be approved by God?

Understanding indeed is required, for the subject Peter brings to us here is the ultimate end of the world as we know it. There are many theories about this. One thing is certain: the day is coming when God will appear to judge the world. That he is patient with us (and all others) is due to his desire that all of us might have salvation through Jesus Christ.

Patience, however, ends when the Lord returns. In his time, in the manner of his own choosing, and in his complete and awesome power the Lord will return. We should make no rash predictions of when or how—but we should be ready.

Peter speaks of this too.

We must be spotless. The word means "unstained" or "unspoiled." The idea is that we are pure. There is no such thing as a "half Christian."

We must be blameless. The idea in the original is that we have nothing in us that others could carp at. It is not sufficient to know that we are forgiven; we must make every effort to live as Christ would have us live.

We must be at peace with our Lord. The word used is not so much the absence of war as it is "to be as one with." We must be so close to him that we appear to one and all as the brothers we are.

The day is coming. All things material will be no more; the shadows of this world will give way to the reality of God. Then your character will be shown to one and all. Are you ready?

The Eyewitness
1 John 1

The last living Apostle, John, was also the closest friend Jesus had on earth. He was the disciple "whom Jesus loved." In his old age he wrote his Gospel and several letters. In those letters there is a constant them: God is love; God is light.

John is an eyewitness. He is telling those to whom he writes that this is what he has seen. So then, what is it that this eyewitness to the ultimate truth has to say?

God is light. There is no darkness in him. All of us who are human are a mixture of good and evil. There are days when we can call ourselves righteous; there are days which we would rather purge from our memories. But God is eternally the same. He is pure righteousness; there is no evil in him. As light creates the possibility of darkness, so the light of God creates the possibility of the darkness of evil.

Therefore, if we say, "I am a Christian," —that is, we claim to be in fellowship with God, the light—we had best be just that: light. Do we serve as a shining example for others, or do we try to hide our deeds because they will not bear close examination? Hypocrisy is a flashlight with dead batteries.

However, if we are walking in fellowship with him, then our sins will be purified. How can this be? It is simple. We walk in fellowship with him by the grace accorded to us at the Cross. That being so, we must be those who are seen by God as sinless. That can only be accomplished by the righteousness of Jesus Christ. Therefore, He must purify us. We cannot do it ourselves.

Are we truly sinless? It's ridiculous. If you think you are, you are lying to yourself as well as God—and only one of you is deceived by it. Don't tell him how wonderful you are. Rather, tell him your troubles and sins; he will be swift and sure to forgive them.

John writes this letter for a purpose: that your joy may be complete. Can you avoid being a sinner? Certainly not. Can you be forgiven? Of course—but only by walking in the light. One does not come clean by washing in filth, but by washing with clean water. It is true spiritually as well as physically. Come to Him, lean on Him—and be clean.

In Christ—the Test
1 John 2:1-17

One of the frequent challenges of Satan is the whispering voice, "How do you know you are really saved? How do you know that you are really a Christian?" John gives us some practical guidance on the subject.

First, when does such a temptation arise? When we sin, of course. Satan comes and says, "Surely someone who has done what you did cannot possibly be saved. It's all an illusion." But hear the words: you have an accuser (Satan) —but you also have someone who speaks in your defense: Jesus Christ. By his atoning sacrifice he defends you from your accuser.

How, then, do we know that we are "in Christ?" John gives us a simple, deep test: Obedience. Obedience is not only the outward sign of a true Christian, it is also the way in which God's love is made complete. What kind of obedience? We must "walk as Jesus did." In other words, we are to be the imitators of Christ, doing as he would have done in our place.

John then gives us a practical example of this obedience. Do you hate your brother? Does your hatred well up at the thought of one of your fellow Christians? Then you are in darkness, not in light—and you are blind. But if you love your brothers and sisters in Christ, then you are in the light.

There is another test here: do you love the world? By this John means the things this world claims as important:

The cravings for the physical things of this world; wealth, power and possessions.

The cravings for what you see: lust in the sexual sense, envy in the spiritual sense.

The most deadly craving of all: pride, the practice of boasting about what you have and what you do.

If you love these things, you are in darkness. Remember that these things are temporary!

John tells us that this command is an old one, and yet a new one. It is an old one for it is the same one Christ has given us, since the time of the Old Testament. It is a new one because each of us must take it to heart, bringing it into our lives as a fresh new thing. It stands forever; it lives new in us today. It is eternal, for it is the Word of God.

December 2

A Model Prayer
Daniel 9

Mention the Book of Daniel to most Christians and their minds turn instantly to prophecy. This is indeed a good reaction, for Daniel is the key to understanding prophecy, however poorly we do that. But in this passage Daniel shows us why he was favored by God: his prayer life is revealed to us.

Trust in God

Daniel shows this before his prayer begins. He notes that Jeremiah the prophet said that Jerusalem would be desolate 70 years—and the time being up, he turned to God.

Acknowledge God

Daniel starts by acknowledging God for who he is. It is the first step in personal relationships; you cannot have a personal relationship of any kind unless you know who the other person is, and what they are about. Daniel shows us here his conception of God. Listen to the adjectives: great, awesome, righteous, merciful, forgiving. Character is portrayed in action; see the actions of God in Daniel's prayer: keeping his covenant, both for good and for destruction; bringing his people out of Egypt; bringing disaster upon Jerusalem. Here is God the omnipotent; here is God the merciful; here is God the just.

Admit who and what we are

Please note that Daniel begs forgiveness and admits the sins of his people, as well as his own. He is not a man alone but a part of a community—a nation which has sinned greatly. He admits their faults: they don't listen to the prophets; they are unfaithful to God and rebellious. Daniel brings no justification of their conduct, no thought that "at least we're better than..." This is confession, this is pleading— not a lawyer's argument but the plea for mercy and forgiveness.

Ask upon his mercy

Daniel does not make his request based upon any righteousness of his own, or of his people. Rather, he asks God to act for his own sake. He asks him to act because he is merciful; he asks him to act for the people who bear his name.

When you go to prayer tonight, Christian, do you ask God for favors because you are so good a Christian? Or do you ask God for mercy and implore him to act for the glory of his name on earth? Do you know him—and yourself?

The Life of Love
1 John 3:7-24

Sometimes the simplest concepts are the most profound—and the most difficult to grasp. It may be so for this concept too: brotherly love.

John teaches us here what true brotherly love is about. It has been defined as "active goodwill," but there is more to it than that. It is not cold charity, but rather a warm, vibrant and completely positive love for one another. How do you teach such a thing? By example, of course. The example for us is Jesus Christ, who laid down his life for us.

It is good for us to examine the life of Jesus, to meditate upon it—for in that life we see brotherly love portrayed perfectly. We see the key difference between friendship as the world knows it (which is a good thing) and brotherly love (which is the better thing). That difference is sacrifice. The life of sacrificial service is the life of brotherly love.

Your actions betray your thoughts. If your actions show that you cannot sacrifice for your brothers, then this shows that you do not truly love them. But if your actions show you sacrificing for your brothers and sisters, then God promises you rich blessings:

First, your heart will be set at rest before God. Have you ever gone through a period of doubt about your salvation? "Do I really know who Jesus is? Am I just praying to a blank wall?" You cannot analyze your way out of such things. So God gives you the task of sacrificial love—so that your experience in sacrifice may bring you certainty of him.

Are you persuaded that God is not answering your prayers, but you're not sure why? John tells us here that those who truly love are heard. Perhaps the word "sacrificial" is missing from your love from your brothers. Should God hear someone who does not truly love his children?

If we are obedient to his commands, he lives in us, in the form of the Spirit. It is a glad thing, and it is very precious.

Examine yourself, Christian. Are your acts of charity only those you can easily afford, or do you give beyond your comfort? Do you forgive only those who are pleasant? Do your offerings to God—monetary or otherwise—come only from what you can spare? Or do you live sacrificially for the Kingdom of God?

Perfect Love Drives Out Fear
1 John 4

There is nothing so persistent in the world's mind as the idea that fear is the perfect motivator. The story is told of a soldier in the American Civil War (Northern accounts say it was a Rebel; Southern accounts are sure it was a Yankee). The soldier was observed by his captain leaving the battlefield on the run. "Halt," cried the captain, "or I'll shoot!" "Shoot and be *******" replied the soldier; "What's one bullet to a whole hatful?"

Fear has its limits as a motivator. There are those who came to a saving knowledge of Jesus Christ through fear of the grave and hell—but such fear cannot keep a man in the faith very long. For as John tells us, perfect love drives out fear—and perfect love is found only in Jesus.

We understand this. If you have ever worked for someone who believed in petty tyranny enforced by fear—and then had the chance to work for a leader who genuinely loved his people—you know how love quickly replaces fear. It is a much more powerful motivator.

How powerful? It is a well known fact that in war men will risk their lives for their comrades. A "reasonable" man would be cynical about survival; but those who have suffered together have a bond of love that rises above battlefield cynicism.

More common to most of us is the fear of embarrassment. Most people are afraid, for example, of public speaking. But have you ever had a speaker talk about his favorite hobby? No matter how nervous they were to start, within a few seconds the stories come rolling out. Love does that; it drives out fear.

So then, do you love the Lord Jesus? Then do you speak for him? It is not easy, and often the consequences are unpleasant. No one wants to be a freak, even a "Jesus freak." But if you love him enough, you will speak of him constantly.

The word "love" is the key. Jesus is the example of perfect love, and his perfect love was directed at us. If you are his disciple, you will imitate him. You will then become more and more like the perfect love that walked the earth. That love, Jesus, was not a timid man—he who cleared the Temple—but a bold one. Bold in the cause of God; meek in dealing with the repentant sinner. Walk in his steps, and walk boldly. Perfect love drives out fear.

Three Tests
1 John 5

John in this last chapter gives us three tests of a Christian. One may be said to be doctrinal; one may be said to be internal and unseen; the last is external and visible.

The Doctrinal Test

The true Christian believes that Jesus is the Christ—that is, the Messiah promised to the Jews. He tells us that Jesus is born of God—we would say he is the Son of God. In other words, that he is divine. But we must also believe that he is Son of Man—born of Mary, and therefore of flesh and blood like us.

The Trinity is a great mystery. It is not required that we understand it perfectly. It is required that we believe that Jesus is the Christ, Son of God, Son of Man.

The Inward Test

No one can see love in the heart of another—only in the outward signs of it. But the inward test is still there: do you love the children of God, or are you going through the motions? This love starts with the love of God. If you cannot love God, who is holy, pure, perfect and lovely, how can you love his children—many of whom are no such thing? But—as is true in most earthly cases—if you love the parent, loving the child is easy enough. Especially if you remember being a child yourself—which all of us still are, for we are children of God.

The practical test

If you truly love God, then it will show in your actions. How is this? You will obey his commands.

Is this hard, or easy? It depends upon your view. Suppose I give you the task of moving several hundred bags of cement, of fifty pounds each, Even if you are very strong to begin with, the task will soon wear you out. But if I give you a forklift at the same time, then the task becomes much easier.

The Spirit is our "forklift." He empowers us to do the will of God—the command of God, if you please—and therefore the task is easy. "My yoke is easy, my burden is light."

Christian, ask yourself: do I believe that Jesus is who he says he is? Do I love God—and thus his children? And does it show in my obedience to his commands? Take this yoke upon you—it is easy; the burden is light.

Obedience and Love
2 John

John, it appears, has given us a tautology. He tells us that God has commanded us to love one another. But what does it mean, to love? He says that this is love: that we walk in obedience to his commands. And what is his command? That we walk in love.

It seems to go in a very tight circle. But behind this seeming circle is a great truth.

It is easy to say, love your neighbor. The test of that love, however, is in the action. It comes in the time of forgiveness; it comes in the time of sharing suffering; it comes in the time of digging deep to help a friend in need. These are responses to a situation. Such responses are not formed in the intellect, but in the habits. If your habits—your obedience, if you will—are in order, your love will bear fruit in action.

But how do you form such habits? It is an act of the will, guided by the intellect. You must purpose to do such things. You must prepare to do such things. You must, in other words, will them.

See how these things come together in this example—taken from real life: I know a man who decided that the care of the poor cannot be neglected. It is beyond any one man to care for all the poor; but at least one can mitigate the lot of the next poor man you meet. So he always carried a dollar bill in his front pocket—to give to the next beggar he met. He decided before the time arrived; he prepared and then he acted.

Could it be that our lack of charity towards others comes from failure in this realm? We say on Sunday that we should love our neighbor as ourselves. We see the beggar by the road and say to ourselves, "I wish there was something I could do." We missed the connection; we have broken John's circle. Prepare yourself in your mind; then in your pocket—and your actions will be easy enough.

Decide that you will love one another; make it a purpose of your life, as your Lord did. Prepare to love one another, as your Lord did, in prayer and in practice. Then go out and do it, as your Lord did— even to the Cross.

Do you love Him? Then obey his commands. He commands you to love one another. Purpose, prepare—and then practice the love and obedience of your Lord.

Love of Being First
III John

It is a bit sad that Diotrophes is mentioned only here. He wanted to be a big actor in the early church; he gets only a bit part, and that a villain.

Why does a man act the way he did?

Most of us enjoy being a big frog—even if we have to work hard to keep the puddle small. Christ wants a river which flows, not a puddle to splash in.

The quest for power, and the ego gratification that go with it, are not limited to the office. It is pleasing to know that other people think you are great.

The word "my" has some impact. We think of "my" house or "my" car; do we think of "my" church in the same way? If so, do we act like we own it?

There is also the numbers game. Those who count attendance can always prove their popularity. The trouble is simple: attendance is the blossom; Christ is looking for the fruit.

Fruits, indeed, are what give this man away. You can see it clearly in his actions:

Gossip—the Greek word is used of water at a rolling boil. It is an apt symbol. It takes much energy and at the end produces nothing but hot, sticky air.

The love of being first—which is a good definition of pride. Do recall, it was through pride that Satan fell.

Refusal of hospitality—which is astonishing for the ancient world. This would be extremely rude.

Why does the man behave like this? How is it that someone who calls himself a Christian can do this? The answer is simple, and sad. He has not given first place to Christ, but to himself. The love of being first has pushed aside the love of Christ.

You don't have to be a church leader for this to happen to you. It is perhaps more commonly found in those who are older, but it can happen at any age. The key question is this: who is Lord? Who is first in your life? If you call yourself a Christian, you have proclaimed that Jesus is Lord. Do you act like it—or do you love putting yourself first?

Scoffers Among You
Jude

One of the more troublesome things about the church is the number of people in it whose actions cause it shame. Most people can understand the backslider—the alcoholic who relapses into the bottle, the drug addict going back to his habit. These are sorrowful things, and we should assist such people as best we can. But Jude shows us a much more severe case.

There are those among us who are a disgrace in a completely different way: these are the false leaders. Jude shows us their character:

They are presumptuous toward any authority. In the name of Christ, but acting in their pride, they tell the Christian to reject authority and rebel.

They pollute their own bodies—indeed, it is a polite expression for sexual sin.

They are shepherds who feed only themselves—in short, they are in it for the money. Perhaps it's for the salary, or because the church is a good place to make business contacts.

They grumble and find fault—unless flattery is required to advance their business.

So, having warned us, what does the writer tell us to do? Throw such out immediately? It would be difficult; for many others do the same thing without such hypocrisy. As Paul told the Romans to overcome evil with good, so Jude tells us to build ourselves up in the faith.

We are to be merciful to those who doubt, not critical. In the face of such hypocrisy, who can blame those who doubt the character of the true church? To those who are in danger of hell, we are to reach out the hand of Christ, always remembering that we too are sinners.

Jude sounds severe—especially for so short a letter. But in this case he must be severe, for it is the Pharisee among us who causes us so much trouble. Have you ever wondered if you are such a person? Jude gives you a test. Are you merciful to those in doubt, or do you condemn them? Do you reach out to the sinner on his way to hell, or do you keep yourself apart from such people? Remember, even Paul was such a man—once.

The Revelation of Jesus Christ
Revelation 1:1-20

Note that this is a *revelation*—an unveiling of a mystery. As such, we are entitled to ask (and have answered) some of the detective's questions. In the process, however, we need to observe also the style in which they are answered.

To whom was it addressed? *To his servants.* First of all, that means us, and all Christians of all times. The church is one. God has sent us this revelation and, as Paul assures us, all Scripture is inspired of God. So we may safely conclude that this book was meant to be understood. But Holmes, why did he send this particular book? To show us what must soon take place.

This, first and foremost, means that this is a book of prophecy. In my opinion, this rules out any thought that the poetic interpretation (which denies prophecy in this book) is possibly complete. It is, as noted, always correct.

The word "soon" in this text is ambiguous in the Greek. It can mean "soon" or "suddenly" —and of course the historicist and preterist take the first meaning, and the futurists are convinced of the second.

Finally, there is "how" the revelation is delivered. It is clear that it originates with God. This is important in the light of :

(Mat 24:36 NIV) "No one knows about that day or hour, not even the angels in heaven, nor the Son, but only the Father.

The message is delivered from the Father to the Son, who commends it to an angel to deliver to John. The method is impressive; this is intentional. Sometimes the medium is the message; a warning can be delivered in jest, or in deep solemnity. The latter usually carries more weight. Winston Churchill once tried to send a very short, personal note with certain intelligence data to Stalin—before the Germans invaded Russia. His ambassador (a hack politician who evidently had no sense of style) simply handed the note in, instead of making a formal presentation of it. Churchill, in his history of the Second World War, lamented this bitterly, for he felt if delivered with due pomp and ceremony (and starkness) it might have been heeded—and saved the Soviets so much surprise destruction.

The same thought applies to us. This is the most solemn of messages. It is our responsibility to heed it.

Forsaken Love
Revelation 2:1-7

God praises; God criticizes. Note that the criticism has a purpose: it is to cause repentance. God does not criticize or discipline us because He is vindictive; He does so to produce repentance. For the experienced Christian, there is a lesson here:

> Remember what you were like when you were first a Christian? Remember the love and enthusiasm? Is there some reason you should not be so now?

> Repent, therefore, and regain that first love.

> Then repeat what you did at first.

It is interesting that athletic coaches spend so much time on the basics. We see why God does it here; he points it out clearly that the Lord of the church, the head, is Jesus Christ. Jesus will have his bride spotless, as we shall see later. Thus, he will not be satisfied as long as there is something to criticize (pleased with progress, but not satisfied).

The Nicolaitans were a heresy that sprang from Nicolaus, a deacon. Nicolaus (one of the seven deacons in Acts, according to Eusebius) wrote that the body "must be abused" (an early form of "no pain, no gain" —actually, he made the statement with regard to his repentance of jealousy of his wife) and was misinterpreted to mean that the body should really be abused—as in promiscuous sex and drunken orgies. This sect taught that the body was evil and should be given over to evil (while keeping the mind and spirit pure, of course!) Note that the Lord hates the *practices* of the Nicolaitans, not the sinners themselves.

The view (under different names) is still with us, and still causing trouble. There are those who will tell you that "sex is beautiful" and therefore conclude that any sex, no matter when or with whom, must therefore be approved by God. "How could a loving God condemn something so beautiful?" Hear the word of the Lord from the Lord, not from those who think they know better.

What happened to Ephesus? The city is a ruin. It housed one of the seven wonders of the ancient world (the temple of Diana of the Ephesians); it was a rich city on a major trade route; it has been a ruin for centuries. The lampstand has been removed. He who has an ear, let him hear.

Thyatira
Revelation 2:18-29

It is no accident that the description of the Christ is the one with the eyes like blazing fire—for here He penetrates behind the disguises to the heart.

The church appears to be a blessed church. It is full of love and faith, showing perseverance—all admirable qualities in any church. Indeed, these qualities are *growing*. If you or I were to walk into this church, we'd be impressed. What's wrong? Jezebel.

Jezebel was the wife of King Ahab, and the power behind the throne. She was the one who connived to get Naboth's vineyard; threatened Elijah (remember the showdown on Mt. Carmel?) and finally was killed at the hands of Jehu. She is a figure of backstage intrigue who introduces "compromise" ("it doesn't matter what you believe as long as you're sincere"). Adultery, from the earliest of the prophets, is taken as symbolic of idolatry.

Some hold that this is the time when the worship of Mary and the saints, the use of statues (idols, to some) in the Roman Catholic and Eastern churches grows rapidly. It is the age of faith; it is the age of idolatry.

Note then the admonition of the Lord: "Hold on." He does not impose any great obligation. He says, simply, hold on. Don't plunge in to the "dark secrets of Satan" but hold on to the faith. Surely this is great assurance for the Christian in the dark.

And the reward? He gives two things:

He mentions that the overcomer will have authority with Him. This is explicitly proclaimed in Matthew 19:28.

He will give him the "Morning Star." At the end of Revelation this is clear: the Morning Star is Jesus . We shall have Him.

This last would have had special appeal to the saints of the middle ages. Thomas Aquinas—practically the definition of the Mediaeval church—has a legend about him. After writing his *Summa Theologica* God appeared to him, saying "Thou has written well of me. What would you have for your reward?" "Only thyself, Lord; only thyself."

So what will you have? Will you have worship in comforting signs and symbols, or will you have the real thing? Will you take the appearance of idolatry, or the "only thyself" of Jesus Christ?

Laodicea
Revelation 3:14-22

The church is in the world, and this church is of the world. So the titles of Christ begin by telling us three things:

He is the "Amen" —the Hebrew thought here is the word "truly".

He is the faithful witness—the one who has seen God, as no one else has. He is therefore the one person this world is looking for—and denying the existence of.

He is the ruler of creation. The worldly church takes God's laws of the creation for granted, not knowing who gives these laws.

This church is given no praise—only condemnation. There is no "Yet" in Laodicea. This is in keeping with Christ, who asks that a man be for him or against him (Mark 9:40). This church thinks it has the best of both worlds: Christ and riches; it has neither.

So Christ admonishes them—and in their own language:

He tells them to buy gold—true, incorruptible riches—from him (and Laodicea was a banking center for Asia Minor)

He tells them to get white clothes—purity—(and Laodicea was famous for its mass-production clothing industry)

He tells them to buy salve for their eyes, that they might see, spiritually (and this to a town which had a famous medical school—which exported eye salve all over the known world.)

So Christ rebukes them—but does so in love (see Prov. 27:6).

To the overcomers a simple promise is made; you will sit with me on the throne I am given (i.e., you will share my authority).

There is one last word: "I stand at the door and knock." Christ knocks; the meal he would share is (in the Greek) the main meal of the day. He would not just "sup" with you; he would feast.

Many think this describes the church of our day. Perhaps it is so; but the advice is good at any time. Do you chase the things of this world, or the things of true riches? Do you care how you appear to God—holy or filthy?

Have you appealed to him for the spiritual medicine which will open your eyes—that you might see Him?

Sea of Glass
Revelation 4:1-11

The stones listed here—jasper, carnelian and emerald—have some history. As we shall see at the end of Revelation, they have a more important duty as well.

Jasper is found on the breastplate of the High Priest (Exodus). It is a green quartz. It is also used as a description of the first foundation of the New Jerusalem, and one of the gates.

Carnelian is found nowhere else in the Bible but in Revelation. It is used as a gate of the New Jerusalem. It is a dusty red quartz. Translated as "ruby" in the Hebrew, it is the first stone in the High Priest's breastplate. Jasper is the last. Hence, these two stones are the "first and last" of the Tribes of Israel.

Emerald (which is descriptive here, as are the others). It forms the fourth foundation of the New Jerusalem. The fourth son of Israel was Judah, from whom came Christ.

The thunder and lightning, the rumbles are known before (see Chapter 1); we are clearly in the presence of God the Father.

The sea of glass bears a little closer examination. The description here would be quite unusual for the time, for glass in the Roman period was rarely "clear." The best that could be hoped for was a transparent glass, with color in it (i.e., a tint that was not opaque). Such glass was hard to get; clear glass was nearly impossible. Commentators see these possibilities:

The rareness of the glass—along with the precious stones—imply a vast wealth.

The clearness of the glass implies purity.

The use of the word "sea" implies a vast distance between mortal man and God.

Interestingly, we have a picture of this sea before Revelation. That picture was found in Solomon's temple, in which there was a great bronze basin called the Sea. Taking the concept of Hebrews 9 (that the tabernacle was a picture of heavenly things) to cover the Temple as well, we would see the bronze Sea of Solomon as the picture of the glass sea of God.

The point of all this? That God has, from the time of ancient Israel, been telling us of things to come. This is yet another vision of the glory that will be revealed. He is the great creative artist, and his picture is yet to be unveiled. To some, it will be the terror of the end; to us, the glory of eternity.

The Titles of Christ
Revelation 5:5-7

Five titles are given for Christ:

"Lion of the Tribe of Judah"

A reference to the Messianic prophecy in Genesis 49:8-10, it is also a reference to Christ the King.

"Root of David "

A reference to Isaiah 11:1 and 10, in which it is prophesied that David's line would produce the Messiah. Recall that one of the favorite titles of Christ (his own favorite) was "Son of David"

"Lamb that was slain"

This takes a bit more elaboration. The title is used once outside Revelation—by John, in John 1:29, quoting John the Baptist. It is fitting that a *prophet* would utter these words, for all the Old Testament points to the sacrifice of Jesus for our sins.

Two "sevens"

Recall that seven implies completeness. Seven horns, therefore, means complete .... what? A horn is used in three ways:

Prophetically (see the horns on the animals in Daniel) it means a king.

In the Old Testament, it may be a symbol for power.

It may also be a symbol for honor (see Psalm 89:17)

So we see Christ as king, Christ in power, Christ in complete honor.

Seven eyes

Finally, there are the seven eyes. Eyes would relate to seeing, seven to completeness, hence this would imply the omniscience of God. There is nothing so strange to happen that God does not know it. (See, for example, Zechariah 4:10.)

The Sum of it all

Christ is shown to us in this brief setting as the one prophesied from the beginning of time—one specifically to come to be "the Lamb of God," the sacrifice for our sins. For this, God has given him all power and authority. Being God, he is omniscient. There is no one greater among those who have walked the earth.

Christians are often comforted by the fact that Jesus is their friend. But he is not only a friend but Lord, King and Savior. We love him as friend; are grateful for salvation—but do we call him Lord? See Him in glory, tremble and bow down.

A Work of Art
Revelation 6

Is it just a coincidence that the living creature resembling the lion, the kingly beast, introduces the conquering rider on the white horse?

Or that the living creature resembling the ox, the animal of sacrifice, introduces the rider on the red horse of blood?

Or that the living creature resembling man, who brought spiritual death into the world, introduces the black horse of death and mourning?

Or that the living creature resembling an eagle, the swiftest of the four, introduces the pale horse of pestilence?

This is a work of art of the highest order.

Consider the altar shown here. The altar seen here is taken, of course, from the Tabernacle—the earthly type of heavenly things.

> The Jew was taught that the blood of an animal was its life; and therefore they could not eat the blood—only the meat of a sacrifice (Leviticus 17:11-14).

> The blood was to be poured out *at the base of the altar.* (Leviticus 4:7) —in other words, the "life" in the symbolic sense flowed under the altar!

> The altar is not in heaven—it is in the world. Remember that the Holy of Holies is the type of Heaven; the outer court contains the altar.

> Christians accept the idea that martyrdom is a form of being poured out as a sacrifice, an offering, to the Lord (Philippians 2:17)

Therefore, virtually all interpreters hold that these are the souls of those who have been martyred for their faith in Jesus Christ.

There are many theories for interpreting this book of Revelation. But one thing is certain—here, as elsewhere in the New Testament, the message is clear: those who trust in the name of the Lord will face martyrdom; they will become sacrificed for the cause of Christ. Some will see death for it; others will see suffering. These souls—and those left behind—cry out, "How long?" To this no answer can be given but, "Until God's good time." But take heart, Christian! This book is given that you might be certain that his time is coming—and you shall see his face, and be glad.

Flawless
Proverbs 30:5-6

Writing is a passionate exercise. When the words show up on paper just as you wanted them to, there is a great feeling of having created something. No wonder, then, that the original creative artist, the Lord God, does not like to have us be his editors.

Editing someone else's work is a temptation too. Editing God's work is tempting because:

We may feel that he has been too strict in some areas. After all, he wrote this work some time ago, and times have changed. Surely he'd appreciate our efforts at bringing his thinking up to date.

Sometimes we think that God did not go far enough. We see something that obviously needs correcting and—oh so clearly—we see that God must agree with us.

Even more often is the personal case. God needs a little help when we are counseling someone; we therefore amplify his original version to make it suit the person to whom we are speaking.

All these temptations have the same difficulty: we, the mortal human beings, are telling God that he missed something. And we're here to help him out.

We're not. First, of course, it is absurd to think we have anything to contribute to God's righteousness. Next, it is utterly presumptuous to put ourselves above him this way. But to make it clear, God has (here and elsewhere) made it a clear violation of his commandment to us.

It is interesting to note that the word translated "flawless" can also be translated "pure." In the word of God we have the pure form of God's communication to man, culminating in the Word of God, Jesus, the Christ. We are not to substitute our opinions for his commandment.

It goes further than that. In verse 5 "word" in the Hebrew means "commandment." In verse 6 a different Hebrew word is used, one meaning "speech." Even in the slightest of speech we are not to add to God's words. So when your friend comes to you for counsel, seeking the wisdom of God, do not substitute your own. Rather, give him the pure, flawless commandment, the very speech of God Himself.

True Riches
Proverbs 30:7-9

The Definition of Wealth

To truly understand wealth, and what God desires in your stewardship of it, you must first define it. Most of us see wealth in terms of money, but it is not so. Wealth does not occur when your possessions are many *but when your needs are few.*

Why do our advertisers so diligently court teenagers? It is because they are wealthy! Think about it; what are their needs? Do they need a house, or car, or food? No, you provide all those things (one way or another) to them. So the small amount of money they have is wealth indeed (and our advertisers know it). You, on the other hand, having so much more money (but greater needs) may indeed be poor. Is there anyone so wealthy as a newborn baby?

The Right Amount of Wealth

That being said, we see here the secret to riches in God's kingdom. This is a special case of "lead us not into temptation." For indeed, if I work hard and become wealthy in the world's eyes, is it not a temptation to say, "I did it myself?" If I think that I alone have done this, Satan will soon point out how many troubles seem to be solved with money. Gradually, then, God recedes from my thought.

Bitter poverty is another case. Would I steal to feed my children? Likely enough. So therefore I should ask God to keep me from both these extremes: "Lead me not into temptation."

Stewardship

If God has been so gracious as to keep you from either temptation (which is not necessarily a function of your paycheck), then comes the question: what does He want me to do with the money? This is not about tithing. Rather, it is about stewardship. The money is yours only for a while (if you think not, make out your will and see). If your heart is set upon the Lord, he will give you ample opportunity to use your money in imitation of him—and he will provide ample resources for his call.

But in all this give thanks that you are not loaded with money. J. Paul Getty was asked how much money was "enough." He answered, "More." He was a billionaire; but in truth he died a poor, needy man—"in want." Thank God for the right amount of money.

They Did Not Repent
Revelation 9

It is a difficult thing to pronounce upon the Book of Revelation. The theories and interpretations are many, the arguments even more, but there are words in this book which must be heeded. At the end of the two "trumpets" described here comes a sad, sad phrase: "they did not repent."

Some among us hold that these sentences apply to the very near future. If that is so (and the warning is valid at any time) then we must ask:

Do we practice idolatry today? Of course, we call it something else; after all, "it doesn't matter what you believe as long as you're sincere."

Murder? (Name it abortion). How shocked and infuriated we are when someone calls it that.

Sorcery? (The Greek word is *pharmakia*, from which we get our word pharmacy—which clearly indicates the drug connection).

Sexual immorality (the Greek is *porneia*, from which we get pornography).

Theft? In particular, theft by sleight of hand, as the original word implies?

Sadder than that: we do not repent, but we justify such behavior. It's "New Age" worship (or old age materialism); abortion is a "right" (which is exercised over a million times a year in our nation alone); drugs are now "recreational" (and so much more fun than doing sit-ups); pornography is now "being realistic" (those who oppose it are "puritanical") and theft is now "economic Darwinism—the survival of the fittest."

Placing a new label on old slime does not mean it will stick. Be assured that God is not deceived. The troubles described in this passage have happened before. The choices before us are simple. Either we, as a people, repent and turn back to our God—or we will continue to decline. Confident in our technology, we think it cannot happen to us. We are mistaken.

For each one of us, there is a choice. Will we continue to tolerate idolatry, murder, drugs, pornography and theft? Or will we rise up and be "intolerant?" Sometimes, being intolerant is being courageous.

Sealed Up
Revelation 10

It is a very curious thing. Of all the books in the Bible, none surpasses Revelation for its visual imagery. John, in each chapter, finds new wonders to describe. Here we have an angel robed in a cloud, with a rainbow, a face like the sun and legs like fiery pillars. Surely, one would think, the artists of the world would rush to portray the magnificent events of these prophecies.

Yet it seems that only three have even approached the subject. Durer (most famous for his praying hands charcoal sketch) did a series of woodcuts on the Apocalypse. El Greco portrayed the fifth seal. And Michaelangelo, in his magnificent Sistine Chapel ceiling, portrayed the triumphant return of Christ. Other than that, there seems very little that great artists have done with this most picture laden of books. Why?

Perhaps it is this: an artist must have comprehension of his subject. The Mona Lisa is held to be one of the greatest works of art; many have wondered what was behind that smile. We don't know—but surely the artist did. If there is no comprehension, then how can the artist portray the subject?

In this passage we see, explicitly, that such comprehension may indeed be beyond us. John hears the seven thunders. He is about to write them down. But the voice from heaven commands him to seal them up.

There is some speculation about this, but one likely theory is that these thunders are sealed to make sure that we understand that we do not understand. Some of the evidence is withheld so that we may not claim to know all. It is God's intention that we may be sure of his purpose. It is His intention that we may be sure of his power. It is his intention that we may be sure of his control of the future. It is not his intention to hand us a road map or investment guide to the stock market.

God has shown us enough that we should have faith in his purpose, power and control. He alone holds the mystery. He alone knows "when." Sufficient evidence is given to produce faith. Enough is withheld so that such faith is not destroyed by false confidence.

So do not fear. God reigns. He has shown you, in pictures, his purpose and intention—the return of our Lord, the judgment and the New Heaven and New Earth. Patience, Christian.

The Nature of God
Psalm 139

It is a human characteristic to cast God in the form of a man. God knows that; this is one reason Christ came in the flesh. But we must remember that God is far above us. The Psalmist gives us some very pointed reminders here:

The Omniscience of God. Have you ever sat in the waiting room of the principal's office, trying to figure out just what to say? Have you ever done the same thing with God? It is useless; he hears your mind's deliberations. You cannot hide it from him, so when you bring your self-justification to him, he has already heard the plotting that went behind it.

The Omnipresence of God. Many of us separate our lives into little compartments. God is wonderful and powerful on the weekends, when we go to church. When Monday comes, no one would know. It is as if God had vanished. He has not; he is still there, and we would do better to acknowledge him every day.

One "place" which most of us are sure is unseen by God is, surprisingly, the darkness. Whether it is our bedroom behavior or simply our hidden fears in the night, he knows. He is there.

Time does not limit God. For many of us the knowledge that a thing cannot be done in our lifetime is equivalent to saying that it cannot be done at all. It is not so with God; he is eternal. He sees you before you were born; your days are numbered by Him alone.

The Precious Thought of God. One common theme of the Psalms is the greatness of the Law. Here we see something greater: the thought of God. Some hold that God willed the universe into existence. His thought is far above our own, and precious indeed.

So why, then, does the Psalmist give advice to God? Surely God has thought of slaying the wicked by now! It is not so much advice as a cry; a cry to this wonderful God, asking him, "Why?"

Indeed, we often give advice to God, and we often wind up asking Him, "Why?" The question is usually presumptuous.

The Psalmist answers his question. God need not answer our cry for explanation; we need to place ourselves before Him. It is not God that needs advice, but man that needs reconciliation. That begins with repentance, so the Psalmist asks God to search him for sin. Will you do the same? Will you ask the Omniscient to show you where you need to repent?

Overcoming Satan
Revelation 12

How does one overcome Satan? There are three ways pictured here:

By the blood of the Lamb. If you are not a Christian, or if you are a Christian trying to rely on your own strength, Satan will overpower you, sooner or later. Later, if you are strong and well principled; sooner, if you are weak and opportunist—but it will happen. This is particularly a trap for the intelligent, who think they are capable. Satan is much stronger than we imagine—but Christ infinitely stronger.

By the word of testimony. In sharing your faith, you strengthen your faith—the best defense is a good offense. Why should Satan have the initiative in your combat with him? We are commanded to be ready with a defense of the faith at any time. For this we should be prepared; we need to know what we are going to say. More than that; we need to take courage to heart and not just prepare, but speak.

In martyrdom—which is to say, in your love for Jesus Christ. This is simply an example that no man can serve two masters. If you love Jesus more than anything else—more than life itself—he will keep you with him. Here we see such in its ultimate test, death. How is it that one can die for Jesus? The answer is simple, really. They did not love their lives so much. If you love Jesus more than life itself, then what is death? He who holds the keys to death and hell will not fail the one who loves Him more than life.

There are many theories as to what represents what in this book. But this lesson is plain. This is the way to overcome the one who is the enemy of man, Satan. We are told here that he is "filled with fury, because he knows his time is short." Against such we can do little in our own strength—but Christ's strength is perfected in our weakness.

Overcome Satan with the blood of the lamb—rely on Christ.

Overcome Satan with the word of testimony—tell others the good news of Jesus Christ.

Overcome Satan with the love you have for Christ. Fear God, dread naught.

Lord, Come Quickly
Psalm 141

The Psalmist is a man who understands the way to the Lord's heart.

Prayer

He begins his plea with prayer; indeed, he prays that his prayer may be heard. How many of us use prayer as a last resort! Yet the secret of those great in the faith has always been the life of prayer.

Stand Guard

"Lead us not into temptation." This plea is seen here also. It is seen first in words. How many times have you spoken and regretted it? How many times have you said something false, and then had to continue the lie to keep up appearances?

Words lead into action, starting with the heart. The Psalmist asks two things to keep his actions in check: that his heart will be kept from evil—and that he will not keep company with those who are evil. Bad company still corrupts good morals.

Rebuke

Here there is wisdom! Did you ever resent someone giving you what they thought was good advice? There is a skill of giving good advice; there is a virtue of taking it. Indeed, if the rebuke of a wise man saves me much pain, I am in his debt. And if that rebuke saves my soul? Sometimes hard words are sweet in the end.

Faith in God's Sovereignty

So often we are discouraged by what we see in the world. The evil seem to be well off; the righteous, poor. But wait! God is still in control. For a short time there is arrogance; then there is scandal, then bitter complaint. The righteous man knows who rules and reigns.

Fixed on You

As he began with prayer, so he ends with devotion. No matter what the temptation, no matter how worthy the rebuke, no matter how much the evil prosper, the man of God knows what to do. Fix your eyes upon your heavenly Father, take refuge in him. The wicked will be undone by their own wickedness; pay them no mind. The righteous man still lives by faith.

The 144,000
Revelation 14

The study of this book is somewhat difficult because of the various interpretations, but even in that the constancy of God can be seen. Consider the 144,000 mentioned here for the second time:

He has not lost one—the same number, through all the trials.

The Lamb is in their midst—the characteristic of the saints.

The 144,000 have the name of the Father on their foreheads. This could mean

ownership—for He bought them.

loyalty—for they have shown it.

dependence—for we are dependent upon him.

safety— just as American citizens used to be able to depend upon their government to come to their aid; just as Paul was "a Roman born," so the saints should see their safety in the Name.

The song itself is unmistakable. The song shows forth

power (do we not sing of the power of praise?)

unmistakableness. The song belongs to the redeemed; you cannot mistake the real thing.

the harp implies a melodious soothing (little David, play), which may signify grace.

Finally, these are "first fruits". Firstfruits are well known to the Old Testament.

Firstfruits were considered to be the best—and therefore to be sacrificed to God. ("Give of your best to the Master.")

There were no lies in them—as there should be no artificial ingredients in our produce.

Like the sacrifices of the Old Testament, they were "without blemish"

And—most important in this context—first fruits are the symbols of the harvest to follow. The Day is coming. Those who are redeemed will be harvested into glory; the condemned into eternal hell. God is faithful; He has promised it; it will be so. Will you be ready?

Song Of Moses
Revelation 15

Though the variations in interpretation of the Revelation of John are quite numerous, there are some points that most interpretations have in common. When these points give us a picture of the character of God—as we have here—they are well worth hearing:

Glass was rare and expensive in John's time, indicating the cost of the Cross. It is a measure of God's love.

The glass is transparent (which was unusual in this day), indicating purity

The size indicates immense distance, symbolic of the omnipresence of God.

To which is added fire, a symbol of judgment.

So we have here, in symbols, a picture of God's love, purity, omnipresence—and wrath. For this book speaks of the Day of Judgment. For those who deny God, it will be a terrible day. But for those who love Him, it will be a glorious day. That glory, that wonder, is shown in the Song of Moses recorded here. There is much debate about who are those singing—but the message of the singers is clear enough:

They emphasize the *great deeds* of God.

They tell us that God is both just and faithful (true).

They exhort us to fear God (and thus have nothing else to fear; if these are martyrs, it is advice from those who know).

Finally, they tell us that God alone is holy—and that all the nations shall worship Him.

A fair Sunday School lesson, that! The song is almost entirely a quotation from the Old Testament. Some scholars see in the Old Testament songs some prophetic points, but there is one key point: this is the song of those who have triumphed. In that song we see no notes of "look what I did." We see only the notes of "Look what God did."

Consider the work of God in your life. Has he not done great things for you? Is he not both just and faithful? He is holy. So then, put your trust in him completely, without reservation. Fear God—and have nothing else to fear, forever.

Just in His Judgments
Revelation 16

There is here a recurrent theme of Scripture: God is just. Just as recurrent is the objection from mankind: how can a loving God execute such punishments upon the earth?

The thought is often well intentioned, but misguided. We are so often told that we should not be vengeful. Indeed, we should not, for who are we, imperfect as we are, to pass righteous judgment upon our fellow mortals? But God is righteous, and his judgments are indeed true, for He is perfect. The Scripture thus tells us that vengeance is His.

But why vengeance at all? Why is there punishment at all? After all, our prison systems have long ago given up the idea of punishment as a motivation—we now seek reform (or at least warehousing for a while). So why does God deliver punishment, shown here in what may be a future tense?

First, we forget that God is patient and kind. If God were to strike down humanity for its sins, none of us would be here, for the sins of mankind have mounted up for centuries. But God, the merciful, wants to give all men a chance to repent.

In some sense, however, God must punish—or there is no fear in the wicked. God created the universe; in so doing he created physical and moral law. If you ravage your environment wickedly, you get the punishment of living in it. If you ravage your environment morally, the same applies.

God has also ordained lesser powers to enforce his judgment in the form of our governments. By so doing, he permits us to learn justice while dispensing it—and perhaps for some to cause repentance.

But ultimately there must come a day when justice is delivered. If by our pleas and playing on God's mercy that day could be delayed forever, it would mean that evil would exist forever on the hope that it would change. Hell on earth would block the arrival of heaven.

Until such a day of justice—and purging—this sinful world will remain as it is, or worse. But when He comes to judge, He also comes to renew.

Even so, come, Lord Jesus! Once as a babe, now as a King.

Called, Chosen – and Faithful
Revelation 17:14

Tucked away amidst these magnificent pictures is an exquisite description of the saints of God.

Called—like those in the Old Testament, where God was very specific about his call. He called Abraham, Moses, Samuel. He called to Israel (which very often did not listen). In this age, He calls to all of us (2 Th 2:4).

Note that we do not seek him; He seeks us. If God did not call to us, how could we ever know him? Now, however, through the Gospel and by the blood of Christ, each and every one of us is called by God. But we are not called like a mob of anonymous souls; each of us is also chosen.

Chosen—Abraham, Israel (the people) and David were all among "the chosen" —and Mark 13:20 calls those of us chosen "the elect." Some are chosen for specific tasks (e.g., Paul); but all of us are chosen by God (1 Th 1:4) according to the foreknowledge of God (1 Peter 1:2).

It is dismaying to think that many Christians just want to blend in with the woodwork of the church. No activity, no service, just go to worship, sing and pray, and be anonymous. But God did not choose us that way. He has chosen each of us for specific service—and we need to find out what it is.

But this too is not sufficient. We must be **faithful.** We have only to look at those Old Testament examples to see it; we must be faithful, even to the point of death (Rev 2:10). It is of no use to recognize the call, determine to what service God has appointed us—and then not be faithful in doing it. Note that the phrase is "faithful." It is not sufficient to start upon God's tasks; he expects us to continue what we start. We may not have the privilege of finishing such service. That's God's choosing. We may be asked to pick up the service from some other saint and carry it on all our lives, only to hand it to another, younger saint. Such is the common case, for example, for those who preach the Gospel. Ours is not to expect the finish; ours is to be faithful at the task. God will give the increase, never fear.

There it is. You were called by God to salvation. You have been chosen by him for his appointed service. Will you be faithful in carrying out that service? This life is but a little time; you are his for eternity.

Three Dirges
Revelation 18

There are three dirges—songs of woe—in this chapter.
The Dirge of the Kings
Note that they mourn—but offer no help. Words substitute for action now that Babylon is of no more value.

Royalty is known for its extravagance (especially in Rome); as the extravagance is, so is the terror of example. (That could have been me!) This is "one of those examples by which God teaches the law to kings."

Babylon now becomes an object of pity. It is one thing to experience misfortune; it is entirely another to be subjected to pity for it. Especially if your chief virtue is pride.
The Dirge of the Merchants
Look at this list! What a pile of luxuries, and it is this that the merchant laments. Think of the profit margins! Think of the carriage trade! Think of the fools who would rush to buy anything they thought fashionable and rare. Anything that makes me better than the crowd.

The worst of this traffic: the bodies and souls of men. Can this be even today? Surely we have outlawed slavery? Or have we, wage slaves? Have you never seen those so dedicated to their work that they could be said to be slaves to it? Do we trade in them? Why do you think we have employment firms whose nickname is "headhunter?"

The key is selfishness. The merchants care nothing for Babylon—but everything for the lost customer.
The Dirge of the Workers
And who are the workers lamenting for? Not for Rome/Babylon; for themselves. In all three laments we see the same thing: they are astonished at how quickly Babylon is fallen; they lament for their own loss.

There is the point. For the proud there will come only pity—and that from a distance. For the greedy will come the sure loss. For those who sell themselves to the system of greed and pride, the lament is equally certain. The lament will come, the dirge will be sung—but the believer will heed the angel's advice to "come out of her, my people." Set your mind on things above, and never share this lament.

Hallelujah
Revelation 19

Hallelujah, in the New International Version, occurs only here in the entire Bible. Other translations have it in the Old Testament, but all agree that this is its only location in the New Testament. This passage is the source of Handel's famous "Hallelujah Chorus." The word itself is a composite one, "Hallel + Jah (short for Jahweh)" or "Praise the Lord."

Who, then, so praises the Lord?

-a multitude, at the beginning and end. Some commentators see angels in the first and the saints in the second.

-then the elders and four living creatures, getting closer to the throne.

-then a voice from the throne itself, echoed by the multitude again.

The elders, the voice, the four living creatures echo the hallelujah; only the multitude says *why.*

Why: There are three categories of why God should be praised, and it is good for us to examine them:

There are his *attributes.* Aquinas assures us that God is his attributes, and these attributes are great: Salvation (for which we should be grateful); glory (in which we should be awestruck) and power (which is unlimited)

There are his *judgments.* Only God can judge righteously, for only He

can see the heart and know the intent

is pure and therefore unprejudiced

has the wisdom to know the right judgment, and the power to enforce it.

Finally, because he is omnipotent, and he reigns. It may not have been clear to all before this—but it is now.

Worthy to be praised: Have you ever noticed that a goodly part of the Psalms that praise God do so by commanding others—even rocks and trees—to praise Him? Perhaps this seems odd to us because we have lost the concept that anything is worthy—intrinsically—of praise. We have become like Oscar Wilde's cynic: we know the price of everything—and the value of nothing.

On Satan
Revelation 20

If there is one thing quite difficult for people to believe in these days, it is Satan. The image is one of the red suit, tail and pitchfork, which is laughable. It is also not Satan.

This passage brings up one of the central mysteries about Satan. We can understand why he would be bound; but why would God allow him to be released?

> Some suggest that during the Millennium faith will become so easy that a final test is necessary.

> Others suggest that this is simply the sign of the fact that sin is ever present in man.

> Perhaps it's just this: tell me why God allowed Satan in the first place, and then you'll know why he is released here.

Satan shows up in different character here than in our time. He is not the ruler of Hell (Milton appointed him that in *Paradise Lost*, but Milton knew better than to believe it). Indeed, as this chapter makes clear, the lake of fire was intended for Satan, not for mankind. Mankind was intended for a very different destiny: eternal fellowship with God himself. So how, then, does a person wind up in this lake of fire?

It is by choice. God sends no one to hell. A person chooses to go there by his (or her) actions. God puts no one on the railroad train to hell. He just informs us of exactly where the train makes its last stop.

The language of Revelation is symbolic, and there is much debate about what this all means. But certain things are clear. If you are not in the Book of Life, you have chosen this end.

It is eternal; there is no hope of escape or redemption.

It is eternal separation from God.

It is eternal torment.

More than that, there is debate. But then, this should be sufficient.

Who, then, is in this Book of Life? There is much argument here too. But one thing again is certain—the owner of the book is Jesus Christ. He writes down the names, or leaves them out. Seek him, and do so daily. "What a friend we have in Jesus" —and all the more so on the day that book is opened and read.

Flood the Altar
Malachi 2:13-16

There is something terribly sad about this passage. It portrays a people who do not know that God sees, and is not mocked. With great effort the men (whom God has appointed as those who have spiritual leadership in their families) go to the altar of God—only to be frustrated. Is it the case, sir, that God does not answer your prayers? Then perhaps you should pay attention to his word.

The concept is familiar to us today under a different name: "Trophy Wife." A man—usually a "successful" one—divorces his wife and marries a much younger, attractive woman. This is altogether too common today. But consider what our approval of this idea really means:

- It means that we are a society which is completely unfair to women. No woman is "forever young." If growing old is a cause for divorce, what should women do about it?
- It means we tolerate a man who would break his sworn word merely for pleasure. Marriage is nothing if it is not an exchange of solemn vows, sacred promises. We throw away our integrity to satisfy our lust.
- It means we think so little of God as to imagine He does not care. This despite the fact that marriage is God's institution.

Note the phrasing here: the reason God does not answer such a man's prayers is that He is a witness between him and his wife. God is saying, "I was there when you exchanged those vows—and I am here now to testify against you." Marriage is precious to him; you break it at your extreme peril.

What is a man to do, then? God gives us two answers:

- "Guard yourself in your spirit." You take marriage so lightly because you take God so lightly. Return to him in prayer, study and meditation. Ask his forgiveness and seek his strength.
- "Do not break faith." As your prayer ministers to the inner man, so your actions show it. Keep your word. Be a man of integrity. This is not so much passion as promise.

The Jews had a saying: "Beware! God counts a woman's tears." Love your wife as Christ loved the church—in will as well as in passion—and see how God honors and blesses the man who keeps his commandments.

Fleeting Beauty
Proverbs 31:25-31

In this discourse on the "ideal wife," the writer fulfills the primary function of Proverbs: to give wisdom to the young. As the year ends it is customary to look back at what has happened and reflect upon it. As we mature, it is also wise to take stock of what we have learned—and pass that wisdom on to the next generation. Here we find wisdom—for choosing a wife, or for knowing the blessing of the one you have.

Strength and Dignity. Dignity is not much praised in our time; it is more often fodder for comedy. It is fun to puncture the pompous. But a certain dignity becomes a woman. It says to one and all that she is not her husband's shadow or servant, but a child of God, loved by Him, in and of herself. If her husband honors this, her children will indeed have the respect to "arise and call her blessed."

Wisdom and Faithful Instruction. How many of us first learned the Gospel at our mother's knee! But there is more than that. If your wife is a woman of wisdom, O husband, you will profit greatly from her counsel in private. God has given her words for your ears; listen well.

The "bread of idleness." Many of us dream of a day when we can retire and do nothing—and then spend retirement working harder than ever. Good habits die hard! Hard work is the key to many things; a woman's diligence (for example, in her relationship to her husband) will make her home a place of delight for herself, her husband and children.

Charm and Beauty. When a man is young charm and beauty are everything in a woman. But charm is a skill. Beauty is the gift to youth; it will fade. When charm is seen through and beauty vanishes, the real woman underneath is revealed. If that woman is one who loves the Lord, that time will reveal a woman of true beauty and charm which never fades.

It is the last day of the year. Husband, look back. Is this a picture of your loving wife? If it is, then God has richly blessed you. Have you given him thanks for such a blessing as this? Have you shown your love and gratitude by loving her as Christ loves the church?

Count your blessings, O Christian, and greet the New Year with the joyful heart of one who loves the Lord.

(Psa 1:1-3 NIV)

Blessed is the man who does not walk in the counsel of the wicked or stand in the way of sinners or sit in the seat of mockers. {2} But his delight is in the law of the LORD, and on his law he meditates day and night. {3} He is like a tree planted by streams of water, which yields its fruit in season and whose leaf does not wither. Whatever he does prospers.